REGNUM

The Holy Spirit, Spirituality and Leadership

Essays in Honour of Younghoon Lee

Series Preface

Regnum Studies in Mission are born from the lived experience of Christians and Christian communities in mission, especially but not solely in the fast growing churches among the poor of the world. These churches have more to tell than stories of growth. They are making significant impacts on their cultures in the cause of Christ. They are producing 'cultural products' which express the reality of Christian faith, hope and love in their societies.

Regnum Studies in Mission are the fruit often of rigorous research to the highest international standards and always of authentic Christian engagement in the transformation of people and societies. And these are for the world. The formation of Christian theology, missiology and practice in the twenty-first century will depend to a great extent on the active participation of growing churches contributing biblical and culturally appropriate expressions of Christian practice to inform World Christianity.

Series Editors

Marina Behera	Research Tutor, Oxford Centre for Mission Studies
Paul Bendor-Samuel	Director, Oxford Centre for Mission Studies
Michael Biehl	Retired, former Executive Secretary for Mission Studies
Bill Dyrness	Former Dean of the School of theology, Fuller Seminary
Tony Gray	Director, Words by Design
Paul Woods	Asia Graduate School of Theology – Alliance

REGNUM STUDIES IN MISSION

The Holy Spirit, Spirituality and Leadership
Essays in Honour of Younghoon Lee

Edited by
Wonsuk Ma and
Robert P. Menzies

Copyright © Wonsuk Ma and Robert P. Menzies 2024

First published 2024 by Regnum Books International

Regnum is an imprint of the Oxford Centre for Mission Studies
St. Philip and St. James Church
Woodstock Road
Oxford, OX2 6HR, UK
www.regnumbooks.net

The rights of Wonsuk Ma and Robert P. Menzies to be identified
as the editors of this work has been asserted by them
in accordance with the Copyright, Designs and Patents Act 1988.

All rights reserved. No part of this publication may be reproduced, stored in a retrieval system, or transmitted, in any form or by any means, electronic, mechanical, photocopying, recording or otherwise, without the prior permission of the publisher or a license permitting restricted copying. In the UK such licenses are issued by the Copyright Licensing Agency, 90 Tottenham Court Road, London W1P 9HE.

British Library Cataloguing in Publication Data
A catalogue record for this book is available from the British Library

ISBN: 979-8-8898-3875-3
eBook ISBN: 979-8-8898-3876-0

Typeset by Words by Design

Cover photo @Yoido Full Gospel Church. 2018
Inner photo @Yoido Full Gospel Church, 2019

Distributed by Fortress Press in the US, Canada, India, and Brazil

Lee ministering to the Aetas in the Philippines

Congratulatory Greetings from
World Christian Leaders

Rev Dr Lee Younghoon, it has been my great privilege to get to know you through the partnership of Yoido Full Gospel Church with the Oxford Centre for Mission Studies. This partnership has flourished primarily because of your personal commitment to the Kingdom of God rather than an exclusive focus on local or denominational loyalties. Generosity, graciousness, and humility overflow in your every encounter, and I have personally been encouraged and refreshed whenever we have met. May God give you strength for as long as your days and continue to use you as an ambassador and champion of His grace. Thank you!

Dr. Paul Bendor-Samuel
Executive Director, Oxford Centre for Mission Study, Oxford, U.K.

Congratulations Dr. Lee. As a global leader, only eternity will reveal the true impact of your life and influence. Thank you for modeling excellence in spiritual leadership. I have been blessed by your friendship and encouraged by your ministry. I am confident that this book will be a tremendous blessing and resource to Kingdom leaders around the world.

Rev. Doug Clay
General Superintendent, General Council of the (US) Assemblies of God

Thank you, Rev Dr Lee Younghoon, for your ministry which has been exercised in a humble and gracious way around the globe. As Chairman of the board of the Oxford Centre for Mission Studies and now as Co-Chaplain, I have seen the partnership of Yoido Full Gospel Church with the OCMS, which has been so beneficial. May you continue to be an ambassador for the Lord Jesus in the months and years ahead.

Professor David Cranston, D.Phil FRCS (Eng). FRCS (Ed).
Associate Professor of Surgery (Emeritus), University of Oxford

Honor to those to whom honor is due. It is indeed an honor to celebrate the life, ministry and continuing legacy of one of the greatest Christian leaders of our time, Dr Younghon Lee of Yoido Church. We celebrate him as a humble and prayerful servant of our Lord and Saviour Jesus Christ, with a sturdy spirit and consuming zeal. With unwavering fidelity to Pentecostal convictions, Dr Lee has also demonstrated a trans-denominational embrace – and a healthy collaboration across many churches. We join in celebrating him as a preacher and teacher par excellence – many generations rise to call him blessed for his godly influence on their lives.

May those who read this book and study the life and ministry of Dr Younghoon Lee be inspired to follow the Lord Jesus Christ even more closely and ever more dearly in the power of the Holy Spirit.

Rev. Dr. Casely Baiden Essamuah,
Secretary, Global Christian Forum

Dr. Lee, I send my grateful congratulations to you on this occasion. Your ministry has inspired millions in the global Body of Christ. God has used your faithfulness to extend grace and blessing not only in Korea, but far beyond. Your sincere desire to nurture bonds of Christian unity and fellowship to overcome the church's painful divisions throughout the world is an inspiring model of witness. Thank you for your commitment and service on behalf of the Gospel of our Lord.

Rev. Wesley Granberg-Michaelson
President, Global Christian Forum Foundation
General Secretary Emeritus, Reformed Church in America

Congratulations, Dr Lee. Thank you for continuing with the founding vision of Yoido Full Gospel Church. Your understanding of the transforming power of the Gospel in the church and the wider society brings the church to the center of the world's realities. This book is a resource for the churches when the world is searching for hope.

Rev. Dr. Nicta Lubaale
General Secretary, Organization of African Instituted Churches

Dr. Younghoon Lee, with deepest appreciation, I celebrate your life and global contribution to the expansion of God's Kingdom. Your influence, as a Christian Statesman, is reaching to the ends of the earth. Your clear proclamation of Christ's redemptive mission continues to guide the Church with prophetic and spiritual insight. Thank you for your commitment to Truth crossing national, cultural, and religious boundaries. I thank God for your voice and sincerely congratulate you on 70 years of life and Gospel service.

Bishop LaDonna Osborn
President, Osborn Ministries International, Tulsa, OK, USA

Dear Reverend Lee, dear friend and brother in Christ. Since we have worked together in such different places as the Knesset in Jerusalem, my home country Germany, the WCC General Assembly in Busan, or sitting at the same table with the President of Korea at the Korean National Prayer Breakfast, and since I have seen many different sides of your ministry, I take the liberty to evaluate your ministry as a whole and to congratulate you on a very rare gift of God, which is the interweaving of the local and the global Christian faith. Although your local church has always come first, and you have become a role model for many pastors around the world, at the same time, you have taken your responsibility as the leader of the largest church in the world very seriously, giving leadership to Korean and Asian Christianity as well as on a global level. You have combined loyalty to your local Christian roots with working for the revival and loving cooperation of the whole Church of God in all denominations and on all continents. May God greatly reward you for all you have done for His Church!

Prof. Dr. Thomas Schirrmacher, Former Secretary General of World
Evangelical Alliance, Archbishop Communio Christiana within
Continuing Evangelical Episcopal Communion

Contents

Foreword One	xi
Foreword Two	xiii
Preface	xv
List of Contributors	xxi

Younghoon Lee and Korean Christianity
Myung Soo Park 1

Bibliography of Younghoon Lee
Ho Sung Kim 25

Part 1
THE HOLY SPIRIT AND SPIRITUALITY

The Void Pastor David Yonggi Cho Left, Too Large to Be Filled
Younghoon Lee 39

The Spirit and Moral Fortitude: Understanding the Spirit's Role
in Luke's Temptation Narrative
Lora Angeline E. Timenia 51

The Realism of the Working of God's Spirit and the Revealing Power
of the Biblical Book of Acts
Michael Welker 63

The Challenge of Demythologising the Devil
Frank D. Macchia 75

Simultaneous Prayer: A Pentecostal Perspective
Robert P. Menzies 89

An Analytical Study of Holiness and Spirituality:
Biblical and Practical Features
Julie C. Ma 105

Digital Pneumatology: Presence and Power of the Holy Spirit
in the Metaverse
Alex Guichun Jun 115

The Church as a Healing Community: An African Perspective
Opoku Onyinah 129

Pentecostal Glocal Ethics
Hanna Larracas 141

Community Engagement After Pentecost: Apostolic Forays
Then and Now
Amos Yong 151

Divine Healing as a Characteristic of the Holy Spirit
Movement in Korea
Jun Kim 165
Contending for the Faith: Pentecostalism and the Reshaping
of World Christianity
J. Kwabena Asamoah-Gyadu 179
Revival in the Borneo Jungles
Hwa Yung 193

Part 2
THE HOLY SPIRIT AND LEADERSHIP

Megachurches in Global/World Christianity: North and South
Philip Jenkins 209
Christianity Moving South – Walter Hollenweger's Propositions
Revisited: A Conversation
Casely B. Essamuah and Jean-Daniel Plüss 225
The Significance of the Voice of the Spirit in Pentecostal Spirituality
and Leadership in the Malaysian Assemblies of God
Eva Wong Suk Kyun 235
Asian Pentecostalism as a Growth Engine for Global Christianity:
Potentials and Challenges
Wonsuk Ma 249
Korean Pentecostalism, Shamanism, and Intercultural Theology
Allan H. Anderson 265
Yoido Full Gospel Church and Ecumenism
Cecil M. Robeck, Jr. 277
The "Power Paradox" in Spiritual Leadership
Ivan Satyavrata 289
An Emmaus Walk with Ancient Mothers and Fathers:
From the Sawdust Trail to the Ecumenical Patriarchate
Harold D. Hunter 301

Foreword One

From the second half of the twentieth century, global Christianity has witnessed two seismic shifts. The first is the southward move of Christian growth and impact. In 1900, only 18 of 100 Christians lived in the Global South (Africa, Asia, Latin America, and Oceania). One hundred years later, in 2000, this number changed to 67. And this shift is expected to grow to 77 of 100 by the year 2050![1]

The second global seismic shift is the birth, growth, and diversification of Spirit-empowered Christianity. From its obscure beginning in the early twentieth century, this new Christian movement expanded rapidly from the second half of the century. From less than one million in 1900, it grew to 644.2 million in 2020, and is expected to reach 1.03 billion by 2050! By then, every three out of ten Christians will be Spirit-empowered. The annual growth rate of the Spirit-empowered movement is also staggering: 1.58% each year between 2020 and 2050. This is compared to 0.75% annual growth for the world's population and 1.03% for Christianity.[2]

Within these radical changes in global Christianity, Yoido Full Gospel Church was born through the visionary leadership of Dr. David Yonggi Cho. Grappling with the post-war devastation and grinding poverty of Asia, the church in Seoul grew to become the largest church in the world and brought powerful transformation to the nation. It well represented the dynamic expansion of Spirit-empowered Christianity in the Global South. When Dr. Younghoon Lee was elected as the second senior pastor of the church, a new generation continued the founder's charisma, vision, and leadership. As a pastor, evangelist, global Christian statesman, and scholar, Dr. Lee has been a leading voice of dynamic Christianity in the Global South. This was well demonstrated when he delivered a keynote address at the Centenary of the Edinburgh Mission Conference in 2010.

I have had the privilege of working closely with Dr. Lee for decades and have found him to be an amazing friend and leader. In 2022, he and his leadership team hosted the 26th Pentecostal World Conference at Yoido Full Gospel Church with the theme of Pentecostal Revival in the Next Generation. He is passionate about reaching the world and today's young people with the Gospel.

Younghoon Lee is a man full of the Holy Spirit, with his spirituality rooted in the life-giving and wonder-working ministry of Jesus. His leadership is Spirit-empowered. His lifelong message of absolute obedience, positivity, and thanksgiving is grounded in both Scripture and the Spirit. This book, contributed by his colleagues and friends, celebrates his life's milestone of reaching seventy

---

[1] Todd M. Johnson and Gina A. Zurlo, *World Christian Encyclopedia*, 3rd ed. (Edinburgh: Edinburgh University Press, 2020), 4.

[2] Todd M. Johnson and Gina A. Zurlo, *Introducing Spirit-Empowered Christianity: The Global Pentecostal and Charismatic Movement in the 21st Century* (Tulsa, OK: ORU Press, 2023), 34.

years of age. Fittingly, the book takes up three components that have helped shaped his life: The Holy Spirit, spirituality, and leadership. I add my congratulations for God's gracious and powerful hand upon one of the great Christian leaders of our generation. I also look forward to more years of working together with Dr. Lee to see everyone in the world have an opportunity to know Jesus as their Saviour by the year 2033, the 2,000th anniversary of Christ's death, burial, resurrection, the giving of the great commission, the Spirit's outpouring, and the birth of the church.

Rev. Dr. William M. Wilson
President, Oral Roberts University
Chair, Empowered21 and the Pentecostal World Fellowship

Foreword Two

On behalf of the World Council of Churches' fellowship of 352-member churches, it is my great honour to join the Church around the world in celebrating the life and ministry of Rev. Dr. Younghoon Lee on the occasion of his 70th year in the Lord.

From his calling to today, Younghoon Lee has been an exemplary friend in Christ, preacher of the Gospel, and minister to the church. He has contributed to the growth of the church, not only in Korea, but throughout the world. His commitment to Christian unity helped bring about a much-prayed rapprochement between the Pentecostal and ecumenical movements. His support for the WCC as the leader of a sister church is deeply appreciated. The legacy of Younghoon Lee's ministry is a remarkable witness to the power of unity in the spirit.

The story of Yoido Full Gospel Church is of faithfulness to the glory of God, the love of Christ, and the gifts of the Holy Spirit. Through his pioneering ministry, Brother Lee has shared the Gospel with countless people, helping to grow Christ's church through salvation and sanctification, and its mission and generous acts of love. For his contribution to the growth of the church, we give thanks.

Both the ecumenical and Pentecostal movements are rooted in the early twentieth-century renewal of the church by the power of the Holy Spirit. For too long, our movements were separated by ignorance and pride. The commitment of Younghoon Lee to our common apostolic faith and unity in Christ has helped reshape the ecumenical landscape, breaking down barriers between us for the sake of our unity in Christ, in Korea, and around the world. For his passion for Christian unity, we give thanks.

Through his leadership in the Pentecostal World Fellowship, his involvement in the Global Christian Forum, and his support for the Joint Consultative Group between the WCC and Pentecostals, Pastor Younghoon Lee has been among the great champions for the unity that Christ prayed for, "that they may all be one … so the world may believe" (John 17.21). The WCC fondly and with deep gratitude remembers the role of Younghoon Lee and the support of Yoido Full Gospel Church in hosting the WCC 10th Assembly in Busan in 2013. For decades of partnership and service, we give thanks.

The legacy of your ministry, Brother Younhoon is a remarkable witness to a deep love for the Lord, for his faithful, and for his church. This book, therefore, is a fitting recognition and celebration of his worldwide influence and leadership. May God's blessing on your life and ministry continue so that the world may know the love of God in Christ through the power of the Holy Spirit.

Yours in Christ,
Rev. Prof. Dr. Jerry Pillay
General Secretary, World Council of Churches
Geneva, June 2024

Preface

Over the past century, the Korean church has witnessed one of the greatest revivals in the history of Christianity. From a small, battered community ravaged by the dysfunction of a nation torn apart by war, the Korean church has blossomed into the large, dynamic, and influential body that we know today. Evidence of its vitality and power abound. It can be seen in the many missionaries this dynamic church has sent around the world. It can be heard in the sounds of fervent prayer that mark its worship services. It is dramatically symbolised in the history and influence of Yoido Full Gospel Church (YFGC). Sixty-five years ago, who could have imagined that Seoul, Korea, would be home to the largest church in the world?

Yoido Full Gospel Church

Although many churches and denominations have contributed to this amazing revival, it is evident that the rapid rise of Christianity in Korea has been propelled by a strong reliance on the power of the Holy Spirit. The remarkable history of YFGC has mirrored the remarkable growth of Pentecostal Christianity worldwide over this same period. Today, it is impossible to speak of worldwide Christianity without acknowledging the significant role and contributions of the Korean church and the Pentecostal movement. Indeed, those of us from the West must acknowledge that the centre of global Christianity has moved. It is no longer found in the traditional churches of North America or Europe but rather in the Pentecostal and Charismatic communities of Lagos, São Paulo, Manila, Beijing, and Seoul.

The YFGC was founded on 18 May 1958. In very humble circumstances, David Yonggi Cho began to proclaim the good news of Jesus to a Korea ravaged and divided by war. In the face of tremendous hardships, suffering, and hopelessness, Cho declared that salvation and hope are found in Jesus Christ. Pastor Younghoon Lee has beautifully picked up Cho's mantle and carried on this ministry of proclaiming the Gospel of Jesus Christ in the power of the Spirit. Now, a little over sixty-five years later, YFGC is the largest church in the world.

Dr. Younghoon Lee

We, the editors, have had different paths of engagement with the church and Dr. Younghoon Lee. In May 2007, I (Robert Menzies) was invited by the YFGC to speak at a theological symposium, lecture in their seminary (The Yong San Theological Seminary), and preach in the YFGC's Friday evening service. I travelled to Seoul and spent a week there, ministering in various settings. It was there that I also met Pastor Lee. My time in Korea at the church and with Pastor Lee was incredibly inspiring. I shall not soon forget preaching in Yoido Church's Friday evening service. What an experience! It was thrilling to see and hear approximately 15,000 Korean believers singing praises to Jesus and praying with great fervour.

Dr. Younghoon Lee led that Friday evening service in which I preached. His leadership gifts and standing in the community were evident. However, I was especially impressed with his graciousness and humility. I had just come from Southwest China, where I was accustomed to speaking in small, house church settings. The sheer volume of people that packed into the massive auditorium that evening left me awe-struck. The huge crowd, strange language, and different customs were all overwhelming, and I'm sure it showed. Yet, I recall with clarity how Pastor Lee went out of his way to set me at ease and assure me that we were family. In various ways, he highlighted that I was worshipping with fellow brothers and sisters, and Jesus was present. His demeanour served to redirect my focus upon that which had brought us to this place: our need and desire to encounter Jesus.

Dr. Younghoon Lee's Spirit-inspired grace and humility are also illustrated in a story told by Robert's brother, Glen Menzies. About a decade ago, Glen, who was at that time serving on the faculty of North Central University (an Assemblies of God school in Minnesota, USA), attended a meeting of the general superintendents of the various Assembly of God churches in the countries of the Asia–Pacific region. Glen attended the meeting as a guest and resource person. The meeting convened in Bangkok. Shortly after their arrival, the various church leaders boarded buses that would shuttle them from their hotel to a banquet hall. One bus had an empty seat, and Glen was directed to take it. Glen noticed that one of the church leaders spoke excellent English and was very friendly. So, turning to this outgoing man and thinking he might have heard of him, he asked, "Are you the general superintendent of Japan?" The man replied, "No. South Korea." Glen was embarrassed by his gaffe but determined to continue. In the US and some countries, the general superintendent of the Assemblies of God is required to leave his or her pastoral duties in order to assume this role as the leader of the denomination. So, Glen then asked, "Do you pastor a church?" This unassuming church leader responded simply, "Yes, I do." It was only later that Glen learned that he had been speaking to the pastor of the world's largest church: Pastor Younghoon Lee of Yoido Full Gospel Church. Glen remarked how Pastor Lee treated him with kindness and warmth throughout those meetings, even after these memorable missteps. That was a lesson in spiritual leadership that Glen will never forget!

I (Wonsuk) have had a longer relationship with Rev. Dr. Lee. We collaborated in several eras as part of the same denomination, the Korean Assemblies of God. Firstly, I regularly participated in his efforts to establish Korean Pentecostal theology during his leadership years at the International Theological Institute (ITI) of Yoido Full Gospel Church (YFGC). He and Dr. Vinson Synan also visited the Asia Pacific Theological Seminary, where I served as a missionary professor and administrator. In 1998, during the Pentecostal World Conference hosted by YFGC, he hosted the historic launch of the Asian Pentecostal Society.

Secondly, he and several Pentecostal scholars agreed to begin a symposium on non-Western Pentecostalism as a pre-conference programme of the triennial Pentecostal World Conferences (PWCs). When we had the Los Angeles symposium in 2001, he served as the president of the Bethesda Christian University, Anaheim, California. About a dozen studies were presented at this

Preface   xvii

successful academic conference, graciously hosted by Lee at his university. This voluntary academic programme continued in connection with the 2004 Johannesburg conference. The symposia encouraged non-Western Pentecostal scholars, as the balance of global Christianity was moving southward. They also complemented the PWCs, as the World Alliance for Pentecostal Education was formed in 2009 and endorsed to serve as the Education Commission by the Pentecostal World Fellowship in the same year.[1]

Thirdly, when I served as the executive director of the Oxford Centre for Mission Studies, Oxford, United Kingdom, he was also elected to succeed Dr. David Yonggi Cho as the senior pastor of YFGC in 2008. We explored a chair sponsored by the church to invest in future Christian leaders strategically. Through Lee's leadership, the church established the David Yonggi Cho chair, and I was honoured to become the David Yonggi Cho Research Tutor of Global Christianity until my departure in 2016. The post was Lee's unique gift to the global church.

Fourthly, Dr. Lee played a significant role in and around the 2010 Centenary of the Edinburgh Missionary Conference. At the conference in Edinburgh, his plenary speech represented the explosive growth of Pentecostal churches, especially in the Global South.[2] In the publication of the massive thirty-five-volume Regnum Edinburgh Centenary Series, his church partially financed two volumes: *Pentecostal Mission and Global Christianity* and *Korean Church, God's Mission, Global Christianity*. Later, he provided resources to select Pentecostal studies published in various titles of the Edinburgh Centenary Series and collect them into a single volume.[3]

Fifthly, my tenure at Oral Roberts University (ORU) in Oklahoma State opened a new era of collaboration. When he spoke at the 2022 graduation ceremony of the university, two programmes were instituted: the Younghoon Lee Dissertation of the Year Award in Studies of Global Spirit-Empowered Christianity was formally introduced to the executive members of the Society for Pentecostal Studies at its 2023 annual meeting held at ORU. Reflecting the global vision of the university and YFGC, the award would recognise the best Ph.D.-level dissertation in the area of global Pentecostal/Charismatic Christianity. The second is the Younghoon Lee Global Leadership Scholarship, intended for ORU's Ph.D. programme.

---

[1] John F. Carter, Paul R. Alexander, and Barry L. Saylor, "Advancing the Vision for Pentecostal Theological Education Worldwide: The Origins and Development of the World Alliance for Pentecostal Theological Education," *Pentecostal Education* 7:2 (Fall 2022), 244–46.

[2] Younghoon Lee, "Christian Spirituality and the Diakonic Mission of the Yoido Full Gospel Church," in Kirsteen Kim and Andrew Anderson, eds., *Edinburgh 2010: Mission Today and Tomorrow*, Regnum Edinburgh Centenary Series 3 (Oxford: Regnum Books, 2011), 85–97.

[3] Younghoon Lee, Wonsuk Ma, and Kuewon Lee, eds., *Pentecostal Mission and Global Christianity: An Edinburgh Centenary Reader* (Oxford: Regnum Books, 2018).

This personal friendship and partnership were born from mutual respect and support of each other's ministries. Once, Lee said, "Wherever you go, let's work together." Thus, I celebrate the relationship with this great man of God.

The Book

This volume, then, is a fitting tribute to one of the key leaders of this dynamic church, Yoido Full Gospel Church, and this divinely birthed movement that bears the name of Pentecost. It is difficult to overstate the enormity of the challenge that following in the footsteps of the founding pastor of the world's largest church represents. Yet this is precisely what Younghoon Lee has done. And he has done so with grace, humility, and a strong sense of his own need for and dependence on the power of the Holy Spirit.

The impact of Pastor Lee's ministry, chronicled in various ways through the chapters of this book, speaks for itself. Yoido Full Gospel Church continues to thrive under Pastor Lee's leadership, and the global church is all the richer because of this fact. In this volume, an international group of Christian leaders testifies. They do so by highlighting some of the important lessons that the global church can learn regarding the work of the Holy Spirit as expressed in our spiritual practices and experiences and, more specifically, in how we envision leadership in the church. We offer this book as a tribute to Younghoon Lee, but even more so as a testimony to the transforming power of the Gospel of Jesus Christ, which is energised by the work of the Holy Spirit and an expression of the love of the Father.

The book has three themes: the Holy Spirit, spirituality, and leadership. After a deep reflection on Lee's life and ministry, an extensive bibliography follows. Then, the contributions are divided into two: spirituality and leadership. The editors took "the Holy Spirit" as the transversal, marking and influencing Lee's spirituality and leadership. However, this division proved challenging, as many studies include both areas. We, the editors, wanted both established and young scholars to form a team for this volume. With Lee's enduring commitment to the new generation, the book is a fitting tribute.

Acknowledgements

It is fitting to acknowledge those who made this project a reality. The contributors eagerly joined the project when the editors first approached them. In various ways, each contributor has a unique relationship with Dr. Lee. We are pleased that the contributors form a strong international and ecumenical team with expertise in diverse areas. We, the editors, express our deepest appreciation to them. The second group is the world's Christian leaders, who warmly congratulated the honoree and the book. Then, the team at Regnum Books of Oxford deserves our commendation. From the inception of the project, Paul Bendor-Samuel and his team provided their professional guidance and enthusiastic support. I (Wonsuk) also acknowledge the valuable help of Jamie Riddle, my assistant, in managing the project.

Preface

This book is the third Festschrift we have collaborated on as co-editors. This friendship-based collaboration well represents this book's nature: the honoree's friends added their studies to a single volume in order to honour Dr. Lee. As friendships are God's gift, so also is this book a gift to a world that is yearning for the life-giving and life-flourishing work of the Holy Spirit. To God be the glory!

Editors, Summer 2024

Contributors

Allan H. **Anderson** is Emeritus Professor of Mission and Pentecostal Studies at the University of Birmingham, England, where he has been since 1995. Previously, he was a theological educator and missionary in South Africa. He is the author of many articles and books, including *To the Ends of the Earth* (2013), *An Introduction to Pentecostalism* (2014), and *Spirit-Filled World* (2018).

J. Kwabena **Asamoah-Gyadu** is the immediate past President of the Trinity Theological Seminary, Legon, Ghana. He is the Baeta-Grau Professor of Contemporary African Christianity and Pentecostal Theology at the Seminary. He has published extensively on Pentecostal/charismatic studies in Africa. He is a member of the Lausanne Working Group and a Fellow of the Ghana Academy of Arts and Sciences.

Casely B. **Essamuah**, an ordained Methodist minister from Ghana, is Secretary of the Global Christian Forum. With degrees from Ghana, Harvard and Boston University, he has worked for two decades in global missions at evangelical churches in the USA. As a reflective practitioner of his faith, he is a bicultural bridge builder straddling the spheres of Global South and North while working in missions, ecumenism, the church, and the academy. His publications include *Genuinely Ghanaian: A History of the Methodist Church Ghana, 1961-2000* (2010).

Harold D. **Hunter** is the Ecumenical Officer of the International Pentecostal Holiness Church, an Adjunct Professor at ORU Graduate School of Theology, co-chair of the PCCNA–USCCB Dialogue, and chair of the PWF Creation Care Task Force. A past president of the Society for Pentecostal Studies and recipient of the 2022 SPS Lifetime Achievement Award, Hunter organized the first global conference for Pentecostal scholars known as Brighton '91 that featured Professor Jürgen Moltmann and brought together all major Christian traditions from five continents.

Hwa Yung is a Bishop Emeritus of the Methodist Church in Malaysia. He worked as a pastor, then taught at Malaysia Theological Seminary and also Trinity Theological College, Singapore. From 2004-2012, he was the Bishop of the Methodist Church in Malaysia. Formerly, he has served on the Trustees Council of the Oxford Centre for Mission Studies, including as Chair, and the International Board of the Lausanne Movement and also as President of the International Fellowship of Evangelical Students (2011-2019).

Philip **Jenkins** is a Distinguished Professor of History at Baylor University, where he serves in the Institute for Studies of Religion. He has published 35 sole-authored books, including *The Next Christendom: The Coming of Global Christianity* (2002), *Climate, Catastrophe, and Faith: How Changes in Climate Drive Religious Upheaval* (2021), and *A Storm of Images: Iconoclasm and* xxii

Religious Reformation in the Byzantine World (2023). Many books have been translated into sixteen languages.

Alex Guichun **Jun** is the Yoido Pentecostal Research Tutor at the Oxford Centre for Mission Studies in Oxford, United Kingdom. He is also an ordained minister who has served in various local churches in both Korea and the UK. He is interested in discovering the local knowledge of a particular congregation situated in a specific time and space to enhance his and others' understanding and skills in ministry and mission, by comprehending the congregants' lived experiences and the local contexts.

Ho Sung **Kim**, a New Testament scholar, is a senior associate pastor at Yoido Full Gospel Church in Seoul, Korea. In addition, he also directs the International Theological Institute, serves as the vice president of the Westminster Graduate School of Theology, and is the dean of Yongsan Theological School. He is also an adjunct professor at Hansei University and a Bible translator for the Korean Bible Society.

Jun **Kim** is a Korean Pentecostal scholar, currently serving as the Academic Dean and a faculty member at Asia Pacific Theological Seminary in the Philippines. He also serves as the vice president of the Asia Pentecostal Society. An ordained minister with the Korean Assemblies of God, he has been engaged in missionary work in the Philippines since 2004. His research interests include Asian Pentecostalism and divine healing movements, with a focus on historical theology. His recent publication is *The Korean Healing Movement* (2024).

Hanna **Larracas** serves as a grief counselor at hospices in California. Her research project involves creating grief support groups for bereaved family members, which aim to create opportunities/facilitate spaces where the bereaved can accompany one another and make space for compassion both inter and intra-personally. She is the 2022 Younghoon Lee Scholar for the PhD program at Oral Roberts University.

Younghoon **Lee** is Senior Pastor of Yoido Full Gospel Church in Seoul, Korea. He has held various leadership positions, such as President of the National Council of Churches in Korea (NCCK, 2011), President of the Christian Council of Korea (CCK, 2009–2011), and President of the United Christian Churches of Korea (UCCK, 2018–2022). In 2024, he was awarded the Peony Order of the National Medal for contributing to South Korea's campaign to improve the national birth rate. His books include *The Holy Spirit Movement in Korea* (1996), *The Power of Faith* (2018), and *365-Day Thanksgiving QT* (4 vols., 2021–2024).

Julie C. **Ma** is a Professor of Missiology and Intercultural Studies at Oral Roberts University, Tulsa, Oklahoma, USA. Previously, she served as a Korean missionary to the Philippines and Research Tutor of Missiology at Oxford Centre for Mission Studies, Oxford, UK. She served as the president of the Asian Pentecostal Society and a general council and executive committee member of

Edinburgh 2010. Her publications include *Mission Possible: Biblical Strategies in Reaching the Lost* (2016).

Wonsuk **Ma** is a Korean Pentecostal, presently serving as Distinguished Professor of Global Christianity and Executive Director of the Center for Spirit-Empowered Research, Oral Roberts University, Tulsa, Oklahoma, USA. He also serves as Co-Chair of the Global Network of Spirit-Empowered Scholars of Empowered21. He previously served as Executive Director of the Oxford Centre for Mission Studies, Oxford, United Kingdom. His latest book is *Mission in the Spirit: Formation, Theology and Praxis* (2023).

Frank D. **Macchia** is Professor of Systematic Theology at Vanguard University of Southern California and Associate Director of the Centre for Pentecostal and Charismatic Studies at Bangor University, Wales (UK). He has been involved in conciliar and bilateral ecumenical conversations and has published widely in the fields of systematic and Pentecostal theology. His recent books include *Tongues of Fire: A Systematic Theology of the Christian Faith* (2024), *Introduction to Theology: Declaring the Wonders of God* (2024), and *Jesus the Spirit Baptizer: Christology in Light of Pentecost* (2018).

Robert P. **Menzies** is the Director of the Asian Center for Pentecostal Theology. He has lived in Southwest China for almost three decades and taught at Bible schools and seminaries in over a dozen nations. His writings on New Testament pneumatology have served as a catalyst for fresh thinking in this area. He has written eleven books, including *Spirit and Power: Foundations of Pentecostal Experience* (2000) and *Pentecost: This Story is Our Story* (2013).

Opoku **Onyinah** is a Christian leader from Ghana. He currently teaches at Pentecost University in Ghana, where he served as the founding rector. He is the Co-chair of the Global Network of Spirit-Empowered Scholars of Empowered21 and previously served as chairman of the Church of Pentecost worldwide. His latest publications include *Apostles and Prophets: The Ministry of Apostles and Prophets throughout the Generations* (2022).

Myung Soo **Park** is Professor Emeritus of Church History and founder and director emeritus of the Institute for Study of Modern Christianity, Seoul Theological University, South Korea. He also served as President of the Church History Society in Korea as well as President of the Korean Association for Political and Diplomatic History. Among his many books is *A Sound Like of the Blowing of a Violent Wind* (in Korean, 2012), a historical and political/diplomatic study of Korean Pentecostalism.

Jean-Daniel **Plüss** holds a PhD in Religious Studies from the Catholic University of Leuven, Belgium that focuses on the interpretation of narrative elements in worship. He chairs the European Pentecostal Charismatic Research Association and is president of the Swiss Global Christian Forum Foundation. Since 1996, he has been involved in various international ecumenical dialogues and is the

Pentecostal co-chair of the Lutheran-Pentecostal Dialogue. He teaches in theological seminaries and ecumenical institutes in Asia and Europe, has written numerous articles on Pentecostalism, and has published a book on the history of Swiss Pentecostalism. He is on the editorial board of the *Journal of Pentecostal and Charismatic Christianity*.

Cecil M. **Robeck**, Jr. serves as Senior Professor of Church History and Ecumenics and Special Assistant to the President for Ecumenical Relations at Fuller Theological Seminary. He has been an ordained minister with the Assemblies of God for over fifty years. His historical specialty is the Azusa Street Mission and revival. His ecumenical work has included international dialogues with Catholics, Reformed, Lutheran, and other Christians, as well as membership in the Commission on Faith and Order of the World Council of Churches and participation in the annual meeting of the Secretaries of Christian World Communions. He is one of the founding members of the Global Christian Forum.

Ivan **Satyavrata** served as Senior Pastor of the Assembly of God Church in Kolkata, from 2006 to 2022, and the Church has since named him Pastor Emeritus. He served for eight years as President of Centre for Global Leadership Development [SABC], Bangalore, and presently Chairs the Board of World Vision International and the Project Rescue Board of Elders. His publications include: *God Has Not Left Himself Without Witness, Holy Spirit: Lord & Life Giver* and *Pentecostalism And the Poor*.

Lora Angeline E. **Timenia** is a Filipina Pentecostal scholar, ordained by the Philippine General Council of the Assemblies of God. She is a faculty member of Asia Pacific Theological Seminary and the book review editor of the Asian Journal of Pentecostal Studies. She previously served as secretary of the Accreditation Commission of the Asia Pacific Theological Association. She authored the book, *Third Wave Pentecostalism in the Philippines*.

Michael **Welker** is Senior Professor and Director of the Research Center International and Interdisciplinary Theology at the University of Heidelberg, Germany. He has been a frequent guest professor and has given many endowed lectures in many parts of the world.

Eva **Wong** Suk Kyun presently serves as Director of the Malaysia Pentecostal Research Centre, Editor of the *Malaysian Pentecostal Journal*, and lecturer at Bible College of Malaysia. She also serves on the Asia Pentecostal Society Executive Committee and co-leads the Scholar Leaders Women's Peer Leader Forum. She has a PhD in Theology (Pentecostal Studies) from the Oxford Centre for Mission Studies, United Kingdom. Her upcoming book is entitled *Malaysian Pentecostalism from Classical to Contemporary: The Assemblies of God with reference to Joel 2:28-32* (forthcoming).

Contributors

Amos **Yong** is an Asian American Pentecostal, presently serving as professor of theology and mission at Fuller Theological Seminary in Pasadena, California, USA. He is the author or editor of five dozen books, including, most recently, *The Holy Spirit and Higher Education: Renewing the Christian University* (2023), and *Revelation*, a volume in Westminster John Knox's Belief: A Theological Commentary on the Bible series (2021).

Younghoon Lee and Korean Christianity

Myung Soo Park

Introduction

The most significant change in Korean Christianity after liberation was the emergence of Yoido Full Gospel Church (YFGC), led by Rev. Yonggi Cho. Starting the church in a shabby tent right after the Korean War, his church grew to become not only the largest in Korea but also in the world. Rev. Cho, who started as a small church pastor, then became a representative figure in Korean and global Christianity. In 2008, Cho stepped down as the senior pastor, and Dr. Younghoon Lee succeeded him. Many people were deeply interested in how Lee would lead YFGC and the Pentecostal denomination after Cho. Many large churches in Korea face challenges when their founders step down, and because of those precedents, the overall succession process was worthy of concern. However, as of 2024, Lee has been leading the church with stability. Not only has the number of believers increased, but his stature within the Korean Christian community has also become more solid. From a historical perspective, this study aims to examine how Lee has led YFGC as the successor to Cho.

For the purpose of examining this objective, the author will first explore Rev. Lee's growth and preparation. While Cho initiated his Christian journey in an unbeliever's home, Lee comes from a lineage of faith that has carried on the early Christian beliefs of the Korean church. He was originally part of the mainstream Presbyterian Church in Korea before transitioning to Full Gospel Church. Consequently, Lee's connections with the broader Korean church community were more extensive than those of Cho.

Next, we will examine how Lee led YFGC when he became the senior pastor. In this context, the key factor will be his established relationship with his predecessor, Cho. Lee defined himself as the spiritual son and disciple of Cho, choosing a path of continuity and expansion rather than discontinuity and transformation. This approach can be considered successful and as enabling stability for YFGC.

Lastly, we will explore Lee's relationship with the Korean church. While Cho founded the largest church in Korea, it is difficult to claim that he represented the Korean church. Lee, however, had deeper roots in Korean Christianity, and so more easily became a representative of the Evangelical Korean church while embracing both progressive and conservative elements.

Lee's Years of Growth and Preparation

Lee's Spiritual Heritage: Presbyterianism

Younghoon Lee's Christian faith has its roots in his great-grandfather, who was originally a Cheondogyo believer. His great-grandfather, Jae-Sik Lee, embraced

Christianity following the teachings of missionary William Baird, who had come to Pyongyang at the time. During his youth, Jae-Sik Lee became a dedicated believer and even explored the mountains to cut trees with an axe to build a church.[1]

This strong faith was passed down to his son, Won-Geun Lee. Missionaries who were working in Pyongyang at the time encouraged Won-Geun Lee and his colleague, Mueong-Seon Kim, to pursue further education abroad. Kim followed their counsel and eventually became the director of Severance Hospital. However, Won-Geun Lee, a ninth-generation descendant, had to abandon his dream of studying abroad due to his parents' disapproval. Instead, he engaged in business. At the same time, he actively participated in the March 1st Movement in 1919 and was imprisoned for six months.[2] Eventually, Won-Geun Lee became an elder at the Seo-Moon-Bak Church in Pyongyang. He married Chang-Hee Moon and became the father of nine children (four sons and five daughters). The Seo-Moon-Bak Church was established as a separate congregation from the Jang-Dae-Hyun Church, which had been initiated by the missionary Maffett A. Samuel. Won-Geun Lee imported sewing machines from Japan and ran a business within the Pyongyang region. He also served as the chairman of the Pyongyang Sewing Machine Cooperative. Currently, Won-Geun Lee's descendants number around 135, and thirteen of them have pursued the path of becoming pastors.

The challenges Won-Geun Lee faced after the liberation on 15 August 1945 were significant due to the Soviet Union's occupation of North Korea. As a response, Won-Geun Lee, like many others, left Pyongyang and relocated to the Jangyeon in the Hwanghae Province. His decision to settle in Jangyeon was influenced by his friend, Pastor Jong-Sam Kim, who was actively involved in ministry in that area. Before the liberation, Won-Geun Lee had arranged the marriage of his second son, Kyung-Seon Lee, to Sun-Sil Kim, the youngest daughter of Jong-Sam Kim. The Jangyeon region was originally known for its active trade with China and later became famous as a summer resort for missionaries. Within this open-minded region, there was the Sorae Church, regarded as the first church in Korea. Jong-Sam Kim, as part of the eighth graduating class of Pyongyang Theological Seminary, served as an itinerant pastor overseeing churches in this area. Shortly after the liberation, Won-Geun Lee established the Korean Establishment Preparation Board, and he became chairman in this region.

During that period, Christians in Hwanghae Province played a crucial role in leading the Korean Provisional Commission. Soon after the liberation, on 17

---

[1] Dr. Younghoon Lee's spiritual heritage has been introduced in a series titled Soon-hee Bok, "신앙의 명가: 이영훈 목사, 4 대째 이어진 신앙의 유산" [The Prestigious Family of Faith: Pastor Younghoon Lee, Inheritor of Faith for the Fourth Generation], *The Full Gospel Family Newspaper* (17 March, 31 March, 7 April, 14 April, 21 April, 2019). The information above is primarily derived from this content.

[2] In 2016, the government recognised these contributions and honoured him as an independence patriot.

Younghoon Lee and Korean Christianity   3

August, Ju-Sam Yang and Gyu-Gap Lee in Seoul reached out to elder Chang-Mo Moon (a medical doctor), who initiated the Haeju Provisional Commission with Jae-Yong Jeong, a Methodist from the Kyungshin School. On 20 August, this committee was officially established in the Hwanghae Province, with Elder Eung-Soon Kim appointed its chairman. Eung-Soon Kim later joined forces with Ryang-Wook Kang to establish the pro-communist Korean Christian Federation. Kang, initially employed as an accountant in Won-Geun Lee's company, pursued theological studies and eventually became a minister. He was the elementary teacher of Il-Sung Kim, the founder of the Democratic People's Republic of Korea (North Korea) and Kim's great-grandfather-in-law. Kang later served as vice premier in North Korea. However, it did not take long for the Haeju Provisional Commission to be transformed into a People's Committee led by the Communist Party, with Deok-Young Kim, a member of the Communist Party, as its chairman.[3]

One day, Kang approached Elder Won-Geun Lee, acknowledging the changing times and emphasising the need to cooperate with the Communist Party for survival. Recognising Won-Geun Lee's personality and his inability to collaborate with the Communist Party, Kang suggested that his best course of action would be to leave North Korea and seek refuge in South Korea. He also mentioned the plan of the People's Army to liberate South Korea in the near future, advising Won-Geun Lee not to take any official positions there. As a result, in June 1948, Lee, along with his family, left everything behind and made his way to South Korea, using a small boat borrowed from Haeju.

As he arrived in South Korea, like many other refugees, he sought sanctuary at Youngnak Church, established by Rev. Kyung-Jik Han, the most famous pastor in Korea after World War II. At that time, Youngnak Church had set up tents in its courtyard to provide shelter for refugees who had fled from North Korea. Lee and his family stayed there for about a month. He later moved with his family to Wonhyo-Ro and established Namyoung-dong Church, where he cared for believers who escaped from North Korea. Formerly a businessman in the North, he transitioned into the role of a preacher, spreading the Gospel.

At that time, Jeju Island was strongly influenced by leftist ideologies, and these groups opposed the establishment of the Republic of Korea government. The Jeju 4.3 incident erupted on 3 April 1948, when a group of 350 individuals, including Dal-Sam Kim from the South Workers' Party, attacked twelve police stations on Jeju Island. The suppression of this group by the police and members of the Northwest Youth Corps resulted in numerous civilian casualties. Jeju Island had originally been within the region of the Southern Presbyterian Church for missions. After liberation, the Jeju Presbytery requested that the mission board assign full-time missionaries to the region. The mission board had entrusted the area to the Talmage family. Father, John Van Neste Talmage and son, John Edward Talmage, had been engaged in missionary activities there even

---

[3] Myung Soo Park, "해방 후 건국준비위원회와 기독교의 역할" [The Korean Provisional Commission (Chosen Keunkook Chunbi Wiwohoe) after the Liberation and the Role of Christianity], in *The Foundation of the Republic of Korea and Christianity* (Seoul: Book Korea, 2014), 81–83.

4   *The Holy Spirit, Spirituality and Leadership*

before liberation. Instead of maintaining resident missionaries, they decided to send Korean evangelists to this area. Won-Geun Lee, who had recently arrived from North Korea, was chosen for this mission.[4] The Talmage family considered Lee suitable for investigation to recover the churches in Jeju Island. It is believed that Rev. Kyung-Jik Han, who had close associations with the Southern Presbyterian missionaries, played a crucial role in facilitating this connection.

As he arrived on Jeju Island, Lee reconstructed Namwon Church and established prayer centres in Wimi and Pyoseon, which later become Wimi Church and Pyoseon Church. Furthermore, he founded a high civil education centre, demonstrating his commitment to youth education. Lee devoted approximately two and a half years to this mission. After completing his mission on Jeju Island, he collaborated with Rev. Kyung-Jik Han, founding Busan Youngnak Church. He requested his eldest son, Kyung-Hwa Lee, serve at Busan Youngnak Church, where he served as an elder for the rest of his life.[5]

From the Presbyterian Church to Full Gospel Church

After the war, Won-Geun Lee moved to Seoul and lived in Sangdo-dong. Then in 1964, he began living with his second son, Kyung-Seon Lee, in Seodaemun. Although he had originally been Presbyterian, he started attending the Seodaemun Full Gospel Church, located just a five-minute walk from his home. During this period, the Seodaemun Full Gospel Church was undergoing a revival under the leadership of Rev. Yonggi Cho, who had taken over this church from the missionaries. After attending early morning prayers for about three months, Lee gathered his family together and said, "Starting this week, our entire family will attend the Full Gospel Church. I've been listening to Pastor Yonggi Cho's sermons for three months, and I've experienced great grace. He is a young minister filled with the Holy Spirit, and his words overflow with grace." In this way, Lee and his second son's family officially became members of the Full Gospel Church. As a result, one of his grandsons, Younghoon Lee, also joined the Full Gospel Church.

Prior, Younghoon Lee had attended Chung-Hyun Church, where he diligently studied the Bible and consistently received recognition for his effort. However, as he joined the Full Gospel Church, he learned about the importance of receiving baptism through the Holy Spirit and speaking in tongues. As he dedicated himself to Bible study, he prayed for the experience of Holy Spirit baptism and speaking in tongues. In February 1966, during a revival meeting led by Cho, he received the baptism of Holy Spirit and began speaking in tongues.

---

[4] Jong-sun Cha, *제주기독교 100 년사* [The 100-Year History of Christianity in Jeju], (Seoul: Qumran Publishing House, 2016), 240–43. When the Korean War broke out on 25 June, Tayo Han, along with Harold Voelkel (Oak Ho Yeol), was active in the Geoje Island prisoner camp.

[5] Youngnak Church, *영락교회 50 년사* [The 50-Years History of Youngnak Church], (Seoul: Youngnak Church, 1998), 128. According to page 128, it is recorded that Kyung-Hwa Lee was documented as a construction committee member for Busan Yeongnak Church.

Younghoon Lee and Korean Christianity

This marked his full conversion to the Full Gospel Church. However, his spiritual journey did not end there. About a year after receiving the gift of speaking in tongues, while he was in the second year of middle school, Seodaemun Full Gospel Church organised a revival gathering with Rev. Otis Keener, the founder of the Hong Kong Christian Charismatic Assembly, as the guest speaker. Rev. Keener was a deeply devoted preacher. Through his ministry, Younghoon Lee received a powerful anointing of the Holy Spirit and a calling to ministry.[6]

After graduating from high school, Lee was confronted with a decision regarding his theological studies. He had the option to choose between Yonsei University and Full Gospel Theological Seminary (now Hansei University). When he sought advice from Rev. Cho on which path to pursue, Cho encouraged Lee to pursue broader studies. As a result, he enrolled in the School of Theology at Yonsei University and completed his theological studies there. Then, he transferred to Full Gospel Theological Seminary, from which he graduated in 1978. Cho, who had not received a sufficient theological education, seemed to believe that the next generation of leaders needed it. Upon graduating, Lee took on the role of editing director at YFGC's Yeongsan Publishing Company (now known as Seoul Logos). Shortly thereafter, the Full Gospel Education Institute was established at YFGC, and Lee became one of its founding members. Within the church, his primary role was to educate the members in the Full Gospel faith. His endeavours eventually led him to the International Theological Institute (ITI).

In 1982, after serving several years at the Full Gospel Education Institute, Lee pursued studies in the United States. Cho generously provided monthly scholarships of $1,000 to support Lee's education. However, it came as a surprise that Lee did not choose to study at a school aligned with the Pentecostal tradition. Instead, he chose to study at Westminster Theological Seminary in Philadelphia, renowned for its conservative Reformed theology. The seminary was not favourable to the Pentecostal movement, but Lee's Pentecostal faith remained unchanged. He engaged in dialogues with many conservative Presbyterian leaders and revisited his early upbringing within the Presbyterian tradition.

During his time at Westminster, Lee pursued a Master's degree and later continued his academic journey in religious history at Temple University. It is worth noting that Temple University is a liberal arts institution that does not emphasise any particular Christian tradition. At that time, the school committee had employed progressive theologians like Paul Matthews van Buren. Nevertheless, Lee used this opportunity to research the Pentecostal movement in

---

[6] Younghoon Lee, "절대긍정과 성령충만의 순복음 사역자" [Absolute Positivity and Spirit-filled Full Gospel Minister], in *Biographies of Christian Leaders in the 100 Years of the Korean Christianity I*, revised version (Seoul: Qumran Publishing House, 2017), 239–40. Derived from Younghoon Lee, "어제도, 오늘도, 내일도 도우시는 하나님" [The God Who Helps Us Yesterday, Today, and Tomorrow], Sunday Worship Sermon, Yoido Full Gospel Church, 21 May 2023.

South Korea and earned his Master's degree in 1992 and his Ph.D. in 1996.[7] He connected the Korean Pentecostal movement with the pre-existing Korean Holy Spirit movement. This would be a key distinctive for his later career as pastor of YFGC. For while Cho understood the Korean Pentecostal movement through its relationship with the Pentecostal movement in the United States, Lee's perspective toward the Korean Pentecostal movement was rooted in Korean religious tradition. Korean Presbyterianism had a long-standing history of engagement with Pentecostal spirituality, with Pyongyang serving as a crucial centre. As one example of this, Won-Geun Lee, who emerged from this tradition, embraced Cho's Pentecostal message within only three months of attending Cho's early morning prayer.

During his time as a student in the United States, Younghoon Lee also took on pastoral responsibilities. Upon his arrival in 1985, he took the role of pastor at Washington Full Gospel Korean Church, which had been without a pastor. He successfully balanced his studies with his pastoral duties, commuting between Philadelphia for his academic pursuits during the weekdays and returning to Washington, DC on weekends to minister to his congregation. He was so effective that he was able to raise $2.7 million in construction donations from his immigrant congregation. This substantial contribution enabled the construction of a worship hall capable of accommodating 1,000 people at Washington First Korean Church. Importantly, Lee was not just a theologian; he was a pastor who provided guidance to the daily struggles of believers, and a Full Gospel minister who conquered obstacles through the power of the Holy Spirit.

Director of International Theological Institute and Pastoral Ministry

In 1992, after completing his doctoral studies, Lee returned to Korea. The period between 1982 and 1992, during which Lee pursued his studies in the United States, was a challenging time for YFGC. During that era, the most influential Christian denomination in South Korea was the United Presbyterian (Tonghap) group, in which Yeongnak Church held a prominent role. Despite YFGC surpassing Yeongnak Church in terms of numbers, its influence in the South Korean religious landscape was not commensurate with its size.

In this context, the Tonghap group raised in 1983 the "Yoido Full Gospel Church Heretic Controversy." It had to do with the relationship between speaking in tongues and the baptism of the Holy Spirit, as well as issues related to healing and blessings. Coming from the Reformed theological tradition, the Tonghap Presbyterian denomination accused YFGC of being pseudo-Christian.

---

[7] Younghoon Lee, "The Holy Spirit Movement in Korea: Its Historical and Theological Development" (Ph.D. diss., Philadelphia, Temple University, 1996). This article was published in 2009 by Regnum Books International in Oxford, along with forewords by Pastor Cho Yonggi and Andrew Walls.

Younghoon Lee and Korean Christianity

7

This accusation by one of Korea's most influential denominations was an extremely disturbing incident with potentially devastating consequences.[8]

The year 1984 marked a significant milestone in the Korean church: the centennial of Korean (Protestant) Christian missions. The principal leader for the event was Rev. Kyung-Jik Han of Yeongnak Church. Its massive gathering in Yoido Plaza required cooperation from YFGC. Contrary to his denomination's accusation of Yoido Church, Han selected Rev. Yonggi Cho as one of the key speakers for the Centennial Anniversary Celebration. This decision signified Han's acknowledgment of Cho in the context of this nationwide celebration.

In 1988, the National Council of Churches, whose members were from progressive denominations in South Korea, issued the "88 Declaration," criticising the anti-communist stance of conservative South Korean Christianity. This declaration challenged one of the most fundamental aspects of South Korean Christianity. In response, conservative and Evangelical denominations, led by Han, established the Christian Council of Korea to emphasise Evangelical unity. This council was an organisation in which most Korean churches, including YFGC, participated. In 1992, the World Holy Spirit Great Revival took place in South Korea, where revivalists from most denominations came together. Cho took the role of president and keynote speaker, while Rev. Hyun-Kyun Shin, a prominent revivalist from the Tonghap Presbyterian Church, became the vice president. This signified that Cho was accepted as a part of the Korean church community, contrary to the resolutions of the Tonghap denomination.[9]

Under these circumstances, Younghoon Lee returned to South Korea. During this period, YFGC recognised the need for the systematic development of Pentecostal theology to safeguard its faith from any disputes and controversies. For this purpose, the church established the International Theological Institute in 1993 with Lee as its founding director. Lee's effort in the systematic development of the Full Gospel faith resulted in the publication of two volumes, titled *The Faith and Theology of Yoido Full Gospel Church*. The book exposited how Cho's theology was in line with Pentecostal theology, rooted in the revival movements of the eighteenth and nineteenth centuries in the United States. It claimed that this Pentecostal theology was reconstructed in the Korean context in the early twentieth century. During that era, various cults in Korea were promoting doctrines that seemed to emerge without any historical Christian roots. Lee also posited YFGC as a unique denomination by asserting that Cho's theology aligned with the internationally recognised Pentecostal faith. As part of this process, in 1994, the Tonghap Presbyterian denomination officially

---

[8] For further information, see International Theological Institute, *여의도순복음교회의 신앙과 신학* [The Faith and Theology of Yoido Full Gospel Church], (Seoul: Seoul Publication, 1993), 243–311.

[9] For further information, read Myung Soo Park, "한국기독교총연합회와 한국교회의 복음주의 운동" [The Evangelical Movement of the Christian Council of Korea and Korean Church], in *Changes of the Korean Church and the Evangelism Movement* (Seoul: Duranno Academy, 2011).

recognised the Pentecostal theology YFGC as a valid theological tradition.[10] In this process, Lee played a crucial role in guarding and establishing Pentecostal theology within the Korean Christian context.

While developing Pentecostal theology, Lee invited prominent scholars around the world and leading scholars from other denominations to analyse and present the significance of Cho's theology. During this period, the Pentecostal movement remained a relative minority in Korea. However, the global theological community had already begun to recognise Pentecostal Christianity as one of the most influential movements of the twentieth century. Through the studies of these scholars, the Korean Christian community came to understand that the Pentecostal movement was not a temporary phenomenon. Even non-Pentecostal scholars assessing the YFGC provided valuable insights into understanding the Pentecostal movement. Among them were Harvey Cox, a religious scholar in Harvard, and Jürgen Moltmann in Tübingen, Germany.

However, Lee's role extended beyond that of a theologian. He consistently engaged in pastoral responsibilities with his academic pursuits. During his leadership over the YFGC, Lee also served as the president of Bethesda University in the United States, where he managed both theological education and administrative duties. In 2000, he was appointed to lead Tokyo Full Gospel Church, and in 2005, Los Angeles Full Gospel Church. Throughout his pastoral endeavours, Lee's primary emphasis was prayer. By adhering to a disciplined daily prayer routine, he kept the fervent faith of Pentecostalism and effectively addressed various challenges. His pastoral model was influenced by Cho. In 2006, Lee returned to YFGC as the acting senior pastor, and in 2008, he took on the role of the second senior pastor of YFGC.

Lee's Leadership over Yoido Full Gospel Church

The Democratic Succession and the Relationship with Pastor Yonggi Cho

The most significant challenge faced by large churches in South Korea is the selection of a successor. Many churches encounter difficulties in the process of selecting a successor, leading to divisions in their aftermath. However, YFGC effectively addressed this challenge, and the transition from Cho to Lee proceeded smoothly, mostly because they adopted a highly democratic procedure for this process.

In most cases, the lead pastor plays the predominant role in selecting their successor. However, in January 2005, during an executive committee meeting of the church, Cho, nearing the age of seventy, announced his retirement and stated that the selection of his successor would follow democratic procedures in

---

[10] International Theological Institute, 여의도순복음교회의 신앙과 신학 [The Faith and Theology of YFGC], 246.

Younghoon Lee and Korean Christianity 9

accordance with the church's bylaws.[11] However, the church members suggested a five-year extension, and Cho accepted a three-year extension, requesting that a successor be chosen to work alongside him. In October 2006, a recommendation for a successor was received, with seven candidates that included Lee. In the same month, an operating committee composed of elder representatives conducted the initial round of voting, shortlisting three candidates. Lee received the highest number of votes among them. In November of that year, a second round of voting occurred with all 940 elders of the church. Once again, Lee was the top choice and was ultimately selected as the final candidate. Subsequently, on 8 July 2007, YFGC conducted a vote by all its members, wherein Lee received 98% approval for his leadership. In May 2008, he took the role of the second senior pastor of the church, succeeding Cho, the founding pastor. Because the church membership actively participated in this entire process, the baton-pass from Cho to Lee occurred with little trouble.

The latter's appointment through such a democratic process held significant implications for the South Korean church community. Many prominent churches faced criticism for the practice of passing down pastoral positions to their children, effectively creating a system of hereditary leadership transition. In fact, Cho upheld his congregation's power to appoint consistently. During the final selection process within the YFGC conference, Cho was asked for his opinion when three candidates emerged as the top choices. He responded, "Since all three individuals are my disciples, it doesn't matter who it is. I encourage you to pray and vote under the guidance of the Holy Spirit." Afterwards, Lee acknowledged that one of Cho's significant contributions was the adoption of a democratic procedure for selecting his successor, which is rarely seen domestically or internationally. He believed that such a democratic approach to appointing successors in large churches served as a model for the future.[12]

The democratic succession process within YFGC also had an impact on South Korean society. In an editorial, the *Hankook Ilbo* daily newspaper noted that Cho, who held considerable influence in the succession process, actively advocated for a democratic procedure, effectively breaking the cycle of hereditary leadership succession within Korean Protestantism. The *Munhwa Ilbo* daily newspaper pointed out that Cho rightfully held absolute authority in selecting his successor, yet chose the next pastor through secret balloting among elders, which was an exceptionally rare occurrence.[13]

Consequently, Lee now emphasises democratic procedures in the succession process within the South Korean church community. He views the term "hereditary" as wrong. He claims that Korean churches possess the power to determine their future pastors independently, and eligibility for the position

---

[11] Yoido Full Gospel Church 60-Year History Compilation Committee (hereafter, "60-Year Committee"), 의도순복음교회 *60 년사* [The 60-Year History of Yoido Full Gospel Church] (hereafter, "The 60-Year History"), (Seoul: Seoul Logos, 2018), 157.

[12] 60-Year Committee, 여의도순복음교회 *60 년사* [The 60-Year History], 158.

[13] 60-Year Committee, 여의도순복음교회 *60 년사* [The 60-Year History], 168, rephrased.

should not be limited exclusively to the children of the current senior pastors. If they meet the qualifications, they may be included as candidates. The issue arises when these processes are not carried out democratically and are manipulated by the current senior pastors in a coercive or intentional manner to pass leadership on to their children.[14]

In the context of leadership transition, Lee is conscious of his position as Cho's successor. He consistently emphasises Rev. Cho's significance to the extent that he refrains from comparing himself to him. He elevates Cho to a level where he describes himself as a mere associate pastor as long as Cho is present with them. Lee does not see his relationship with Cho as that of a predecessor and successor, but rather as that of a mentor and disciple, or father and son. This perspective is influenced by his Asian way of thinking.[15]

The relationship between Lee and Cho can be traced back to Lee's grandfather, Won-Geun Lee, who was a listener of Cho's sermons and led the entire family to move to the Full Gospel Church. Afterward, Lee's parents became dedicated members of the YFGC. His father, Kyung-Seon Lee, was not only an injured Korean War veteran but also a successful businessman. He was devoted to the Full Gospel Church and, like his father, served as its chairman when the first elder council was organised at YFGC in 1978. His mother, Sun-Sil Kim, worked as the head of the women's department and became an honorary pastor after retirement. Therefore, Lee's whole family was a Full Gospel family, and it was natural for Cho to trust his successor.

Within Lee's congregation and leadership team, Cho was both a valuable asset and significant challenge, particularly concerning various issues related to Cho's family. Because of this, some suggested suspending Cho's preaching at YFGC. In response, Lee emphasised that many people at YFGC still wished to hear Cho's sermons, and he respected their rights. Furthermore, regarding the conflicts involving Cho's sons associated with the *Kukmin Ilbo*, Lee asserted that he remained neutral. While he held deep respect for Cho, he chose not to involve himself in Cho's family-related matters.[16]

---

[14] Yong-sam Kim, "사회에 기여하는 교회, 나누고 섬기는 교회 만들겠다: 세계 최대 교회 여의도순복음교회 이영훈 담임목사" [Establishment of a church dedicated to societal contributions, emphasising sharing and serving: The biggest church Yoido Full Gospel Church Senior Pastor Younghoon Lee], *Monthly Chosun* (January 2010), n.p.,
https://monthly.chosun.com/client/news/viw.asp?nNewsNumb=201001100039/, accessed 29 July 2023.

[15] Sung-dong Kim, "대형교회의 적극적인 나눔은 시대적인 요구이다: 세계 최대 여의도순복음교회 이끄는 이영훈 당회장 목사" [The active sharing of large churches is a modern necessity: Senior Pastor Younghoon Lee who leads the biggest church Yoido Full Gospel Church], *Monthly Chosun* (December 2013), n.p.,
https://monthly.chosun.com/client/news/viw.asp?ctcd=E&nNewsNumb=201312100032&page=13/, accessed 29 July 2023.

[16] Ibid.

Lee's Ministry and Theology: Succession and Advancement

The primary reason Lee was well-suited to succeed Cho in leading YFGC was his deep understanding of Cho's faith and Pentecostalism. Lee had served for a long time as the director of the YFGC, where he organised and presented Cho's theology. This effort helped various denominations in Korea to understand the essential theological position of the Full Gospel Church. Cho himself possessed a remarkable ability to express his faith in appropriate language. His articulation covered important theological aspects such as salvation, fullness of the Holy Spirit, divine healing, blessing, the second coming, the Pentecostal five-fold ministry, the three-fold salvation applied to specific life issues (spiritual well-being, prosperity, strong body), and the four dimensions of spirituality (thinking, dreaming, believing, speaking). In this sense, Cho was a pioneering and influential leader. Lee did not deviate from this existing framework. He faithfully inherited the emphases of his spiritual mentor.

Yet, Lee reinterpreted and advanced Cho's theology from his own perspective. His first principle is the absolute sovereignty of God and God-centeredness.[17] This is something he learned from his grandfather. Growing up, Lee learned to prioritise God through daily family worship. From his parents, Lee learned the importance of living a life where God holds the highest priority. This signifies his adherence to a conservative Presbyterian tradition that has the potential to prevent the idolisation of specific individuals.

Lee's second principle involves having faith, being filled with the Holy Spirit, and what he calls "absolute positivity." In his book, *The Miracles of Absolute Positivity*, Lee offers a fresh perspective on the faith and theology discussed earlier. He emphasises the concept of "fivefold-positivity" (positivity toward oneself, others, work and mission, environments, and the future), and also "triple training" (positive language, absolute gratitude, and sharing love).[18] As a leader in YFGC, Lee had possessed a profound understanding of the Holy Spirit's role in Christian faith and carried on the spirit of Cho. However, by introducing new language, Lee adds a fresh interpretation of how the Spirit transforms the lives of believers based on an absolute affirmation of God's work.

Lee's third guiding principle centres on the concept of "Little Jesus' spirituality." While being filled with the Holy Spirit characterised Cho's faith development, the concept of "Little Jesus" represents a new direction pursued by Lee. Traditionally, the core message of the Full Gospel movement is blessing. For many impoverished Koreans, the message of blessing became synonymous with the Gospel itself. However, as the decades passed, Koreans began seeking deeper meaning beyond mere blessings. In this changing landscape, Lee encountered Father R. A. Torrey III, a significant figure at the Jesus Abbey, and

---

[17] 60-Year Committee, *여의도순복음교회 60 년사* [The 60-Year History], 169–74. This is a summary of Pastor Younghoon Lee's faith and theology.

[18] Younghoon Lee, *절대 긍정의 기적* [The Miracle of Absolute Positivity], (Seoul: Institute for Church Growth, 2023), 10–11.

spent approximately three weeks there in 1977.[19] He immersed himself in Father Torrey's spirituality, which connected the Pentecostal experience with traditional monastic self-denial. The spirituality of the Little Jesus is the cross of Christ which leads to liberation from sin, illness, and poverty through self-sacrifice or self-emptying. The baptism in the Spirit brings spiritual gifts but also a strong drive to embrace Christ's holiness, sanctification, and love for missional work. During this period, the *Shinangge*, issued by the Full Gospel Church, serialised Torrey's "Letters from the Valley."

This intentional choice represents a response to the previous criticism that the Pentecostal movement had focused excessively on gifts.

The Institutional Reconstruction and Growth of the Church

Alongside Lee's appointment as the senior pastor, YFGC initiated a process of organisational reconstruction. Prior to his retirement, Cho had already come up with plans to establish approximately twenty significant satellite churches. Beyond the primary sanctuary located in Yoido, YFGC had a network of church sites spread across the Seoul metropolitan area. These would be mutually interdependent and influenced by the main sanctuary in matters of personnel and finances. Many assistant pastors, trained under Cho, held leadership positions on these campuses. As part of his retirement plan, Cho decided to grant them each independence.

The process of granting autonomy to these satellite churches, and transitioning them into independent churches, had been around for several years. However, with Cho anticipating his retirement, there was a significant push to expedite this transition. Although the decision was made in 2007, the actual transition of these branch churches into independent congregations began after the appointment of Lee. This transition, initiated in early 2009, concluded by the end of the same year and resulted in the establishment of approximately twenty independent branch churches. This decision held great significance for YFGC. At the time of Lee's inauguration as the senior pastor, the registered members numbered around 780,000, with an attendance of approximately 300,000. But after independence, the total number of registered members decreased from 780,000 to 430,000.[20]

Yet, the independence of branch churches aligned with Lee's ministry vision. He believed that it was no longer desirable for the Korean church to be led solely by charismatic single leaders, and that the church should move away from

---

[19] Younghoon Lee, "절대긍정과 성령충만의 순복음 사역자" [Absolute Positivity and Spirit-filled Full Gospel Minister], 229.

[20] Yoido Full Gospel Church began in 1958 with just five believers, but by 1979, it boasted a congregation of 100,000 members. In 1992, the church's membership had grown to 700,000. However, starting in 1990, it began to grant independence to twelve branch churches located in the outskirts of Seoul. As a result, during the 1990s, Yoido Full Gospel Church's membership maintained around 700,000 members. See Kim, "사회에 기여하는 교회, 나누고 섬기는 교회 만들겠다: 세계 최대 교회 여의도순복음교회 이영훈 담임목사" [Establishment of a church...], n.p.

centralisation towards regional decentralisation.[21] Following the footsteps of Cho, Lee and YFGC encouraged senior leaders to work together as a team in ministry under Lee's leadership. The satellite churches each had independent authority over personnel and finances, but still operated under the overarching spiritual leadership of Cho within the larger framework of YFGC. Currently, these churches have congregations ranging from 10,000 to 15,000 members each on average. As part of their collaboration, all churches under the Full Gospel framework participate in live broadcasting of the Sunday afternoon service (featuring Cho's sermons) at 1 pm from YFGC. Additionally, each branch church allocates 10% of its church finances to the non-profit organisation "Full Gospel Mission," which is affiliated with YFGC. This contribution supports various ministries, including overseas missions.

In addition to the church's structural reorganisation, Lee encourages a powerful Holy Spirit movement. The strength of YFGC lies significantly in its Holy Spirit and prayer movements. In this way, Lee has successfully blended Pentecostal traditions with those of the historic Korean church, which placed great emphasis on early morning prayer gatherings and Friday all-night prayer gatherings. Lee restructured the Friday night prayer gatherings, launching the "Friday Night Holy Spirit Prayer Meeting." These meetings on Friday evenings provide substantial time for prayer and testimonies. These changes offer opportunities for attendees to receive the abundant grace of the Holy Spirit through a variety of speakers and programmes.

Lee also introduced the "Twelve Basketfuls Early Morning Prayer Meeting" in 2009, shortly after taking on the role of senior pastor in 2008. This event, typically observed by most Korean churches as a special prayer gathering at the beginning of the year, is embraced by YFGC to start the new year with prayer dedicated to God. This endeavour received significant enthusiasm when it was started and has continued to be held annually. The Twelve Basketfuls Early Morning Prayer Meeting has created a new tradition involving around 650 churches, including affiliated main sanctuaries, branch churches, and related organisations. Beyond this, special early morning prayer meetings are also conducted during Holy Week and Thanksgiving.

Under the leadership of Lee, YFGC underwent a transformation initiated by Cho but given fresh vision and momentum by Lee. The branch churches gaining greater independence, combined with theological adjustments and Spirit-empowered prayer movement, has yielded a growth rate of about 10,000 to 15,000 members annually. Considering the challenges faced by many churches in Korea, this growth can be seen as quite remarkable.

Helping Hands: Relief Work and Volunteer Services

Generally, YFGC has been widely known as a church that emphasises blessings. However, Lee has made efforts to establish a connection between God's blessings and the act of sharing and caring for our neighbours. He believes that the essence of the church lies in sharing God's love with our neighbours. In his

---

[21] 60-Year Committee, 여의도순복음교회 60 년사 [The 60-Year History], 175.

inaugural address as the senior pastor, when asked about his desired objectives, he stated, "What I would like the most is for our church to remain as a community church that embraces and provides support to the marginalized, the impoverished, and the powerless. I find myself deeply reflecting on the observation that, consciously or unconsciously, our church's focus appears to be shifting from serving the working class to serving the middle class and the more affluent."[22]

Lee asserts that this marks a significant transformation in the ministry of YFGC. He explains, "While the practice of sharing and caring persisted in the past, its main focus was on growth and revival during the 1960s and 1970s, primarily centred around individual salvation. Now, as the church has matured, the next phase involves reaching out to society. Such societal outreach fundamentally entails the act of sharing." Lee's passion and conduct are rooted in the experiences he gained during his college years. While attending university, he engaged in volunteer work in a resettlement community located in Nanji Island. This experience opened his eyes to the impoverishment that people lived in within Seoul. Subsequently, he developed the belief that he should make a meaningful contribution to helping those in need when given the opportunity. Now, he is actively fulfilling a long-standing aspiration. Lee believes that the church, which was criticised by some for its efforts in individual concerns, will find its way forward through helping hands: relief work, volunteer services, societal engagement.

Lee's dedication to relief work and helping others is not a temporary effort; instead, it is a well-defined and institutionalised commitment. He has established the practice of allocating one-third of the annual budget towards assisting those in need. Currently, YFGC's annual budget stands at approximately 100 billion won, with around 35 billion won allocated to support relief work, volunteer service, and missionary initiatives. Lee believes that this is something large-scale churches can accomplish. These large churches have substantial budgets, enabling them to take on tasks that may exceed the capabilities of smaller congregations. Similar to how the accumulation of capital has shaped modern industrial society, the significant contributions to large churches can be systematically directed to aid individuals facing challenging circumstances.

In the context of conducting relief work, YFGC's most vital channel is established through the NGO organisation known as "Good People." Good People is an internationally registered humanitarian development organisation affiliated with the United Nations. YFGC is a major supporter of Good People, with Lee currently serving as its chairman. Good People's operations can be classified into four main categories: international initiatives, domestic programmes, charitable endeavours, and humanitarian assistance efforts. Their international projects encompass areas such as healthcare, education assistance, sanitation, and income enhancement activities. Domestically, they engage in child support, medical aid, and crisis family support programmes. Their sharing initiatives include Hero Race (treating rare diseases), Love's Hope Box

---

[22] Kim, "대형교회의 적극적인 나눔은 시대적인 요구이다: 세계 최대 여의도순복음교회 이끄는 이영훈 당회장 목사" [The active sharing...], n.p.

(providing assistance to those in need), and Good People Medical Volunteer Service (offering support to the medically underserved). Additionally, humanitarian support programmes provide immediate responses to sudden crises. [23] These actions by Good People exemplify the extent to which YFGC is dedicated to conducting relief work/helping hands in a professional and comprehensive manner.

YFGC actively participates in various significant relief and volunteer initiatives, one notable example being the "Ansan Hope Sharing Project." Ansan is an area that suffered greatly due to the tragic *MV Sewol* incident in 2014, considered one of the most significant disasters in South Korean history. From the very beginning of this tragedy, YFGC consistently visited Ansan to express solidarity and actively contribute to the local economy. The church's dedication extended through a total of twelve visits until 2017, with the aim of empathising with and supporting those who endured immense suffering. In this, Lee has displayed a strong commitment to the task of healing the wounds of the public. [24]

Another societal transformation activity YFGC engages in is organising job fairs to address the issue of unemployment. The church noticed that there were a significant number of entrepreneurs and companies seeking employees, while many young people were looking for employment. Since 2014, YFGC has been facilitating connections between these two demographics through annual job fairs. They have even expanded their efforts to include job fairs for the elderly, providing new employment opportunities not only for youth but for senior citizens.

Another critical issue prevailing in Korean society is the low birth rate, which poses a substantial threat to the nation's future. Lee is deeply concerned about this problem and has taken initiatives within YFGC to encourage childbirth. Currently, the church provides financial incentives for childbirth, offering 2 million won for the first child, 3 million won for the second, 5 million won for the third, and 10 million won for the fourth and subsequent children. It is important to acknowledge that while these financial incentives may not completely resolve the problem, they serve as a means to encourage childbirth within the church's community.

Lee in the Global Pentecostal Movement

Rev. Cho was a highly significant figure in the global Pentecostal movement. His ministry extended beyond the boundaries of Korea and had a worldwide

---

[23] See "인도적 지원사업" [Humanitarian assistance], n.d., n.p,
https://www.goodpeople.or.kr/kor/business/legacy-donation.html/, accessed 5 August 2023.
[24] Gil-yong Yoo, "특별 인터뷰, 이영훈 여의도순복음교회 담임목사의 따뜻한 리더십" [Special interview, the warm leadership of senior pastor of Yoido Full Gospel Church, Younghoon Lee], *The Joongang* (May 2015), n.p.,
https://jmagazine.joins.com/monthly/view/305953/, accessed 29 July 2023.

impact. But since his passing in 2021, one of Lee's tasks now is to determine how to continue that international ministry. Fortunately, his academic career has equipped him with a deep understanding of global Pentecostalism, and he has established strong connections with Pentecostal scholars, including Vinson Synan, a prominent historian of the American Pentecostal movement. Synan, who was the dean of the School of Divinity at Regent University, jointly operated the doctoral programme in ministry with YFGC. Lee played a crucial role as Synan's Korean counterpart, engaging in academic exchanges with globally renowned scholars like Cecil M. Robeck Jr. (Fuller Theological Seminary) and Allan Anderson (University of Birmingham) while overseeing the International Theological Research Institute.

Lee has also carried on Cho's distinctive three-fold blessing, which was acquired during his interactions with Oral Roberts in the United States. Consequently, YFGC and Oral Roberts University continue in strong relationship. In 2022, Oral Roberts University invited Lee to be their commencement speaker for their graduation ceremony. During this prestigious event, he was introduced as a leader continuing Cho's legacy in guiding the global Pentecostal movement and awarded an honorary Doctor of Theology degree.[25]

The core of Cho's international ministry was carried out through his organisation, Church Growth International (CGI), which he established in 1976. He collaborated with pastors and scholars worldwide to promote the growth of the Korean church and learn from them. CGI held one year in Korea and another year travelling abroad, organising conferences for church growth. Cho visited major cities in over 100 countries and held more than 600 conferences. Even after retiring from YFGC, CGI continued to be influenced by Cho's leadership until his passing.

When Lee took the position of president of CGI in 2022, succeeding Cho, this marked a significant transition where Lee inherited another critical dimension of Cho's ministry. He restructured the board of directors and organised a conference under the theme "Pentecostal Revival for the Next Generation." The conference featured international speakers such as François Possehl (France), Bob Rogers (USA), Hendrik Bolster (Australia), and John Milton Rodriguez (Colombia).[26] He then led the 100th anniversary of the Pentecostal Church in Indonesia in March 2023, and visited City Harvest Church in Singapore, encouraging them to experience revival. In June, Lee hosted the "Fire

---

[25] Ui-jung Hwang, "이영훈목사, 오랄로버츠대 졸업예배서 첫 한국인 설교" [Pastor Lee Younghoon, the first Korean to preach the Oral Roberts University graduation service], *Asia Today* (8 May 2022), n.p., https://www.asiatoday.co.kr/view.php?key=20220501010000429&ref=search/, accessed 5 August 2023.

[26] Bo-hyuk Lim, "이영훈 목사, 국제교회성장연구원 총재에 추대" [Pastor Younghoon Lee inaugurated as president of Church Growth International], *Kukmin Ilbo* (7 October 2022), n.p., https://www.kmib.co.kr/article/view.asp?arcid=0924267196/, accessed 5 August 2023.

Conference," a massive gathering of interdenominational groups in Taiwan, marking the largest event held in the country since the beginning of the pandemic. During this conference, Lee proclaimed that it would not be long before one-third of Taiwan's population returned to the Lord, laying the foundation for the Gospel's expansion in China. In July, he travelled to Kenya, where he led a pastor's conference attended by over 3,000 New Year's Day leaders from seven neighbouring countries, as well as a public assembly attended by 20,000 people. Kenya had been visited by Cho thirty years prior, and the president of Kenya, William Ruto, invited Lee to the presidential palace to convey his gratitude.

Because Cho was such a central figure in the Korean and global Pentecostal movements, numerous gatherings were held in Korea and it is the task of Lee and YFGC to carry on this tradition. The World Pentecostal Conference, an event involving Pentecostal churches around the world, was held in Korea in both 1973 and 1998. Following this tradition, Lee hosted this conference in Seoul in October 2022. The core message of the conference emphasises the ongoing global spiritual awakening among the new generation and highlights the significant role of the Korean church.[27] Notably, leaders from the Pentecostal churches in seventy-three countries gathered at the DMZ Peace Park to pray for the reunification of the Korean Peninsula, and this prayer meeting was attended online by 1.5 million believers worldwide.

Through all this, it is important to note that Lee has not simply replicated Cho's ministries. While Cho primarily focused on healing ministry within the Pentecostal context, Lee explains the historical background of the Pentecostal movement and its current global significance when he travels abroad. Simultaneously, he introduces Korea's prayer and Bible study movement. By doing so, he is nurturing the seed planted by Cho into a more mature state. This demonstrates that Lee is carrying forward Cho's ministry in a progressive manner.

Lee and the Unity Movements

The Unity Movement of the Korean Church

After the period of liberation, Korean Christianity underwent a significant transformation with the emergence of the Pentecostal movement. It originated on the outskirts of the Korean church during the Korean War and gradually moved to the centre of the Korean church, with YFGC playing a crucial role in nurturing this development. Rev. Cho maintained close ties with revivalists in Korea during this period, actively collaborating with them during revival gatherings. As the Full Gospel Church went through a heresy dispute with the Presbyterian Church in the 1980s, it began to consider the necessity of aligning

---

[27] Kyung-bae Choi, "(파워인터뷰) 이영훈 목사 '오순절 운동, 다시 부흥으로 나아갑시다'" [(Power Interview) Pastor Younghoon Lee, "Pentecostal movement, let's move to revival again"], *CBS NoCut News* (11 October 2022), n.p., https://www.nocutnews.co.kr/news/5830663/, accessed 5 August 2023.

with mainstream Korean churches. In line with this perspective, YFGC joined as a founding member of the Christian Council of Korea (CCK) under the leadership of Pastor Kyung-Jik Han in 1989. Given the conservative nature of the Full Gospel Church, this move was a natural progression.

However, Cho's collaborative efforts did not end there. In 1996, the Assemblies of God joined the National Council of Churches in Korea (NCCK). During that time, the ecumenical movement centred around the World Council of Churches (WCC) and the NCC faced criticism from many churches due to its progressive faith and theology. To address these issues, they attempted to incorporate the Pentecostal denomination. Walter J. Hollenweger, who conducted the initial comprehensive study on the Pentecostal movement, served as the first Secretary for Evangelism in the Division of World Mission and Evangelism of the WCC. As Cho had been involved in heresy disputes during the 1980s, he believed that joining mainstream gatherings was key to avoiding such disputes. While there was a membership invitation from the WCC, Cho chose to join only the Korean NCC. This decision integrated the Full Gospel Church into the mainstream denominations in Korea. However, it was exceptionally rare for a denomination belonging to the Pentecostal tradition to align with the progressive organisation represented by the NCC.

Lee, however, has been able to bridge the conservative and progressive traditions within the Korean church more naturally. He originally grew up in the Presbyterian tradition, with many ministers from the conservative side of the church in his maternal extended family. He was nurtured in a conservative faith environment. During his studies in the United States, he attended Westminster Theological Seminary, which is traditionally Reformed. However, during that time, he also received a liberal theological education. As mentioned, his initial theological education was at the progressive Yonsei University in Korea, with a doctoral degree completed at Temple University, known for its liberal approach. This experience helped him go beyond the boundaries of conservatism and progressivism and led him to a place where he places importance on experiential aspects of faith without strict doctrinal constraints. In this sense, he believes Pentecostalism has aspects that harmonise well with other traditions. So, while actively engaging in various unity movements, Lee maintains his own identity and brings what he feels is the best to the Korean church. For example, when he emphasises social welfare, he does not advocate for a social revolution, as emphasised in liberation theology, but emphasises initiatives that help neighbours in need through love. In this regard, his emphasis lies in Christian service to society rather than structural reform.

This bridging of traditions has not been without bumps. After YFGC joined the NCCK, Lee became the head of its theological committee, and in 2011, its chairman. This was controversial because the NCCK represents the progressive faction of Korean Christianity, and Lee is not fundamentally a progressive. He attended the WCC conference in Busan as well, where a significant division existed among the conservatives regarding participation in the WCC. Some advocated for rejecting WCC involvement, while others believed it was crucial to engage with the organisation to broaden the Evangelical perspective. The latter argument was initially put forward by Cho and Lee when they joined the

NCCK. Korean Evangelicals attempted to include North Korean human rights issues in the final statement of the WCC conference, led by prominent figures including Lee himself, as well as Sang Bok Kim, and Jong Yun Lee.[28] Unfortunately, despite their efforts, the statement was not ultimately adopted, and the idea that the participation of pastors like Cho and Lee in the NCC would bring about change did not yield significant results.

His attempt to work with progressive figures continued to be rocky. In 2014, he became the chairman of the Christian Council of Korea (CCK). Following the establishment of the CCK in the late 1980s, most churches in Korea joined, and the organisation became a representative voice of Korean Christianity on the national stage. However, CCK encountered prolonged conflicts over the selection of its chairman, leading a significant portion of its members to form the Communion of Churches in Korea (CCIK). Lee took up the position of chairman during a period in which CCK was striving to restore its historical credibility with the aim of revitalising CCK, an institution with a robust historical legitimacy. Lee hosted the World Evangelical Alliance (WEA) leaders' conference, a global united movement of Evangelicals, in Korea to exert Evangelical influence comparable to that of the WCC. However, his efforts to host the WEA meeting in Korea faced challenges within the divided landscape of the Korean church and failed.

At that time, the conservative Evangelical churches in Korea were divided into two organisations, the Christian Council of Korea (CCK) and the Communion of Churches in Korea (CCIK). In such a situation, many believed that these two entities could not collectively represent Korean conservative Evangelical Christianity. As an alternative, the Council of Denominational Leadership in the church of Korea emerged. This organisation brought together prominent denominational leaders in South Korea to discuss current issues within Korean Christianity. By the end of 2016, this organisation was restructured and renamed as the United Christian Churches of Korea (UCCK) to represent the Korean church. The majority of Korean denominations participated in this council and Lee was one of its founding members. The UCCK is proud of its extensive membership, which includes 60,000 churches and approximately 11.5 million believers, representing an estimated 95% of the Korean church. Notably, even the Methodist Church in Korea, which had not participated in the Christian Council of Korea, joined the UCCK. As of 2023, Lee is the chairman of the UCCK and currently serves as its executive. This means he now not only serves as the senior pastor of South Korea's largest church but has also become a pastor representing the entire Korean church.

Lee and the Public Policy of Korean Christianity

As a prominent leader within the Korean church at large, Lee is dedicated to representing the church's interests and conveying its perspectives on various

---

[28] Kim, "대형교회의 적극적인 나눔은 시대적인 요구이다: 세계 최대 여의도순복음교회 이끄는 이영훈 당회장 목사" [The active sharing...], (December 2013), n.p.

issues to the government. Firstly, Lee reflects the societal consciousness held by conservative/Evangelical churches in Korea. He firmly acknowledges that South Korea is a nation founded on the principles of liberal democracy and rejects communist ideology completely. When Suk-Yeol Yoon was elected as the president, Lee supported him, emphasising the importance of upholding liberal democracy rooted in Christian values. In response, President Yoon recognised that contemporary democracy has deep roots in Christian principles, specifically referencing Calvin's political theology.

Lee makes his anti-communist stance very clear in other ways. As a descendant of North Korean Christians, he holds a highly negative view of the idolisation of Il-sung Kim and the Juche faction that supports North Korean ideology. He states:

> Juche ideology is contrary to both the identity of Christianity and the identity of South Korea. Juche ideology elevates Il-sung Kim into an eternal spiritual idol, promoting the idea that he should be followed. It is even documented in the World Religious Yearbook as a religion with 25 million believers. The infiltration of Juche ideology into our society is highly dangerous. As 80% of the Korean church is conservative, Juche ideology cannot penetrate conservative churches. The church must diligently work to guard our identity against the Juche Faction.[29]

Furthermore, Lee believes that the South Korean government should fairly assess the influence of Korean Christianity on Korean society and educate their students about that. Korean Christianity has long been recognised as having a significant impact on Korean modern and contemporary history. Through Christianity, not only schools and hospitals but also modern ideas such as democracy and individual freedom have been introduced to Korean society. However, public education does not adequately acknowledge this role of Christianity; instead, it often portrays Christianity as fostering Western imperialism and Japanese aggression. Korean church historians have therefore been making efforts to correct these inaccuracies, especially in history textbooks, and Lee has strongly supported these endeavours.[30] Further, he has sponsored the publication of *The Founding of the Republic of Korea and Christianity*, under

---

[29] Geun-mi Lee, "기성의 입장에서 권력에 휩싸여 있으면 정치도 교회도 후퇴: 이영훈 여의도순복음교회 목사" [Politics and churches retreat when entrenched in power: Yoido Full Gospel Church Senior Pastor Younghoon Lee], *Monthly Chosun* (December 2022), n.p., https://monthly.chosun.com/client/news/viw.asp?ctcd=c&nNewsNumb=202212100026/, accessed 29 July 2023.

[30] "이영훈 대표회장, 교과서 국정화 찬성입장 밝혀" [Younghoon Lee, the president of the Christian Council of Korea, expresses his affirmation in favour of the nationalisation of textbooks], *Veritas* (20 October 2015), https://veritas.kr/articles/18820/20151020/%EC%9D%B4%EC%98%81%ED%9B%88-%EB%8C%80%ED%91%9C%ED%9A%8C%EC%9E%A5-%EA%B5%90%EA%B3%BC%EC%84%9C-%EA%B5%AD%EC%A0%95%ED%99%94-%EC%B0%AC%EC%84%B1%EC%9E%85%EC%9E%A5-%EB%B0%9D%ED%98%80.htm#google_vignette/, accessed 5 August 2023, n.p.

the leadership of the Church History Society in Korea.[31] This publication contains contributions from Korean historians about the foundational role of Christianity in the establishment of the Republic of Korea.

Recently, Lee has had to get involved in one of the most contentious issues within the Korean church: homosexuality and opposition to the Anti-Discrimination Law. In fact, there is an ongoing global cultural battle centred around debates regarding homosexuality, which primarily centres on whether there should be freedom to openly discuss the subject. Advocates for homosexuality argue that debating it constitutes discrimination, so anti-discrimination laws are necessary to forbid discussions against conservative views. However, Korean Christianity takes a different stance, rooted in the biblical tradition against homosexuality and all forms of sexual deviance. As such, Lee has asserted that:

> The entire nationwide church stands united in its opposition to the Anti-Discrimination Law. According to conservatism, Confucian tradition, and the 5,000-year history and Christian tradition, "human beings fundamentally exist as male and female, mutually interacting and respecting each other's dignity." The Korean church is prepared to make great efforts to prevent the passage of the Anti-Discrimination Law.[32]

Similarly, the issue of Islamisation carries equal importance to that of homosexuality. Islam is currently gaining prominence in Korean society through various channels, particularly by seeking to establish a presence in the Korean economy using Middle Eastern financial resources and leveraging this influence to promote its religion. The concern arises from Islam's historical stance towards other religions and cultures, which poses a significant threat to Korean culture and Christianity. For example, Islam denies monogamy in Korean society and restricts religious freedom. Consequently, the spread of Islam could endanger the foundation of Korean society. However, Korean society seeks to accommodate Islam due to economic reasons, labour force supply, and multiculturalism.

Korean Christians are well aware of how Islam has affected and deconstructed European Christian societies. Therefore, Korean Christianity actively opposes these developments through strong resistance movements. Lee, specifically, emphasises the need to differentiate between peace-loving Muslims versus extremists within the Islamic community who want sharia law or support terrorist acts for the advancement of Islam within a peaceful Korean society.[33]

---

[31] Myung Soo Park, Kyo-sung Ahn, Kwon-jung Kim et al., "대한민국 건국과 기독교" [The Foundation of the Republic of Korea and Christianity], (Seoul: Book Korea, 2014), 11.

[32] Younghoon Lee, "기성의 입장에서 권력에 휩싸여 있으면 정치도 교회도 후퇴: 이영훈 여의도순복음교회 목사" [Politics and churches retreat when entrenched in power: Yoido Full Gospel Church Senior Pastor Younghoon Lee], *Monthly Chosun* (December 2022), n.p.

[33] Young-chul Cho, "'통일전도사' 이영훈 여의도순복음교회 담임목사" ["Unification evangelist" Younghoon Lee, senior pastor of Yoido Full Gospel Church],

A last critical issue facing the Korean church was the coronavirus pandemic, which brought the church into conflict with the government, as it did in many nations. During the pandemic, Korean churches confronted two main challenges. The first was related to the form of worship: should online worship be allowed, or should only in-person worship be permitted? Some conservative churches strongly advocated for in-person worship, asserting that true worship should take place in a physical church building as a communal experience. Conversely, some churches embraced online worship and believed it should continue in the future. Lee advocated for a harmonious coexistence of both online and in-person worship, stating that "both online and offline worship should go hand in hand."[34] While obeying governmental policies by refraining from physical gatherings, he also suggested ways to enable in-person worship as much as possible. In fact, YFGC pioneered video worship early on, which could seamlessly connect into online worship. The YFGC has valued physical gatherings from its origins, but this adaptability surfaced as one of its strengths.

During the COVID-19 era, the economic challenges faced by the Korean church posed another significant challenge. Lee has consistently believed that the Korean church should extend its care to the underprivileged, who became even more prominent during the pandemic. YFGC therefore allocated a budget of 15 billion KRW to help those affected, including 1 million KRW to small business owners, 500,000 KRW to recipients of basic living support, 500,000 KRW to families with two children, and 1 million KRW to households with three or more children. Additionally, they extended financial aid of 1 million KRW per household to disadvantaged families in the Seoul metropolitan area. In particular, Lee aimed to help areas where government assistance was insufficient and strove to instill hope in those communities.

Lee and the Reunification of the Korean Peninsula

YFGC has taken proactive steps to seek opportunities and engage in missionary efforts in response to changing circumstances regarding the Korean Peninsula. Following South Korea's democratisation in 1987, which established press freedom, Rev. Cho founded the *Kookmin Ilbo* newspaper. During the administration of President Moo-Hyun Roh, when inter-Korean exchanges were taking place, Cho aspired to establish a cardiac hospital in North Korea. In 2007, plans were developed for the construction of the "Cho Yonggi Cardiac Hospital" in Pyongyang, with a capacity of 280 beds and an initial construction cost of 20

ShinDong-a (November 2018), n.p.,
https://www.donga.com/SHINDONGA/people/article/all/13/1513354/1/, accessed 29 July 2023.

[34] Myung-hee Lee, "(신년 특별대담) 한국교회, 통렬한 자기반성과 성찰 통해 제2도약 이루자" [(New Year's Special Interview) Korean churches, let's take a second leap forward through stinging self-reflection and introspection], *Kukmin Ilbo* (5 January 2022). n.p.,
https://www.kmib.co.kr/article/view.asp?arcid=0924225955&code=23111111&sid1=chr/, accessed 29 July 2023.

billion KRW. However, due to events like the *Cheonan* sinking during the presidency of Myung-Bak Lee, inter-Korean relations deteriorated, and this project could not progress. Lee, however, fervently believed in the importance of completing this project initiated by Cho.

In 2014, President Geun-hye Park, perceiving shifts in North Korea's internal political landscape, believed that unification led by South Korea would be realised in the near future. In that same year, Lee established the Korea Peace Foundation to pray for the peace and unification of the Korean Peninsula while actively striving to provide humanitarian assistance to North Korea. Through this foundation, he proposed allocating 1% of the total funds of the entire Korean church to prepare for unification. However, at the time, North Korea strongly opposed President Park Geun-hye's unification policy, perceiving it as a policy aimed at the North Korean regime collapse. Also, in 2018, Lee visited the area of North Korea that opposed the construction of the Cho Yonggi Cardiac Hospital in Pyongyang. However, this could not proceed due to ongoing sanctions on North Korea, a situation that has remained unchanged during the subsequent government led by Seok-Yeol Yoon.

Pastor Younghoon Lee holds conflicting emotions toward North Korea, as he is of North Korean descendants. He recognises North Korea as a nation with shared ancestry and regards reunification as the destiny of the Korean people. Nevertheless, he firmly opposes sentimental reunification proposals, emphasising that they could lead to various complications, especially in the situation of North Korea's nuclear weapons possession. He has said, "From a religious perspective, reunification should neither be rushed nor delayed. Each issue should be systematically addressed within the overarching framework of denuclearization. It's not a matter of one side advancing ahead of the other. North Korea is a highly organized society, and wise handling is essential."[35]

Ideologically, Lee identifies two critical factors that contributed to the successful reunification of Germany. First was the power of Christianity. Despite the ideological division between the two German states, Germany had a long-standing Christian identity, which played a crucial role in the reunification process. Second was the freedom of travel. Despite numerous conflicts, Germany maintained continuous exchanges, ultimately leading to reunification. Lee believes that for reunification, it is essential to focus on continuous exchanges rather than confrontations between North and South. That is, he asserted that instead of closing the Kaesong Industrial Complex, further developing of it and the opening of North Korean society would be more effective.[36] Moreover, as a Christian minister, he believes in the mission to spread the Gospel in North Korea, which could aid reunification in the long term.

---

[35] Cho, "'통일전도사' 이영훈 여의도순복음교회 담임목사" ["Unification Evangelist"...], (November 2018), n.p.

[36] Ibid.

Conclusion: From the Outskirts to the Centre

After liberation, YFGC began humbly on the outskirts of Seoul. However, it has since grown to become the world's largest church, first under the leadership of Reverend Yonggi Cho. In 2008, a significant transition took place when Dr. Younghoon Lee succeeded to that role. This attracted considerable attention as people wondered how Lee would preserve and carry forward the legacy of Cho. Yet, Lee did faithfully preserve the Cho's ministry while adding his own unique character. Succession and development were more important to him than discontinuity and change.

Most of all, Lee faithfully shared and honoured the Korean Pentecostal legacy of Cho, having grown up and ministered at YFGC before his promotion. He not only matured within the context of the Pentecostal tradition but studied it historically and theologically. In this regard, one of Lee's most important tasks was to develop the Pentecostal faith established by Cho and mature it by infusing it with both historical contributions and his unique conceptions. Lee's continuation of Cho's legacy while advancing it can be observed in the following ways:

First, Lee has positioned YFGC as one of the mainstream Christian churches in South Korea. Although the church was previously one of the largest in the world, its prominence within the Korean church did not necessarily align with its size. Unlike Cho, Pastor Younghoon Lee comes from a Presbyterian background, which is a predominant denomination in South Korea. He received a comprehensive education that extended beyond the Pentecostal theological teachings, encompassing both progressive and conservative perspectives. This background has elevated YFGC to a central position within the Korean church, extending its influence within but also beyond the Pentecostal denomination.

Secondly, Lee has served as the chairman of union associations representing various streams of Korean Christianity. Through these roles, he has effectively communicated the stance of the Korean church to Korean society. Currently, the Korean church faces various critical issues such as Islamisation, anti-discrimination legislation, revisionist education, and North Korean policy. Pastor Lee has played a crucial role in conveying the Korean church's perspective on these issues to both Korean society and the government.

Thirdly, Lee has made efforts to sublimate what could be called "full gospel" to a "whole gospel," by placing a strong emphasis on holistic evangelism and missions. In the past, YFGC was criticised for focusing on individual faith while neglecting societal issues. In response, Lee has emphasised comprehensive salvation and theologically supported it. His stance has led YFGC to initiate outreach and societal transformation in areas like unemployment, declining birth rates, and basic economic assistance in times of need.

Lastly, Lee departed from the era of the single charismatic leader and pursued collaborative ministry with his colleagues. While Cho was an exceptional figure in the Korean Pentecostal movement, Lee finds himself in a position where he must lead the denomination through collaborative relationships with fellow Pentecostal ministers. He prefers to work as a leader within a team rather than as a charismatic figure. In the era of democratisation, Lee is guiding YFGC toward new horizons.

Bibliography of Younghoon Lee

Compiled by Ho Sung Kim

Books

Expository Preaching Books

에베소서: 하나님께서 기뻐하시는 교회 [Ephesians: The Church in Which God Is Pleased]. Seoul: Seoul Logos, 2009.

빌립보서: 예수, 우리의 기쁨 [Philippians: Jesus, Our Joy]. Seoul: Seoul Logos, 2009.

골로새서: 영광의 소망 예수 그리스도 [Colossians: The Hope of Glory in Jesus Christ]. Seoul: Seoul Logos, 2010.

사도행전 1: 성령이 너희에게 임하시면 [Acts 1: When the Holy Spirit Comes Upon You]. Seoul: Seoul Logos, 2010.

사도행전 2: 든든히 서가는 교회 [Acts 2: A Church That Is Going Strong]. Seoul: Seoul Logos, 2011.

사도행전 3: 복음의 지경을 넓히시는 성령님 [Acts 3: The Holy Spirit Who Expands the Horizons of The Gospel]. Seoul: Seoul Logos, 2011.

사도행전 4: 열방을 향한 하나님의 마음 [Acts 4: God's Heart for the Nations]. Seoul: Seoul Logos, 2011.

사도행전 5: 위대한 여정의 시작 [Acts 5: The Beginning of a Great Journey]. Seoul: Seoul Logos, 2011.

갈라디아서: 내 안에 그리스도께서 사시는 것이라 [Galatians: I No Longer Live, But Christ Lives in Me]. Seoul: Seoul Logos, 2011.

사도행전 6: 와서 우리를 도우라 [Acts 6: Come and Help Us]. Seoul: Seoul Logos, 2012.

사도행전 7: 주 예수께 받은 사명 [Acts 7: The Mission Received from the Lord Jesus]. Seoul: Seoul Logos, 2012.

사도행전 8: 끝나지 않는 복음의 열정 [Acts 8: The Never-Ending Passion for the Gospel]. Seoul: Seoul Logos, 2012.

요한복음 1: 말씀이 육신이 되어 [John 1: The Word Became Flesh]. Seoul: Seoul Logos, 2013.

요한복음 2: 영원히 목마르지 아니하리라 [John 2: You Shall Never Thirst]. Seoul: Seoul Logos, 2013.

요한복음 3: 나는 선한 목자라 [John 3: I Am the Good Shepherd]. Seoul: Seoul Logos, 2013.

요한복음 4: 서로 사랑하라[John 4: Love One Another]. Seoul: Seoul Logos, 2014.

요한복음 5: 내가 세상을 이기었노라[John 5: I Have Overcome the World]. Seoul: Seoul Logos, 2014.

창세기 1: 저녁이 되고 아침이 되니[Genesis 1: And It Was Evening, and It Was Morning]. Seoul: Seoul Logos, 2015.

창세기 2: 너는 복이 될지라[Genesis 2: You Shall Be Blessed]. Seoul: Seoul Logos, 2016.

창세기 3: 네 이름이 무엇이냐[Genesis 3: What Is Your Name?] Seoul: Seoul Logos, 2017.

창세기 4: 꿈꾸는 자가 오는도다[Genesis 4: Here Comes That Dreamer]. Seoul: Seoul Logos, 2017.

데살로니가전후서: 그리스도를 본받는 교회[1 & 2 Thessalonians: The Church Imitating Christ]. Seoul: Institute for Church Growth, 2016.

출애굽기 1: 하나님이 그들을 기억하셨다[Exodus 1: God Remembered Them]. Seoul: Seoul Logos, 2018.

출애굽기 2: 야훼께서 너희를 위해 싸우시리니[Exodus 2: God Will Fight for You]. Seoul: Seoul Logos, 2019.

출애굽기 3: 내가 거기서 너희를 만나리라[Exodus 3: I Will Meet You There]. Seoul: Seoul Logos, 2019.

사도행전 강해 1–3 [A Commentary on the Acts of the Apostles 1–3 (40th Anniversary Edition)]. Seoul: Christian Literature Society of Korea, 2018.

야고보서: 행함이 있는 믿음[James: Faith in Action]. Seoul: Institute for Church Growth, 2019.

디모데전후서: 영적 지도자의 길[1 & 2 Timothy: The Path of a Spiritual Leader]. Seoul: Institute for Church Growth, 2019.

사무엘서 1: 야훼께서 여기까지 우리를 도우셨다[1 Samuel 1–15: Thus Far Has the Lord Helped Us]. Seoul: Seoul Logos, 2020.

사무엘서 2: 나 야훼는 중심을 보느니라[1 Samuel 16–31: The Lord Looks at The Heart]. Seoul: Seoul Logos, 2022.

사무엘서 3: 네 왕위가 영원히 견고하리라[2 Samuel 1–14: Your Throne Will Be Established Forever]. Seoul: Seoul Logos, 2023.

사무엘서 4: 야훼께서 큰 구원을 이루시니라[2 Samuel 15–24: The Lord Brought About a Great Victory]. Seoul: Seoul Logos, 2023.

Academic Books

With Euntae Lim and others. *하나님 나 그리고 기적*[God, I, and Miracle]. Seoul: Kookmin Ilbo, 1999.

Translated. Synan, Vinson. 세계 오순절 성결운동의 역사 [The Holiness Pentecostal Tradition]. Seoul: Seoul Logos, 2004.

The Holy Spirit Movement in Korea. Oxford: Regnum Books, 2009.

Translated. Doudera, Ralph J. 행복한 부자 불행한 부자 [Happy Rich, Unhappy Rich]. Seoul: Seoul Logos, 2011.

With Myongjin Ko and others. 내 영혼의 멘토들 [Mentors of My Soul]. Seoul: Institute for Church Growth, 2012.

Edited with Wonsuk Ma and Kuewon Lee. *Pentecostal Mission and Global Christianity: An Edinburgh Reader*. Seoul: Regnum Books, 2012.

The Power of Faith. Seoul: Seoul Logos, 2018.

Following Jesus. Seoul: Seoul Logos, 2020.

Edited. 희망의 목회자(영산 조용기 목사 평전 [A Pastor of Hope: A Critical Biography of Youngsan Yonggi Cho]. Seoul: Seoul Logos, 2022.

Only by Prayer. Seoul: Institute for Church Growth, 2022.

Only by the Holy Spirit. Seoul: Institute for Church Growth, 2022.

The Cross: Foundation of the Full Gospel Faith. Seoul: Institute for Church Growth, 2022.

English–Korean Parallel Sermon Series

돌을 내려놓으라 [Put Down the Stone]. Rev. ed. Seoul: Seoul Logos, 2012.

치료자 예수 그리스도 [Jesus Christ The Healer]. Seoul: Seoul Logos, 2013.

하나님께서 인정하시는 믿음 [The Faith That God Acknowledges]. Seoul: Seoul Logos, 2013.

십자가의 은혜 [The Grace of the Cross]. Seoul: Seoul Logos, 2014.

성령의 시대 [The Era of the Holy Spirit]. Seoul: Seoul Logos, 2015.

네 눈물을 보았노라 [I Have Seen Your Tears]. Seoul: Seoul Logos, 2016.

하나님의 영광의 때 [The Time of the Glory of God]. Seoul: Seoul Logos, 2016.

영원한 감사 [Eternal Thanksgiving]. Seoul: Seoul Logos, 2017.

꿈과 희망을 노래하라 [Sing Songs of Dreams and Hope]. Seoul: Seoul Logos, 2017.

그 중의 제일은 사랑이라 [The Greatest of These Is Love]. Seoul: Seoul Logos, 2018.

용서의 위대한 힘 [The Great Power of Forgiveness]. Seoul: Seoul Logos, 2022.

성숙한 그리스도인 [A Mature Christian]. Seoul: Seoul Logos, 2023.

Sermon Series

영적 성장의 길 [Spiritual Growth]. Seoul: Seoul Logos, 2012.

감사의 기적 [The Miracle of Thanksgiving]. Seoul: Duranno, 2013.

기도의 기적 [The Miracle of Prayer]. Seoul: Duranno, 2013.

십자가의 기적 [The Miracle of the Cross]. Seoul: Duranno, 2014.

믿음의 기적 [The Miracle of Faith]. Seoul: Duranno, 2015.

작은 예수가 되는 길 [The Way to Become a Little Jesus]. Seoul: Seoul Logos, 2015.

내가 너희를 쉬게 하리라 [I Will Give You Rest]. Seoul: Seoul Logos, 2016.

3 분 만화 설교 [3 Minutes Cartoon Sermon]. Seoul: Seoul Logos, 2017.

이영훈 목사의 말씀 365 [Scriptures 365 of Pastor Young Hoon Lee]. Seoul: Seoul Logos, 2017.

오직 십자가(목회의 길 40 년 총서) [Only Cross]. Seoul: Christian Literature Society of Korea, 2018.

오직 말씀(목회의 길 40 년 총서) [Only Scripture]. Seoul: Christian Literature Society of Korea, 2018.

오직 성령(목회의 길 40 년 총서) [Only the Holy Spirit]. Seoul: Christian Literature Society of Korea, 2018.

오직 믿음(목회의 길 40 년 총서) [Only Faith]. Seoul: Christian Literature Society of Korea, 2018.

오직 기도와 감사(목회의 길 40 년 총서) [Only Prayer and Thanksgiving]. Seoul: Christian Literature Society of Korea, 2018.

그리스도인의 영적 성장 [Christian Spiritual Growth]. Seoul: Seoul Logos, 2020.

사랑의 기적 [Miracle of Love]. Seoul: Seoul Logos, 2021.

강하고 담대하라 [Be Strong and Courageous]. Seoul: Seoul Logos, 2023.

위대한 하나님의 사람 1 아브라함: 기적을 창조하는 믿음 [Great Man of God 1 Abraham: A Faith That Creates Miracles]. Seoul: Seoul Logos, 2024.

Training Books

제자의 길 (1) [The Path of Discipleship 1]. Seoul: Seoul Logos, 2010.

4 차원의 영성 리더십 학교 [4-Dimensional Spirituality Leadership School]. Seoul: Institute for Church Growth, 2010.

4 차원의 영성 전도학교 [4-Dimensional Spirituality Evangelical School]. Seoul: Institute for Church Growth, 2010.

Bibliography of Younghoon Lee

4 차원의 영성 리더십 대학 [4-Dimensional Spirituality Leadership College].
Seoul: Institute for Church Growth, 2010.

4 차원의 영성 중보기도 학교 [4-Dimensional Spirituality Intercession
School]. Seoul: Institute for Church Growth, 2011.

제자의 길 (2) [The Path of Discipleship 2]. Seoul: Seoul Logos, 2011.

하나님의 말씀 (1–3) [The Word of God (1–3)]. Seoul: Seoul Logos, 2011.

MTS 정규과정 개정판 성령학교 교재 [Holy Spirit School: MTS Regular
Course]. Rev. ed. Seoul: Institute for Church Growth, 2012.

MTS 정규과정 개정판 성령학교 지침서 [Holy Spirit School Guide Book:
MTS Regular Course]. Rev. ed. Seoul: Institute for Church Growth, 2012.

MTS 정규과정 개정판 큐티학교 교재 [QT School: MTS Regular Course].
Rev. ed. Seoul: Institute for Church Growth, 2012.

MTS 정규과정 개정판 큐티학교 지침서 [QT School Guide Book: MTS
Regular Course]. Rev. ed. Seoul: Institute for Church Growth, 2012.

MTS 정규과정 개정판 성경가이드학교 교재 [Bible Guide School: MTS
Regular Course]. Rev. ed. Seoul: Institute for Church Growth, 2012.

MTS 정규과정 개정판 성경가이드학교 지침서 [Bible Guide School Guide
Book: MTS Regular Course]. Rev. ed. Seoul: Institute for Church Growth,
2012.

MTS 정규과정 개정판 신앙입문학교 교재 [Faith Introduction School: MTS
Regular Course]. Rev. ed. Seoul: Institute for Church Growth, 2012.

MTS 정규과정 개정판 신앙입문학교 지침서 [Faith Introduction School
Guide Book: MTS Regular Course]. Rev. ed. Seoul: Institute for Church
Growth, 2012.

MTS 정규과정 개정판 기도학교 교재 [Prayer School: MTS Regular Course].
Rev. ed. Seoul: Institute for Church Growth, 2012.

MTS 정규과정 개정판 기도학교 지침서 [Prayer School Guide Book: MTS
Regular Course]. Rev. ed. Seoul: Institute for Church Growth, 2012.

MTS 정규과정 개정판 가정행복학교 교재 [Family Happiness School: MTS
Regular Course]. Rev. ed. Seoul: Institute for Church Growth, 2012.

MTS 정규과정 개정판 가정행복학교 지침서 [Family Happiness School
Guide Book: MTS Regular Course]. Rev. ed. Seoul: Institute for Church
Growth, 2012.

MTS 정규과정 개정판 전도자훈련학교 교재 [Evangelist Training School:
MTS Regular Course]. Rev. ed. Seoul: Institute for Church Growth, 2012.

MTS 정규과정 개정판 전도자훈련학교 지침서 [Evangelist Training School
Guide Book: MTS Regular Course]. Rev. ed. Seoul: Institute for Church
Growth, 2012.

MTS 정규과정 개정판 예배학교 교재[Worship School: MTS Regular Course]. Rev. ed. Seoul: Institute for Church Growth, 2012.

MTS 정규과정 개정판 예배학교 지침서[Worship School Guide Book: MTS Regular Course]. Rev. ed. Seoul: Institute for Church Growth, 2012.

MTS 운영매뉴얼[Course Manual: MTS Regular Course]. Rev. ed. Seoul: Institute for Church Growth, 2012.

MTS 정규과정 개정판 새가족양육자학교 지침서[New-Comer Fosterer School Guide Book: MTS Regular Course]. Rev. ed. Seoul: Institute for Church Growth, 2013.

MTS 정규과정 개정판 새가족양육자학교 교재[New-Comer Fosterer School: MTS Regular Course]. Rev. ed. Seoul: Institute for Church Growth, 2013.

MTS 정규과정 개정판 소그룹리더학교 지침서[Small Group Leader School Guide Book: MTS Regular Course]. Rev. ed. Seoul: Institute for Church Growth, 2013.

MTS 정규과정 개정판 소그룹리더학교 교재[Small Group Leader School: MTS Regular Course]. Rev. ed. Seoul: Institute for Church Growth, 2013.

더 나눔 1 인도자용[The Nanum Vol.1 Guide Book]. Seoul: Institute for Church Growth, 2014.

더 나눔 1 교재[The Nanum Vol.1]. Seoul: Institute for Church Growth, 2014.

더 나눔 2 인도자용[The Nanum Vol.2 Guide Book]. Seoul: Institute for Church Growth, 2014.

더 나눔 2 교재[The Nanum Vol.2]. Seoul: Institute for Church Growth, 2014.

작은 예수의 영성[The Spirituality of the Little Jesus 1–2]. Seoul: Nexus CROSS, 2014.

말씀과 진리 1–3 [The Word and Truth 1–3]. Bible College Textbook. Seoul: Institute for Church Growth, 2014.

구역예배공과 성령이 이끄는 삶 (1–2) [Home Cell Group Study (1–2): A Life Led by the Holy Spirit]. Seoul: Seoul Logos, 2015.

구역예배공과 성령이 이끄는 삶 (3–4) [Home Cell Group Study (3–4): A Life Led by the Holy Spirit]. Seoul: Seoul Logos, 2016.

천국 시민의 삶[The Life of a Heavenly Citizen]. Seoul: Institute for Church Growth, 2016.

구역예배공과 성령이 이끄는 삶 (5–6) [Home Cell Group Study (5–6): A Life Led by the Holy Spirit]. Seoul: Seoul Logos, 2017.

구역예배공과 성령이 이끄는 삶 (7–8) [Home Cell Group Study (7–8): A Life Led by the Holy Spirit]. Seoul: Seoul Logos, 2018.

구역예배공과 성령이 이끄는 삶 (9) [Home Cell Group Study (9): A Life Led by the Holy Spirit]. Seoul: Seoul Logos, 2019.

영적 지도자 훈련학교 [The School of Spiritual Leadership]. Seoul: Institute for Church Growth, 2019.

예수님의 참 제자 (1) [True Disciple of Jesus 1. A]. Seoul: Seoul Logos, 2019.

예수님의 참 제자 (2) [True Disciple of Jesus 1. B]. Seoul: Seoul Logos, 2019.

LTC1 예수님의 리더쉽 [LTC1 The Leadership of Jesus]. Seoul: Seoul Logos, 2020.

4 차원 절대긍정학교 [The 4th Dimension Absolute Positivity Training School]. Seoul: Institute for Church Growth, 2023.

Other Books

펜사콜라 기적의 현장 브라운스빌 교회 [Pensacola Field of Miracles Brownsville Church]. Seoul: Kookmin Ilbo, 1997.

십자가 순복음 신앙의 뿌리 [The Roots of the Full Gospel of the Cross]. Seoul: Institute for Church Growth, 2011.

365 일 작은 예수 [365 Days of Little Jesus]. Seoul: Institute for Church Growth, 2011.

신앙생활 [Faith Life]. Seoul: Seoul Logos, 2011.

충성된 일꾼 [Loyal Workers]. Seoul: Institute for Church Growth, 2012.

감사, 행복의 샘 [Gratitude, a Fountain of Happiness]. Seoul: Beautiful Companion, 2013.

성령과 교회 [Holy Spirit and Church]. Seoul: Institute for Church Growth, 2013.

물댄동산-가정예배서 (1–2–3) [Well-Watered Garden – Home Worship Book (1–2–3)]. Seoul: Institute for Church Growth, 2013.

물댄동산-가정예배서 (4–5–6) [Well-Watered Garden – Home Worship Book (4–5–6)]. Seoul: Institute for Church Growth, 2014.

물댄동산-가정예배서 (7–8–9) [Well-Watered Garden – Home Worship Book (7–8–9)]. Seoul: Institute for Church Growth, 2014.

물댄동산-가정예배서 (10–11–12) [Well-Watered Garden – Home Worship Book (10–11–12)]. Seoul: Institute for Church Growth, 2014.

성령 운동의 발자취: 하나님성회 교회사 [The Footsteps of the Holy Spirit Movement: History of AG of Korea]. Seoul: Seoul Logos, 2014.

감사 플러스 긍정 플러스 [Gratitude Plus Positivity Plus]. Seoul: Beautiful Companion, 2014.

성령과 함께 [With the Holy Spirit]. Seoul: Shinangge, 2014.

내가 믿나이다 [I Believe]. Seoul: Institute for Church Growth, 2015.

순전한 감사 넘치는 은혜 [Sheer Gratitude, Overwhelming Grace]. Seoul: Beautiful Companion, 2016.

변화된 신분 변화된 삶 [Changed Identity, Changed Lives]. Seoul: Institute for Church Growth, 2017.

기도, 은혜의 통로 [Prayer, a Channel of Grace]. Seoul: Institute for Church Growth, 2017.

치료의 광선을 비추리니 [I Will Shine a Healing Ray]. Seoul: Institute for Church Growth, 2017.

모든 일을 사랑으로 행하라 [Do All Things in Love]. Rev. ed. Seoul: Institute for Church Growth, 2017.

참 기쁨 [True Joy]. Rev. ed. Seoul: Institute for Church Growth, 2018.

성령운동의 발자취 [The Footsteps of the Holy Spirit Movement: History of AG of Korea]. 40th anniversary edition. Seoul: Christian Literature Society of Korea, 2018.

성령과 한국교회 [The Holy Spirit and the Korean Churches]. 40th anniversary edition. Seoul: Christian Literature Society of Korea, 2018.

감사로 시작하는 365 [Start with Gratitude 365]. Seoul: Seoul Logos, 2020.

2022 감사 QT 365 [2022 Gratitude QT365]. Seoul: Seoul Logos, 2021.

오직 성령으로 [Only by the Holy Spirit]. Seoul: Institute for Church Growth, 2022.

신앙을 이해하다 [Understanding Faith]. Seoul: Institute for Church Growth, 2022.

2023 감사 QT 365 [2023 Gratitude QT365]. Seoul: Seoul Logos, 2022.

오직 기도로 [Only by Prayer]. Seoul: Institute for Church Growth, 2022.

성공에 이르는 12 가지 지혜 [12 Wisdom for Success]. Seoul: Institute for Church Growth, 2023.

절대긍정의 기적 [The Miracle of Absolute Positivity]. Seoul: Institute for Church Growth, 2023.

절대긍정 120 말씀 캘린더 [Absolute Positivity 120 Word Calendar]. Seoul: Institute for Church Growth, 2023.

하늘의 멜로디 [Melody in Heaven]. Seoul: Institute for Church Growth, 2023.

2024 감사 QT 365 [2024 Gratitude QT365]. Seoul: Seoul Logos, 2023.

Academic Articles and Presentations

"성령운동과 에큐메니칼 운동" [Holy Spirit Movement and Ecumenical Movement]. *Pentecost* 11 (1979).

"The Holy Spirit Movement in Korea." *Collected Works* 4 (1993).

"한국교회 성령론을 말한다 <좌담>" [Spirituality in the Korean Church; Colloquium]. *Monthly Ministry* 210 (1994).

"The Pauline Conception of Baptism in Ephesians." *Teaching Theory Series* 5 (1994).

"한국 교회 교육과 영성훈련" [Korean Church Education and Spiritual Training]. *Pastoral and Theological Journal* 59 (1994).

"한국 교회 성령 운동이 나아갈 길" [The Way Forward for the Holy Spirit Movement in the Korean Church]. *The Holy Spirit and Prayer* (1995).

"번영 신학과 고통의 신학: 번영 신학에 대한 성경적 교훈" [Prosperity Theology and the Theology of Suffering: Biblical Lessons on Prosperity Theology]. *Bible and Theology* 17 (1995).

"The Yoido Full Gospel Church: Its History and Structure." *Report for 95 AWF and World Congress of the Sung-Kyul Church* (1995).

"Biblical Teachings on Prosperity Theology." *World Evangelical Fellowship Conference* (1995).

"Luther's View of Law and the Gospel in Christian Life." *Teaching Theory Series* 6 (1995).

"Karl Barth's View of the Gospel and Law in Christian Life." *Teaching Theory Series* 7 (1995).

"번영 신학에 대한 성서적 이해" [A Biblical Understanding of Prosperity Theology]. *The Papers on the 40th Anniversary of the Ministry of Rev. Youngsan Yonggi Cho* 2 (1996).

"현대 성령론 평가: 현대 성령 운동의 역사적 고찰" [Evaluating Contemporary Spiritualism: A Historical Review of the Modern Spirit Movement]. *Bible and Theology* 20 (1996).

"The Case for Prosperity Theology." *Evangelical Review of Theology* 20 (1996).

"The Holy Spirit Movement in Korea: Its Historical and Doctrinal Development." Ph.D. Dissertation, Philadelphia, Temple University, 1996.

"Augustine's Doctrine of the Trinity." *Teaching Theory Series* 8 (1996).

"The Holy Spirit Movement in Korea in the Nineteen-Sixties and Seventies."
Teaching Theory Series 9 (1996).

"교회 안에서 벌어지는 천사이해의 문제점" [The Problem with Angelology
in the Church]. *Pastoral and Theological Journal* 92 (1997).

"The Yoido Full Gospel Church and the Pentecostal Movement." *Teaching
Theory Series* 10 (1997).

"Korean Pentecost: The Great Revival of 1907." *Teaching Theory Series* 11
(1997).

"21 세기를 향한 성령 운동의 원리" [The Spread of the Pentecostal
Movement and the Azusa Revival]. *The Ministry of the Holy Spirit in the
21st Century* (1998).

"여의도순복음교회의 신앙과 신학" [Faith and Theology of Yoido Full
Gospel Church]. *The Holy Spirit and Spiritual Awakening: The 7th
International Theological Seminar* (1998).

"오순절 운동의 확산과 아주사 부흥 운동" [Principles of the Holy Spirit
Movement for the 21st Century]. *The Ministry of the Holy Spirit in the 21st
Century* (1998).

"오순절 운동이 한국교회에 미친 영향" [The Impact of the Pentecostal
Movement on the Korean Church]. *Pentecostal Theological Debates* 1
(1998).

"한국 교회의 전도와 교회성장" [Evangelism and Church Growth in the
Korean Church]. *Theological Thought* 100 (1998).

"Witness and Unity from Pentecostal Perspective in Relation to Korean Church
History." *Christian Church and Ecumenical Organization* (1998).

"삼중축복에 대한 오순절 신학적 이해" [Pentecostal Theological
Understanding of the Threefold Blessing]. *First Full Gospel Theological
Symposium* (1999).

"삼중축복 신앙의 오순절 신학적 이해" [A Pentecostal Theological
Understanding of the Threefold Blessing Faith]. *A Theological
Understanding of the Threefold Blessing by Dr. Yonggi Cho* (2000).

"Korean Pentecost: The Great Revival of 1907." *Asian Journal of Pentecostal
Studies* 4 (2000).

"한국 오순절운동과 신유" [Korean Pentecostalism and Divine Healing].
Holiness Church and Theology 11 (2004).

"조용기 목사의 성령론이 한국 교회에 미친 영향" [The Impact of Pastor
Cho Yonggi's Theology of the Holy Spirit on the Korean Church]. *Journal of
Youngsan Theological* 2 (2004).

"한국교회의 부흥과 교회성장" [Revival and Church Growth in the Korean
Church]. *Spirituality and Divinity* 21 (2005).

"영산 조용기 목사의 '좋으신 하나님 신앙'이 한국 교회에 미친 영향" [The
Impact of Pastor Youngsan Cho Yonggi's Faith in a Good God on the

Korean Church]. *2005 Youngsan International Theological Symposium* (2005).

"여의도순복음교회의 구역 조직과 역사" [District Organization and History of Yoido Full Gospel Church]. *Church Growth* (August 2005).

"영산 조용기 목사의 '좋으신 하나님 신앙'이 한국 교회에 미친 영향" [The Impact of Pastor Youngsan Cho Yonggi's Faith in a Good God on the Korean Church]. *Journal of Youngsan Theology* 7 (2006).

"오순절 운동의 어제와 오늘 그리고 내일에 대한 전망" [Yesterday, Today, and Tomorrow in the Pentecostal Movement]. *Shinangge* (June 2006).

"오순절 사건의 세계 확산에 대한 교회사적 조명" [An Ecclesiastical Look at the Global Spread of the Pentecostal Event]. *2nd National Association of Seminarians and Graduate Students Spirituality* (2007).

"조용기 목사의 성령론이 한국 교회에 미친 영향" [The Impact of Pastor Cho Yonggi's Theology of the Holy Spirit on the Korean Church]. *The Ministry and Theology of Youngsan II* (2008).

"한국의 성령운동에 있어서 조용기 목사와 여의도순복음교회의 공헌" [The Contributions of Pastor Cho Yonggi and Yoido Full Gospel Church to the Holy Spirit Movement in Korea]. *Pastor Cho Yonggi's Church Growth as the World Takes Notice* (2008).

"여의도순복음교회, 새로운 50 년을 바라보며" [Yoido Full Gospel Church Looks Ahead to the Next 50 Years]. *Christian Thought* 606 (2009).

"조나단 에드워즈의 종교적 감성에 대한 이해와 목회적 적용" [Jonathan Edwards' Understanding and Pastoral Application of Religious Sensitivity]. *Korean Church Renewal Seminar Resource Book* (2010).

"기독교영성과 사회윤리" [Christian Spirituality and Social Ethics]. *13th Annual Meeting of the Academy of Christian Science* (2010).

"Christian Spirituality and the Diakonic Mission of Yoido Full Gospel Church." *An Academic Seminar to Commemorate the 100th Anniversary of the Edinburgh Missionary Conference* (2010).

"한반도 통일에 관한 한국교회의 역사적 역할 인식" [Recognise the Historical Role of the Korean Church in the Reunification of the Korean Peninsula]. *2010 Youngsan International Theological Symposium* (2010).

"영산의 십자가 영성과 제자사역" [Cross Spirituality and Discipleship at Youngsan]. *Journal of Youngsan Theological* 20 (2010).

"예수 그리스도의 십자가: 영산의 50 년 목회와 영성의 뿌리" [The Cross of Jesus Christ: The Roots of 50 Years of Ministry and Spirituality at Youngsan]. *2011 Youngsan International Theological Symposium* (2011).

"Christian Spirituality and the Diakonic Mission of the Yoido Full Gospel Church." In *Edinburgh 2010: Mission Today and Tomorrow.* Edited by Kirsteen Kim and Andrew Anderson. Regnum Edinburgh Centenary Series 3. Oxford: Regnum Books, 2011.

"목회적 관점에서 본 개혁주의 생명신학과 신학 회복 운동" [Reformed Life Theology and the Theological Restoration Movement from a Pastoral Perspective]. *5th Reformed Forum on Life and Theology* (2012).

"The Holy Spirit and Mission Spirituality: The Case of Yoido Full Gospel Church." In *Mission Spirituality and Authentic Discipleship*. Edited by Wonsuk Ma and Kenneth R. Ross. Regnum Edinburgh Centenary Series 14. Oxford: Regnum Books, 2013.

"Church Growth: Reflections on Yoido Full Gospel Church." In *Pentecostal Mission and Global Christianity*. Edited by Wonsuk Ma, Veli-Matti Kärkkäinen, and J. Kwabena Asamoah-Gyadu. Regnum Edinburgh Centenary Series 20. Oxford: Regnum Books, 2014.

"Charismatic Tradition in Korea." In *Korean Church, God's Mission, Global Christianity*. Edited by Wonsuk Ma and Kyo Seong Ahn. Regnum Edinburgh Centenary Series 26. Oxford: Regnum Books, 2015.

"그리스도의 마음을 품으신 한경직 목사님" [Pastor Kyung-Jik Han with the Heart of Christ]. *Pastor Kyung-Jik Han's 12th–15th Anniversary Celebration Resource Book* (2016).

"Responding to Human Needs: A Case Study of Yoido Full Gospel Church." In *Good News to the Poor: Spirit-Empowered Responses to Poverty*. Edited by Wonsuk Ma, Opoku Onyinah, and Rebekah Bled. Tulsa, OK: ORU Press, 2022.

Part 1

THE HOLY SPIRIT AND SPIRITUALITY

The Void Pastor David Yonggi Cho Left, Too Large to Be Filled[1]

Younghoon Lee

The Passing of Pastor Cho

Pastor Cho, who had been fighting for his life for over one year and two months while still holding onto his dream of world missions, was finally embraced by the Lord.[2] Except for the period when visits were banned due to COVID-19, I visited him in the hospital every week and believed that he would get well. I wanted to see him get out of the hospital and stand in front of the congregation again, because I did not know how I would manage this megachurch and congregation alone without the Emeritus Pastor. As if he knew my feelings, when I prayed fervently in the hospital room, he held my hand tightly and prayed with me with his whole body. It was exceedingly encouraging and good to see him just lying there, but the void in my heart that he left behind remains an emptiness that cannot be filled even after a year.[3]

For fifty-eight years, starting from my fourth grade in elementary school, Pastor Cho has been my hero, life mentor, and teacher of faith. The first time I heard him preach was when I was eleven years old. The way he smiled and gently spoke to me remain beautifully intact within my heart. His loving presence seemed almost ubiquitous: when I played on the side of the road, when he visited my home, the moment I brought my Yonsei University application and received his prayers, his words of encouragement during my studies in the United States, and many other fond memories. Every fall, memories of our time together come flooding back, and I dearly miss him. There is no one else in this world who can replace him, someone who has consistently taught me with warmth and guided me with love.

My Family's Introduction to Pastor Cho

It was through my grandfather that I first encountered Pastor Cho as a child. My grandfather, Elder Won-Geun Lee, was a man I genuinely admired for his

---

[1] This chapter is an English version of the author's reflection on his special relationship with David Yonggi Cho, first published in *Shinangge* (September 2022) to mark the first anniversary of Cho's passing.

[2] Seong-ho Paik, "세계 최대 단일교회 여의도순복음 창립자 조용기 목사 소천" [Pastor Yonggi Cho, founder of the world's largest single church, Yoido Full Gospel Church, dies], *The JoongAng Ilbo*, 15 September 2021, 16.

[3] Mi-na Lee, "희망의 목회자, '영산 조용기 목사 1주기 추모예배' 열려" [First anniversary memorial service held for "Young San Pastor Yonggi Cho, the Pastor of Hope"], *The Full Gospel Family Newspaper*, 16 September 2022, 1.

integrity and life experiences. He had attained a level of spirituality that proved challenging for me to reach. Indeed, he commanded so much respect that even esteemed leaders of the Korean church, such as Pastor Kyung-Jik Han of Youngnak Church and Pastor Shin-Myung Kang of Saemoonan Church, would bow to him as a senior in the faith.[4]

It was around the time I entered the fourth grade of elementary school when my grandfather came to live with us. He was an active servant of the Lord. At the request of missionary John Talmage from the Southern Presbyterian Mission (PCUSA), he went to Jeju Island to establish Namwon Church and several other churches. He also collaborated with Pastor Kyung-Jik Han to assist refugees who had evacuated during the Korean War,[5] founding Busan Youngnak Church. He encouraged his eldest son and his wife to serve the church in Busan. After many years of active service for the Lord, my elderly grandfather decided to settle down and move in with my father,[6] who was the second son. The reason behind this decision was that my grandfather was active in Seoul and did not want to move to Busan, where his eldest son lived and served as an elder in Busan Youngnak Church. Around that time, my grandfather's youngest daughter, my aunt, had emigrated to Canada, and she asked my father to host my grandfather in her house, located at 45 Naengcheon-dong, Seodaemun-gu. Coincidentally, the Full Gospel Central Church was situated next door, and Pastor Cho's house was just three houses down.

This coincidence turned out to be a life-changing event that would forever alter our family's trajectory. While not everyone in the neighbourhood became a member of the Full Gospel Church or developed a close relationship with Pastor Cho, my family was an exception. We had a spiritually driven grandfather who made attending church a daily ritual for early morning prayer. To accommodate this, we needed to find a nearby church after he had moved to our new home. Initially, we attempted to attend the closest church affiliated with the Presbyterian Church of Korea, which happened to be Saemoonan Church. This choice was particularly fitting because my grandfather had previously fostered a strong and trusting relationship with the senior pastor, Pastor Shin-Myung Kang. Pastor Kang had served as an educational pastor at Seo-Moon-Bak Church, the largest church in Pyongyang, where my grandfather had held a key elder position in the past.[7]

---

[4] Younghoon Lee, "신앙의 명문가를 이루게 하소서 2" (hereafter, "명문가") [Let us become a prestigious family of faith 2] (hereafter, "A prestigious family"), *Shinangge* (April 2016), 29.

[5] Yoido Full Gospel Church 60-Year History Compilation Committee (hereafter, "60-Year Committee"), *여의도순복음교회 60 년사* [The 60-Year History of Yoido Full Gospel Church] (hereafter, "The 60-Year History") (Seoul: Seoul Logos, 2018), 161.

[6] Lee, "명문가 17" [A prestigious family], *Shinangge* (July 2017), 30–31.

[7] Younghoon Lee, "선진국 되려면 부자가 재산 과감히 내놓아야" [To become a developed country, the rich must give up their wealth], *The JoongAng* (September 2014), 106.

The Void Pastor David Yonggi Cho Left   41

However, there was one problem. During the Japanese occupation, my grandfather developed health issues in his legs after a six-month imprisonment due to his participation in the independence movement.[8] Attending Sunday and Wednesday services was not a problem; however, walking thirty to forty minutes for early morning prayers was nearly impossible. This was when there were no private cars and no early morning public transportation available. Therefore, my grandfather had no choice but to attend the nearby Full Gospel Central Church for early morning prayer. It was during this time that he met Pastor Cho for the first time.[9]

My Fateful Introduction to Pastor Cho

I wonder what my grandfather thought when he first met Pastor Yonggi Cho. It must have been challenging for him to open up his heart, because he had been a lifelong Presbyterian, learning his faith from missionary Baird in Pyongyang. Despite this, my grandfather attended early morning prayer daily at the Full Gospel Church for three months. Another three months later, in April 1964, something extraordinary happened in our home. My grandfather gathered our family and had a profound message to share. Even as a fourth-grader, I remember that evening vividly. "Starting this Sunday, our family will be attending the Full Gospel Church. There is a young pastor, not even in his thirties, who is gifted with the Word and full of the Holy Spirit."[10]

Why did he want us to change churches when he could have just attended the Full Gospel Church for the early morning prayers? It was a difficult decision of faith made by my grandfather after a long time of contemplation. It seemed unthinkable that a man with not much time left on earth, a man who had faithfully devoted his life to serving the Presbyterian Church as an elder, would take a gamble by abandoning the Presbyterian Church, which he had been a part of all his life, to join the Full Gospel Church. Moreover, it was an extremely challenging decision because the Assemblies of God was an almost non-existent denomination at the time, with a completely different worship style from that of Presbyterianism. It was labelled as heresy and ignored by other denominations. Unsurprisingly, there was heavy opposition from those close to and around my grandfather.

It was a hard pill to swallow, even for my parents, who were attending Chung-hyun Presbyterian Church in Chungmuro at the time. In fact, its senior pastor, Chang-In Kim, said, "Absolutely not," and opposed the idea.[11] For my parents, it was challenging to separate from the church community, all of whom were

---

[8] Lee, "명문가 22" [A prestigious family 22], *Shinangge* (December 2017), 30.

[9] Soon-hee Bok, "신앙의 명가 1: 신앙 명문가의 태동과 기초 – 조부 이원근 장로의 신앙과 믿음" [The prestigious family of faith 1: The origin and foundation of prestigious family of faith – the faith and belief of Elder Won-geun Lee, my grandfather], *The Full Gospel Family Newspaper*, 17 March 2019, 6.

[10] 60-Year Committee, *여의도순복음교회 60 년사* [The 60-Year History], 162.

[11] Lee, "명문가 6" [A prestigious family 6], *Shinangge* (August 2016), 28.

fellow refugees from the northern part of Korea. I can only imagine how difficult it must have been for my father, who was born in Pyongyang, and my mother, who was born in Jangyeon, Hwanghae-do (now in North Korea).

Considering these challenges, my grandfather must have given this decision much thought before reaching his final conclusion. He set aside all human conditions and rationale, making the difficult decision solely from a faith perspective. Despite Pastor Cho being a young twenty-nine-year-old, my grandfather decided that his message was more fitting for the spiritual journey of our family. This move was not just a request; it was a command that he made for all of us in the family.

Eventually, my parents grasped the deep meaning behind my grandfather's decision and willingly obeyed. They soon became key members at the Full Gospel Church. My father eventually served as the senior elder, and my mother took on roles such as precinct cell leader and evangelist.[12] I followed my grandfather and parents and also became a member of the Full Gospel Church. Finally, my fateful meeting with Pastor Cho took place.

Why Was I the Only One Left at the Full Gospel Church?

My parents were not the only ones who struggled with switching churches during that time. I did not like leaving my friends at Chung-hyun Church behind, and I did not like the unfamiliar and awkward worship style. Coming from a fourth-generation Presbyterian family accustomed to solemnity, stillness, and silence, my entire family experienced a culture shock.[13] Everything about the Full Gospel Church felt strange to me. From the fast-paced hymns sung to the beat of big drums and enthusiastic clapping, to the loud prayer sessions where the congregation cried out as if they would destroy the church building, to the sermons delivered in a rapid-fire cannon blasting with a thick Gyeongsang provincial accent, I felt as though I was living in a different universe under the same Seoul sky. For a while, I had a difficult time adjusting to the church as a child.

But why was I, the second son among four sons and one daughter, the only one who remained at the Full Gospel Church? My older brother, who graduated from Seoul National University of Engineering, became an elder at a Presbyterian church in the United States. My older sister diligently nurtured her spiritual faith and became a senior deaconess at a Methodist church. My younger brother became a missionary affiliated with the Methodist Church, serving in Kenya. My youngest brother became an ordained deacon in the Global Mission

---

[12] Bok, "신앙의 명가 3: 믿음의 가정을 세운 아버지와 어머니 '한 마음 한 뜻' 주의 일에 헌신한 부부" [The prestigious family of faith 3: Father and mother "one heart and one mind" devoted to the Lord's work], *The Full Gospel Family Newspaper*, 7 April 2019, 6.

[13] Sung-Sik Cho, "조성식 기자의 Face to Face 4: 여의도순복음교회 담임목사 이영훈" [Face to face with reporter Cho Sung-Sik 4: Yoido Full Gospel Church Senior Pastor Younghoon, Lee], *Shindong-a* (May 2009), 20.

Church.[14] Out of all of my siblings, why did I become a pastor affiliated with the Assemblies of God?

As I look back over the years, I find it fascinating that I was the only one who stayed in the Full Gospel Church while all of my siblings branched out into other denominations. It is even more amazing to think that out of my grandfather's 140 descendants, all of them were Presbyterians, Methodists, Holiness, Baptists, and so on, except for me. I was the only member of the Assemblies of God. As a result, I can only say that my grandfather's decision to change churches was to move me from the Presbyterian Church to the Full Gospel Church. I like to think that it was his foresight to build a bridge of destiny between Pastor Cho and me. It is a bit of a stretch, but I find God's guidance truly amazing.

An Early Turning Point in My Life

I had this particular thought hit me one day. If one of my five siblings had to be chosen, all of whom attended church from a young age and received thorough religious education from my grandfather, why was I, the second son, chosen and not my older brother, a brilliant student at Seoul National University who ranked first or second in his class at Seoul High School? The single most important answer I can come up with is this: the baptism of the Holy Spirit, and the filling of the Holy Spirit!

God does not look on the outside but at the centre of one's heart: "... The Lord does not look at the things people look at. People look at the outward appearance, but the Lord looks at the heart" (1 Samuel 16:7).

There was one thing that made me stand out from my siblings. I loved the church, and I loved Pastor David Yonggi Cho. I prayed passionately to receive the Holy Spirit, which Pastor Cho urged us daily to seek.[15] I prayed earnestly and persistently. After two years of prayer, I received the Holy Spirit after attending a five-day church revival.[16] God answered the prayers of a thirteen-year-old boy who did not know anything about the process but faithfully and persistently prayed. My life changed completely from the day I received the Holy Spirit.[17]

From an ordinary little boy, a remarkable transformation took place in my life. Whenever I went to the service, tears welled up in my eyes, and I was able to comprehend the Word of God better. Hymns constantly came out of my lips, and my eyes were fixated on nothing but Jesus. At times, tears streamed down my face, and I repented for my sins, wondering how I could have sinned so much as a child. I loved Pastor Cho's sermons and attended every adult service at the church that I could. I also went to as many week-long revivals that always took place at the church. Receiving the Holy Spirit was an early turning point in my life.

---

[14] Lee, "명문가 42" [A prestigious family 42], *Shinangge* (August 2019), 40–41.

[15] Lee, "명문가 6" [A prestigious family 6], *Shinangge* (August 2016), 29–30.

[16] Lee, "명문가 46" [A prestigious family 46], *Shinangge* (December 2019), 41.

[17] 60-Year Committee, *여의도순복음교회 60 년사* [The 60-Year History], 162–63.

I continued to grow in my faith even after graduating from high school. At church, I served as the president of the middle school and high school groups. At school, I was a self-proclaimed pastor excited to share the Gospel. When I was the class president during my first year at Daegwang High School, I arrived early at school, went through my class attendance sheet, and prayed for each individual by name so that they might come to meet Jesus Christ, our Lord and Saviour.[18] Looking back on those times, I wonder if I was more passionate back then than I am now.

My life changed since I came to the Full Gospel Church, met Pastor Cho, and received the Holy Spirit. From that point, I could not think of anything else other than Jesus. I loved studying the Bible, and I was most excited when I could bring my friends to church. Pastor Cho was significant. Throughout my school years, he was my hero.

Becoming a Pastor Looking up to Pastor Cho

I had many opportunities to see Pastor Cho up close since I was a young student. I was happy just to see him. He was also excited to see me and poured out his love towards me. I thought this was the case because I was nurturing good faith. Later, I happened to realise that it was because of my famous elder grandfather and my faithful parents who served the church diligently.

When I was taking my entrance exams for middle school, high school, and college, I always sought out and asked for Pastor Cho's advice before deciding on which school I wanted to go to. I brought my applications with me to Pastor Cho and received his prayers before taking the entrance exams.[19] That was how influential he was. I always looked up to him and wanted to be just like him, so I naturally took the path of serving the Lord. I became a pastor and went to the United States to further my theological studies, all under his guidance.

Even after becoming a pastor, I continued to look up to Pastor Cho and decided that, to be like him, I needed to learn from him as my mentor. Therefore, I was obedient to him, believing that God was speaking to me through him. I tried to look at the bigger picture behind each of Pastor Cho's requests, understanding that God wanted to use me for his Kingdom, and I faithfully obeyed. There were times when I did not understand the purpose behind each responsibility that was given, but I obeyed and did my best to fulfil each task. When Pastor Cho asked me to stand, I stood up. When he asked me to go, I went. This was how I served him.

When he asked me to further my theological education by studying in the United States, I obediently replied, "Yes." When he asked me to urgently return to Korea after I became the senior pastor of the Full Gospel Church of Washington, DC and oversaw the successful construction of the sanctuary, I obediently replied, "Yes."[20] When he asked me to return to the United States to

---

[18] Lee, "명문가 43" [A prestigious family 43], *Shinangge* (September 2019), 39–40.
[19] Lee, "명문가 10" [A prestigious family 10], *Shinangge* (December 2016), 28–29.
[20] 60-Year Committee, *여의도순복음교회 60 년사* [The 60-Year History], 163.

get Bethesda University accredited, I obediently replied, "Yes." When he asked me to go to Tokyo, Japan, and establish a church right after getting Bethesda University accredited, I obediently replied, "Yes." When he asked me to return to Korea after I bought an ideal building for the Tokyo church at a bargain, held the first service, and served the Full Gospel Tokyo Church, I obediently replied, "Yes."[21] There were times when I was hesitant to leave because I felt there was still work left to be done at each of his requests, but I always willingly obeyed.[22]

Pastor Cho's Unexpected Words, "Thank You, Pastor Lee!"

I never thought that at the age of fifty-five, I would succeed Pastor Cho to become the second senior pastor of Yoido Full Gospel Church in 2008. He was still going strong, and no one could picture the church without him. I do not know exactly why I was chosen, but I do clearly remember the major events and the processes that led up to my appointment.

As mentioned earlier, I never spoke out against Pastor Cho's requests but faithfully obeyed him. He knew this as well, and he casually handed me the requests that he wanted me to follow. However, there was one time when he asked me for my wishes first. This was when I was serving as the vice senior pastor of Yoido Full Gospel Church. In June 2005, he called me one day and greeted me warmly, to the point that something felt off. He spoke to me in a toned-down and warm voice and said, "There seems to be a big problem at the LA Full Gospel Church in the United States ... [and] the congregation asked for you to be sent over ... Would you be all right with going to Los Angeles?"

At this point, I had just returned from serving two years as the senior pastor at the Full Gospel Tokyo Church in Japan. My wife, who had earned her Ph.D. in the United States, was teaching full-time at a university. Our only child, Sung Eun, whom we had after seventeen years of marriage, was nine years old and was now living a relatively comfortable life for the first time. I was fifty-two years old. I wanted to stop travelling and settle down in Korea.

Understanding my situation, Pastor Cho seemed to feel remorseful about sending me into another phase of having to pack our belongings and face the hardships of moving to another country. In the forty years I have known him, I have never seen him speak so softly and gently as when he asked me if I was willing to go to Los Angeles. It was the first time he reacted this way, and out of awkwardness, I gave my immediate response, "Yes, I will go!"

"Pastor Lee, thank you so much!" he replied with great relief and gave my hand a firm squeeze. As I listened to his warm expressions of gratitude, which were different from his usual charismatic demeanour, I had a sudden realisation. As Pastor Cho entered his seventies, his heart had become softer.[23] There was something touching about the ageing Pastor Cho. As I closed my day and headed back home, my footsteps only became heavier with each step. I felt incredibly

---

[21] Lee, "명문가 38" [A prestigious family 38], *Shinangge* (April 2019), 38–41.

[22] Lee, "명문가 12" [A prestigious family 12], *Shinangge* (February 2017), 30–33.

[23] Lee, "명문가 13" [A prestigious family 13], *Shinangge* (March 2017), 30–32.

sorry for my wife, because I put her back into the position of having to pack our belongings for an international move. I did this to my wife six times, something that other people would not do to their wives even once, and I had nothing to say if anyone called me a terrible husband.[24]

Reunited with Pastor Cho in Los Angeles

I quickly wrapped up my affairs at Yoido Full Gospel Church and moved to Los Angeles, where I assumed the position of the senior pastor at LA Full Gospel Church in July 2005. This church, founded in 1975, was the oldest and largest church outside of Korea affiliated with Yoido Full Gospel Church. However, several elders had problems with one another and constantly fought, inflicting deep scars and bringing chaos due to the conflicts. Prior to this assignment, I had served as a senior pastor twice at Full Gospel Church of Washington, DC and Full Gospel Tokyo Church, but this responsibility was the greatest challenge that I was to face.

From experience, I knew that disputes within the church were not easy to resolve using human methods or solutions. Therefore, as soon as I assumed the senior pastor position, I strongly encouraged the congregation to attend early morning prayers so that they could pray, love, forgive one another, and strive towards a healthy, united church once again.[25] By the grace of God, it was not long before all the problems that once plagued the church were resolved peacefully, and I was able to report the good news to Pastor Cho.[26]

After nine months apart, I had the opportunity to meet and reunite with Pastor Cho again. In April 2006, the Centenary Anniversary of the Azusa Street Revival was held in Los Angeles, and Pastor Cho was invited as the main speaker for the event.[27] At that time, Dr. William Wilson (now the Chair of the Pentecostal World Fellowship) was the president of the convention, and I was the chairman of the convention's planning committee. Therefore, I was able to host Pastor Cho and look after him during his stay in the United States. To utilise his short stay to the fullest, I held the thirty-first North American Full Gospel Conference at my church, LA Full Gospel Church, for three days. After the conference, I invited Pastor Cho as the guest speaker for the revival held at the main sanctuary.

With the two different conferences and revivals, many members of the congregation were able to be filled with the Holy Spirit and restore their faith. This was a big help towards my ministry afterwards. I expressed the deepest thanks to Pastor Cho, and he thanked me for stabilising and revitalising the LA Full Gospel Church and shared words of encouragement. On the day I saw Pastor

---

[24] Lee, "명문가 29" [A prestigious family 29], *Shinangge* (July 2018), 34–35.

[25] 60-Year Committee, *여의도순복음교회 60 년사* [The 60-Year History], 164.

[26] Bok, "신앙의 명가 5: 4 대째 이어진 신앙의 유산" [The prestigious family of faith 5: A legacy of faith for four generations)], *The Full Gospel Family Newspaper*, 21 April 2019, 6.

[27] Jae-hyung Park, "영혼 추수, 오직 성령과" [Harvesting souls, only with the Holy Spirit], *The Full Gospel Family Newspaper*, 7 May 2006, 1.

The Void Pastor David Yonggi Cho Left

Cho off for his return trip to Korea, who could have known that in just six months, I would resign from the senior pastor position of LA Full Gospel Church and return to Korea? Was it possible that Pastor Cho knew of this? I do not think he did at that time. Only God knew.

Pastor Cho's Sudden Retirement Announcement

Suddenly, events began to unfold that no one could have anticipated or planned for. Pastor Cho announced his retirement abruptly and instructed the church to elect his successor through a democratic process.[28] There had been a lot of speculation among the pastors, disciple pastors, and missionaries of Yoido Full Gospel Church about who the successor would be. At that time, I did not even think about the position because I was already over fifty years old and had no ambitions for the senior pastor role. I was solely committed to the revival of LA Full Gospel Church. I had only been the senior pastor at this church for a little over a year, and it did not seem right to return to Korea.

But shortly afterward, I received a call from Yoido Church informing me that I had been included in a shortlist of seven candidates recommended for the senior pastor role. Candidates were required to be fifty-five years old or younger. Out of the seven candidates, the sixth voting committee held a secret ballot, and I received the most votes, followed by Pastor Myung-Woo Choi of Gangdong Church and Pastor Kyung-Hwan Ko of Wondang Full Gospel Church. We were selected as the three finalists.[29] For reference, the initial list of seven candidates included Pastor Yong-Dal Ha, Youth Mission Director; Pastor Sam-Hwan Kim, Yoido Full Gospel Kimpo Church; Pastor Seung-Ho Yang, Full Gospel United Church of New York; and Pastor Yong-Bok Kim, London Full Gospel Church.[30]

Events between the Votes

It was the day after the sixth voting committee's vote when unusual events began to unfold. The final vote was to be opened by a special committee in two weeks, and I planned on waiting patiently to hear back on the results. In the meantime, I heard rumours that the other two finalists were campaigning, exerting consistent pressure through various methods for me to step down. As it turned out, the two groups were against me becoming the senior pastor, and although their numbers were small, they were quite vocal about their views.

At the time, I seriously considered dropping out from the candidate list. I heard many rumours that, if the opposition was strong, even if I did become the next senior pastor, I could be falsely accused and driven out of the position. Since

---

[28] Younghoon Lee, 영산 조용기 목사 평전: 희망의 목회자 [The Critical Biography of Rev. Young San Yonggi Cho: The Pastor of Hope] (Seoul: Seoul Logos, 2022), 286.

[29] "조용기 목사 후임자 3 명으로 압축" [Pastor Yonggi Cho's successor narrowed to three], *CBS NoCut News*, 30 October 2006, https://www.nocutnews.co.kr/news/207655?c1=262&c2=269 [accessed 7 Feb 2024].

[30] 60-Year Committee, 여의도순복음교회 60 년사 [The 60-Year History], 157–58.

the influence of the founding pastors was extremely powerful, the competition for the second senior pastor position was very fierce and filled with poison and spite.

I felt extremely uncomfortable, to the point that I submitted a letter to drop out of the final voting session to Pastor Cho. Then, the two groups that pushed for my resignation urged me to return to Korea the following Sunday and declare my resignation vocally before the vote. When I consented, they sent a report to Pastor Cho that stated, "Pastor Lee has decided to come to Korea and declare his resignation in person." After Pastor Cho received this report, he told me, "You do not have to come to Korea against your own will." My plans to return to Korea were effectively cancelled.

The Second Senior Pastor of Yoido Full Gospel Church

As scheduled, a special committee gathered two weeks after the initial voting phase. In the secret ballot, I was selected as the second senior pastor of Yoido Full Gospel Church. 12 November 2006 was a day that I will never forget.

It was incredible to think that just a year and four months before this day, I was boarding a plane to Los Angeles without ever imagining becoming the senior pastor of Yoido Full Gospel Church. The final results were as follows: I received the most votes, 435; Pastor Myung-Woo Choi received 285; Pastor Kyung-Hwan Ko received 204; and there were 9 invalid votes.[31] I believe that it was not only by the grace of God that I was elected to the highest position, but also because of Pastor Cho. The opposition groups spread rumours that Pastor Cho had eyes on a different candidate; however, before the actual voting began, Pastor Cho told the committee, "All three of these candidates are disciples that I love equally. Vote with the guidance of the Holy Spirit." After that, his statement allowed the members to vote freely.

After the result was finalised, Pastor Cho gave me a personal phone call while he was returning home in his car. I could see his big smiling face through the phone. "Pastor Lee! The next senior pastor of Yoido Full Gospel Church is you! Congratulations! Please return back to Korea as soon as possible." I can never forget the warmth and delight with which he, in his distinctive accent, congratulated me. It still resonates in my ears. It was the most moving and memorable moment of my life.

In accordance with the decision made by the special committee, I soon returned to Korea and served as the interim senior pastor for a year and a half. After passing a final confirmation vote in the session, I formally became the second senior pastor of Yoido Full Gospel Church on 21 May 2008.[32] In front of

---

[31] 60-Year Committee, *여의도순복음교회 60 년사* [The 60-Year History], 158.

[32] "이영훈 여의도순복음교회 담임목사 취임" [Younghoon Lee inaugurated as senior pastor of Yoido Full Gospel Church], *Yonhap News*, 21 May 2008. https://n.news.naver.com/mnews/article/001/0002094850?sid=103 [accessed 7 Feb 2024].

all the elders, I said, "I will serve Pastor Cho as my father and humbly serve the church for the rest of my life."

Even after I took office, I heard rumours that a few elders talked negatively about me behind my back. They said, "Let us see how long he will last in that position. Maybe three or four months? Possibly a year?" They continued to spread false rumours about me, attempting to drive a wedge between Pastor Cho and me. They fabricated evidence to frame me negatively and slander me.[33] Although there were times when Pastor Cho grew suspicious of me due to these accusations, thankfully, he knew my character well and disregarded all allegations. Until the day he went to be with the Lord, he trusted and respected me. Despite my many shortcomings as a disciple, through Pastor Cho's teachings and mentorship, I believe I was able to lead Yoido Full Gospel Church well without making any major mistakes.

Pastor Cho, the Only One who Understood My Heart

Even in the smallest of churches, the position of a senior pastor requires one to bear tremendous responsibilities in serving God, making the role challenging and daunting. In society, if salaried managers fail to fulfil their duties, they might be displaced from their position, and that would be the end of it. However, when a pastor commits him- or herself to a church, representing the body of Christ, and fails to shepherd the Lord's sheep, there is no price that can repay the failure. Senior pastors carry this immense responsibility, and my church happened to be Yoido Full Gospel Church, the largest church in the world.

After fifteen years as a senior pastor and two years since Pastor Cho passed away, I have come to a realisation. The senior pastor position bears the weight of a heavy burden, and I must carry it alone without the guidance of someone who has been in my shoes. It is now that I realise and understand the pressure and loneliness that Pastor Cho must have felt during his fifty years of ministry as he founded and crafted the world's largest church, Yoido Full Gospel Church.

When Pastor Cho was still with us, it was comforting to have someone I could turn to in times of trouble. Amidst the sea of voices from the 1,500 elders and the loud voices that could render you powerless, Pastor Cho was the only person who understood my struggles. He had watched me grow up since I was a fourth-grader in elementary school and knew my parents and grandfather well.[34]

There were times when I was misunderstood by Pastor Cho because of those who slandered me and vowed to remove me from the senior pastor position. However, he tried to understand me to the best of his ability. He poured out his support and encouragement during my senior pastor-elect phase and allowed my leadership to flourish. The more I think about it, the more I realise that I have received much love and support from Pastor Cho, and I can never thank him enough. It was not because I was good, but because Pastor Cho knew all too well the misunderstandings and challenges that a senior pastor was bound to face in a

---

[33] Lee, "명문가 40" [A prestigious family 40], *Shinangge* (June 2019), 41.

[34] Lee, "명문가 5" [A prestigious family 5], *Shinangge* (July 2016), 37.

vibrant megachurch like Yoido Full Gospel Church.[35] Even now, when I see people trying to slander me with false charges and fabricated scenarios, I miss Pastor Cho because he was always a strong fence that protected me.

Pastor Cho, the great man of God, is no longer with us and is currently in heaven, far away from us. Just as it has brought deep sadness to the congregation, my heart is also empty and full of sorrow. The pain of losing my spiritual mentor continues to pain me and pierce my heart. My feelings for Pastor Cho remain the same as when I first met him at the age of eleven. I miss him so much, and when I face difficult obstacles and troubles by myself, I think about how privileged and happy I was working for and alongside Pastor Cho in bettering the Kingdom of God. I believe Pastor Cho is looking down from heaven, praying for the spiritual growth of the congregation and me. And here I am, as I kneel before God in early morning prayer today to fulfil the task he has entrusted to me.

Someday, when my time comes, and the Lord calls me, I want to find Pastor Cho and tell him, "Pastor Cho! I have had a hard time. I really have!" All I want to hear are his words of comfort in that warm voice. "Pastor Lee! You have done a great job. Thank you for all of the work you have done!" As I write this, I miss him more dearly today than ever.

---

[35] Lee, "명문가 40" [A prestigious family 40], *Shinangge* (June 2019), 40–41.

The Spirit and Moral Fortitude: Understanding the Spirit's Role in Luke's Temptation Narrative

Lora Angeline E. Timenia

Introduction

Luke's Contribution to New Testament Pneumatology

Most Lukan theologians agree that Luke's pneumatology is greatly indebted to the Jewish tradition of the Spirit; that is, the Spirit is understood as the Spirit of prophecy. Eduard Schweizer, for instance, strongly contends that the Spirit was seen as the source of prophetic utterance in late Judaism and that Luke's writing demonstrates congruence with this post-exilic tradition.[1] G. W. H. Lampe concludes, "To Luke, the Spirit means the Spirit of prophecy primarily."[2] On the other hand, Max Turner asserts that in Luke, this "Spirit of prophecy," which functions (among other things) to prophetically and missiologically empower, is received upon conversion-initiation.[3] Robert Menzies disagrees with Turner's assertion and argues that the gift of the Spirit of prophecy is a *donum superadditum*, a distinct missiological empowering received after conversion.[4] Roger Stronstad extends Menzies' claim, noting that in Luke, the outpouring of this prophetic/missiological anointing signals the dawn of the prophethood of all believers; believers in Christ are no longer just priests but also prophets of God's Kingdom.[5]

Lukan Spirit of Prophecy: Exclusive or Inclusive?

Though the discussion on Luke's contribution to Christian pneumatology has been largely exhausted, there remains a sub-theme that needs further clarification. Does Luke's concept of the Spirit, as the Spirit of prophecy, include moral empowerment? Hermann Gunkel, Eduard Schweizer, and Robert Menzies

---

[1] Eduard Schweizer, "'The Spirit of Power': The Uniformity and Diversity of the Concept of the Holy Spirit in the New Testament," *Interpretation* 6 (1952), 259–78.

[2] G. W. H. Lampe, *God as Spirit* (Oxford: Clarendon, 1977), 65.

[3] Max Turner, "The 'Spirit of Prophecy' as the Power of Israel's Restoration and Witness," in I. Howard Marshall and David Peterson, eds., *Witness to the Gospel* (Grand Rapids, MI: Eerdmans, 1998), 327–48; c.f. Darrell Bock, *A Theology of Luke and Acts: Biblical Theology of the New Testament* (Andreas J. Kostenberger, ed.; Grand Rapids, MI: Zondervan, 2012), 213–19.

[4] Robert Menzies, "The Spirit of Prophecy, Luke-Acts and Pentecostal Theology: A Response to Max Turner," *Journal of Pentecostal Theology* 15 (1999), 53–55, 68–72, https://doi.org/10.1177/096673699900701503.

[5] Roger Stronstad, *The Prophethood of All Believers: A Study in Luke's Charismatic Theology* (JPTSS 16; Sheffield: Sheffield Academic Press, 1999), 59.

answered with negative responses. Gunkel argued that the Lukan (non-Pauline) community viewed the Spirit in Jewish terms; that is, as the Spirit of prophecy who endows one with power for miracles or spectacular works, not with piety.[6] In a similar vein, Schweizer argues for a narrower theme, emphasising the Spirit of prophecy in Luke as the enabler of inspired speech and glossolalia, which are not necessary for salvation and do not directly cause ethical transformation.[7]

Menzies, who to a certain extent follows Gunkel's and Schweizer's thesis, carefully explains that Luke's pneumatology is consistently non-soteriological, prophetic, and missiological; that is, Luke never presents the Spirit of prophecy as the agent of salvation (contra Turner) or the *sine qua non* of Christian existence (contra Dunn).[8] Menzies, however, does not imply that Luke's understanding of the Spirit is incomplete. Instead, Luke's narrative emphasises the Spirit's prophetic/missiological functions without necessarily contradicting the same Spirit's soteriological/ethical functions found elsewhere in Scripture.[9]

However, these arguments for the exclusive conception of the Spirit of prophecy are challenged by scholars who favour a broader or inclusive understanding. Turner argues that Luke does not merely adopt the Jewish concept of the Spirit of prophecy; rather, Luke also modifies it to include other functions of the Spirit, including revelatory wisdom, Charismatic edification, ethical transformation and inspired preaching and praise.[10] For Turner, Luke's pneumatology is not unique since, like Paul's and John's writings, the Spirit is the source of "charismatic wisdom which links the believer to Christ."[11]

James Shelton also favours a broader understanding of the Spirit of prophecy, proposing that the Lukan Spirit functions in two ways: abiding and infilling.[12] The Spirit in Luke-Acts not only abides in human agents (e.g., John, Jesus, and Simeon), but also occasionally fills them for vocational tasks of preaching the Kingdom, interpreting Scripture, or "confronting enemies of the true Israel."[13]

---

[6] Hermann Gunkel, *The Influence of the Holy Spirit: The Popular View of the Apostolic Age and the Teaching of the Apostle Paul*, trans. R. A. Harrisville and P. A. Quanbeck II (MN: Fortress Press, 2008 [1888]), 15, 99; c. f. Robert P. Menzies, *Empowered for Witness: The Spirit in Luke-Acts* (New York, NY: T & T Clark, 2004), 19–20.

[7] Schweizer, "'The Spirit of Power': The Uniformity and Diversity of the Concept of the Holy Spirit in the New Testament," 268.

[8] Menzies, "The Spirit of Prophecy, Luke-Acts and Pentecostal Theology," 52–54; James D. G. Dunn, *Baptism in the Holy Spirit: A Re-Examination of the New Testament Teaching on the Gift of the Spirit in Relation to Pentecostalism Today* (London: SCM Press, 2010 [1970]); Turner, "The 'Spirit of Prophecy'," 213–19.

[9] William W. Menzies and Robert P. Menzies, *Spirit and Power: Foundations of Pentecostal Experience* (Grand Rapids, MI: Zondervan, 2000), 201–8.

[10] Max Turner, "Spirit Endowment in Luke-Acts: Some Linguistic Considerations," *Vox Evangelica* 12 (1981), 58, 66–67.

[11] Menzies, "The Spirit of Prophecy, Luke-Acts and Pentecostal Theology," 55.

[12] James B. Shelton, *Mighty in Word and Deed: The Role of the Holy Spirit in Luke-Acts* (Eugene, OR: Wipf and Stock Publishers, 1991), 9.

[13] Shelton, *Mighty in Word and Deed,* 9.

The Spirit and Moral Fortitude   53

Luke Timothy Johnson adds to this broad concept by including moral righteousness in the Lukan Spirit's prophetic function. [14] For Johnson, the prophetic Spirit not only grants inspired oracular gifting but also embodies faithfulness to God and his Word.[15]

Ultimately, these opposing views indicate divergences in the various scholars' purview of Luke's pneumatology. The issue of Luke's inclusion or exclusion of moral empowerment amongst the Spirit's functions remains a topic of discourse that has both theological and pragmatic relevance.

Contribution of the Current Study

The current study offers a modest contribution to the ongoing discussion by interpreting the role of the Spirit in Luke's temptation narrative through narrative analysis. The choice of narrative analysis has to do with the genre of Luke's writing – historical-theological narrative.[16] Since Luke presents his theological message in narrative form, one should not neglect critical narrative methods in one's analysis of the Spirit's role in Luke's account of the temptation of Jesus.

Specifically, this study will employ deductive plot analysis through the study of (1) the narrative's plot development and (2) the Spirit's narrative role. The current researcher seeks to answer two questions: what is the role of the Spirit in Luke's temptation narrative? How does the significance of the Spirit's role in the temptation narrative impact our understanding of Lukan pneumatology?

In the interim, the study proposes that Luke presents the Spirit of prophecy as the one who aided Jesus in embodying moral fortitude in the temptation narrative.[17] As such, the study suggests that Luke includes moral fortitude in the prophetic functions of the Spirit.

Luke's Temptation Narrative: A Deductive Plot Analysis

Summary and Thesis of the Narrative

Luke's temptation narrative (Luke 4:1–13, 14) describes the crucial testing that Jesus experienced as the Son of God.[18] Before this, he was affirmed as the Son of God, endowed with the Spirit, and ancestrally connected to David and Adam (Luke 3). John Nolland, commenting on Luke's prophetic Christology, explains,

---

[14] Luke Timothy Johnson, *Prophetic Jesus, Prophetic Church: The Challenge of Luke-Acts to Contemporary Christians* (Grand Rapids: Eerdmans, 2011), 39, 46.

[15] Johnson, *Prophetic Jesus,* 42–47.

[16] I. Howard Marshall, *Luke: Historian & Theologian* (Downers Grove, Ill: IVP Academic, 1970), 52. See also, Ju Hur, *A Dynamic Reading of the Holy Spirit in Luke-Acts* (London: T&T Clark International, 2004), 28.

[17] Moral fortitude is defined in this study as the firmness to do what is right amid adversity.

[18] Joel Green comments that Jesus' temptation narrative reflects Jewish tradition, where fidelity to God is proven through testing. Joel Green, *The Gospel of Luke* (NICNT; Grand Rapids: Eerdmans, 1997), 221.

"Jesus is the one upon whom (as in Isa 42:1) God has seen fit to place his Spirit: in deed and word there is, thus, a declaration of divine approval of Jesus as he stands on the threshold of his privileged role in the purposes of God."[19] Jesus, born by divine parthenogenesis (Luke 1:26–38), is royal, priestly, and approved by God. He is also, as Luke portrays, the unique bearer of the Spirit.[20]

Just before he started his ministry, "Jesus, full of the Holy Spirit, left the Jordan and was led by the Spirit into the wilderness" (Luke 4:1). Yuri Phanon, commenting on Luke's repeated mention of the Spirit, writes, "Luke's intention was to emphasize how the Holy Spirit was involved in the temptation narrative."[21] Robert Tannehill interprets this as Luke's way of indicating that the Spirit is the instigator of a series of events.[22] Undeniably, it was under the Spirit's directive that Jesus entered the wilderness to be tempted for forty days (Luke 4:2a).

Luke reports three temptations: first, the temptation to exploit his power to satisfy his hunger (Luke 4:1–4); second, the temptation of earthly authority and glory if he worshipped the devil (Luke 4:5–7); and third, the temptation to escape messianic suffering based on his privileged Sonship (Luke 4:9–12).[23] David Bryan argues for a chiastic structure in Luke's temptation narrative.[24] He states that the second temptation (Luke 4:5–8) is the centre of the pericope.[25] In the second temptation, the devil tempts Jesus with authority and glory in exchange for devil worship (Luke 4:4–7). Jesus responds with a passage linked to the *Shema*, "Worship the Lord your God and serve him only!" (Luke 4:8; Deut 6:13). Bryan supports his proposition by comparing Luke's account with that of Matthew. If the second temptation is at the centre, both versions highlight "authority and allegiance to the one true God over heaven and earth" as its central thesis.[26] His proposition makes sense if one interprets the narrative as a test of filial obedience.[27] Moreover, the other two temptations point to dependence on and faithfulness to God in conjunction with filial obedience. Hence, the central idea of the narrative as a test of Jesus' filial obedience to God, the Father, makes sense.

---

[19] John Nolland, *Luke 1:1–9:20* (Word Biblical Commentary 35A; Grand Rapids: Zondervan, 2000), 165.

[20] Stronstad, *The Prophethood of All Believers*, 43.

[21] Yuri Phannon, "The Work of the Holy Spirit in the Conception, Baptism, and Temptation of Christ: Implications for the Pentecostal Christian Part II," *Asian Journal of Pentecostal Studies* 20:1 (2017), 61.

[22] Robert C. Tannehill, *The Gospel According to Luke (The Narrative Unity of Luke-Acts: A Literary Interpretation*, vol. 1) (Philadelphia: Fortress Press, 1986), 56–58.

[23] Nolland, *Luke 1:1–9:20*, 178–83.

[24] David K. Bryan, "The Center of Luke's Temptation Narrative," *The Catholic Biblical Quarterly* 82:3 (2020), 407–23.

[25] Bryan, "The Center of Luke's Temptation Narrative," 420.

[26] Bryan, "The Center of Luke's Temptation Narrative," 420.

[27] Nolland, *Luke 1:1–9:20*, 182.

The Spirit and Moral Fortitude   55

Although most Lukan scholars espouse that Luke reversed the order of the second and third temptations to emphasise a Jerusalem climax,[28] Bryan's proposition also holds weight because his premise highlights Jesus' filial obedience. Bryan proposes this chiastic structure for the narrative:

A 4:1a: Jesus returns from the Jordan
    B 4:1b–4: Temptation: stone into bread
            C 4:5–8: Temptation: all authority in exchange for worship
    B' 4:9–13: Temptation: throw yourself off the temple pinnacle
A' 4:14a: Jesus returns to Galilee[29]

In this chiastic structure, the temptation against obedience and faithfulness to God is central to the conflict. Tannehill also notes that through this conflict, Jesus' identity, role as Son of God, and understanding of his mission were clarified.[30]

Interestingly, there seems to be a subliminal link between Luke 4:1 and 4:14.[31] In 4:1, Jesus is full of the Spirit and led by the Spirit, while in 4:14, Jesus returns to Galilee in the power of the Spirit. Although Green considers verse 14 separate from the narrative,[32] Luke seems to be bookending the event with the activity of the Spirit. This bookending indicates the crucial role of the Spirit from start to end of the narrative. Menzies proposes that it forms a redactional bridge that emphasises the "pneumatic significance of the temptation account."[33] Since 4:15 is potentially linked to 4:14, one can suggest that 4:14–15 serves as both a conclusion to Jesus's preparation and a link to the beginning of his public ministry.[34]

Hence, after overcoming all three temptations, Jesus lives up to his identity as the Son of God, demonstrates filial obedience, and returns to Galilee empowered by the Spirit (Luke 4:14). He begins his public ministry with a prophetic anointing and with positive acclaim throughout the countryside. In Luke 4:14, Nolland describes Jesus as "an impressive pneumatic figure operating in the

---

[28] Richard B. Hays, *Echoes of Scripture in the Gospels* (Waco, TX: Baylor University Press, 2016), 266; Joseph A. Fitzmyer, *The Gospel According to Luke: Introduction, Translation, and Notes*, vol. 1 (Garden City, NY: Doubleday, 1982), 507; Francois Bovon, *Luke 1: A Commentary on the Gospel of Luke 1:1–9:50 (Hermeneia*; Minneapolis, MN: Fortress Press, 2002), 139; Luke Timothy Johnson, *The Gospel of Luke (Sacra Pagina*; Collegeville, MN: Liturgical Press, 1991), 76; Nolland, *Luke 1:1–9:20*, 179–80.

[29] Bryan, "The Center of Luke's Temptation Narrative," 411.

[30] Tannehill, *Luke*, 59.

[31] Bryan suggests that that Luke 4:1 and 4:14 form an inclusion. Bryan, "The Center of Luke's Temptation Narrative," 413.

[32] Green, *The Gospel of Luke*, 220.

[33] Menzies, *Empowered for Witness: The Spirit in Luke-Acts*, 145.

[34] Menzies, *Empowered for Witness: The Spirit in Luke-Acts*, 144.

sphere of the Spirit and with the power of the Spirit at his disposal."[35] In summary, Luke's temptation narrative established Jesus' Sonship, filial obedience, and Spirit empowerment.

Plot Development

Analysing Luke's temptation narrative with the premise that the second temptation is the centre of the narrative, one can construct the following plot development:

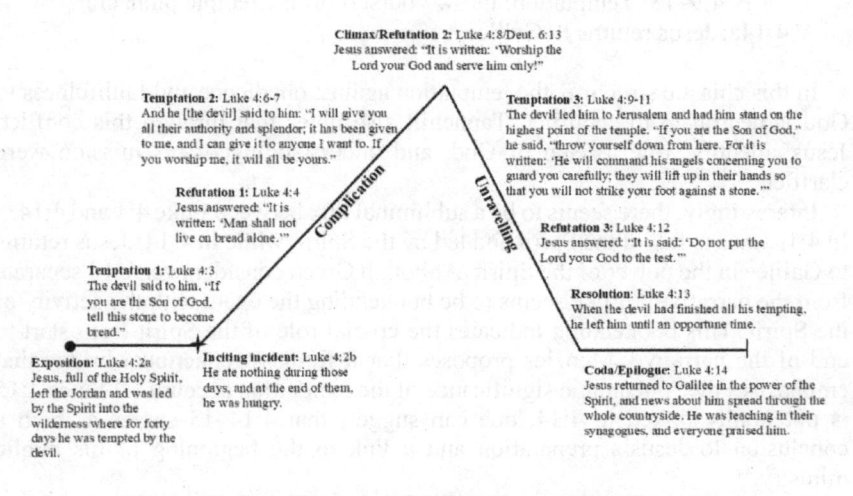

Figure 1. Plot Diagram of Luke's Temptation Narrative

Yairah Amit's five-stage pediment structure for biblical narratives serves as the basis of the diagram.[36] It consists of the exposition (which sets out the background elements and the inciting incident), the complication or crisis that brings on the change (climax/pivot), the unravelling (which reveals the consequences of the change), and the denouement with its resolution and coda/epilogue.[37]

Exposition

Luke's temptation narrative starts with a clear exposition. The setting is an "undesignated wilderness in the Jordan."[38] The characters are Jesus, the devil, and the Holy Spirit. The immediate context is the Spirit's leading of Jesus into the wilderness right after the latter's water baptism and Spirit reception. It is in this undesignated wilderness that Jesus experienced being tempted by the devil.

---

[35] Nolland, *Luke 1:1–9:20*, 187.

[36] Yairah Amit, *Reading Biblical Narratives: Literary Criticism and the Hebrew Bible* (Minneapolis, MN: Fortress Press, 2001), 46–48.

[37] Amit, *Reading Biblical Narratives,* 46–48.

[38] Green, *The Gospel of Luke*, 220.

The Spirit and Moral Fortitude   57

The inciting incident of the narrative is Jesus' hunger – that is, because he fasted for forty days in the wilderness, he was hungry. At the narrative level, Jesus' hunger is an inciting incident because it starts the plot's motion. Jesus, who was affirmed as the Son of God and who, as the narrator infers, was a man full of the Holy Spirit, was experiencing human frailty. As such, in the case of any human temptation, weakness can serve as an opening to the devil's insidious attacks.

Complication

Indeed, the devil steps into the narrative by first attacking Jesus' human frailty, his hunger. The first temptation tries to subvert Jesus' filial dependence on God, the Father, by misleading him to use his Spirit-power to satisfy his needs. Jesus refutes this temptation by quoting Deuteronomy 8:3, which affirms his dependence on God's provision. Jesus' response is the first step to unravelling the devil's scheme of subverting his Sonship and misconstruing his mission.

The devil ups the game by bringing Jesus to "a high place and showed him in an instant all the kingdoms of the world" (Luke 4:5). The devil, by using such a visionary spectacle, offers Jesus dominion over the inhabited earth in exchange for his worship. Jesus' response is pivotal to the entire experience. He quotes a line from Deuteronomy 6, which is directly connected to the *Shema*, "Worship the Lord your God and serve him only" (Luke 4:8; Deut 6:13).

Jesus' response is pivotal because the entire temptation experience aims to compromise his identity as the Son of God and his obedience to the Father.[39] Once compromised, Jesus would fail to uphold his identity and role in God's plan of salvation. He would also be an unworthy bearer of the Spirit and an unworthy recipient of the promised everlasting Kingdom in Luke 1:32–33. His overcoming of such temptation evinces his understanding of true Sonship and obedience to the Father.

The devil's plot unravels quickly with Jesus' unwavering obedience to the Father. As a result, the devil directly challenges the status of Jesus' Sonship by offering an alternative to the suffering of his messianic task. He leads Jesus to Jerusalem and the temple's highest point. There, the devil tempts Jesus to test God's concern for his Son. "If you are the Son of God," the devil said, "throw yourself down from here. For it is written: 'He will command his angels concerning you to guard you carefully; they will lift you in their hands so that you will not strike your foot against a stone'" (Luke 4:9–11).

At the narrative level, the devil's last attempt is akin to a taunt. Using Jesus' faithfulness to the Father and his reliance on Scripture, the devil brings to the fore the messianic task of the Son, which will include rejection, suffering, and death in Jerusalem, and uses the promises of Psalm 91 to confuse him. It's as if the devil was saying: "If God considers you his Son, he will not let you go through such pain. He'd command his angels to guard you. If you jump from this

---

[39] Green, *The Gospel of Luke*, 223.

temple (the symbol of God's presence and refuge), you'd receive God's supernatural deliverance and, at the same time, pain-free messianic glory."[40]

Jesus's response completely unravelled the devil's deception, saying: "It is said: 'Do not put the Lord your God to the test'" (Luke 4:12). In the Greek text, Luke uses the word *eirētai*, a hapax legomenon, which translates, "It has been said."[41] Jesus, knowing what the devil was up to with his erroneous quote of Scripture, declares a truth learned by the people of Israel and transmitted from oral to written tradition: "Do not test God." Commenting on Jesus' response, Nolland writes: "He quotes from Deut 6:16. At Massah, the people confronted God (Moses) about preserving their lives (Exod 17:3). But the faithful man does not seek to dictate to God how he must express his covenant loyalty and fulfil his promises. That would put God to the test and a failure to believe that God will do well by his Son."[42] The devil's last attempt was for Jesus to "test" God. Jesus refuses him and chooses to remain loyal and obedient to the Father, regardless of suffering and death.

This theme of obedience to the Father amid future persecution and suffering is programmatic for Jesus' public ministry. Martin Mittlestadt, referring to Simeon's prophecy of Jesus in Luke 2:29–32, explains that from the outset, Jesus' rejection and suffering were integral to God's plan.[43] Jesus accepted this and wholly submitted to God's plan of salvation through his death. His response demonstrates unwavering obedience to God and faithfulness to his divinely appointed mission.

Denouement

The devil's plot completely unravels in the face of Jesus' moral fortitude. The conflict between Jesus and the devil resolves with the latter's temporary exit (Luke 4:13). The narrative's resolution is brief and clear-cut: the devil finished tempting Jesus and left him until an opportunity arose.

Luke adds an epilogue to this brief ending. He writes in verses 14–15, "Jesus returned to Galilee in the power of the Spirit, and news about him spread through the whole countryside. He was teaching in their synagogues, and everyone praised him." This passage can be considered a coda – an epilogue that provides a satisfactory conclusion to a story. Readers of a narrative want to know what happens to the main character after the conflict ends. In Jesus' case, after emerging victorious over the antagonist, he returns to Galilee with the power of the Spirit. He also receives positive acclaim throughout the countryside for his teaching and powerful ministry. From a reader's perspective, this epilogue is

---

[40] Green comments that the devil's use of the temple setting was apt to Psalm 91 since the passage promises God's refuge to those who seek shelter from him. Green, *The Gospel of Luke*, 271.

[41] Nolland, *Luke 1:1–9:20*, 181.

[42] Nolland, *Luke 1:1–9:20*, 35A:181.

[43] Martin William Mittlestadt, *The Spirit and Suffering in Luke-Acts: Implications for a Pentecostal Pneumatology* (London: T & T Clark, 2004), 47; Stronstad, *The Prophethood of All Believers*, 48–49.

The Spirit and Moral Fortitude 59

satisfying. It is also effective in transitioning from the inauguration narratives (Luke 3:1–4:14) to the start of Jesus' public ministry in Galilee.

The Spirit's Narrative Role

Noticeably, the Holy Spirit (or the Spirit) is only mentioned three times in the narrative. Twice in the exposition (Jesus, *full of the Holy Spirit*; Jesus was *led by the Spirit* into the wilderness), and once in the epilogue (Jesus returned to Galilee in the *power of the Spirit*). Using Greimas's Actantial Model, six roles or actants emerge from the narrative: the sender, the subject, the helper, the opponent, the object, and the receiver.[44] Luc Herman and Bart Vervaeck explain that the subject performs the action and achieves a specific object, the helper aids the subject in their quest, the sender provokes or inspires the subject, the receiver benefits from attaining the object, and the opponent aims to thwart the subject's quest.[45] The model of this system of roles is as follows:

```
sender →      object      → receiver
                ↑
helper →      subject      ← opponent
```

Figure 2. Greimas's Actantial Model

Herman and Vervaeck affirm that one actant can perform multiple roles, since these roles are abstract and should not be confused with actual characters.[46]

The Holy Spirit's Role in the Exposition

In this narrative, the Holy Spirit fits Jesus' role as both sender and helper. At the exposition of the narrative, Luke records how the Holy Spirit instigated the temptation event by leading Jesus into the wilderness to be tempted. The Holy Spirit's role here is as the sender, who directs the subject (Jesus) to begin the sequence of events that will result in the narrative's object achievement.

However, the Holy Spirit doesn't just act as the sender because, *before* the temptation event, he already descended upon Jesus (Luke 3:21–22). The phrase "full of the Holy Spirit" in Luke 4:1 refers to the abiding of God's presence and power in a human agent. Remember that the preceding context of this narrative was Jesus' baptism and Spirit reception at the Jordan. Jesus, affirmed as the Son of God, also received the Spirit of God and was led by the same Spirit to be tested as God's Son. In Lukan parlance, being "full of the Holy Spirit" meant full access to the Spirit's presence and power.

---

[44] Adapted from A. J. Greimas, *Sémantique Structural: Recherche de Méthode* (Paris: Larousse, 1966), 180, quoted in Luc Herman and Bart Vervaeck, *Handbook of Narrative Analysis* (Lincoln and London: University of Nebraska Press, 2001), 52.

[45] Herman and Vervaeck, *Handbook of Narrative Analysis*, 52–53.

[46] Herman and Vervaeck, *Handbook of Narrative Analysis*, 53.

At the narrative level, this meant that, though he led Jesus into the wilderness to be tempted, the Spirit already endowed Jesus with his presence and power to face the devil's temptation. Shelton comments, "he [Jesus] was filled to conquer temptation."[47] Hence, one can see the role of the Spirit in the exposition of the narrative as both sender and helper. He sets the plot in motion but also endows beforehand "the help" the subject needs to unravel the complications. This double role of the Spirit is not contradictory since these two roles (sender and helper) are abstract roles that the same person can fulfil.

The Spirit's Role in the Plot Action

Though the name of the Holy Spirit does not appear in the plot action (from the complication to the unravelling), there is evidence of his full abiding in the subject. Jesus, who was described as "full of the Holy Spirit," demonstrated evidence of the Spirit's power and presence through his inspired speech.[48] Here the role of the Spirit as a helper comes into play. Adapting Greima's model to Luke's temptation narrative, the systemisation of roles appears as follows:

$$\textbf{sender} \rightarrow \quad \textbf{object} \quad \rightarrow \textbf{receiver}$$

$$\uparrow$$

$$\textbf{helper} \rightarrow \quad \textbf{subject} \quad \leftarrow \textbf{opponent}$$

Figure 3. Adapted Model of Roles for Luke's Temptation Narrative

The Holy Spirit, as explained above, acted as the sender, the one who directed the subject into the quest. The subject is Jesus, the one "who carries out the action and strives for a specific object."[49] The object is the goal of the quest. In the temptation narrative, the object of the quest is to embody true Sonship (through filial obedience).[50] Jesus' baptism experience in the Jordan (Luke 3:21–22) predicated this event. The one identified as the Son of God, on whom the Holy Spirit bodily descended, is now tested for his filial obedience.

The Holy Spirit himself leads Jesus to the testing but also endows him with his presence and power to help him in the quest. The opponent is the devil, who seeks to thwart Jesus' success. However, the Spirit helps Jesus overcome the devil's seditious temptations through *inspired speech*. Notice how in the narrative, Jesus' inspired scriptural responses were able to refute the devil's rhetoric. As a result, Jesus achieves the object of the quest: the embodiment of true Sonship.

---

[47] Shelton, *Mighty in Word and Deed*, 59.

[48] Shelton proposes that the phrase "full of the Holy Spirit" has a specialised function in the Lukan text. As used elsewhere, "fullness" results in *inspired speech*. This, however, doesn't preclude other meanings. Shelton, *Mighty in Word and Deed,* 59.

[49] Herman and Vervaeck, *Handbook of Narrative Analysis*, 52.

[50] Nolland, *Luke 1:1–9:20*, 178, 182.

The Spirit and Moral Fortitude   61

The Role of the Spirit in the Denouement

In the narrative's epilogue (Luke 4:14), the Spirit empowers Jesus for his public ministry. Using the same systemisation of roles, the Spirit acts as the sender and helper. The epilogue serves as a redactional bridge (á la Menzies) that provides a satisfactory ending to the inauguration narrative and a transition to Jesus' public ministry.[51] The Holy Spirit now sends Jesus into public ministry. He also helps Jesus through an endowment of power. The proof of Jesus' Spirit empowerment is his inspired verbal ministry, which resulted in positive acclaim throughout the countryside.

Theological Synthesis

One can deduce that the role of the Spirit in Luke's temptation narrative is both sender and helper – that is, he is the one who led Jesus into the wilderness to be tempted, but also the one who provided the necessary aid to overcome the temptation. The temptation event is shared among the Synoptics, indicating that testing God's Son was essential to God's salvation history. Luke's unique contribution to this event, however, is highlighting the Spirit's action from the start to the end of the event.

As a sender, Luke records that the Spirit instigates a sequence of events in Jesus' life and preparation for ministry. His direction, however, is purposeful and connected to the plan of God. As the helper, the Spirit endows Jesus with his presence and power. His presence and power manifested in Jesus' *inspired speech* (á la Shelton), which was spiritually effective in refuting the devil's rhetoric. As a result, Jesus remained steadfast in his obedience to the Father.

Since the devil's temptations were moral, the Spirit's aid was a needed reinforcement to Jesus' moral fortitude. However, the Spirit's aid was not the only contributing factor to his moral fortitude. One must also consider Jesus' actual relationship with God. Because Jesus had a solid relationship with God, he chose to remain obedient and fulfil his mission even in the face of bodily pain, fatigue, and temptation.

Hence, from Luke's temptation narrative, one can deduce that Jesus' moral fortitude came from (1) his genuine relationship with God, (2) the Holy Spirit's reinforcement, and (3) his choice to obey and fulfil his mission in the face of testing and temptation.

Conclusion

In conclusion, Luke's unique contribution to New Testament pneumatology is his emphasis on the Holy Spirit as the Spirit of prophecy. The Lukan Spirit, who endows prophetic anointing, enables his recipients to function prophetically (here with inspired speech). Furthermore, Luke's pneumatology includes the Spirit's role as a reinforcing agent of moral fortitude. Luke's temptation narrative, analysed through deductive plot analysis, demonstrates that the Spirit guided and supported Jesus' display of moral fortitude. In the face of the devil's

---

[51] Menzies, *Empowered for Witness: The Spirit in Luke-Acts*, 145.

temptation and with the weakness of his humanity, Jesus was able to refute the devil's seditious temptations with the aid of Spirit-inspired scriptural responses. Although Jesus' moral fortitude was due partly to his actual relationship with the Father, the Spirit's reinforcement through *inspired speech* was a necessary component of his overcoming.

Therefore, the Spirit's role in Luke's temptation narrative signifies a correlation between prophetic anointing and moral fortitude. The Spirit that grants prophetic anointing also reinforces moral fortitude. Luke's concept of the Spirit of prophecy is broad in its inclusion of the Holy Spirit's multifaceted roles in the biblical narrative.

The Realism of the Working of God's Spirit and the Revealing Power of the Biblical Book of Acts

Michael Welker

Senior Pastor Dr. Younghoon Lee and I share a concern for theological realism. We respect and praise the reality of the Holy Spirit and its working, not only in ecclesial, but also in social, cultural, and political contexts. The Holy Spirit is not a metaphysical entity to be captured in ultimate and last thoughts. The Holy Spirit should not be reduced to mere mental capacities such as conscience, self-conscience, rationality, and reason, and neither should the human spirit.

To be sure, the divine Spirit captures, fills, and transforms the human spirit; it enters human hearts, and through the hearts, the human body. It enlightens the human mind and soul and gives orientation to the human consciousness. In all this, it is much richer than a merely intellectual and transcendental spirit. However, the divine Spirit does not only generate all these powers and transformations in individual hearts and minds, but above all, it shapes the real lives of a multitude of communities. The significant biblical notion of the "pouring of the Spirit" gives a vivid impression of this real power "from on high." The divine Spirit does not only "overcome" individual persons, but, to be precise, a multitude of individuals, groups, and communities, and acts as a great transformative power.

It is crucial to see that the working of the Spirit endows human life with specific gifts and qualities. God's Spirit is a spirit of benevolence and love, of justice and freedom, of truth and peace. For Christians, it is most clearly revealed in the pre- and post-Easter life and work of Jesus Christ, with Christ's prophetic, pastoral, beneficial, and humble royal radiations.

Younghoon Lee and I also share a strong appreciation of the biblical book of Acts, with its theology of the Holy Spirit in continuous connection with historical events and experiences. In the following, I would like to share some thoughts on our shared theological interests and concerns. In the first part, I intend to deal with Dr. Lee's theological and pneumatological realism in his impressive book on the Holy Spirit movement in Korea. In the second part, I reflect on the rich teaching about the Holy Spirit in the book of Acts; above all, on the important message of the outpouring of the Spirit. In the third part, an appendix, I will turn to a famous, but only partly biblically inspired, witness of the pouring of the Spirit in the twentieth century. It demonstrates the urgent need to theologically connect a pneumatological realism with a careful biblical orientation.

The Reality of the Holy Spirit and the Realism of the Spirit's Working: *The Holy Spirit Movement in Korea*

Younghoon Lee's book *The Holy Spirit Movement in Korea: Its Historical and Theological Development*[1] is an impressive witness to the reality of the Holy Spirit and the realism of its working.

The heading "The Holy Spirit Movement" subsumes several movements with different focuses: "The Pentecostal Movement," "The Neo-Pentecostal (Charismatic) Movement," and the complex "Neo-Charismatic Movement," including the so-called "Third Wave" and the "New Apostolic Movement" (cf. pages 3–5). The book also unfolds the rich "Religious Background of the Holy Spirit Movement in Korea" with its roots in shamanism, Buddhism, Confucianism, and Christianity. "All the religions took root in the context of the Korean religious soil, and influenced one another" (11).

From this starting point, the book explores "the religious, social and historical background of Korean Christians and the life of the Korean churches by discussing the process of the indigenization of Christianity in Korea" (1). It is an approach that enables Younghoon Lee to exhibit a non-excluding and non-defensive open-minded realism, which, however, does not neglect the important power of discernment. In sharp short sketches, he identifies the influences of shamanism, Buddhism, and Confucianism on Christianity (cf. 11–18), but also gives reasons for their loss of impact in past centuries. Throughout the book, he is concerned with the continuing impact of the non-Christian traditions on Korean Christianity. Furthermore, he offers perspectives on the introduction of Catholicism to Korea since the sixteenth century, and he takes into account the Japanese invasion.

His main interest, however, focuses on the growth of Protestantism in general and the Holy Spirit movements in six particular periods of the twentieth century and the beginning of the twenty-first century. These periods are marked by 1) a great revival; 2) the Japanese occupation as a colonial power and its attempts "to destroy the spirit of the nation" (41); 3) the Korean War and the division of the country, the co-suffering with the oppressed North Koreans, by the emergence of new religious sects and the beginnings of the Korean Pentecostal movement; 4) political dictatorship, rapid economic growth but also hard divisions between urban and rural developments and the widening gap between the rich and the poor, and finally, conflicting theological and ecclesial reactions to these developments; 5) the ecumenical movement and enormous new church growth in Korea; and 6) a "globalization of Christian mission" (122), growing social engagement, and environmental stewardship among Korean Pentecostals.

The growth of Korean Protestantism in general and the Holy Spirit movements in particular over a century was not only accompanied by many experiences and events of joy and gratitude but also by long periods of suffering and pain. The Japanese occupation in the second period, the Korean War at the beginning of the third period, and the dictatorship in the fourth period brought fear and persecution, suppression, imprisonment, and even death for countless

---

[1] Oxford: Regnum Books, 1996; Eugene/Oregon: Wipf & Stock, 2009.

The Realism of the Working of God's Spirit   65

people. The emergence of religious sects and inner-religious and interreligious conflicts, the rapid economic growth and growing tensions between urban and rural developments, and the increasing separation between rich and poor people, but also ambivalent repercussions of the processes of globalisation and social and ecological challenges generated many questions and doubts with respect to God's good guidance in the sustaining, rescuing, and ennobling working of God's Spirit. Younghoon Lee's impressive book does not gloss over or conceal these sad and dark sides of the past century in Korean history.

The Korean Holy Spirit movement in the first period of the twentieth century "started in 1903 at Wonsan and reached its peak in 1907 at Pyongyang" (24). Younghoon Lee comments, "… through this movement, Korean Protestantism experienced the powerful gifts of the Holy Spirit for the first time." Christians "came to feel the excitement of their faith" and witnessed "the exceptional growth of the Korean church" (ibid.). It is characteristic of Dr. Lee's theological realism that he does not only emphasise "the explosive growth in the Korean church" but also the important roles of individual theologians, pastors, bishops, and other religious leaders.[2] Rather, he focuses on the impacts not only on adults but also on children and students; he illuminates different dynamics in different denominations.

Moreover, he attests to "some negative outcomes." New styles of faith generated problems: "… first, people are likely to become apathetic to society and the present life when the future life and hope for the future are exclusively emphasized; and on the other hand, when the present life is overly emphasized, people are likely to focus on personal well-being, and to care more for the material blessings of the present" (33).

The second period (1920–1940) was shaped by the Japanese occupation of Korea, the strong opposition of Christian churches and schools, and a "terrible persecution for the Korean church" (41). This brought about a decline of the Korean church, as well as developments in revival movements (Ik-doo Kim's Healing Ministry; Yong-do Lee's theology and religious practice aiming at a mystical union with Christ).

Here again, Younghoon Lee offers a very subtle evaluation. On the one hand, the revival movements contributed to the growth of the Korean church, even in oppressed and depressing situations, but on the other hand, they showed tendencies towards eschatological escapism, a strong emphasis on the dualism of flesh and spirit, and the lack of a self-critical discernment of the spirits in the church.

The third period (1940–1960), after the liberation from the Japanese occupation, saw the outbreak of the Korean War, the beginning of strong divisions in the Korean Presbyterian churches, and the emergence of about 200 new Korean syncretistic religions. In the midst of many chaotic developments, "the Holy Spirit movement kept going" (66) and "the Pentecostal faith, which was first brought to Korea by Mary C. Rumsey" in 1928, inspired that

---

[2] Cf. the important role of Sun-ju Gil, who "baptized more than 3000 people and built more than sixty churches" (34–39, 35) and developed a strong emphasis on future eschatology.

movement. Mary Rumsey was a Methodist and missionary who had been impressed by the rapid growth of the Pentecostal movement in the United States. She won the support of several Korean theologians even under the Japanese occupation.

The third period saw the consolidation of Pentecostal theology, originally evolving from the Holiness movement and John Wesley's doctrine of sanctification, with a strong concentration on the differentiated baptism in the Holy Spirit. [3] Many Pentecostal churches throughout the country were established.

In the fourth period (1960–1980), Korea was under the dictatorship of President Jung-hee Park, who "curtailed free speech, put anti-government leaders in detention, and laid off anti-government professors" (77). This political development was connected with rapid economic growth, an increase in the urban population, a decrease in the rural and agricultural population, and above all, a growing gap between rich and poor people. As a consequence, "anti-government elite group(s)" inside and outside the churches emerged (cf. ibid.), and along with this, various tensions among the more politically, socially, or theologically concerned persons in these groups arose.

Younghoon Lee summarises: "… the difference between the rich and the poor became more noticeable; social anarchy ensued. An alienated group of people was formed who were socially and financially oppressed" (77). "Against this social background, there arose two types of the Holy Spirit movement: the Minjung theology of the elite and the revival movement by and for the people" (78). Dr. Lee emphasises the more sceptical conservative voices with respect to the Minjung theology. These voices saw deficiencies in the Christological and trinitarian theologies of the Minjung supporters and a strong emphasis on moral and political issues inspired by the success of liberation theologies in various parts of the world in this era. Minjung theologies, however, received a strong international and ecumenical resonance. Was this just owed to the "spirit of the time" and the moral, legal, and political horror brought about by a dictatorial regime and an unbalanced economic development?

Several Korean and international theologians emphasised an enormous Christological and biblical strength at the core of Minjung theology. This was highlighted by the German theologian Jürgen Moltmann in his book *Erfahrungen theologischen Denkens*. Moltmann compared a discovery by the Korean theologian Byung-Mu Ahn with the central discovery by Luther regarding God's justice and righteousness in Romans 3:28. Ahn's was a discovery in the gospel of Mark. The Greek word *ochlos* – for "the people," "the mass" – was translated as "Minjung." Mark used the word *ochlos*, but not *ethnos*, *laos*, or other more neutral terms. *Ochlos* was the suffering but often silent lower and disadvantaged part of society. This part of the people is quite excited about Jesus' work and teaching. Jesus has mercy on the *ochlos* (Mark 5:34; 6:34); he teaches them and proclaims God's reign, even from a boat (2:13; 4:1 and 5:21); they are witnesses to and impressed by his healing (5:24; 9:14f; 10:46). Those

---

[3] Cf. Ig-jin Kim, *History and Theology of Korean Pentecostalism* (Zoetermeer, The Netherlands: Uitgeverij Boekencentrum, 2003).

The Realism of the Working of God's Spirit   67

who want to persecute Jesus fear the *ochlos* (11:18; 12:12). This does not mean that the members of the *ochlos* are saints. For instance, at the beginning of Mark, they block the access to a sick person whom Jesus wants to heal so that he and his helpers have to go through the roof of the house. And at the end, they go along with those who cry: "Crucify him!" (Mark 15:15).

It is obvious that Jesus is full of empathy for the multifariously suffering *ochlos*, that he cares for them and, in this way, identifies with them. But is it adequate to speak of an identity between Jesus and the *ochlos*, Jesus and the Minjung? It is, however, the *ochlos* that he calls in the central words of Mark 8:34–38: "If any man would come after me, let him deny himself and take up his cross and follow me ... Whoever wants to be my disciple must deny themselves and take up their cross and follow me. For whoever wants to save their life will lose it..." The call for discipleship in suffering is connected with an eschatological promise. One should thus not juxtapose Jesus' theological and pastoral concerns with his diaconal and social concerns.

Younghoon Lee explains that Minjung theology "is deeply related to the Koreans' unique mindset *han*." With Andrew S. Park's *The Wounded Heart of God: The Asian Concept of Han and the Christian Doctrine of Sin*,[4] he unfolds: "*Han* is an Asian, particularly Korean, term used to describe the depths of human sufferings." "*Han* is a repressed anger mixed with depression over a situation that cannot be changed" (79).

Traumatising past experiences and present sufferings come together in the abyss of *han*: the colonisation by the Japanese, the sufferings in the Korean War and the ongoing division of the country, the co-suffering with the people under the repressive regime in the North, but also memories of the dictatorship in the South in the fourth period, the ambivalence of the fast economic growth under the dictatorship with social divisions between urban and rural communities, and an increasing gap between the rich and the poor in the country.

In the attempts to counter and overcome the multifaceted challenges of *han*, Minjung theology also referred to and made use of aesthetic practices, drawing on and engaging non-Christian religious traditions in Korea. Its "struggle does not engage in direct confrontation, but is often hidden behind *talchum* (mask dances), *mindam* (storytelling), and *pansori* (dramatic solo performances that use songs and poems)."[5]

All these impulses caused "conservative scholars (to) criticize the Minjung theology, saying it cannot be considered a theological movement, but it can be considered a social one" (81). This critique could be underscored by the enormous success of gigantic revival meetings and evangelistic crusades in the 1960s and 1970s. "The growth of the Korean church in the 1970s is worth noting: the Christian population in 1974 was 3 million; in 1978, four years later, it had grown to seven million. This indicates that Christians were added to the Korean church at an average rate of one million per year. According to the 1978 statistics,

---

[4] Nashville,TN: Abingdon, 1993, 15.

[5] Sam Kyung Park, "The Notion of Liberation in Minjung Theology – Focusing on First Generation Minjung Theologians" (a paper drawing on a Ph.D. dissertation, Drew University, 2009).

six new churches were born daily in South Korea." Although Younghoon Lee is quite impressed by the power of the evangelistic activities in the Presbyterian Church, in the Holiness Church, and, of course, in the Holy Spirit movement, he also acknowledges the strength "of the contributions of Minjung theology (which) lies in its calling for attention to society, especially to the plight of the oppressed. The evangelical group had been focusing on personal salvation and the growth of the churches, and was not very much interested in the oppressed, if at all. Therefore, the evangelical group obviously needs to be more concerned about the socio-political and economic situation and must elaborate on how to lift the burden of *han* from the people" (83).

In this respect, he sees positive developments in the fifth period (1980–2000). Confrontations between conservative and liberal groups of the Korean churches became less vigorous or even began to stop. A growing ecumenical cooperation, the joining of activities in revival movements of various denominations, and all this was greatly supported by the Holy Spirit movement. Younghoon Lee underscores the enormous development of megachurches in Korea. "The world's largest Pentecostal, Presbyterian, Methodist, and Baptist churches were all found in Korea." He highlights the life and ministry of Yonggi Cho and the fantastic development of Yoido Full Gospel Church, which became "the largest single congregation in the world with a membership of 755,000 by the end of 2007" (93).

In this fifth period, he sees a strong development in connecting spiritual and social concerns in the life and teaching of the churches. The establishment of "cell units" in the church, each practising worship, prayer, and fellowship, and the encouragement of women leaders with respect for their status was brought together with a deep respect for the message of the outpouring of the Spirit (see the next part on Acts) and the richness of the gifts of the Spirit. The strong concern for the spiritual dimension of healing and the non-defensive acknowledgement of shamanistic healing-oriented impulses in Korean history energised spiritual and church growth. Many social activities and a growing institutionalisation of social concerns in the Korean churches continued into the sixth period at the beginning of the twenty-first century.

The sixth period (2000–today) has seen new attempts to overcome at least some of the divisions between the North and the South in Korea. There is a growing impact of the Pentecostal churches on other spiritual and ecclesial developments in the processes of globalisation. The beginning of concerns and activities with respect to environmental stewardship and their fast growth are also documented in this rich book.

The book summarises the reasons for the most impressive success story of church growth in the midst of many long periods of distress and suffering. It names the rich religious soil with roots in shamanism, Buddhism and Confucianism. It points to the instability of the Korean society and public life as a cause for the desperate search for stability and spiritual satisfaction. It finally names challenges and potential sources for weakening the powers of spiritual and ecclesial life: the danger of sectarianism, a lack of social concerns, a lack of doctrinal standards, and the danger of too strong an emotionalisation of public and ecclesial life (138f).

The Realism of the Working of God's Spirit   69

In the second part, I will deal with some of the future challenges listed at the end of the book: "The traditional emphasis on the person and work of the Holy Spirit among the Pentecostals should continue, but in the healthy and wider context of Christian theology." The appreciation of the spiritual resources of the Korean Holy Spirit movement should not block an appropriation of outside influences in (self-)critical discernment. A strong orientation towards a substantial theology and a sound set of practices in church life should help to ensure vigilance and discernment to guard against social and religious currents, indigenous as well as foreign. The traditionally mission-oriented Pentecostal movement should not lose its missionary energies in the global call and in confrontation with global challenges (cf. 140–144).

Biblical Lessons in the Book of Acts

The notion of the "outpouring of the Spirit" in Acts 2 and Joel 3 is breathtaking in many aspects: spiritual, theological, moral, political, and conceptual. It challenges modes of traditional thinking in many fields of experience. Traditional thinking – religious and secular – focuses on clear bipolar, dualising concepts: God and human, I and thou, heaven and earth, and so on. The pouring of the Spirit, however, addresses a multitude of recipients: male and female (in patriarchal societies), old and young (in gerontocratic societies), maidservants and menservants (in slaveholder societies, which were a matter of course in antiquity) (Acts 2:17f). Not just one revolution – many revolutions take place in one event!

With this outpouring of the Spirit, God speaks, and Jesus Christ speaks to human persons according to the book of Acts (Acts 1:2, 5; 2:33). What a powerful speaking and acting! And what a great empowerment of those who receive the Holy Spirit (Acts 1:8; 2:38; 4:8, 31; 6:3, 5, 10; 7:55, 59). The working of and empowerment by the Spirit is central to the Pentecost event. But it reaches back to a history long past (e.g., David, Isaiah, and the prophets spoke empowered by the Spirit, Acts 1:16; 4:25; 28:25). The working of the Spirit has an impact on human beings from many countries, traditions, and languages – another revolution for a world full of nationalism, chauvinism, xenophobia, and other excluding hostilities. It bestows wonderful gifts of the Spirit that can be communicated and shared among human beings (Acts 8:17–19).

Acts 9:31 says, "the church throughout all Judea and Galilee and Samaria had peace and was built up: and walking in the fear of the Lord and in the comfort of the Holy Spirit it was multiplied" (see also Acts 11:24). Acts 10 records Peter's preaching about Jesus' being anointed with the Holy Spirit, giving Jesus the power of "doing good and healing all that were oppressed by the devil," is connected with another outpouring of the Spirit: "the Holy Spirit fell on all who heard the word" (Acts 10:44). The Jews and even Peter "were amazed, because the gift of the Holy Spirit had been poured out even on the Gentiles" (Acts 10:45; cf. also Acts 11:15 and Acts 15:7–19). Acts 13:52 mentions the connection of joy with the experience of receiving the gift of the Holy Spirit: "… the disciples were filled with joy and with the Holy Spirit."

In Acts 16, we do not only hear about the orienting and guiding power of the Holy Spirit, but also about the Spirit's forbidding and not allowing power. It is not clear whether these orientations were gained in the communication of the community, or by individual inspirations. It is remarkable that the last chapters of Acts deal with problems of discerning the spirits. In Acts 16, "a slave who had a spirit of divination and brought her owners much gain by soothsaying" seems to speak the words of truth by following Paul and "crying: these men are servants of the Most High God, who proclaim to you the way of salvation" (Acts 16:17f). But instead of being happy about this prophetic support, Paul practises an exorcism – and the spirit "came out (of her) that very hour." Chapters 18–20 speak of the divine Spirit and human spirits, of believers who had "never heard that there is a Holy Spirit" (Acts 19:2), about the working of an "evil spirit," but also that the Spirit testifies to Paul from city to city that "imprisonment and affliction await" him (Acts 20:23; cf. Acts 21:11).

We owe a complex pneumatological orientation to the book of Acts. The passage on the outpouring of the Spirit and the Spirit baptism is clearly its most important part.

A Famous but only Partly Biblically Inspired Witness to the Outpouring of the Spirit in the Twentieth Century[6]

In October 1978, Karol Wojtyła from Poland was elected pope. Eight months later, in June 1979 – during the second of his over one hundred trips abroad – he visited his homeland and celebrated his first mass there on Victory Square in Warsaw. He concluded with a prayer that electrified his fellow Poles: "And I cry – I who am a son of the land of Poland and who am also Pope John Paul II – I cry from all the depths of this millennium, I cry on the vigil of Pentecost: Let your Spirit descend! Let your Spirit descend and renew the face of the earth, the face of this land! Amen."

Everyone in Poland understood what he said – except perhaps the communist government, which allegedly wondered whom, exactly, he had summoned. The CIA? A year later, in 1980, strikes erupted in the country, leading to the founding of the labour union Solidarity and –despite numerous violent setbacks – enduring social, political, and freedom-based transformations in Poland and elsewhere. Two decades later, during his eighth, penultimate, journey to Poland, John Paul II spoke once more at the site of his legendary 1979 address:

> Is not all that happened at that time in Europe and the world, beginning with our own homeland, God's response? Before our eyes, changes of political, social and

---

[6] This section intends to show that the biblical witnesses can provide great power of orientation concerning the working of the Spirit, but that it is important to listen to them carefully. I take up some passages from my Gifford Lectures on "natural theology": see M. Welker, *In God's Image: An Anthropology of the Spirit. The 2019/2020 Gifford Lectures at the University of Edinburgh* (Grand Rapids: Eerdmans 2021), 21–24. Its Korean translation is by Hae Kwon Kim and Kang Won Lee, edited with an introduction by Hae Kwon Kim, published by Presbyterian Church of Korea (2022).

The Realism of the Working of God's Spirit
71

economic systems have taken place, enabling individuals and nations to see anew the splendor of their own dignity. Truth and justice are recovering their proper value, becoming a challenge for all those who are able to appreciate the gift of freedom.

Justice, truth, and freedom, as mentioned in this speech – along with peace and love – are themes that consistently stir the hearts of people in many cultures. They are also central themes in the Bible. Indeed, Paul in the New Testament and other biblical traditions explicitly associate these concepts with the activity of the Holy Spirit.

In the Old Testament, the classical biblical witness to the "outpouring" of the divine Spirit is the prophet Joel, chapter 3, verses 1–5; and in the New Testament, Acts, chapter 2, verses 1–13. It is highly noteworthy that biblical accounts of the outpouring of the Spirit explicitly include women and even maidservants (slaves) and young people; that is, *not* merely the men who traditionally had the last word in such communities. The New Testament account in Acts, moreover, also mentions the salutary effects that the outpouring of the Spirit had on numerous other nations, races, and languages. The Pope does not address the highly charged and even revolutionary consequences that these biblical witnesses have for the status and treatment of women and against the subordination of young people in patriarchal and gerontocratic communities – not to speak of chauvinistic, xenophobic, and racist environments.

But for a moment, let us concentrate on the notion itself of the outpouring of the Spirit. This phenomenon implies that the divine Spirit can be "invoked," that is, petitioned to descend upon human beings – but also that those receiving this outpouring are, in their own turn, "summoned" to respond in a life-changing way. *The outpouring of the Spirit is a realistic event* that, even within the context of "natural theology" (expected in the Gifford lectures), can be conveyed particularly by way of its effects on human circumstances. John Paul II also spoke about social, political, economic, and moral transformations with tangible changes for individuals, an entire nation, and even international relations. And to describe the weave of virtues and values he discerned being mediated by the Spirit, he turned to the grand concepts of truth, justice, freedom, and human dignity.

I have called this a "multimodal and multipolar working of the Spirit." The expression "multimodal" has been commonly used only since the twentieth century, particularly since the digital revolution, and primarily in connection with linguistics, media studies, psychology, philosophy, and economics. In business communication, multimodality can, for example, enhance customer satisfaction by providing several contact possibilities between customers and the business, such as text messaging, chats, and social media. Media are multimodal if, for example, they deliver information not just by way of a single medium such as a text, but through other media as well, such as speech and images that not only specify a message more clearly but also actually shape it.

By contrast, one speaks of "multipolar" constellations whenever a given constellation (of people, social entities, or even an arrangement of nerve cells) possesses several centres or several poles. The idea of a multipolar world order, for example, envisions a political arrangement with several power centres, enabling the world to be stabilised (or destabilised) by different states or power blocks.

But why, in this present inquiry concerning the human spirit and the divine Spirit and their cooperative activities, might we profit from a multimodal and multipolar approach? The advantage of understanding the spirit by way of such an approach is that it offers wholly new insights against dominant forms of the traditional understanding of the spirit. Previous perspectives on the spirit and its effects were distorted by, among other things, attempts to come to an understanding by way of culturally rooted bipolar thinking. The notions of the spirit and its effects tended to be reduced to simple relationships (God–person; human being–fellow human being; my interior intellectual, moral, and religious dialogue; the relationship between the act of thinking and what is thought). In situations where one sensed that the spirit was somehow "more" than could be articulated by bipolar reductions, the remedy in many religious and even secular communities was simply to view it as a mysterious, nebulous, incomprehensible, numinous power. One shifts, as it were, from unequivocal bipolarity over to diffuse plurality and assumes that the divine Spirit is a numinous, transcendent power that descends upon creatures from the beyond like wind and rain. The figure of the outpouring of the Spirit "from above" – conceived in a less than rigorous manner – and various biblical statements seemed to support such vague notions. A reflection on John Paul II's invocation and summoning of the Spirit in Warsaw in 1979, however, provides us with a considerably different perspective.

Although the Pope was convinced that God did indeed respond to the invocation, that response did not come about in some ghostlike, indeterminate fashion. Instead, a large number of people were concretely, profoundly moved, and inspired to think, communicate, and act anew and indeed in new ways. In the historical case under consideration here, a considerable role was played by a distinct consciousness not only of divine power but also of open support by the head of the Roman Catholic Church. A key factor in all situations involving the outpouring of the Spirit, however – both past and present – is that the resulting interplay between people does *not* simply remain diffuse and aimless. What emerges is a focused movement. A great many individuals act together, doubtless sometimes even in conflict with one another, and yet always in "re-action" to one another, and it is together, collectively, that their actions bring about grand results. Plural developments of this sort, developments that cannot be traced back to simple cause-and-effect chains, are described as "emergent." As a rule, emergent developments initiated by the outpouring of the Spirit cannot be guided or stopped by simple intervention and are permeated by a healthy measure of free decisions and actions and thus sometimes take surprising turns.

It is extremely important to keep in mind that these developments always focus on specific content, for the divine Spirit does not impart this or that arbitrary impulse. Although even influential thinkers such as Hans Küng or Charles Taylor have repeatedly asserted that people need "some kind of

The Realism of the Working of God's Spirit

religiously or morally imparted orientation,"[7] this view ignores the important notion of a discernment of spirits. After all, there are not only freedom-oriented spirits but also evil, destructive, and subversive spirits. Think of an evil spirit that spreads hate in a country. The view that a spirit and its effects are, from the outset, exclusively good is as naive and foolish as the view that morality and religion are always and in all their manifestations charitable and good. Here, the differentiation between the divine Spirit, which is always conducive to life, and other spirits, whose effects can be good or evil, is essential.

It is deeply regrettable that the powerful message of John Paul II on the outpouring of the Spirit is deficient in its biblical orientation. It does not reveal that the outpouring of the Spirit addresses and ennobles male and female, old and young, and even subordinated and enslaved people in human societies. There was obviously a need to protect monohierarchic, patriarchal, and gerontocratic conditions and structures in religious and political communities. We can only guess why the powerful developments in Poland, followed by many economic developments and progresses in societal freedom after 1980, were gradually blocked, and the Spirit of freedom, justice, equality, and truth was not allowed to unfold according to the biblical witnesses.

A serious theological and spiritual biblical orientation and respect for the realism of the powers of the Spirit of God should help and guide us in the future to discern the spirits and to follow the Spirit of Christ, a Spirit of benevolence and love, of justice, freedom, truth, and peace.

---

[7] Charles Taylor, *Sources of the Self: The Making of the Modern Identity* (Cambridge: Cambridge University Press, 1989), 28. See also the erroneous assumption in Taylor, *Sources of the Self*, 48 that orientations in the moral sphere unfold similarly to those in the natural sphere; see Hans Küng, *Global Responsibility: In Search of a New World Ethic* (Chestnut Ridge: Crossroad, 1991); and my review "Hans Küngs 'Projekt Weltethos': Gutgemeint – aber ein Fehlschlag," *Evangelische Kommentare* 26 (1993), 354–56.

The Challenge of Demythologising the Devil

Frank D. Macchia

Spiritual warfare, in which demonic spirits are opposed and even cast out, is an important aspect of Pentecostal ministries, especially outside the West. How this warfare is interpreted and practised certainly needs to be questioned, but it should not be dismissed. In particular, we need to take seriously the reality of the demonic assumed in it and not simply reject it out of hand as mythological and, therefore, irrelevant to the Charismatic ministry of the church today. It is for this reason that I discuss the topic of the challenge involved in "demythologising the devil."

The Biblical Challenge of the Demonic

Before we confront the challenge of "demythologising" the demonic, we need to recognise that opposing the demonic is not a minor theme in the New Testament nor in the history of Christian thought. Granted, the sovereignty of God in the Old Testament leaves little room for demonic activity in decisive opposition to God. Walther Eichrodt points out that a satanic adversary is even pictured as part of the heavenly court in Job (Job 1:6). This adversary is allowed to function within the boundaries of the permissive will of God.[1] In 1 Chronicles 21:1, a satanic adversary is indeed placed in opposition to God. In this verse, evil results in the context of judgements that were attributed to God (2 Sam. 24:1) and are now attributed to an opposing supernatural adversary. Such examples, however, are not numerous. One finds in the Old Testament not much more than "glimmerings of the idea of a superhuman being hostile to God."[2] By contrast, the New Testament grants the satanic and the larger category of the demonic a significant role to play in that which opposes God's redemptive mission in the world. The background for granting much more prominence to the demonic in the New Testament can be traced to later Judaism, which, under apocalyptic influence, granted greater attention to the demonic. A sharper focus on eschatology tends to raise the question of the final struggle that will occur between those aligned with divine purposes and the forces of evil and darkness. Some have speculated that this change between the Testaments may also be due to a possible Persian dualistic influence on Judaism, which gave rise to a more robust role for the demonic in its opposition to God (a more prominent attention to a dualistic opposition between good and evil).[3] The overarching victory of the sovereign reign of God is thus qualified to allow for genuine opposition (a

---

[1] Walther Eichrodt, *Theology of the Old Testament*, Vol. 2, trans. J. A. Baker (Philadelphia: Westminster, 1962), 205.

[2] Ibid, 207.

[3] Ibid, 209.

qualified dualism between good and evil in which the good is still assured the victory). The most compelling reason for the rise of attention paid to the demonic in the New Testament in my view comes from the Gospel itself, referring us to the coming of the light in Christ, for the darkness is expected to be revealed more prominently in contrast and opposition to *him* as the revelation of the light of God. The Word of the Father was always the light that will overcome the darkness that threatens creation (John 1:5).

The Gospels thus launch Jesus' ministry with his defeat of satanic temptation in the wilderness, which concludes in Matthew 4:10 with Jesus' statement, "Away from me, Satan!" When Peter rebukes Jesus later for predicting his future death on the cross, Jesus responds by repeating something similar to that earlier rebuke: "Get behind me, Satan!" (Mark 8:33). Christ resists Satan in his entire journey to the cross. Moreover, the Gospels feature numerous cases in which people are delivered from demons by Christ: "When evening came, many who were demon-possessed were brought to him, and he drove out the spirits with a word and healed all the sick." (Matt 8:16). As this verse shows, the Gospels do not regard all sickness as directly demonic in nature (notice how the two categories of the demonic and sickness are kept distinct). Yet, the deliverance of people from demonic torment was an important element of Jesus' healing ministry and mission to inaugurate God's reign or Kingdom in the world. Notice Christ's announcement that "if it is by the Spirit of God that I drive out demons, then the Kingdom of God has come upon you" (Matt 12:28). He then characterises his mission as "tying up the strong man" (which in context is the devil) to "carry off his possessions" (v. 29). In inaugurating the Kingdom of God, Christ acts decisively to strip the devil of his ill-gotten bounty by freeing humanity of his deception and oppression. The coming of the liberating reign of God through Christ and the power of the Spirit is significantly signalled by the defeat of demonic powers.

Notice also how Peter summarised to the Gentile household of Cornelius what was fundamental to the proclamation of Christ's redemptive mission:

> You know what has happened throughout the province of Judea, beginning in Galilee after the baptism that John preached – [38] how God anointed Jesus of Nazareth with the Holy Spirit and power, and how he went around doing good and healing all who were under the power of the devil, because God was with him (Acts 10:37–38).

Deliverance from the power of the devil is an important component of the Gospel. Hebrews 2:14–15 even points out that the Son of God shared in the flesh of humanity so that in his death and resurrection, he could deliver us from the devil who wields a tormenting influence by using the power of death as a weapon: "Since the children have flesh and blood, he too shared in their humanity so that by his death he might break the power of him who holds the power of death – that is, the devil." Surely, the author of Hebrews would have added the point to Paul's statement that death is the "final enemy" defeated by Christ (1 Cor 15:26) and that the devil will also fall with it. Paul would have agreed, since he wrote that Christ on the cross "disarmed the powers and authorities," making "a public spectacle of them," and "triumphing over them" (Col 2:15). Ernst Käsemann correctly notes that for Paul the liberty of the

The Challenge of Demythologising the Devil   77

children of God involves the defeat of demonic powers, which is the fruit of the crucifixion as well as the expression of the dawning Kingdom of God in the Holy Spirit. [4] Also significant is Gustaf Aulén's argument that the classical understanding of the atonement from the New Testament to Luther involved a "Christ as victor" over sin, death, and the devil motif:

> The New Testament idea of redemption constitutes in fact a veritable revolution; for it declares that sovereign divine love had taken the initiative, broken through the order of justice and merit, triumphed over the powers of evil and created a new relation between the world and God.[5]

In line with Aulén's thesis, the Book of Revelation indicates that the devil's defeat also has missional and eschatological significance. Satan, "who leads the whole world astray," is hurled down to earth as a prelude to his final demise at Christ's return. The saints triumph over Satan by the blood of Christ poured forth out of love for humanity on the cross, which is the basis of Satan's final demise:

[10] Now have come the salvation and the power
   and the kingdom of our God,
   and the authority of his Messiah.
For the accuser of our brothers and sisters,
   who accuses them before our God day and night,
   has been hurled down.
[11] They triumphed over him
   by the blood of the Lamb
   and by the word of their testimony;
they did not love their lives so much
   as to shrink from death (Rev 12:10–11).

In the end, the devil is hurled into the great lake of fire, never to deceive and torment humanity again (Rev 20:10). The demonic may be said in the New Testament to have not only individual and social but also vast cosmic and eschatological significance.

In the New Testament, the demonic is indicative of the ultimate significance of evil as a transcendent power that opposes God and the divine triumph in history and in all of creation. To be sure, there is no unqualified dualistic struggle in the Bible to speak of between God and the demonic in the sense that the two are in any way comparable in significance and power. Indeed, God alone is sovereign as Lord of creation; the Old Testament makes this point abundantly clear. God is, therefore, the one who is guaranteed to win in the opposition of dark powers to God and to those who are aligned with God's cause of love in the world. According to the Prologue of John's Gospel, Christ mediates creation as the Word of the Father *and* as the one who cannot be overcome by the darkness that will threaten it (John 1:5).

---

[4] Ernst Käsemann, "The Saving Significance of Jesus' Death," 45, in *Perspectives on Paul*, trans. Margaret Kohl (Mifflintown, PA: Sigler Press, 1996), 32–59.

[5] Gustaf Aulen, *Christus Victor: An Historical Study of the Three Main Types of the Idea of Atonement* (New York: Macmillan, 1969), 155.

Yet, one is reminded when speaking of the demonic that there is still indeed a genuine opposition to God involved and a great deal at stake when it comes to the challenge laid at the feet of believers to resist demonic temptation and influence. There are texts that warn Christians to take the opposition of the devil with utmost seriousness. Submitting to God involves resisting the devil (James 4:7). We are to put on the whole armour of God to withstand the devil's schemes (Eph 6:10–17). Of course, we stand only in the might and victory of Christ (Eph 6:10), but we must still stand! And note the dire warning of 1 Peter 5:8: "Be alert and of sober mind. Your enemy, the devil, prowls around like a roaring lion looking for someone to devour." Satan wished to "sift Peter as wheat," perhaps meaning that Satan willed to shake his faith so violently that Peter would fall. But Christ prayed for Peter's endurance (Luke 22:31). We need to bear in mind that the power of the demonic lies in the area of deception, thriving where humanity gives itself to sin and death in all dimensions of human and creaturely life. Exaggerating the role of the demonic can indeed end up eclipsing human responsibility. Our best resistance to the devil is in our submission to God's will in the world (James 4:7). Indeed, in the preface to his famous *Screwtape Letters*, C. S. Lewis has done well to warn us not to exalt or overly glorify the demonic, but he also warns us not to neglect it or place it into the ash heap of outmoded mythology.[6] It is to the latter part of this warning that we now turn. Dare we demythologise the devil?

Bultmann, Barth, and Blumhardt

What is demythologising? To answer this question, we will turn to Rudolf Bultmann, who is most often associated with this term. We will focus on how he applied the term to demonology. To do so, it helps to explore how he responded to the story of the deliverance of a woman from demonic possession under the care of a German pastor named Johann Blumhardt. In response to this story, Bultmann penned the following words in his *Kerygma und Myth*: "Die Blumhardtischen Geschichten sind mir ein Greuel" ("The Blumhardt stories are an abomination to me").[7] What was it about the Blumhardt story that so revolted Bultmann? Johann Blumhardt was a nineteenth-century pietist who became a Reformed church pastor in the small town of Möttlingen in southern Germany. He considered the entire village as his congregation, including those who did not attend his church. He gave part of his meagre income away to feed the poor of his village and spent long hours praying with anyone who was in need. Over time, he began to counsel a young woman named Gottlieben Dittus, who complained of fainting spells, hysteria, and bouts of depression. She was also plagued with thoughts of suicide. She claimed to have had visions of spirits speaking to her. And, while under a spell, she was known to have spoken in voices not her own. Needles and nails were found coming from her scalp, which

---

[6] C. S. Lewis, *Screwtape Letters* (London: Geoffrey Bles: The Centenary Press, 1942), 9.

[7] Rudolf Bultmann, *Kerygma und Myth* (New York: Harper, 1948), 150.

The Challenge of Demythologising the Devil   79

she could have placed there to injure herself. Pastor Blumhardt soon learned that she and her sister, Katarina, were raised by a deplorable aunt with occult connections, who had dedicated Gottlieben to Satan. At first, Blumhardt thought Gottlieben to be in need of a *Seelssorger* (pastoral counsellor). But he gradually began to detect a dark dimension to her problems. In describing this story, Barth notes that Blumhardt did what any courageous minister faithful to Christ would do: in the power of Christ he took her side against the darkness. According to Barth, Blumhardt opposed that debilitating darkness "in relation to which there must not be adaptation into something willed by God but revolt, protest, and angry negation."[8] In one counselling session, when Gottlieben seemed under the spell of a dark presence, Blumhardt was gripped by the thought that he could not abandon her to the darkness that seemed to be engulfing her. The thought kept coming to him, "Who is the Lord?" Since it is Christ, Blumhardt believed that resignation was not an option. He put her hands together and asked her to pray, "Lord Jesus help me!" The symptoms temporarily subsided. Months later, a prayer vigil in the dead of night led to Gottlieben's deliverance. Her sister, who was also claiming to be tormented by spirits, was delivered as well. A demon was reported to have cried out from Gottlieben at the point of their deliverance that "Jesus ist Sieger" (Jesus is Victor). Their change was sudden and remarkable. The villagers who knew Gottlieben found her sudden change so shocking that news spread quickly of the event, both by word of mouth and the local press. Blumhardt was soon ministering at his little church to overflowing crowds that now met daily to accommodate the many people who came to hear him preach. Significantly, he took the occasion to proceed beyond Gottlieben's deliverance to speak of God's victory in Christ and in the outpouring of the Spirit to liberate people amid all forms of physical oppression and torment, even urging Christians to groan for the liberty of the entire creation from the grip of evil and suffering. He eventually established a retreat centre nearby in the German village of Bad Boll dedicated to the preaching of the Gospel and the healing of the sick. Gottlieben followed him and his extended family there. She married and led a normal life as a member of Blumhardt's extended household. She is buried today on the grounds of that centre, and the statement on her gravestone in large letters reads, "Jesus ist Sieger" (Jesus is Victor). That a demonic cry would end up her epitaph may sound strange. But the moment of that cry was her deliverance, and it came to characterise the banner under which she lived and was further healed in the loving acceptance of the Blumhardt household.[9]

Bultmann considered this story an abomination to him in part because of the sensational press that it received at the time Gottlieben's deliverance occurred (1843). For Bultmann, the story was unfortunately preoccupied with chilling details of a battle with demons, highlighting an element of the New Testament world picture that seemed to him to obscure rather than highlight the existential relevance of the Gospel. He held that the course of history over the past 2,000

---

[8] Karl Barth, *Church Dogmatics*, Vol. III, Pt. 3: The Doctrine of Creation, trans. G. W. Bromiley and R. J. Ehrlich (Edinburgh: T & T Clark, 1961), 371.

[9] Frank D. Macchia, *Spirituality and Social Liberation: The Message of the Blumhardts in the Light of Wuerttemberg Pietism* (Metuchen, NJ: Scarecrow Press, 1996), 64–68.

years has led to the inescapable conclusion that the New Testament's expectation of the soon-coming Kingdom of God was mythological. Bultmann elaborated by noting: "Just as mythological are the presuppositions of the coming of the Kingdom of God, namely, the theory that the world, although created by God, is ruled by the devil, Satan, and that his army, the demons, is the cause of all evil, sin, and disease."[10] He posed the question as to whether or not in this light the proclamation of the coming Kingdom of God involving the overthrow of demonic powers can have any meaning for modern humanity.[11] He answers in the affirmative, but only if we abandon the mythological worldview assumed in the preaching of Jesus without losing its "deeper meaning." He calls this effort at stripping away the myth while preserving its deeper meaning "demythologizing."[12] What for Bultmann is essential to religious mythology? For Bultmann, religious myths grant transcendent reality objective, this-worldly form, as if, for example, evil has its source in actually existing personal creatures called "demons" that tempt and inflict harm on humans. Demythologising strips away such myths, while maintaining their deeper religious and existential significance. Thus, so-called demonic powers are to be regarded as having a deeper existential significance, as "a power that enslaves every member of the human race," though its source is in humanity rather than in actual demonic beings.[13] Stripping away the myths while maintaining their deeper existential significance has for Bultmann its goal in clarifying the Gospel that is implied within the myths for a new generation of hearers who find the ancient mythological forms of expression to be a stumbling block.

One could thus see Bultmann's desire to demythologise Blumhardt's story as pastoral, or as an effort to liberate the kerygma or the Gospel from the sensationalistic distraction of its ancient mythological mode of communication. But here is precisely where Barth placed the focus of his disagreement with Bultmann. In Barth's view, the thought forms that communicated the ancient expression of the Gospel were not the fundamental issue for the pastor, but rather the Gospel of Christ as liberator that must always occupy the preacher's primary emphasis and loyalty. Pastoral concern was thus mainly served in Gottlieben's case, not by demythologising Gottlieben's assumptions about her demonic possession, but rather by challenging the assumption of her abandonment to darkness by God in the light of the Gospel. For Barth, Blumhardt's battle in Christ's name rightly undermined the dark forces that held Gottlieben in their grip and on behalf of the Gospel of Christ's grace and deliverance that was extended to her instead. Barth thus says of Blumhardt: "He did what every preacher must adequately or inadequately attempt, namely, to make present the

---

[10] Rudolf Bultmann, *Jesus Christ and Mythology* (New York: Charles Scribner's and Sons, 1958), 14–15.

[11] Ibid, 16–17.

[12] Ibid, 18.

[13] Ibid, 19–21.

The Challenge of Demythologising the Devil   81

word of God. He only tried to take seriously the saying in Ps 77:10, which ...
runs, 'The hand of the Most High can change everything.'"[14]

For Barth, Blumhardt's remarkable battle for a young woman's deliverance
was an open window into the concrete relevance of the Gospel for Blumhardt's
time and place, even without demythologising Gottlieben's understanding of her
desperation. Blumhardt entered her world and she understood it, but he did so as
a minister of the Gospel. Hence, he did not leave her world unchallenged. He
called her out of the bondage under dark powers mediated to her through a family
situation that condemned her to a hopeless and self-destructive existence. The
liberation that Blumhardt's Gospel offered to her was not only a matter of the
mind or of the heart (as liberals or pietists might have assumed) but was also
communal and social in nature. Those institutional realities that mediated the
demonic to her would do so no more. The Blumhardt story gives us, according
to Barth, an open window into a Gospel that offers deliverance for the embodied
life of humanity in the midst of a battle that has concrete historical, social, and
even vast cosmic and eschatological significance.

Demythologising in Loyalty to the Gospel: Karl Barth

Barth indeed praised Blumhardt for meeting Gottlieben within the world of her
existence as it was mediated to her and as she beheld it, in the throes of demonic
possession and abandonment, and did so with the liberating Gospel in hand.
Barth, however, was also willing in the context of secondary, theological
reflection to think about the demonic creatively, in other than strictly literal
terms. But Barth was insistent that the Gospel of Christ is our fundamental
loyalty and the lens through which the demonic was to be reinterpreted for our
time. The result was an understanding of the demonic that is realistic though not
literal. And the standard of interpretation would not be cultural or existential but
kerygmatic (in loyalty to the Gospel). In the process, mythological elements
involved in cultural images of the demonic (even those found in Scripture) can
be understood, even pruned, in loyalty to what the Gospel requires of our
interpretation. Reading Barth on the demonic makes it clear that he pays no
attention to popular myths about demons as spirits of deceased people or
subhuman creatures with horns and hooves. He also dismisses the notion of
demons in the New Testament as fallen angels (Jude 6). He dismisses the notion
of demons as actually existing personal beings. Using the Gospel as his
hermeneutical lens, Barth turned from taking what he regarded as mythological
ideas surrounding the demonic to focus instead on the outer darkness that negates
all that God elects for creation in Christ. This darkness is for Barth the notion of
the demonic demanded by the Gospel. It is the deep negation of all that is willed
by God in Christ, the final Nothingness (*Nichtige*) that negates the Gospel.[15] As
the ultimate negation of the light which is Christ, the demonic is for Barth the
mystery of iniquity. Barth writes of the devil, "He is certainly not a creature of

---

[14] Ibid.
[15] Karl Barth, *Church Dogmatics*, Vol. III, Pt. 3, 519–31.

82   *The Holy Spirit, Spirituality and Leadership*

God. He may, perhaps, be merely the cause of the unfounded nature of sin. The devil is, as I say, the impossible possibility, which cannot be defined."[16]

So, Barth demythologises, not in faithfulness to a modern scientific worldview, but in the name of biblical "realism" or the worldview called forth in the Bible by the Gospel. In Barth's view, he demythologises the Bible on the demonic for the sake of the Bible, or to bring to clearer expression what the Bible itself implicitly reaches beyond the limits of its own time-bound language to say about the demonic. As Barth put the matter in the prefaces of his Romans Commentary, he "does not exclude a criticism of the letter by the spirit, which is, indeed, unavoidable," for it is "precisely a strict faithfulness which compels us to expand or to abbreviate the text, lest a too rigid attitude to the words should obscure that which is struggling to expression in them and which demands expression."[17] To probe this matter further, we turn to the Ghanian theologian Esther Acolatse and her interaction with Barth's approach to the demonic.

Esther Acolatse's Contextual Demonology

Loyalty to the Gospel has contexts. Esther Acolatse has written a significant book exploring the question of deliverance from demonic oppression and possession in African contexts (and by implication, other contexts) today. Though she mentions the Blumhardt story, she does not elaborate on it nor explore the Barth–Bultmann tension over it. Yet, she does utilise quite a bit of space taking up Bultmann's challenge. She maintains that Bultmann did not see clearly enough the complex ways that the Bible deals with ancient mythology. The Bible deals with the mythology prevalent in its ancient cultural contexts by taking it up and transforming it into a witness to what God is doing and will do. The limitations of ancient myths are overcome and used poetically to bear witness to truths implied by the divine promises and acts of redemption. So, she largely follows the Gospel-mandated devotion to biblical realism advocated by Barth, as well as by Brevard Childs, who was himself inspired by Barth.[18] There is an exception, though. Acolatse still regards demons as personal beings that actually exist. Acolatse's major response to Barth's idea that demonic powers are not created, personal beings is to ask, "… if God exercises his will positively and negatively should there not be an ontology corresponding to both?"[19]

In the end, Acolatse qualifies Barth and takes issue with Bultmann by viewing the demonic as actually existing beings, apart from humanity and in opposition to God. Her reasons for preserving the demonic as an actually existing reality are

---

[16] Karl Barth, *Gespräche* 1959–1962, Gesamtausgabe, Band 25, herausg. Eberhard Busch (Zürich: Theologischer Verlag Zürich, 1995), 113.

[17] Karl Barth, *Epistle to the Romans* (Oxford: Oxford University Press, 1968), 18–19 (from the preface).

[18] Esther Acolatse, *Powers, Principalities, and the Spirit* (Grand Rapids, MI: Eerdmans, 2018), 97–126. See Brevard Childs, *Myth and Reality in the Old Testament*, Studies in Biblical Theology 27 (Naperville, IL: A. R. Allenson, 1960), 102.

[19] Acolatse, *Powers*, 147.

The Challenge of Demythologising the Devil

four-fold. First, she maintains that we have to bring the devil into our understanding of Christ's victory because the Scriptures do. As I noted above, the pages of the New Testament speak of the victory over the demonic powers as important, not only to the practical ministry of the church, but to the very kerygma or proclamation of the Gospel itself, for Christ disarmed the powers on the cross. Her second answer is based on tradition. The church down through the centuries has stood by the Scriptures in its denial of Satan, and implicitly calls the modern church to do likewise. So, she applies not only the Scriptures but also the weight of tradition to modern interpreters who would like to eliminate a realistic view of the demonic from the church's ministry and theology. Thirdly, Acolatse's argument is ecumenical. Not only past tradition but large segments of the church today, especially where Christianity is gaining its centres of strength outside of the West, stand with the historic church and the Scriptures in resisting the demonic powers in their witness to Christ. And, fourthly, she makes the theological argument that removing the reality of the demonic powers as the Scriptures portray them causes us to lose from view the supernatural depth and expanse of divine power as revealed at the cross and present in the work of the Spirit in the world today. It is especially with this last point that Acolatse's argument implicitly captures the central point as Blumhardt saw it; namely, a rediscovery of the power of God somewhat lost to the church today.[20]

But Acolatse recognises the challenge raised by her stance. Does not the belief in the existence and involvement of the devil bind the Gospel to a worldview that is prescientific, making scientific insights seem irrelevant? Does it not have the effect of elevating human suffering to the level of the supernatural, handicapping our efforts to understand and combat it through medical or social scientific means? Does it not lead us to the simplistic conclusion that all we need to do is pray to bind the spiritual forces in order to achieve personal healing and social renewal? Even worse, does it not create a moral dualism in which *we* occupy the light and all who oppose our views and methods are demonised? Acolatse admits that the kind of extreme belief in the ever-present threat of demonic spirits evident in African worldviews can lead to such problems. But she is also convinced that even more problematic is the reductionistic rejection of the demonic in the West exemplified by Bultmann that fails to recognise a transcendent dimension to evil that does not have its source in humanity. So, Acolatse takes Karl Barth as her major dialogue partner in attempting a middle path between naturalistic demythologising and an all-too-mythical preoccupation with the demonic in her African context. She also wishes to steer a course between African supernaturalism and Western naturalism, the path of a biblical realism that opens us to both supernatural and natural means of healing.

In accepting demons as actual beings, Acolatse also wants to conceive of them as still having the ability to function pervasively as the corporate spiritual influence involved in human communities and institutions, as implied in texts like Ephesians 6:11 and Colossians 2:15, such as we have in the work of Walter

---

[20] Ibid, implied throughout her book, especially her introduction, 1–20.

Wink.[21] But, unlike Wink, Acolatse wishes also to maintain that there are actual demons at work that are not reducible to the human corporate or institutional "spirit." Acolatse's way of supporting biblical realism does not seek to abandon the idea of the demonic as consisting of "personal" beings. Here is where the issue in my view becomes complex. Acolatse admits that the Bible that speaks to all cultures authoritatively is *itself* mediated to us through an ancient cultural framework. She knows that biblical realism is not to be naive about the influence of ancient culture on the language and thought forms used in the Bible to bring to expression its diverse witness to the Gospel. But she is not willing to define the personality of demonic powers implied in Scripture as merely part of an outmoded cultural worldview. So, how can the demonic exercise vast personal, social, and institutional influence if they are personal beings of given times and places?[22] And in what way may we call them "personal"?

Demythologising the Devil: My Response

Here is how I've understood Barth on the demonic as Nothingness, or as the ultimate negation of God's elect will for creation in Christ. It might help to realise that the fundamental issue for Barth when it comes to the demonic is not primarily creation but rather election, as revealed in the Christ event. Creation for Barth is subordinate theologically to election in Christ. For Barth, God creates with the goal of conforming creation to Christ. Christ is elect to be the inauguration of the new creation, including the new humanity, for which creation is made. This is why Nothingness for Barth is not obvious to human reason. It's only accessible through the lens of election as revealed in Christ. The darkness is only understood in contrast to the light. If left to the lens of unaided human wisdom, we would trivialise this Nothingness and its chaotic lure, justify it, see it as willed by God, or deny it altogether. Nothingness is only known from the lens of election as revealed in the Christ event. From *that* lens, it becomes clear to us that Nothingness is not directly willed by God, nor can it be part of creation. The Nothingness has been overcome by Christ but for now still exists until the fulfilment of the Kingdom of God in all of creation. As such, it exists not as essential to creation itself but rather as that which threatens it and is thus opposed by God. For Barth, demons are this Nothingness in its concrete and diverse "dynamic" in the world.[23] This is why Barth refuses to see demons as created, personal beings who are fallen angels. It's also why he views the demonic as a mystery, and why he refuses to say he "believes" in demons. It is nonsensical in Barth's view to believe in that which has no existence in creation as elected in and for Christ.

Yet, Barth still sees Nothingness as a dynamic and destructive threat to what is elected for creation in Christ. How are we to understand this? To explain it,

---

[21] See, for example, Walter Wink, *Naming the Powers: The Language of Power in the New Testament* (Philadelphia: Fortress Press, 1984).

[22] Acolatse, *Powers*, 141–43.

[23] Karl Barth, *Church Dogmatics*, Vol. III, Pt. 3, 523.

The Challenge of Demythologising the Devil   85

Michael McClymond has provocatively used the image of a black hole. A black hole is neither a thing nor an entity. Yet, it "draws everything near to its immensely powerful gravitational field and then collapses it." McClymond elaborates:

> Physical objects will be pulled into the black hole so violently that they will be drawn into spaghetti-like strings, and lose all trace of their original form as they are compacted in ultra-dense matter. Essential to this process is *a transition from form to formlessness* – a loss of distinctness and individuality. Applying this analogy to spiritual realities, we might say that the demons are a destructive emptiness that causes human beings entering their gravitational field to lose their character and personhood, to cave in on themselves, and ultimately to become sub-human.[24]

Demons for Barth are neither things nor personal entities, but they still have a potentially destructive agency in the world. Though Barth has not used the analogy of black holes (unknown in his time), it does fit well what he has said about the demonic as a dynamically destructive Nothingness.

As potentially creative as Barth's theory of the demonic is, there are potential problems with it. I don't have a problem with a destructive "Nothingness" as a description of evil so long as one views it as the privation of all that is good and thus as the corruption or distortion of the good. However, by expanding the *demonic* into a larger theory of evil in this way, Barth has arguably granted the demonic exaggerated significance beyond the boundaries of the biblical witness. The demonic certainly may be viewed as devoured by evil or Nothingness and bound to stand for and serve it, but evil is a larger category theologically. Moreover, though lore about the devil being "Lucifer" or the "Morning Star" is not biblically applied to the devil (but rather to a King of Babylon, Isa 14:12–22), there is biblical warrant for viewing demons as fallen angels (Jude 6). I don't see how the Gospel mandates we demythologise this.

Demons are indeed created beings, even fallen angels, but are they "personal"? If one simply means by "personal" an agent of action with intentionality, the term might have some currency in relation to the demonic. But "personhood" means more than this. Personhood was created by God with a capacity to love and be loved, especially in relation to God. Can demons be described in this way? Hardly. If demons have lost *all* such capacity, not just the exercise of it but the capacity itself, can they still be called "personal"? Humans maintained essential personhood in their fall. But angels were more exalted at their creation than humans. There is, I think, warrant in the thought that the higher one is exalted, the harder one falls. The nearer to God one is (as angels are), the more intense or radical their self-negation had to be in rebellion towards their Creator. Demons have perhaps lost the spark of their personhood as oriented towards God. They are arguably in that case beyond redemption. There is nothing personal left to redeem.

---

[24] Michael McClymond, "On Giving the Devil (No More) than His Due: Karl Barth, Pentecostalism, and the Demonic," in Frank D. Macchia, Terry Cross, and Andrew Gabriel, eds., *Karl Barth and Pentecostal Theology* (New York: T & T Clark, 2024), (124–42) 134.

So, in what sense may demons be called "personal"? Perhaps we could call them "supra-personal" in origin but "anti-personal" in their fall. They are the final negation of all that is personal. There may be a trace of personhood alive in their intentionality, but such intentionality has lost all freedom and thrives now only in opposition to that essential core that it was always meant to serve but now cannot serve. I wonder in the light of McClymond's response to Barth whether the demonic shouldn't indeed be viewed as "anti-personal" rather than "personal", as we understand that term theologically, for to be entirely anti-God is to be entirely anti-personal as God created it, is it not? I am open to see the demonic as fallen angels because of scriptural teaching (Jude 6), but angelic personalities (if one can use that term of angels) have, in becoming demons, collapsed into themselves by being lured into the Nothingness. They've lost all created form and purpose. They no longer warrant being spoken of as having, ontologically speaking, "personhood." Perhaps there is a point to Barth's hesitance to affirm the personhood of demons, but he has in my view taken that point too far. The biblical witness does grant intentionality to demons. The devil seeks to devour the saints (1 Pet. 5:8). Jesus mentions that the devil wanted to "sift" Peter "as wheat" (Luke 22:31). Though the demonic influence can be pervasive beyond the confines of a finite being so as to be mediated through corporate and institutional corruption, it still has a sinister transcendent intentionality behind it that is not reducible to the human participation involved in it. This is what the scriptural witness seems to require of theological reflection on the demonic.

It is here that I take issue with Bultmann in viewing the demonic as both existentially relevant (holding humanity it its grip) but not transcendent (having its source in human sin). This is not to deny that human sin aligns itself with demonic deception and influence. But I do not regard all human sin and destruction as directly caused by the demonic. I do not mean to blame the devil for everything negative. Notice how James describes the movement from temptation to sin without even mentioning the demonic: "… each one is tempted when he is carried away and enticed by his own lust. Then when lust has conceived, it gives birth to sin; and sin, when it has run its course, brings forth death" (James 1:14–15). Yet, yielding to sin does cause one to align oneself with the demonic, even if demons are not directly involved at their source. Our actions and corporate life can indeed fortify corporate and institutional resistance to God through which the demons could work and attain an enduring influence (I refer to all sorts of institutional realities: family, religious, political, national, etc.). The demonic influence is mediated. Even in Gottlieben Dittus's case of individual demonic possession, her captivity was mediated to her through a family caught in the throes of the occult who created a world of darkness and abandonment into which Gottlieben was introduced and in which she was held captive. They gave her the language, rituals, concepts, and self-image that defined her existence and aligned her with hopeless and destructive demonic purposes. The church becomes by contrast that which is the instrument of the liberating Kingdom of Christ in the power of the Holy Spirit. And no one who confesses Christ as Lord in the communion of saints can also curse him by aligning with the darkness (1 Cor 12:3).

The Challenge of Demythologising the Devil

In the end, why bring the devil into our understanding of evil and the suffering it causes? Could not that which mediates darkness be understood solely in human terms, as Bultmann proposed with his demythologising? In addition to Acolatse's reasons for involving the category of the demonic in our theological reflection, I would like to offer one of my own. There are times when evil as a whole confronts us as so unspeakably dark that no human words and natural causality seem adequate to capture it. There is an implied dimension to it all that transcends the natural. The demonic must not be dismissed because the devil puts a face on evil as it exists in the world, not just in this case or that, but as a vastly historical, cosmic, and, ultimately, eschatological reality: a point that Blumhardt saw so clearly. I do not mean to reduce the darkness of evil to the demonic, but I do believe the demonic represents it. As the light dawns in the coming of Christ, it will expose this darkness, which, in the end, will bear the face of Satan. Though not every case of evil or suffering necessarily arises from his direct involvement, they all serve demonic purposes if aligned against the love of God revealed in Christ. There are indeed natural causes to evil and suffering that can be studied, understood, and eliminated (or at least alleviated). But if they dehumanise and diminish anything that God wills in the world, they serve the demonic intent. To avoid this, we need to seek deliverance and healing by the grace of God. If natural suffering becomes unavoidable, we should seek a redemptive transformation of our suffering by enduring it in a way that turns it into a witness to the grace of God.

Ultimately, the darkness that the devil represents is the grand lie to which humanity had sold its soul and from which Christ as the light of truth has delivered us. It is the lie that the world centres on "me" as its ultimate purpose and point of reference. In saving us from the devil, Christ really does save us from ourselves. To say that "the devil can take a vacation, we destroy ourselves" is not entirely wrong. But it's not entirely accurate either. Corporately mediated evil takes on a life of its own distinct from the individuals who are tempted to yield to it, and it's in this space that the demonic finds its habitation, enduring influence, and apocalyptic significance. The demonic is a mystery that is eschatologically revealed and only known in the light of Christ's victory through the Spirit over darkness, sin, and death. As Barth maintained, the darkness is known only in the light. Only in the light of Christ does it come to true disclosure. It is a conquered reality that can still destroy but which will finally be removed once and for all from creation at the final judgment (Rev 20:10). The myths of the devil as a subhuman creature with hooves and horns are laughable and do indeed require demythologising in order to confront the biblical mystery behind it. That mystery must be probed and not demythologised, if for no other reason than to demythologise the lie that the devil has told us about ourselves. We dare not linger by the devil, never by the lie, but always by the truth that dispels it. A preoccupation with the demonic (naming them, seeking them out, seeing them as directly involved in all that is negative) is unhealthy and distracts us from the call to linger only by Christ in response to every challenge. Our witness to him through speaking his truth in love remains our overwhelming preoccupation (Eph 4:15) and the best means of resistance. "Submit yourselves therefore to God. Resist the devil, and he will flee from you" (James 4:7).

Simultaneous Prayer: A Pentecostal Perspective

Robert P. Menzies

In August of 2014 I was privileged to attend a worship service that formed the prelude to the Centennial Celebration of the Assemblies of God. This special worship service convened at my home church, Central Assembly of God in Springfield, Missouri. I arrived early but found that I was already too late. The sanctuary was packed with people from 120 different nations. But I am not dissuaded easily, so I moved through the throng and attempted to locate a seat in the balcony. Over 3,500 packed into the church, which was filled with the chatter of languages from around the world. I found an empty spot in the aisle on the very top step of the balcony. To my immediate right was a young man from Bangladesh. In front of me was a Christian brother from Africa and to my left was a lady from Venezuela. It was a remarkable scene for Springfield, a rather small and monolithic community in the heart of the Midwest. I remember thinking that there is a lot of talk about diversity in the United States, but here you really have it. The media did not take much notice of this fact, but it was an amazing experience to hear the multiple languages around me as I entered and exited the sanctuary. I also heard an incredible array of languages during our times of corporate prayer.

Pentecostal prayer is seldom quiet and usually marked by a Spirit-led spontaneity. Although Pentecostal worship services centre around worship, prayer, testimonies, and Christ-centred preaching from the Bible, you never quite know what will happen and in what order. Spontaneous prayer and worship might bring the entire congregation to its feet. Times of prayer that invite all of the worshippers simultaneously to cry out in their own tongue – or in Spirit-inspired tongues – are not uncommon. This is true of Pentecostal churches in Africa, Latin America, Asia, Europe, and the United States. So, it was no surprise to find that in this gathering, composed of followers of Jesus from 120 different nations, there were times of prayer and worship that sounded a lot like that first Pentecost. In one stirring moment, I recall hearing a cacophony of sounds uttered by different voices and representing different languages filling the sanctuary. The prayers during that moment of corporate worship were unintelligible but beautiful.

The stunning diversity of the worshippers was not the only remarkable feature of this meeting. I found the unity that knit this diverse group together even more compelling and noteworthy. Here, in the midst of this congregation representing seemingly "every nation under heaven," there was a remarkable unity of faith and purpose. It was not a forced unity that destroys cultural distinctives and individual expression; rather, it was a beautiful unity of shared experience rooted in our common faith in Christ. Our mother tongues may be different, but we all embrace the same Gospel and worship the same Lord.

This experience is not unique to special, large gatherings like the Centennial Celebration I have just described. Whether churches are large or small, whether they are located in the Global North or South, it matters not. Around the world, in many Christian gatherings, but especially in Pentecostal churches, you can hear simultaneous prayer. While simultaneous prayer, "the corporate practice of praying different prayers at the same time,"[1] is indeed a global phenomenon, this form of corporate prayer has been modelled and encouraged in a special way by the Korean church, particularly the Yoido Full Gospel Church (Seoul, South Korea). Indeed, Korean churches and missionaries around the world are known for their fervent prayers, which often take the form of simultaneous prayer. One North American observer described it this way,

> Whenever a group of Koreans is praying, whether as part of a church service or spontaneously in small groups, someone takes the lead, guides the rest of the group in what to pray for, and then says, "Let's pray." At once, everyone prays out loud, according to the direction of the leader.[2]

The impact of this form of corporate prayer, which I have personally witnessed at Yoido Full Gospel Church, is often very powerful. I concur with Diana Hynson's assessment of simultaneous prayer as it is practiced in Korean churches,

> Rather than praying silently or one at a time, the entire class or congregation prays aloud together, creating a kind of Pentecost atmosphere. This swell of prayer, which God understands all at once, creates a thrilling, even mysterious, sense of unity in the wholeness of God's community.[3]

In the following pages, I will respond to a recent, thoughtful critique of the practice of simultaneous prayer offered by Scott MacDonald, a missionary to Africa. I greatly appreciate the biblical focus and clarity of MacDonald's fine article and offer my response as an attempt to foster what I believe to be a much-needed dialogue between Pentecostal Evangelicals and non-Pentecostal Evangelicals on this and related issues. The central question MacDonald addresses is expressed in his article, "Does Acts 4:23–31 Support the Practice of Simultaneous Prayer?"[4] MacDonald suggests that we need to look elsewhere for biblical support for simultaneous prayer, "since Luke only records a single prayer and the spontaneity of the prayer is married to the liturgical recitation of Psalm 2:1–2."[5] MacDonald concludes that with the prayer of Acts 4:23–31, Luke does provide us with a model for our prayers. He simply feels that Luke's record at this point does not support or encourage the practice of simultaneous prayer as described above. We will explore MacDonald's reasons for this judgement

---

[1] Scott D. MacDonald, "Does Acts 4:23–31 Support the Practice of Simultaneous Prayer?" *Themelios* 47:1 (2022), 60.

[2] Tervin Wax, "2 Reminders from the Korean Church about Prayer," *The Gospel Coalition*, 17 November 2016. Cited in MacDonald, "Simultaneous Prayer?" 61.

[3] Diana Hynson, "Learning the Practice of Walking with Christ," *The United Methodist Church: Discipleship Ministries*, 25 January 2011. Cited in MacDonald, "Simultaneous Prayer?," 61.

[4] Scott D. MacDonald, "Does Acts 4:23–31 Support the Practice of Simultaneous Prayer?" *Themelios* 47:1 (2022), 60–69.

[5] MacDonald, "Simultaneous Prayer?" 60.

Simultaneous Prayer: A Pentecostal Perspective 91

below. Our analysis of the prayer of Acts 4:23–31 and MacDonald's arguments will come in three parts: first, we will analyse Luke's account of this important prayer of the early church (Acts 4:23–31); second, we will discuss the form or method of the prayer; finally, we will consider its content.

The Prayer Revisited (Acts 4:23–31)

The Prayer: Nature and Method (Acts 4:23–24)

Immediately after Pentecost (Acts 2), in the first story Luke recounts, we begin to see how relevant and important the promise of the Spirit's enabling is for the newly anointed band of end-time prophets (Luke 12:11–12; Luke 24:49; Acts 1:8). The first story of bold, Spirit-inspired witness (3:1–4:31) takes place in the temple courtyard, centres on the dramatic healing of a man crippled from birth (3:6–10), and through Peter's preaching highlights that Jesus is the "prophet like Moses" (3:22) whom God has "raised up" (3:26).[6] Peter's and John's preaching incurs the wrath of the Jewish leaders, who demand that they stop speaking about the resurrection of the dead "in Jesus" (4:2). Peter's and John's courageous response to this command serves as a model for future generations of Christian disciple-prophets (4:19–20). The prayer that concludes this section includes requests for "great boldness" and "signs and wonders" (4:29–30). It, too, is paradigmatic for future readers of Acts who, Luke assumes, will also face opposition and persecution. While Luke's Christian readers will face persecution, so also will they experience the Spirit's power in response to their prayers (4:31; cf. Luke 11:9–13).

Luke brings this literary unit (Acts 3:1–4:31) to a stirring conclusion with his portrait of the praying church. Upon "their release, Peter and John" return "to their own people" (i.e., a group of believers)[7] and report all that "the chief priests and elders" said (4:23). When the beleaguered group hears of the threats and commands not to speak about Jesus, they respond with *one heart and one mind*. Persecution has a way of focusing the church's attention on its central purpose. When the church has a clear sense of mission – a clear purpose – it is united. So, the disciples "raised their voices together [*homothymadon*] in prayer" in response to their first experience of persecution.

Pentecostals are known for praying loudly and for good reason. Spirit-inspired prayer, particularly that described in Luke-Acts, is seldom quiet (Acts 2:6, 11; cf. Rom 8:15, 26).[8] Luke's description here, "they raised their voices together," also suggests loud, corporate prayer. The plural form of the verb, *airō* ("they raised"), highlights the corporate nature of the group's prayer. The term, *phōnē*, is a singular noun (literally, "voice") and always refers to articulated speech.[9] This construction – the plural form of *airō* ("they raised") with the singular

---

[6] All quotations from the Bible are from the NIV (2011) unless otherwise noted.

[7] This is clearly a smaller group than the full company (5,000 men) noted in Acts 4:4.

[8] Luke 1:15, 41, 67; 3:21–22; 4:14, 18–19; 10:21; 11:13; 12:11–12; 24:48–49; Acts 1:8; 2:4; 4:8, 31; 9:17; 13:9; 10:46; 19:6.

[9] The term occurs over forty times in Luke-Acts.

phōnē ("voice") – is characteristic of Luke. For example, the ten lepers "lifted their voice" and said, "Jesus, Master, have pity on us!" (Luke 17:13). So, also, we read that in Lystra the crowd, upon seeing a crippled man healed through Paul's ministry, "raised their voice" and declared, "The gods have come down to us in human form" (Acts 14:11). In similar fashion, the crowd in Jerusalem "raised their voice" against Paul and shouted, "Rid the earth of him!" (Acts 22:22). These examples demonstrate that Luke frequently describes groups "raising" (plural form of *airō*) their "voice" (singular form of *phōnē*) and then, with a clause introduced by the verb, "saying" or "said" (forms of *legō*), he offers a summary of the content of the group's spontaneous, collective message.[10] The message is always articulated by the various members of the group and generally in a loud and forceful manner. This survey of Luke's language indicates that the prayer he describes in Acts 4:24–30 is neither pre-planned nor coordinated (i.e., liturgical); but rather, spontaneous and corporate, with each member of the group giving voice together (*homothymadon*) to their undoubtedly different but wonderfully harmonious prayers. Thus, Luke's description of the content of the group's prayer (Acts 4:24–30) is either a representative summary that depicts the general thrust of the collective prayers of the group or a record of one person's concluding prayer that achieves this same purpose.

The Prayer: Content and Result (Acts 4:25–31)

The prayer that Luke records highlights four interrelated themes: God's power (4:24); God's plan (4:25–28); God's purpose (4:29–30); and God's promise (4:31). This prayer, like the sermon that precedes it, serves as a model for Luke's readers. This prayer represents a fitting and faith-filled response to opposition and persecution. If this pattern of prayer is followed, it will redirect our focus away from the obstacles before us and centre our vision on the God who has called us to represent him (Luke 10:16).

God's Power (4:24). The disciples' prayer begins in remarkable fashion. They cry out, "Sovereign Lord." Normally, the term "Lord" in the New Testament is a translation of the Greek term, *kyrios*, which appears close to 200 times in Luke-Acts. However, here Luke uses a different term, *despotēs*. This term occurs ten times in the New Testament and elsewhere in Luke-Acts only once (Luke 2:29). This term, the source of our English term, "despot," designates one who possesses all power and authority. This single word is translated with the phrase, "Sovereign Lord." So, it is a remarkable scene. Peter and John have just been arrested, spent the previous night in prison, and been threatened. A small group of disciples gather and learn that the Jewish leaders who are supported by one of the most powerful empires the world has known have commanded them not to preach or teach "in the name of Jesus" (4:18). How does this besieged group respond? By calling out in prayer to the "Sovereign Lord," the *despotēs* in whom all power and authority really reside. All power and authority rests in the "Sovereign Lord" because he is the creator, the one who "made the heavens and the earth and the sea, and everything in them" (Acts 4:24; cf. 14:15).[11]

---

[10] Luke 17:13; Acts 4:24; 14:11; 22:22.

[11] Note also Rev 5:13; 14:7; Exod 20:11; Neh 9:6; Ps 146:6; Amos 9:6.

Simultaneous Prayer: A Pentecostal Perspective

God's Plan (4:25–28). The prayer now shifts to an affirmation of faith, a declaration that the recent crucifixion of the Lord's "holy servant, Jesus," was foretold by the prophets and a part of God's wondrous plan (cf. the divine *dei* of Luke 24:7, 26, 44). This theme is introduced by a quote from Psalm 2:1–2 (LXX): "Why do the nations rage? ...the kings of the earth rise up ... against the Lord and against his anointed one" (4:25–26). We hear echoes of Psalm 2 elsewhere in Luke's writing (Luke 9:35; Acts 13:33) and beyond (Rev 2:27). It is noteworthy that Psalm 2 records the Lord's response to the rebellion of the kings and rulers. Is he worried? Not in the least. Rather, "He who resides in the heavens *will laugh*" (Psalm 2:4 LXX). Acts 4:27–28 explains that these recent events, the conspiracy of "Herod and Pontius Pilate together with the Gentiles and the people of Israel" against the Lord's "holy servant Jesus," are the fulfilment of Psalm 2:1–2. The key verbal link is found in the description of Jesus as the Messiah, the Lord's "anointed one" (*chriō*). Verse 28 states the matter clearly: "They did what your power [*cheir*, literally, "hand"] and will had decided beforehand should happen." The reference here to the "hand" (*cheir*) of the Lord draws upon the rich imagery of the Exodus, for "by a mighty hand the Lord brought" his people out of slavery in Egypt (Exod 13:3 LXX).[12] It also anticipates the disciples' petition, "Stretch out your hand [*cheir*] to heal and perform signs and wonders" (Acts 4:30), which also draws upon the language of the Exodus. "The Lord brought us out of Egypt with great strength and with a strong hand ... and with signs and wonders" (Deut 26:8; cf. 4:34; 7:19).

God's Purpose (4:29–30). At this point, the prayer of the disciples shifts from praise to petition. They first ask the Lord to "consider their threats" (*apeilē*), a reference to the warning (*apeileō*) and threats (*prosapeileō*) of the Sanhedrin (Acts 4:17, 21). The disciples' prayer not only expresses a clear understanding of the Lord's identity – the all-powerful Creator and Lord of history – but it also reflects an admirable grasp of their own identity. With their petition the disciples identify themselves as "your servants" (plural of *doulos*, 4:29). Jesus is *the* Suffering Servant (*pais*) of whom Isaiah prophesied (4:27; cf. 3:13, 26; 4:30; cf. Isa 52:13), but they too are the Lord's servants (*doulos, doulē*, Acts 2:18).[13] As the Lord's servants, they have a *clear purpose*. They have been filled with the Holy Spirit and they are called to bear bold witness for Jesus (Acts 1:8; Isa 49:6). So, they now ask the "Sovereign Lord" to give them "[your servants] great boldness [*parrēsia*] to speak your word" (Acts 4:29). The disciples ask the Lord to give them precisely what Peter and John have just exemplified (4:13, 19–20).

The disciples' petition includes one other important element. In addition to strength for bold witness, the disciples ask the Lord, "stretch out your hand to heal and perform signs and wonders through the name of your holy servant Jesus" (4:30). We have already noted how the references to "hand" and "signs and wonders" evoke well-known descriptions of God's deliverance of Israel from bondage in Egypt (Deut 26:8). Jesus, the prophet like Moses, is now acting through his servants to affect even greater salvation (Luke 24:46–47; Acts 3:17–

---

[12] Cf. Exod 3:19–20; 7:5; 13: 3, 9; 15:6.

[13] Holly Beers, *The Followers of Jesus as the "Servant": Luke's Model from Isaiah for the Disciples in Luke-Acts,* Library of NTS 535 (London: Bloomsbury, 2015), 118–79.

26; 4:10–12). Jesus' salvific work, which provides forgiveness of sins, is also marked by signs and wonders (Acts 2:19; 5:12–16). Just as Peter's and John's witness before the Jewish leaders anticipates the disciples' petition for boldness, so also the healing of the man crippled from birth through "the name of Jesus" (3:6, 16; 4:10) foreshadows the disciples' petition for the Lord to perform signs and wonders. These themes, bold witnesses and signs and wonders, which are crucial for Luke's narrative, are thus highlighted in Luke's first description of the post-Pentecost ministry and prayer life of the early church.

God's Promise (4:31). The impact of the disciples' prayer is described in terms that mirror previous promises in Luke's narrative. Like on the day of Pentecost, a tangible manifestation of God's presence marks the answer to their prayers, the infilling of the Spirit (Acts 2:2–3; cf. Luke 3:21–22): "After they prayed, the place where they were meeting was shaken" (4:31). Then we read, "they were filled with the Holy Spirit." This description of the Spirit's coming indicates that the implicit promise contained in Luke's version of Jesus' teaching on prayer (Luke 11:9–13) once again finds fulfilment in the lives of the disciples. The outpouring of the Spirit on the day of Pentecost (Acts 2:4), as well as Peter's more recent infilling (4:8), anticipate this experience. Luke's message is unmistakable: along with Peter, the other disciples (including Luke's readers) may also share this experience. For some, this reception of the Spirit may be their initial experience (i.e., their baptism in the Spirit); for others, it will be an additional "filling." For all, however, this infusion of the Spirit's power provides precisely what they need. So, "they spoke the word of God boldly [*parrēsia*]." This is a decisive answer to the petition of 4:29, but it also fulfils the prior promise of Jesus: "When you are brought before synagogues, rulers and authorities, do not worry … the Holy Spirit will teach you at that time what you should say" (Luke 12:11–12; cf. 24:47–49; Acts 1:8). While Luke's Christian readers will face persecution (cf. 2 Tim 3:12), so also will they experience the Spirit's power in response to their prayers.

Form: The Method of the Prayer (Acts 4:23–31)

MacDonald's Liturgical Interpretation

Here, we encounter MacDonald's first problem with viewing the prayer in Acts 4 as supporting simultaneous prayer. MacDonald suggests that "while some of the content is spontaneously provided, the overall framework of the Acts 4 prayer is historical and liturgical."[14] MacDonald explains,

> What happened? Presumably, one person prayed. The people may have orally remembered Psalm 2 in unison. The leader interpreted the psalm in prayer and then presented the community's desire for perseverance in boldness. In this time of prayer, the community was of the same mind. And if "voices" was intended to be literal, it could refer to the recitation of Psalm 2. Jewish background, early liturgy,

---

[14] MacDonald, "Simultaneous Prayer?" 66.

Simultaneous Prayer: A Pentecostal Perspective 95

and togetherness all played a part in the Acts 4 prayer, and it led to a unique prayer that was orderly and psalmic yet tailored to the immediate circumstances.[15]

If I read MacDonald correctly, he is suggesting that the community was unified in thought (they were of one mind), but the community's corporate prayer was only articulated by one person, with the possible exception that the group might have chimed in together with the person praying as he or she recites the quotation from Psalm 2:1–2 (probably known to all). In other words, according to MacDonald, this passage *does not* describe a sizeable group of Jesus' disciples simultaneously and spontaneously praying out loud, each one articulating their distinctive prayer in their own words.

MacDonald offers four arguments in support of his liturgical reading of this text. First, MacDonald points to the fact that this prayer is uttered in a Jewish context by Jewish followers of Jesus. The implication is that these Jewish followers of Jesus would be familiar with liturgical patterns of worship in which fixed prayers (like the *Shema,* the *Shemoneh Esreh,* and the *Kaddish*) were recited.[16]

Secondly, MacDonald states "the prayer of Acts 4 starts 'like a liturgical prayer rather than a spontaneous expression.'"[17] Here he refers to the term, "Sovereign Lord" (*despotēs*), the reference to the Lord's creative activity (Acts 4:24), and the quotation from Psalm 2:1–2 found in Acts 4:25–26. All of these features suggest to MacDonald that the prayer of Acts 4 is not an informal, spontaneous prayer uttered by a multitude; but rather, a formal, liturgical prayer offered by a leader with others perhaps joining in for the recitation of the quote from Psalms 2.

Third, MacDonald suggests this liturgical interpretation is supported by the use of the definite article (*ho*) with "prayers" (plural of *proseuchē*) in the description of the early church found in Acts 2:42: "They devoted themselves to … *the prayers.*"[18]

Finally, MacDonald argues that Luke's use of *homothymadon* ("together") speaks of a unity in thought and purpose rather than corporate speech. So, the phrase, the disciples "raised their voices together [homothymadon] in prayer," does not mean that the group literally prayed out loud together. MacDonald concludes, "The early church prayed together, but probably not in the literal sense of speaking simultaneously or in unison. Rather, the togetherness of Acts 4:24 means agreement."[19]

---

[15] MacDonald, "Simultaneous Prayer?" 67–68.

[16] MacDonald, "Simultaneous Prayer?" 65.

[17] MacDonald, "Simultaneous Prayer?" 65. Here he quotes Jaroslav Pelikan, *Acts,* Brazos Theological Commentary of the Bible (Grand Rapids: Brazos, 2005), 78, with approval.

[18] MacDonald, "Simultaneous Prayer?" 65, following Pelikan, *Acts,* 77.

[19] MacDonald, "Simultaneous Prayer?" 67.

My Response: A Charismatic Interpretation

The Jewish Context. I do believe that upon close examination each of MacDonald's points noted above lose their lustre. Let's begin with the Jewish context. The mode of Jewish prayer was varied and included personal, spontaneous prayer (*Ber.* 4:4; 9:4; *Avot* 2:13). But this is especially true of the Jewish Christian setting. Jesus' prayer life and his teaching on prayer was unconventional in Jewish terms. This is illustrated most clearly in the Lord's prayer (Luke 11:2–4). The three occurrences of *Abba* in the New Testament (Mark 14:35–36; Rom 8:15–16; Gal 4:6) demonstrate two surprising and vitally important facts about Jesus' prayer life and his instruction to his disciples regarding prayer. Both of these facts must have shocked and scandalised many of Jesus' Jewish contemporaries.

First, following his own, personal practice (Mark 14:36), Jesus taught his disciples to pray in their mother tongue, Aramaic.[20] He did not follow Jewish custom and teach his disciples to pray in the "religious" language of the Jewish people (Hebrew), the language of their Scriptures and their communal prayers.[21] Jesus broke from these conventions and encouraged his disciples to pray in their heart language. In view of the fact that many rabbis considered Hebrew to be the language of heaven – and thus, by extension, the only language that God heard – this is, indeed, a striking turn of events.[22]

Secondly, again, following his personal practice, Jesus taught his disciples to address God as "Father" (*Abba*) when they prayed. The significance of the term *Abba* has been hotly debated by scholars and theologians. However, this much appears to be clear. *Abba* was clearly a term of respect and could be used by a student addressing his teacher. Yet more commonly, it was also used by a small child when calling out to his or her father. Kenneth Bailey, who served as a missionary in the Middle East for over forty years, discusses the term Abba with a group of Palestinian women. One exclaimed, "*Abba* is the first word we teach our children."[23]

It must have shocked many of Jesus' contemporaries when they heard him or his disciples address God as *Abba*. Although God is often described as being like a father in the Old Testament, nowhere is he there addressed directly as "Father." If we expand our survey of the relevant Jewish literature beyond the Jewish Scriptures, we find that direct address to God in prayer as "Father" is exceedingly

---

[20] Kenneth E. Bailey, *Jesus Through Middle Eastern Eyes: Cultural Studies in the Gospels* (Downers Grove, IL: IVP Academic, 2008), 95.

[21] As Bailey notes, "The Aramaic-speaking Jew in the first century was accustomed to recite his prayers in Hebrew, not Aramaic" (*Jesus Through Middle Eastern Eyes*, 95).

[22] Poirier, *Tongues of Angels*, 16: "b. Sabb. 12b: ... and [did not] R. Yochanan say, 'Everyone who petitions for his needs in Aramaic, the ministering angels will not attend to him, because the ministering angels do not understand Aramaic!'" I want to thank the late Russell Spittler for pointing me to this reference. See Spittler's review of Poirier's *Tongues of Angels* in the *Journal of Biblical and Pneumatological Research* 3 (Fall 2011): 146–52.

[23] Bailey, *Jesus Through Middle Eastern Eyes*, 97.

rare.[24] So, when Jesus taught his disciples to pray in Aramaic and to begin their prayers by addressing God as *"Abba*/Father," he was defying tradition. Jesus rejected the widely held belief that we must use a special "religious" language when communicating with or about God. Additionally, he called and enabled his disciples to enter into a filial relationship with God characterised by deep intimacy. This intimate, filial relationship, so beautifully illustrated in the parable of the Gracious Father (Luke 15:11–32), is powerfully expressed with one word: *Abba.*

In view of the variety of perspectives on prayer in the Jewish, and especially Jewish Christian, communities of the first century, I suggest that we should seek to understand the prayer of Acts 4 against the backdrop of prayer in Luke-Acts. A survey of prayer in Luke-Acts is revealing. Prayer in Luke-Acts is typically informal and Charismatic (i.e., associated with the inspiration of the Spirit). For example, only Luke tells us that Jesus was praying when the Spirit descended upon him at the Jordan River (Luke 3:21–22). Luke alone describes Jesus' ecstatic prayer, when "full of joy through the Holy Spirit," he bursts forth in praise and speaks of his filial relationship with God the Father (Luke 10:21). And it is Luke who interprets the significance of Jesus' teaching on prayer for his readers by rendering the key line, "how much more will your Father in heaven give *the Holy Spirit* to those who ask him!" (Luke 11:13; cf. Matt 7:11). Other instances of informal, spontaneous prayer or teaching emphasising this approach to prayer (Luke 18:1, 10; 20:47) are found throughout Luke's gospel.[25] This trend continues in Acts, with many references that highlight the spontaneous, informal, and Charismatic nature of the disciples' corporate prayers.[26] Luke's narrative also frequently highlights the spontaneous and Charismatic character of the prayers of individuals (Acts 9:11, 40; 10:9, 30; 11:5). When we add to this the Charismatic nature of early Christian worship described in Paul's epistles (1 Cor 14:14–16, 26) and Paul's numerous references to Spirit-inspired prayer,[27] Luke's picture of the prayer life of the early church comes into sharp focus.

The Liturgical Beginning? What shall we make of the term, "Sovereign Lord" (*despotēs*), the reference to the Lord's creative activity (Acts 4:24), and the quotation from Psalm 2:1–2 found in Acts 4:25–26? Do these features indicate that the prayer of Acts 4 is a formal, liturgical prayer offered by a single church leader? MacDonald's conclusion at this point is highly debatable. All of these features sound much more like elements of a spontaneous prayer uttered by a community familiar with the Bible of the early church (the LXX) and directed to

---

[24] Bailey, *Jesus Through Middle Eastern Eyes,* 97.

[25] Luke 5:16; 6:12; 9:18, 28–29; 11:1; 22:40–41, 44–46.

[26] Acts 1:14, 24; 2:4, 42, 47; 8:15–17; 12:12; 13:3; 14:23; 16:25; 20:36; 21:5; 28:8. For the noun "prayer": Acts 3:1; 6:4; 12:5. Acts 6:6 (commissioning prayer) might be more formal, but it probably includes Charismatic and spontaneous elements as well (see Acts 8:15–17; 13:3; 19:6; cf. 1 Tim 4:14; 2 Tim 1:6).

[27] For example, Paul frequently presents speaking in tongues as a form of doxological prayer: 1 Cor 12:2–3, 14:14–17; Rom 8:15–16; Gal 4:6; Eph 5:18–19, 6:18; Col 3:16; 1 Thess 5:19; and Jude 20.

a specific need. The term, "Sovereign Lord" (*despotēs*) is rare, used of the Lord only five times in the NT and only twice in Luke-Acts (Luke 2:29; Acts 4:24).[28] This is not a term that Christians normally used to refer to the Lord and thus it is unlikely that it was part of a liturgical prayer that they utilised. However, it is a term uniquely suited for this specific occasion. What better way to begin their prayer, facing as they were threats of persecution from a powerful foe, by calling out to the *despotēs*, the one who possesses all power and authority? The reference to the God of creation also flows naturally, for it is a wonderful way to acknowledge the Lord's sovereignty. Additionally, the quotation from Psalm 2:1–2, clearly a text of central importance for and well known to the early church (Luke 9:35; Acts 13:33; Rev 2:27; 12:5), fits beautifully into this specific setting, since it affirms the same truth. God is not threatened by these rulers' threats. "The One enthroned in heaven laughs" (Psalm 2:4).

The prayers. What significance shall we attach to the use of the definite article (*ho*) with "prayers" (plural of *proseuchē*) in Acts 2:42: "They devoted themselves to … *the prayers*"? Not much. The argument that this grammatical feature suggests liturgical prayers are in view misses a vital point. The use of the article (*ho*) with "prayer" (*proseuchē*) is simply a matter of Lukan style. "Prayer" with the article occurs nine times in Luke-Acts and only three times without.[29] As we have noted, the form of prayer described in the vast majority of these passages is spontaneous, and a number are clearly Charismatic.

Together in purpose, not speech. Finally, MacDonald's appeal to *homothymadon* ("together") as purely a matter of conviction does not do justice to what Luke actually says. Luke explicitly states that the disciples "raised their voices together [*homothymadon*] in prayer." Luke is fond of the adverb, *homothymadon* ("together"). Acts contains ten of the eleven occurrences of *homothymodon* found in the New Testament.[30] This term speaks of the rich unity and sense of purpose that marked the early church. Additionally, this term calls to mind Luke's earlier description of the disciples praying expectantly for the promise of the Father (Acts 1:14) and their practice of daily sharing fellowship along with prayer and worship (2:46). In view of the strong links that Luke forges between prayer and the inspiration of the Spirit,[31] the use of *homothymadon* ("together") here is not surprising.

David Crump states the matter well, "The community that openly and frequently prays together places itself in a perfect position to witness the Holy Spirit's activity unfurled around them."[32] Pentecostals, who have rightly been noted for their emphasis on "tarrying together" around the altar, will resonate with this declaration, even if we might also want to highlight that, as a result of our prayers, we will also *participate in* the Spirit's work. Pentecostals will also

---

[28] The other occurrences are found in 2 Peter 2:1; Jude 4; and Rev 6:10.

[29] With the article: Luke 6:12; 22:45; Acts 1:14; 2:42; 3:1; 6:4; 10:4, 31; 16:16. Without the article: Luke 19:46; Acts 12:5; 16:13.

[30] Acts 1:14; 2:46; 4:24; 5:12; 7:57; 8:6; 12:20; 15:25; 18:12; 19:29.

[31] Luke 3:21; 11:13; Acts 1:14, 2:1; 8:15–17; 9:17; 19:6.

[32] Crump, *Knocking on Heaven's Door*, 194.

Simultaneous Prayer: A Pentecostal Perspective　　　　99

offer a hearty "amen" to Crump's conclusion, "there is no better place to pray than with the assembled body of Christ."[33]

However, in Acts 4:24 Luke says more than that the disciples shared a unity of purpose. He declares, "they raised [plural form of *airō*] their voices [singular form of *phōnē*] together [*homothymadon*] in prayer to God and said [form of *legō*]." As we have noted, Luke frequently utilises this linguistic construction to describe the spontaneous, collective speech of a multitude of people.[34] The final verb, "and said," introduces a summary of the content of the group's message. In each instance, the context makes it clear that this message is articulated by the various members of the group and generally in a loud and forceful manner. It stretches credulity to suggest that the group in unison declares these exact words (i.e. choral speech). Clearly, Luke is summarising the essence of the various utterances offered by the members of the group. In this instance (Acts 4:24), Luke describes the many members of the group "lifting their voices" and praying together. A natural reading of the text suggests that this involved many different people praying loudly at the same time (i.e. simultaneous prayer).

If we broaden our view and examine more generally Luke's narrative, we can observe Luke's penchant for summarising group speech with a single representative voice. This is a part of Luke's literary art, his narrative technique. So, for example, at Jesus' tomb the two angels declare to the women [seemingly with one voice], "Why do you look for the living among the dead?" (Luke 24:5). The disciples gathered around the risen Lord and "asked him [again, seemingly with one voice], 'Lord are you at this time going to restore the kingdom to Israel?'" (Acts 1:6). The diaspora Jews who had gathered together in Jerusalem on the day of Pentecost were "utterly amazed," so "they asked: 'Aren't all these who are speaking Galileans?'" (Acts 2:7). This literary technique is found literally throughout Luke-Acts.[35]

All of this supports our conclusion that the prayer Luke describes in Acts 4:24–30 is neither pre-planned nor coordinated (i.e., liturgical); but rather, spontaneous and corporate, with each member of the group giving voice together

---

[33] Crump, *Knocking on Heaven's Door*, 195. Crump (p. 181) lists twenty instances of prayer in the book of Acts, which he groups into three categories: (1) prayers with explicit content (Acts 4:23–31; 7:59–60; 8:15; 8:22, 24; 14:23; 26:29); (2) prayers with contextually implied content (6:6; 9:40; 12:5, 12; 13:3; 16:25; 20:36; 21:5; 28:8); (3) uncertain prayer notices without any clear content (1:14; 2:42; 6:4; 9:11; 10:2, 4, 9, 30; 22:17). For category three, Crump acknowledges he is reluctant to attribute contextually supplied content for fear of reading our theological biases into the texts (p. 181, n.4).

[34] Luke 17:13; Acts 4:24; 14:11; 22:22.

[35] A survey of Luke 24–Acts 6, seven chapters in all, reveals that this literary device is employed in the following texts: Luke 24:5, 19, 29, 32, 34; Acts 1:6, 11, 24; 2:7, 12, 13, 37; 4:1, 7, 13, 16, 19; 5:23, 29; 6:2, 11, 13.

(*homothymadon*) to their undoubtedly different but wonderfully harmonious prayers.[36]

Content: The Message of the Prayer (Acts 4:23–31)

Deliverance and Breakthrough

In 2007, I was invited by Yoido Full Gospel Church (YFGC) to speak at a theological symposium, lecture in their seminary (the Youngsan Theological Seminary), and preach in the YFGC's Friday evening service. So, that May, I travelled to Seoul en route to China, where I lived and served at the time, and spent about a week there, ministering in various settings. My time in Korea was very inspiring. The YFGC was founded on 18 May 1958, five days before I was born. In very humble circumstances, David Yonggi Cho began to proclaim the good news of Jesus to a Korea ravaged and divided by war. In the face of tremendous hardships, suffering, and hopelessness, Cho declared that salvation and hope are found in Jesus Christ. Now, more than sixty-five years later, YFGC is the largest church in the world.

The amazing genesis of Yoido Full Gospel Church has mirrored the remarkable growth of Pentecostal Christianity around the world over this past century. Sixty-five years ago, who could have imagined that Seoul, Korea would be home to the largest church in the world? And back then, who could have predicted that the Pentecostal movement would grow with such rapidity that scholars now label it "the most successful social movement of the past century?"[37]

It was wonderful fellowshipping with the believers there, a number being old friends and students. I certainly got a glimpse of why this church has had such a dynamic impact on Korea and, indeed, the world. I shall not soon forget preaching in Yoido Church's Friday evening service. What an experience! It was thrilling to see and hear approximately 15,000 Korean believers singing praises to Jesus and *praying with great fervour*. Yes, I experienced simultaneous prayer in the YFGC, and it was a beautiful sight, an extraordinary sound. This experience reminded me in a fresh way of the power of prayer. It is absolutely amazing to see what God has done in Korea over the past sixty-five years! Korean church leaders will tell you that prayer is a major reason for the amazing revival that has transformed South Korea.

I suspect that the prayers of those initial members of the YFGC back in 1958 were probably different from those of their American counterparts. They were probably somewhat different from their Korean counterparts today. Each individual, each situation, each context often requires a prayer uniquely shaped for a specific purpose or need. Indeed, as the Apostle Paul writes, "the Spirit

---

[36] See also the forthcoming commentary on Acts, co-authored by Craig Keener and Robert Menzies, in the *Word and Spirit New Testament Commentary Series* scheduled to be published by Baker Academic.

[37] Philip Jenkins, *The Next Christendom: The Coming of Global Christianity* (Oxford: Oxford University Press, 2003), 8.

Simultaneous Prayer: A Pentecostal Perspective

helps us in our weakness. We do not know what we ought to pray for, but the Spirit himself intercedes for us through wordless groans" (Rom 8:26). I do appreciate MacDonald's call for us to pray regularly from the Psalms, to emulate OT language and patterns in our prayers, and to acknowledge God's sovereign purposes. MacDonald's pastoral heart is evident in his exhortation: "Let the church militant raise her voice in unity with the church triumphant!" It is also true that balance is needed and that "the wealth of biblical prayer is an easy bridge to unite our times of corporate prayer, instead of dividing through overly personalized prayer practices."[38]

With this pastoral concern in mind, MacDonald notes that "simultaneous prayer is often, though not always, deliverance and 'breakthrough' oriented."[39] He finds this emphasis lacking in the prayer of Acts 4, where the disciples ask for power to persevere rather than for deliverance. Although MacDonald's point here has merit and deserves consideration, it perhaps needs to be balanced with an observation. In this prayer, the disciples note that those who opposed Jesus "did what your power [*cheir*, literally, "hand"] and will had decided beforehand should happen." The reference here to the "hand" (*cheir*) of the Lord calls to mind the Exodus, for "by a mighty hand the Lord brought" his people out of slavery in Egypt (Exod 13:3 LXX).[40] It also anticipates the disciples' petition voiced later in the prayer, "Stretch out your hand [*cheir*] to heal and perform signs and wonders" (Acts 4:30), which also draws upon the language of the Exodus. "The Lord brought us out of Egypt with great strength and with a strong hand … and with signs and wonders" (Deut 26:8; cf. 4:34; 7:19). Thus, an emphasis on deliverance and breakthrough can be seen in this prayer. Of course, the disciples pray that the Lord might enable them to be active participants in bringing this deliverance, this salvation, to others (Acts 4:29–30). And the Lord is not slow in answering their request (4:31).

Orderly Worship

I suspect the real problem that MacDonald and many of my Evangelical brothers and sisters have with the practice of simultaneous tongues is that it appears to be a bit chaotic. A cacophony of sounds confronts the casual observer and little or nothing cognitive is being communicated to the larger group. However, this is precisely where I believe we in the West might learn from our brothers and sisters in Korea, in Africa, and beyond.

Instinctively, we in the West struggle with the notion that unintelligible speech can be edifying and useful. Yet there are numerous examples of that which transcends rational description or understanding serving as a powerful vehicle of communication and an effective means of expressing emotions. Poetry and music, in particular, come to mind. There is, however, an even closer biblical analogy to this kind of non-cognitive (at least to the larger group) yet edifying experience: the many references that present speaking in tongues as a form of

---

[38] MacDonald, "Simultaneous Prayer?" 69 for all the quotes in this paragraph.

[39] MacDonald, "Simultaneous Prayer?" 68.

[40] Cf. Exod 3:19–20; 7:5; 13: 3, 9; 15:6.

doxological prayer.[41] These texts, which describe the Spirit praying through the believer, link speaking in tongues with a strong sense of communion with Christ. This is perhaps most beautifully expressed in the *Abba* prayer of Romans 8:15–16 and Galatians 4:6. Paul declares that "the Spirit himself testifies with our spirit that we are God's children" (Rom 8:16). While the *Abba* prayer references Charismatic prayer more broadly, it includes glossolalic prayer.[42] Furthermore, Paul's words here paint a powerful picture of what happens as the Spirit prays through us. We are caught up in the love of Christ and filled with joy as we begin to glimpse the significance of our divine adoption. Is it any wonder that human words fail to adequately express what we feel? Indeed, if non-cognitive, glossolalic prayers can be edifying, how can we deny that simultaneous prayer, the corporate practice of praying different prayers at the same time, has value?

I would emphasise that Pentecostals together with Paul do understand that there is an important cognitive dimension to our faith and worship. Our mystical, non-cognitive experience of tongues is grounded in the Gospel and biblical teaching. As a result, it is an experience that above all brings praise and glory to Jesus. If speaking in tongues for Paul and Pentecostals is a mystical experience, it is nonetheless an experience centred on Christ. Ulrich Luz, in his essay, "Paul as Mystic," states the matter well. He argues that the gift of the Spirit is the experiential basis of Paul's Christ-mysticism, which centres on "the conformity of the believer with the Lord Jesus in his passion and in his resurrection glory."[43] Luz notes that "the fear and panic at 'enthusiasm' and any *theologia gloriae* which marks out many Protestant theologians is unknown to Paul, for it is not a question of his own glory, but Christ's."[44]

In short, I do believe that there is an appropriate place for simultaneous prayer in the corporate life of the church. However, as with the experience of glossolalic prayer, this practice should be balanced with other edifying forms of prayer, particularly in the corporate setting.[45] This is where MacDonald's suggestions are particularly valuable.

---

[41] 1 Cor 12:2–3, 14:14–17; Rom 8:15–16; Gal 4:6; Eph 5:18–19, 6:18; Col 3:16; 1 Thess 5:19; and Jude 20.

[42] For more on this see Robert Menzies, *Speaking in Tongues: Jesus and the Apostolic Church as Models for the Church Today* (Cleveland, TN: CPT Press, 2016), 139–46.

[43] Ulrich Luz, "Paul as Mystic," in Graham N. Stanton, Bruce W. Longenecker, and Stephen C. Barton, eds., *The Holy Spirit and Christian Origins: Essays in Honor of James D. G. Dunn* (Grand Rapids: William B. Eerdmans, 2004), 140.

[44] Luz, "Paul as Mystic," p. 141.

[45] When the rules that Paul lays down for order in worship in 1 Cor 14:23–24, 27–28 (cf. 14:5, 13, 19) are evaluated in the light of the larger context of Paul's writings, the specific situation addressed at Corinth, and Paul's primary concerns, a rigid application of his "injunction" concerning uninterpreted tongues in our contemporary settings appears to be misguided. For my discussion of this important text and its application, see Menzies, *Speaking in Tongues*, 107–23, 151–52.

Simultaneous Prayer: A Pentecostal Perspective

Conclusion

In his fine article, Scott MacDonald correctly encourages the gathered church to pray regularly from the Psalms, to emulate OT language and patterns in our prayers, and to acknowledge God's sovereign purposes. This exhortation mirrors the prayer of Acts 4:23–31 in many respects. However, I do believe that Acts 4:23–31 describes simultaneous prayer, the corporate practice of praying different prayers at the same time. The Acts 4 prayer, when viewed against the backdrop of Luke's literary style and his emphases on prayer, is seen to be neither pre-planned nor coordinated (i.e., liturgical), but rather, spontaneous and corporate, with each member of the group giving voice together to their different but ultimately harmonious prayers. Even the content of the prayer, which draws upon Exodus imagery, echoes the themes of deliverance and breakthrough prevalent in so many contemporary church settings. In short, the Acts 4 prayer shows considerable continuity with the contemporary practice of simultaneous prayer. Although Christians in the West often struggle with the notion that unintelligible speech, particularly in corporate settings, can be edifying, the Apostolic Church had no such reservations. Those first-century believers saw clearly that the Holy Spirit helps us pray, even in our weakness.

An Analytical Study of Holiness and Spirituality:
Biblical and Practical Features

Julie C. Ma

Introduction

Spirituality in the Christian faith is integrally related to the character of Jesus Christ and what he accomplished in accordance with God's expectations and in accordance with righteousness. Because it is firmly based on the holiness of God, a believer's spirituality soars from trust in actual life and an authentic relationship with God. What exposes a person's virtuous temperament and what it means to be associated with God is their capacity to select the proper circumstances for particular acts, not their acquisition. With the aid of the Holy Spirit, this linkage results in confession, praising, and loving others.[1]

Being holy is living our life in accordance with God's will. This is not feasible for fallen humans without the help of the Holy Spirit, a strong commitment to prayer, Scripture study, repentance with self-reflection, and other spiritual disciplines. All Christian traditions equally share holiness training. Trust is that it has always been a part of the church's doctrines. Studying and pursuing holiness results in Christians' spiritual life becoming more profound.

This paper will examine holiness and spirituality from the biblical and practical perspective, as well as from Pentecostal and non-Pentecostal spiritual orientations, through reflection on the spiritual practice of Christian life. In order for God's churches to reflect holiness in their spiritual life, the study seeks to understand the significance of living holiness as he is holiness. A clear fact is that holiness and spirituality go hand in hand.

Biblical Foundation of Holiness

Holiness as God's Character

The solid warning through biblical teaching is to live a life adequately with the "character of God's own holiness." All aspects of the believer's faith in cleansing and purifying will eventually be connected to God's holiness. Israel is a holy people because they were chosen by a holy God. Holy God commanded, "You should be holy as I am holy." "Be holy for I am holy" is God's anticipation to those entitled to be God's people (Lev 20:7–8; Eph 1:4, 5:27). In other words, from the beginning, the believer's life is built, through faith in Jesus Christ, in its relationship to God, in a "redemptive relationship" that is constantly

---

[1] David Kirkpatrick, "The Trinity and Christian Spirituality," *Southwestern Journal of Theology* 2 (2003), 49.

established by the grace of God, which is an explicit gift. The spiritual life, which consists of sanctification, dedication, and piety, is a life that should be lived in answering to the holy God's enterprise and revealing the nature of holiness.[2] As Brevard Childs notes,

> Righteous before the nations, gloriously holy, sacrificially compassionate, and mysterious beyond comprehension, the celebrated call of Israel's feted prophet is that "there is none other like God" (Isa 6:1–5). The Old Testament is fundamentally a portrait of God's sovereign love freely bestowed upon Israel even as God "grieves in agony because of the sin and rebellion of [his chosen people]."[3]

In other words, God is the only One who is holy, and his holiness is demonstrated in Israel's history in the Old and New Testaments. John's gospel catches the concept of holiness by declaring the distinctiveness of God as the Spirit, indicating that God only should be worshipped "in spirit and in truth" (4:24). The declaration of both Testaments is that God alone is to be given adoration and praise (Ps 86:8–12; 148:1; John 9:24). Although corrupted human beings don't need any longer to depend on the sacrifice for forgiveness of sins, the distinctiveness of God's amazing grace is still generously given as it finds unmatched appearance in the misery of the cross (1 Cor 15:3ff; Rom 3:24–26; 4:25; Mark 10:45). In this performance of divine empathy, God discloses the redemptive character of suffering love, as well as the sacrificial expectations of the life of faith. For those people who have faith, the spiritual teaching is nothing smaller than to "take up one's cross and follow" the Saviour crucified for the sins of humankind (Matt 16:23; Mark 8:34; Luke 9:23). Believers need to be spiritually disciplined on the cross to "strive for peace with all men, and for the holiness without which no one will see the Lord." The overwhelming evidence of God's suffering shown in Jesus Christ's cross and the magnificent presence of the Spirit will be found in the flowing together with God's sovereignty. "God's sacrificial revelation of his holiness and its confession is not only the spiritual ground of the biblical revelation, but it should also become the primary hermeneutical referent in the construction and praxis of the church's theology."[4]

Reflection of the Holiness in God's Creation

God does not limit his holiness to the Israelites and those who are saved by the work of Jesus, but his entire creation is full of God's presence. One of the most remarkable accounts of this idea has been expressed by Isaiah (Isa 6).[5] 6:3 says, "Holy, holy, holy is the LORD Almighty; the whole earth is full of his glory." Isaiah had seen the Lord seated on his heavenly throne, high and exalted (6:1). Beginning with this vision, the account demonstrates three viewpoints: the viewpoint of the seraphim, the viewpoint of the entire earth, and the viewpoint

---

[2] Brevard S. Childs, *Biblical Theology of the Old and New Testaments: Theological Reflection on the Christian Bible* (Minneapolis: Fortress Press, 1992), 359.

[3] Childs, *Biblical Theology of the Old and New Testaments,* 359.

[4] Kirkpatrick, "The Trinity and Christian Spirituality," 50–51.

[5] J. Guillt, "Saintete' de Dier," in Andre Rayez, ed., *Dictionnaire de Spiritualite* (Paris: Beauchesne, 1990), XIV, 186–88.

An Analytical Study of Holiness and Spirituality

of the prophet. Concerning the viewpoint of the seraphim, they are flying heavenly beings, positioned above the throne of the Lord, guarding his holiness.[6] Though they are made as limited creatures, they directly reveal in their Trisagion[7] the holiness of the Lord: "Holy, holy, holy!" Their singing is not an explanation of his holiness; they convey and personify his holy presence in the universe, including the heavenly loftiness of God's creation. They are covered by his holiness.[8]

The entire earth was occupied with the "*kabod*" (the glory of God) as the striking presence of the Lord (6:1–4). Certainly, the earth is earthbound. But Yahweh as a "King has clothed himself with this earthly reality. Now the whole earth is participating in the holiness of the Lord. Not by nature, but by participating in God's choice. Being the clothes of the King, the earth is lightning and impressive revelation of his holiness."[9]

Concerning the prophet,

> Confronted with the holiness of the Lord reflected in his creation, heaven, and earth, Isaiah becomes aware of the unclean lips, his guilt, and his sin. His lips were not essentially unclean. If they were impure as such, they should be removed, but now they are to be purified (6:5–7). The seraph purified the unclean lips of the prophet, his guilt was removed, and his sin was blotted out. Now the prophet could hear the voice of the Lord and present himself as his servant: "Here I am" (Isa. 6:8–9). As we have seen "Here I am" is the embodiment and witness of God's holiness. With the obstacles being removed, Isaiah is no longer hindered to be an instrument in the hand of the Holy One: he hears his voice and is able to say: "Here I am" (6:8).[10]

Correlating to Trinitarianism

The One who is Holy exhibits the "compassionate economy of his being Father, Son, and Holy Spirit in order to draw all of humanity unto himself." There are three scriptural texts that are mostly measured to bear a clear theology of Trinitarianism: 1 Corinthians 12: 3–6; 2 Corinthians 13:14; and Ephesians 4:4–6. Because these are "contextually soteriological," there is an implied spirituality.[11] 1 Corinthians 12 text is essentially noteworthy as it is preceded with the recognition that "no one can say that 'Jesus is Lord' except by the Holy Spirit." In 2 Corinthians 13 the work of three persons, the "grace of Christ," the "love of God," and the "fellowship of the Holy Spirit," is realised.[12]

---

[6] U. Rutersworden, "Saraph," in H-J Fabry & H. Ringgren, eds., *Theologisches Worterbuch zum Alten Testament* (Stuttgart: W. Kohlhammer, 1993), VII, 887–91.

[7] Trisagion is Greek: Τρισάγιον, "Thrice Holy", sometimes called by its opening line, "Agios O Theos", is a standard hymn of the Divine Liturgy in most of the Eastern Orthodox, Oriental Orthodox, and Eastern Catholic churches.

[8] Kees Waaijman, "Holiness in Spirituality," in *HTS Teologiese Studies/Theological Studies* 72:4 (2016), 4.

[9] Waaijman, "Holiness in Spirituality," 4.

[10] Waaijman, "Holiness in Spirituality," 4.

[11] Gordon Fee, "The Spirit and the Trinity," in *God's Empowering Presence: The Holy Spirit in the Letters of Paul* (Peabody, MA: Hendrickson, 1994), 841–42.

[12] Fee, "The Spirit and the Trinity," 841–42.

God's distinctiveness is exposed in its deepest respect in the person of Jesus Christ, who carries on to be dynamic and existing in the world through the presence and work of the Holy Spirit. The significant nature of this disclosure for Christian theology is that God is not confined in his infinity. While God "cannot be moved from outside by an extraneous power," he is "capable of moving himself" so that in the liberty of his "self-disclosure," there is an "expression of the divine economy."[13] Therefore,

> If the community's spirituality was to be tied to the praise of Jesus Christ as the Son of God, then "it cannot be denied that it was [making this confessional investment] in order to testify to the deity of God in his salvation activity." It is to this salvation event that the Spirit gives witness in order to identify and encourage the believer's relationship to the revealed Son."[14]

A clear fact is that the Holy Spirit began to be the performer of God's plan because, without the Spirit, humanity could not be formed into the "image of Christ." The Spirit guides and leads human beings to the Father. Without the Spirit's help, becoming a truly spiritual person is impossible. The Spirit ministers to the believer's life to mollify the physical desires and bring the body to perpetual life. Additionally, the Spirit makes the church living "to guide [it] and maintain it in truth." In all of these actions, the Spirit enables Christians to grow to live passionate life in God.[15]

Holy Living in Material Worlds

The central place of holiness is in the physical world, not in the "transcendent realm." The human being was made with physical form because God wants and yearns for human beings to employ their bodies as the means for accomplishing *qedushah* (holiness). Specifically, believers attain *qedushah* not by evading their bodies but through their physical form and the entire substantial reality in which believers are living as human beings. If God desired an additional class of *mal'akhim* (angels), he would have made other types of *mal'akhim*. He would have made other kinds of incorporeal souls that would have been capable of singing to him, the entire day long, "holy, holy, holy." However, he made human beings with bodies enclosed by substantial things so that human beings could acquire from their "relationship qualities how to conduct all of these aspects of our existence with a sense of holiness."[16] 1 Peter 1:14–16 states, "... do not conform to the evil desires you had when you lived in ignorance. But just as he who called you is holy, so be holy in all you do, for it is written: Be holy, because I am holy."

Accomplishing holiness necessitates an effort, and there are no rapid resolutions to ideas of Christian spirituality. There is no easy way out and no tiny pathway. Holiness needs labour. It necessitates work and entails learning. It

---

[13] Karl Bath, *Church Dogmatics*, trans. and ed. G. W. Bromiley & T. F. Torrance (Edinburgh: T & T Clark, 1932–68), II: 370.

[14] Kirkpatrick, "The Trinity and Christian Spirituality," 55–57.

[15] Kirkpatrick, "The Trinity and Christian Spirituality," 59.

[16] Saul J. Berman, "Holiness, Meaning and Spirituality," *Edah Journal* 2:1 (2002), 6.

An Analytical Study of Holiness and Spirituality   109

needs realisation. It necessitates attention. It needs responsiveness at a profound level.[17]

Empirical Features of Spirituality and Holiness in Christian Life

For the Christian faith, spirituality and holiness are inextricably linked to the work of the Holy Spirit and firmly rooted in God's holiness. The spirituality of the followers soars from inner teaching to outward manifestation in their everyday lives. In this aspect, the function of the Holy Spirit is essential. Furthermore, Christians who have been empowered by the Spirit display their spirituality and holiness in a variety of ways through their participation in Christian spiritual activities which include remorse, worship, relationship, love, the healing ministry, invocation, mission, etc.

Remorse

The idea that Christians are only necessary at the beginning of the Christian life, when we are starting the Christian journey toward the Kingdom, is that repentance and faith are merely the entrance to religion. And the great Apostle seems to support this by urging the Hebrew Christians to pursue perfection while instructing them to discard the foundational tenets of the Christian doctrine and refrain from re-establishing the pillars of repentance from sin and faith in God, which must at the very least imply that they should relatively abandon those tenets in order to move forward toward the goal of the high call of God in Christ Jesus.[18]

And it is unquestionably true that repentance and faith are particularly necessary at the outset. Repentance is the recognition of our complete sinfulness, guiltiness, and helplessness; it comes before we receive the Kingdom of God, which, according to our Lord, is "within us," and faith is the means by which we do so, receiving "righteousness, and peace, and joy in the Holy Spirit."[19]

But, notwithstanding this, there is also repentance and faith (taking the words in another sense, a sense not quite the same, nor yet entirely different) which are requisite after we have "believed the gospel"; yea, and in every subsequent stage of our Christian course, or we cannot "run the race which is set before us." And just as the faith and repentance were required for admittance into God's kingdom, these are also necessary for our ongoing development in grace.[20]

Being remorseful typically entails an inward transformation, a shift in perspective from sin to holiness. However, we today use the term in a very different context because it refers to a particular type of self-knowledge in which

---

[17] Berman, "Holiness, Meaning and Spirituality," 6–7.

[18] John Wesley, "The Scripture Way of Salvation," in Robert E. Coleman, Robert A. Danielson and Faith E. Parry, eds., *Holiness Through the Ages: An Historical Reader of Christian Writers on Holiness* (Wilmore, KY: First Fruits Press, 1997), 160.

[19] Wesley, "The Scripture Way of Salvation," 160.

[20] Wesley, "The Scripture Way of Salvation," 160.

we recognise that, while knowing we are God's children, we are guilty, helpless sinners.[21]

Worship

Worship is a way for the community of Spirit-filled believers to express their spirituality. The act of worshipping God requires more than just human activity; it also entails a profound level of intimacy between God and his people. The Holy Spirit guides and leads believers in worship, frequently working in unexpected ways (John 3:8). The participants fully anticipate that someone from the neighbouring group will act instantly upon the Spirit's prodding. As a result, printed orders of service are absent from church services.[22] Following a brief prayer, a group of young musicians and singers lead the worship. There are no hymnals, and the songs are highly "contemporary," similar to the music of Hillsong in Australia. The atmosphere is upbeat, and the music is loud. As several young girls dance while holding cymbals, the congregation moves forward while clapping and waving their hands.

Preaching on the day of Pentecost, for instance, would recount God's manifestation as "fire," especially the appearance of "tongues of fire" on a specific day. The congregation consistently gives their approval by responding, "Amen." The sermon is concluded with a prayer for the Holy Spirit's baptism. As the participants divide into groups of three and four to pray for one another, the prayer eventually transitions into communal prayer. The entire service concludes with a burst of applause and more enthusiastic singing.[23]

Love with Relationship

Balance is the key to mature spirituality. Christians cannot afford to lose sight of the fact that God is so fascinated by the physical world that he chose to become incarnate in it, even though a certain amount of introversion is necessary for the development of spiritual life. He cares so much about actual people that Jesus took on human form, lived a human life, died, and then resurrected from the dead.[24]

The Christian life does not alternate between periods of action and interaction with others and periods of introspection. Relationships and mature social action are modes of contemplation, and genuine contemplation is the foundation of love and Christian social action. According to Henri Nouwen, if our need for solitude

---

[21] Wesley, "The Scripture Way of Salvation," 161.

[22] Russ Spittler, "Spirituality, Pentecostal and Charismatic," in S. M. Burgess and G. B. McGee, eds., *Dictionary of Pentecostal and Charismatic Movements* (Grand Rapid: Zondervan, 1988), 804–9.

[23] Wonsuk Ma, "Worship and Spirituality," in Kenneth R. Ross, Francis D. Alvarez S. J., and Todd M. Johnson, eds., *Christianity in East and South-East Asia*, Edinburgh Companions to Global Christianity, vol. 4 (Edinburgh: Edinburgh University Press, 2020), 364–74.

[24] Maria L. Santa-Maria, *Growth Through Meditation and Journal Writing: A Jungian Perspective on Christian Spirituality* (Ramsey, NY: Paulist Press, 1983), 40–41.

An Analytical Study of Holiness and Spirituality   111

and prayer is not motivated by a desire to better the lives of those around us, we will quickly grow disinterested in our spiritual lives. On the other side, some individuals now believe that the Christian's main vocation is spent attending to the needs of others. It is observed that finding fellowship in the outside world, in warm and intimate relationships that are growing and expanding, is the best insurance for a safe voyage within. Other than by showing them our love, we have no other method to influence them to be receptive to relationships with God and their fellow humans. Otherwise, people would continue to be fortresses that can be overpowered and brought under control but are closed to new kinds of connections. Therefore, our Christian spirituality is lived out and manifested through love and relationships.[25]

Mother Teresa, who spent sixty-eight years in Calcutta, committed her life to helping the poor, the mistreated, and the abandoned. Pope John Paul II approved the beginning of Mother Teresa's cause for canonisation less than two years after her passing due to her broad saintly reputation and the alleged favours. He approved her heroic traits and wonders on 20 December 2002.[26] She drew on her decades of service in India to express herself in her meditation book:

> People today are hungry for love, which is the only answer to loneliness and great poverty. In some countries, there is no hunger for bread. But people are suffering from terrible loneliness, terrible despair, terrible hatred, and feeling unwanted, helpless, and hopeless. They have forgotten how to smile, they have forgotten the beauty of the human touch. They are forgetting what is human love. They need someone who will understand and respect.[27]

When compared to the reflective side, which measures the justification and appropriateness of such risk and initiative, loving relationships with other people have an unavoidable "plus" on the resolution and decision side of the balance sheet. We can come to our first conclusion about the topic at hand here: a sincere love-relationship with Jesus.[28]

Conversion Through the Power of Divine Healing

The mandate given to the disciples during Jesus' lifetime serves as the foundation for the healing ministry. He attracted his twelve disciples and gave them the power to cast out demons and cure all illnesses. As part of their equipping to effectively lead others to Christ's redemption, those who are sent to preach the Gospel are given the healing gift. Jesus was a shining example of someone who, after being filled with the Spirit, healed a variety of sick individuals. Healing was an important aspect of Jesus' ministry, as stated in Luke

---

[25] Santa-Maria, *Growth Through Meditation and Journal Writing*, 42.

[26] Mother Teresa of Calcutta (1910–1997), https://www.vatican.va/news_services/liturgy/saints/ns_lit_doc_20031019_madre-teresa_en.html [accessed 6 April 2023].

[27] Agnes Bojaxhiu, *The Joy in Loving* (New York: Penguin Books, 1997), 86.

[28] Karl Rahner, *The Practice of Faith: A Handbook of Contemporary Spirituality* (New York: Crossroad, 1982), 137.

112   *The Holy Spirit, Spirituality and Leadership*

4:18, "The Spirit of the Lord is on me because he has anointed me to proclaim good news to the poor."

Within the group of believers who are filled with the Spirit, healing happens frequently. When a church member is unwell physically, other Christians pray for the person and lay hands on them in the hope that God will use them to show off his or her healing power. A healing testimony is essential for boosting churchgoers' spirits and drawing more family and friends to the church. They become closer to him as they receive more heavenly healing.

Non-believers who are healed as a result of a Christian's prayer are compelled to accept Christ. Not just with words, but also with power, with the Holy Spirit, and with a strong conviction, according to 1 Thessalonians 1:5.[29] Dom Bustria, a rural pastor in the Philippines who is now sixty-one years old, had a wonderful healing testimony. Dom suffered from epilepsy for almost twenty-five years. His seizures typically happened once a week. His despair led to the development of various addictions, primarily alcohol. He embraced Christ as his personal Saviour in November 1988 while at the marine base in Diego Garcia. He never experienced another epileptic seizure or longed for his previous addictions after that day. He began sharing the Gospel in small towns before leaving his well-paid job to become a pastor. Medically, even with continued treatment, a chronic case of severe epilepsy is typically not permanently curable. Numerous ancestral worshippers were saved by God through his healing miracles; hence, a house church was naturally started, and eventually, a church was built.[30]

Invocation

Nouwen makes a perceptive analogy to explain the meaning of prayer. He claims that because the Spirit has removed our narrowness and made everything new for us, we are like anxious asthmatics who are cured of their condition. As a result, the new life and breath we receive are actually God's life and breath. Prayer is like the breath of God in us. It is no accident that the majority of contemplatives learn to calm down and become ready for prayer by concentrating on their breathing patterns. When we experience spiritual depression, we forget that grace is exactly what grace is – that prayer is a gift that is precisely the meaning of grace. "The thing to do then is not to try to pray harder, but simply to ask the Spirit to do it for us."[31] Prayer is further explicated,

Prayer of petition is prayer and meaningful before God only if the desire for a determined and even worldly individual good asked for is also at the same time man's absolute surrender to the sovereign decrees of God's will. One cannot come to God in prayer without giving him oneself, one's whole existence, in trustful submission and love, and in acceptance of the incomprehensible God who is

---

[29] R. F. Martin, "The Gift of Healing," in S. M. Burgess and G. B. McGee, eds., *Dictionary of Pentecostal and Charismatic Movements* (Grand Rapid: Michigan, 1988), 352.

[30] Craig Keener, *Miracles: The Credibility of the New Testament Accounts,* vol. 1 (Grand Rapid: Michigan, 2011), 271.

[31] Santa-Maria, *Growth Through Meditation and Journal Writing,* 38.

An Analytical Study of Holiness and Spirituality   113

beyond our understanding not only in his essence but also in his free relationship
with us and must be accepted as such.[32]

Fasting is a long-established practice for Spirit-led Christians and goes hand
in hand with intense prayer. It is perceived as an act of devotion to God and a
close relationship and connection with him. A believer who fasts acknowledges
his dependence on God and reveres him as the Creator of humans and Lord of
his life. This is the spirit of adoration toward God. In order to preserve her people,
Esther fasted for three days (Esther 4:16). Jesus fasted for forty days in the
wilderness before establishing his messianic Kingdom, just as Moses did when
he received the ten commandments on Mount Sinai (Exod 34: 28). The largest
church in the world, Yoido Full Gospel Church in Seoul, Korea, was co-founded
by Jashil Choi, and she routinely fasted and prayed. Choi fasted whenever her
spirit prompted her to. She was adamant that fasting could bring one closer to
God and help one pray more effectively. Her desire for a strict spiritual life led
her to build a prayer mountain that was focused on fasting. This practice was
naturally characterised by prolonged, solemn prayer and frequent fasting. Her
faith grew stronger the more time she spent in prayer and fasting, with a special
emphasis on fasting, seeking the highest prayer mountain.[33]

Mission

The mission was directly influenced by the Spirit's manifestation. He then
breathed on them and told them to accept the Holy Spirit, according to John
20:22, which describes the pre-ascension bestowal of the Spirit. It is crucial to
realise that this verse describes the disciples' experience of receiving the Spirit
of life. Jesus breathes the Spirit of the New Creation into the disciples. The
sending phrase "As the Father has sent me, I am sending you" in the context of
John 20:21–23 points past the Spirit's work of regeneration to an energising
witness.[34] Act 1:8 also notes a comparable command from Jesus Christ before
ascending to heaven. "But you will receive power when the Holy Spirit comes
on you, and you will be my witnesses in Jerusalem, and all Judea and Samaria,
and to the ends of the earth."

The book of Acts details the apostles' participation in God's mission as well
as their preaching of the word. Even after the baptism of the Holy Spirit, they
stayed in Jerusalem. They were hesitant to leave the location and wanted to stay
where they were. Only after experiencing persecution did they scatter to other
places. The Antioch Church was founded as a result of the Jerusalem church's
missionary efforts.

---

[32] Rahner, *The Practice of Faith*, 88.

[33] Julie Ma, "Korean Pentecostal Spirituality: A Case Study of Jashil Choi," *Asian
Journal of Pentecostal Studies* 5:2 (2002), 235–54.

[34] Robert Menzies, "John's Place in the Development of Early Christian
Pneumatology," in Wonsuk Ma and Robert Menzies, eds., *The Spirit and Spirituality:
Essays in Honour of Russell Spittler* (New York: T & T Clark International, 2004), 41–
52.

The missionary expedition sent by the Antioch Church was started by Paul and Barnabas. Signs and wonders are part of their mission. Acts 14: 8–10 details the miracle that Paul's ministry worked in Lystra. When he saw a man who had never been able to walk, he commanded him, "Stand up on your feet," and immediately, "the man jumped up and began to walk." Acts 8: 4–8 notes that Philip preached the Word of God wherever he went. The power of the Holy Spirit was manifested in a city in Samaria, where miraculous miracles were carried out, unclean spirits cried and emerged, and several paralysed and crippled people were healed. The fearful disciples were inspired by the Spirit.

God's power was manifested in numerous ways, especially in the mountain villages of Northern Luzon, Philippines. Exorcism and healing miracles were performed by missionaries and church staff who were inspired by the Holy Spirit. Following are a number of notable healing episodes. One girl, who was eighteen years old and had been mute and deaf for twelve years, was instantly cured. During a revival meeting, the sick lined up for healing prayers in both the morning and evening services. Countless deaf-mutes were cured by God, and the blind were given sight and paralysis was removed. Numerous illnesses, including tuberculosis and others, were cured. One prominent city resident who had a massive goitre was cured. When she prayed for it on Saturday night, it partially faded, and when she came back on Sunday morning, it completely vanished. A man of twenty-eight years of age, who had been a deaf mute all his life, was cured instantly one morning.[35] Through healing mission work, churches were established in different mountain villages, and many non-believers came to the knowledge of salvation.

Concluding Remarks

This paper discussed the biblical foundations of holiness and its various aspects, including its relationship to trinitarianism, its manifestation in God's creation, and its practice in the physical world. The second section covered the empirical characteristics of spirituality and holiness in the various yet crucial aspects of Christian lives, including mission and invocation, and a few others like repentance and love with relationships. It is necessary to reflect Christian qualities based on God's holiness. The holiness of God as revealed in the Bible and the practice of spiritual purity in daily life by believers should go hand in hand. It is clear that the church must revere the Holy Spirit completely and depend on him throughout its spiritual journey. By properly putting it into practice and implementing it in one's spiritual journey, the Christian life will be enriched.

---

[35] Julie Ma, *When the Spirit Meets the Spirits: Pentecostal Ministry Among the Kankana-ey Tribe in the Philippines* (Frankfurt: Peter Lang, 2000), 80–81.

Digital Pneumatology: Presence and Power of the Holy Spirit in the Metaverse

Alex Guichun Jun

Introduction

One distinctive feature that has influenced the ministry and mission of the church since the second half of the twentieth century is digitalisation, or the third industrial revolution that began with the invention of computers and the internet. On the one hand, many theologically conservative Christians were anxious about the rapid development of digital devices and their negative influences on spirituality due to the dichotomic view of secular and sacred things. On the other hand, some churches actively use various digital devices for effective evangelism and ministry. For example, churches used mass media (radio, television, and the internet) to spread the Gospel and Charismatic ministries, such as faith healing, by touching the screen when televangelists prayed.[1] At the beginning of the second decade of the twenty-first century, the fourth industrial revolution began to bring a fundamental change in all aspects of human life and work, including religious practices. Recently, churches have actively used various digital platforms, such as YouTube and Zoom, to conduct online worship services and prayer meetings and to communicate with their members during the COVID-19 pandemic and afterward. According to a survey, approximately 72% of respondents reported that the pandemic changed how they practise their faith, with many adopting new private religious practices in the home or joining online services.[2] A report by the Hartford Institute for Religion Research indicated that 80% of US churches in November 2021 utilised a hybrid worship service in which congregants simultaneously gather in person and online.[3]

One notable trend in religious practice in this contemporary digital age is the launch and development of churches in the metaverse. The first metaverse church (VR Church: www.vrchurch.org) was established in 2016. Since then, there have been many metachurches in virtual space to reach more people by transcending time and distance. The concept of the death of distance by

---

[1] Shane Denson, "Faith in Technology: Televangelism and the Mediation of Immediate Experience," *Phenomenology and Practice* 5:2 (2011), 94.

[2] Manmit Bhambra and Austin Tiffany, "From the Sanctuary to the Sofa: What Covid-19 has Taught us about Sacred Space," *LSE Research Online,* last modified 10 October 2021, http://eprints.lse.ac.uk/id/eprint/110575

[3] Hartford institute for Religion Research, "Navigating the Pandemic: A First Look at Congregational Responses," last modified 14 December 2021, https://www.covidreligionresearch.org/wp-content/uploads/2021/11/Navigating-the-Pandemic_A-First-Look-at-Congregational-Responses_Nov-2021.pdf

technological revolution is fulfilled not only in business and communication,[4] but also in religious practices. Digital technologies converged into the metaverse, enabling the church to be anywhere at any time with anyone. As a church in the metaverse is a fully virtual reality church, every user participates through their avatars in religious activities, such as Sunday worship, small groups, Bible studies, or prayer meetings.

Due to the nature of avatar-mediated interactions, some believers are concerned that religious experiences in virtual spaces cannot be replaceable with the ones in the traditional Christian community. Nevertheless, it is undeniable that believers have been increasingly participating in various religious activities in the metaverse since the pandemic.[5] D. J. Soto, the founder of VR Church, says that a radical shift in terms of theological understanding of the nature of the church and the characteristics of its ministry is coming in the age of digitalisation.[6] Despite these rapid changes in religious practices and phenomena triggered by technological advancement, there has been little theological reflection on them. In particular, no attention has been paid to digital pneumatology to understand the person and the role of the Holy Spirit in the intersection of theology and technology. Therefore, this paper intends to explore the theological possibility of digital pneumatology to understand that the Holy Spirit can present and work in digital spaces in reference to the metaverse.

Digital Pneumatology

Digital pneumatology is a new field of study for the theological exploration of the presence and power of the Holy Spirit in digital spaces. It seeks to understand how the Holy Spirit is presented in digital spaces and how believers experience the work and the power of the Holy Spirit through advanced technology. As no one has done substantial academic writing in this field, digital pneumatology is currently based on the theological presupposition that the Holy Spirit can be present and demonstrate his power and attributes in digital spaces in the same way that he is present and active in physical spaces. It is theologically legitimate to speculate that the presence or the manifestation of the Holy Spirit is not limited by physical boundaries, and his power can be perceptibly experienced in any space, including digital spaces. COVID-19 has played a significant role in developing this theological speculation into a form of digital pneumatology. The classical understanding of the presence and the power of the Holy Spirit can be extended to digital spaces. Churches and mission agencies have used various

---

[4] Frances Cairncross, *The Death of Distance 2.0: How the Communications Revolution will Change Our Lives* (London: Texere, 2001).

[5] Luis Anders Henao and the Associated Press, "Religious People Are Increasingly Attending Worship Service in the Metaverse," *Fortune*, last modified 31 January 2022, https://fortune.com/2022/01/31/virtual-worshipping-services-religion-metaverse/.

[6] Mary Deckert, "The Metaverse and Virtual Reality Church: The Complete Guide," *Church Marketing University*, last modified 22 August 2022, https://churchmarketinguniversity.com/metaverse-church/.

Digital Pneumatology   117

digital platforms to spread the Gospel and form digital communities for worship and fellowship. Robert Wuthnow [7] and Nancy Ammerman, [8] prominent sociologists of religion, and Heidi Campbell,[9] an outstanding scholar in religion and digital culture, commonly say that digital technologies, including the metaverse, can create online and virtual platforms not only for complementing traditional practices and accessing religious resources but also providing new opportunities for enhancing religiosity (or spirituality) in digital spaces. Nicky Gumbel, the founder of Alpha Course, mentioned his theological belief that the Holy Spirit can be present and work through virtual platforms like Zoom. In an interview with Premier Christianity, he stated, "The Holy Spirit is not limited by the technology we use. The Holy Spirit can work through a Zoom call, just as much as He can work through a live meeting."[10]

There are many church leaders and mission agencies who have the same belief as Gumbel that digital platforms will be continually used for their ministries, such as virtual worship services, prayer meetings, and other spiritual practices. Therefore, it is time to deepen our understanding of the evolving relationship between digital technologies and Christian spirituality from the Pentecostal perspective. Recently, there was a great spiritual awakening at Asbury University, Kentucky. Gen Z students who were spiritually hungry and seeking the transforming power from above experienced an outpouring of the Holy Spirit. The occurrence gained widespread popularity on the internet, particularly on the social media platform TikTok, where the hashtag "#asburyrevival" garnered over 100 million views and accumulated more traction throughout the revival gatherings.[11] The university campus could not accommodate the huge

---

[7] See Robert Wuthnow, *The Restructuring of American Religion: Society and Faith Since World War II* (Princeton: Princeton University Press, 1989) and Robert Wuthnow, *Inventing American Religion: Polls, Surveys, and the Tenuous Quest for a Nation's Faith* (Oxford: Oxford University Press, 2015).

[8] See Nancy Tatom Ammerman, *Sacred Stories, Spiritual Tribes: Finding Religion in Everyday Life* (Oxford: Oxford University Press, 2014).

[9] See Heidi Campbell, *When Religion Meets New Media: Media, Religion and Culture* (Hoboken: Taylor & Francis, 2010), Heidi Campbell, *Digital Religion: Understanding Religious Practice in Digital Media* (Abingdon, Oxon: Routledge, 2022) and Heidi Campbell, *Exploring Religious Community Online: We are One in the Network* (New York: Lang, 2010).

[10] "Your Own Personal Jesus: Online Services Swell the Church of England's Congregations," *The Economist*, 4 June 2020, https://www.economist.com/britain/2020/06/04/online-services-swell-the-church-of-englands-congregations [accessed 14 August 2023].

[11] Thomas Lyons, "When a Christian Revival Goes Viral: At Asbury University, in Kentucky, a Student Chapel Service Turned into a Revival that Has Captivated TikTok," *The Atlantic*, last modified 23 February 2023, https://www.theatlantic.com/ideas/archive/2023/02/asbury-kentucky-university-christian-revival/673176/.

influx of more than 15,000 worshippers daily.[12] As a consequence, the university allowed several YouTube channels to do live streaming of the worship services after several days. One of the channels was SermonIndex.net. Over 150,000 people from all over the world joined the live-streaming services for several days. They testified by leaving comments that they also experienced the presence and the power of the Holy Spirit while watching them online in their own places.[13] On the one hand, it is legitimate to raise concerns about the potential risks and dangers of relying on digital technology for spiritual experiences. Some may argue that digital platforms diminish the authentic sense of community and fellowship in the physical spaces and increase the sense of spiritual superficiality and religious consumerism by only accessing online content without physical interactions with other believers in the traditional church contexts. On the other hand, the counterargument is that digital technology has been used to foster spiritual experiences and growth for decades. From the viewpoints of religious phenomenology and empiricism, technology contributed to enhancing and deepening spiritual experiences and growth to a certain degree,[14] although there are still theological challenges and practical limitations remaining in the intersection between digital technologies and spirituality. This debate has opened up a new avenue for theologians and practitioners to move forward from religious phenomenology to digital theology, particularly digital pneumatology, to reimagine the future possibility of Pentecostal theology and ministries in the metaverse for Gen Z and beyond.

Presence of the Holy Spirit in the Metaverse

Grace Rose raises a thought-provoking question, "Will the metaverse leave God and His congregations in the past or will it be an extension of God's creation and support His church beyond our wildest imaginations?"[15] Sönmez rightly pointed out that many Christians are still trapped in the dualistic Christian belief that separates physical spaces and virtual spaces concerning the presence of God, while large numbers of believers have been already utilising technological advancement to form their spiritual communities and interact with the Spirit of

---

[12] Wikipedia, "2023 Asbury Revival," last modified 22 July 2023, https://en.wikipedia.org/wiki/2023_Asbury_revival.

[13] SermonIndex.net, "Asbury University Revival Live 2023 – Feb 15, 2023 (Worship – Part 1)," https://www.youtube.com/watch?v=_FpKv5O2wMI&ab_channel=SermonIndex.net [accessed 14 August 2023].

[14] Don Iannone, "The Two Faces of Digital Spirituality: Contrasting Motives for Digital Spirituality," *KOSMOS: Journal for Global Transformation,* last modified February 2023, https://www.kosmosjournal.org/kj_article/the-two-faces-of-digital-spirituality/.

[15] Grace Rose, "How Will God and the Church Fit into the Metaverse?" *Commentary* 18:1 (2022), 4.

God in digital spaces.[16] The metaverse has already become a new way of life in all aspects, including religious practices in all religions. For example, Muslims can participate in the pilgrimage (the hajj) to the holy Mecca through a digital platform in the metaverse called "Experience Makkah" since 2015.[17] Jewish believers can pray and place a slip of prayer in the Western Wall through the metaverse.[18] These unprecedented digital opportunities have opened a new door for religious people not only to satisfy their religious hunger and promote their religiosity but also to experience their gods in immersive virtual spaces.[19] As the empirical approach of the sociology of religion and religious phenomenology informs that God is already in cyberspace through his Spirit and people encounter Him,[20] it is meaningless to ask questions, such as "Does God exist in the metaverse?" or "Has God entered into the metaverse?"[21] The aforementioned phenomenological human experiences of the presence of the Holy Spirit in the metaverse need to be further reflected theologically to develop digital pneumatology.

Omnipresence of the Holy Spirit

From a biblical and theological standpoint, it is acknowledged that all things were created by God, and nothing was created without him, as stated in John 1. This understanding affirms that virtual spaces are not a product of human creativity but a part of God's creation. Therefore, it is reasonable to claim that

---

[16] Ozan Sönmez, "Context before Technology: The Possible Utopian/Dystopian Elements of the Metaverse with Examples from Great Literature," in Enis Karaarslan, Ömer Aydin, Ümit Cali and Moharram Challenger, eds., *Digital Twin Driven Intelligent Systems and Emerging Metaverse* (Singapore: Springer, 2023), 299.

[17] Lara Katharina Schneider, "Religious Acts in Metaverse: Catholic Christianity," *GRIN*, last modified 15 March 2023, https://www.grin.com/document/1338328#:~:text=A%20metaverse%20makes%20sacred%20sites,confessions%20and%20other%20religious%20rituals.

[18] Luis Andres Henao, "From the Western Wall to Mecca: VR Lets Virtual Pilgrims Explore World's Holy Sites," *The Times of Israel*, last modified 8 August 2022. https://www.timesofisrael.com/from-the-western-wall-to-mecca-vr-lets-virtual-pilgrims-explore-worlds-holy-sites/.

[19] Seiji Kumagi, "Development of Buddhist AI, AR, and VR toward the Establishment of Buddhist Metaverse," *Kuensel*, last modified 10 October 2022, https://kuenselonline.com/development-of-buddhist-ai-ar-and-vr-toward-the-establishment-of-buddhist-metaverse-tera-verse/.

[20] Lavinia Byrne, "God in Cyberspace: Media and Theology Project Public Lectures," Cambridge Theological Federation (2000), https://ctpi.div.ed.ac.uk/wp-content/uploads/2017/12/Byrne-2000-God-in-Cyberspace.pdf [accessed 14 August 2023].

[21] Euronews and Associated Press, "God Has Entered the Metaverse – and Faith in the Virtual World Is Flourishing," *Euronews.next*, last modified 3 February 2022, https://www.euronews.com/next/2022/02/01/god-has-entered-the-metaverse-and-worship-in-virtual-worlds-is-booming.

virtual spaces, such as the metaverse, exist within the universe God created and sustains.[22] This origin of the virtual spaces enables us to have a theological inference for God's presence in the metaverse through the concept of the omnipresence of God. In other words, the concept of God's omnipresence extends beyond the limitations of time and space, allowing him to exist in all corners of the universe and beyond. As the third person of the Trinity, the Holy Spirit is similarly present in all places, reflecting the divine essence of God. This understanding of God's presence in all locations logically extends to the virtual realm, including the metaverse, where the Holy Spirit can also be present. Jeff Reed,[23] the founder of "Thechurch.digital," uses the principle of Henry Blackaby, who is the author of the book *Experiencing God*, to argue that God is always at work around us through his Spirit, even in virtual realms.[24] Therefore, the aforementioned empirical experiences of a divine encounter in the metaverse are only possible if the omnipresent God is present there through his Spirit.

Transcendence of the Holy Spirit

One common feature found in the intersection between pneumatology and the metaverse is the idea of transcendence. In pneumatology, the Holy Spirit is often associated with transcendence and the ability to go beyond the limits of human understanding. Similarly, the metaverse allows people to transcend physical barriers and experience things that may not be possible in the physical world. The Holy Spirit's transcendence refers to the understanding that he surpasses the confines of physical realities. This means that the Holy Spirit is not bound by the limitations of created physical environments but can operate on a transcendent level beyond physical reality. Just as the Holy Spirit is often associated with transcending the limits of human understanding in pneumatology, the metaverse can offer us a way to transcend our limited understanding of the presence of the Holy Spirit beyond the physical world. The transcendent nature of the metaverse allows humans to explore new dimensions and realities beyond our physical senses, including new ways of encountering and connecting with God. This new perspective of digital pneumatology, in light of the transcendence of the Holy Spirit, may enable believers to experience God in ways that were previously impossible in the physical world.

---

[22] Guichun Jun, "Virtual Reality Church as a New Mission Frontier in the Metaverse: Exploring Theological Controversies and Missional Potential of Virtual Reality Church," *Transformation* 37:4 (2020), 300.

[23] Jeff Reed has written two books concerning mission in the metaverse. Jeff Reed, *VR and The Metaverse Church: How God is Moving in this Virtual, Yet Quite Real, Reality* (London: Leadership Network, 2022) and Jeff Read and John Harris, *Sharing Jesus Online: Helping Everyday Believers Become Digital & Metaverse Missionaries* (London: Exponential, 2023).

[24] Jeff Reed, "Blackaby's Experiencing God: Metaverse Edition," *Leadership Network*, last modified 15 March 2022, www.leadnet.org/blackabys-experiencing-god-metaverse-edition.

Immanence of the Holy Spirit

The Holy Spirit is not only transcendental but also immanent in all his creations. On the one hand, the Holy Spirit is beyond humanity's full experience and perception of his attributes and power. On the other hand, his presence and power permeate the mundane so that he is knowable and graspable. In particular, since the outpouring of the Holy Spirit on the day of Pentecost in Acts 2, the indwelling of the Holy Spirit in believers' lives is promised with empirical evidence as he guides, teaches, rebukes, and loves his people with his wisdom, power, and authority. This nonphysical sense of immanence and indwelling of the Holy Spirit in believers may be extended to the metaverse through the embodied relation between humans and their created avatars. Don Ihde, who is a philosopher of science and technology, proposes the four types of human and technology relations. One of them is embodied relations, which can be an appropriate theoretical approach to explain how one can empirically experience the presence of the Holy Spirit in the metaverse through one's avatar. Through its immersive nature, the metaverse plays a significant role in mediating human users' sensory experiences in embodied relations with their avatars. In this theory of Ihde, avatars are not only representatives of their human users through digital anthropomorphism but also the virtual presence of the users through the digital embodiment by the technology's merging of the physical world and virtual world. This immersive nature of interconnectedness between human users and their avatars not only enables the users' cognitive functions to perceive things in the metaverse but also enhances the sense of homogeneity through psychological, emotional, and spiritual intimacy.[25] In particular, this sense of homogeneity between the self and avatars helps believers to have empirical experiences of the presence of the Holy Spirit when they are engaged in collective religious activities, such as worship services or prayer meetings in virtual communities.[26]

Spiritual Communion and Community of Believers

The three aforementioned theological presuppositions grant a legitimate reason for building spiritual communities to worship and fellowship among believers in the metaverse. The promise of Jesus saying, "Where two or three are gathered together in my name, I am there among them" (Matt. 18:20) is also valid and applicable in the metaverse. This carries significant theological implications. Firstly, from the ecclesiological perspective, churches in digital spaces are as equally valid as the traditional churches in physical spaces in terms of their nature and functions. It does not mean that virtual churches can completely replace the value of real-life relationships and the richness of physical

---

[25] Anthony Steed, Ye Pan, Fiona Zisch, and William Steptoe, "The Impact of a Self-Avatar on Cognitive Load in Immersive Virtual Reality," *IEEE Virtual Reality (VR)* (Greenville, SC, 2016), 67–76.

[26] Robby I. Chandra and Noh I. Boiliu, "The Metaverse's Potential Impacts on the God-Centred Life and Togetherness of Indonesian Christians," *Theologia Viatorum* 46:1 (2022).

interactions among believers in traditional church contexts. However, virtual churches can be efficacious in building missional communities and enhancing spiritual experiences collectively when believers together seek God, who is present in virtual spaces. In particular, the idea of fostering communities and engaging in spiritual activities in virtual spaces in the same way that we do in physical spaces can be an inclusive act of practising communion with Gen Z believers, who are digital natives seeking different ways of believing and belonging, and those who are housebound, when physical proximity is not possible. Secondly, from the perspective of pneumatology, the Spirit of God plays the role of fostering communion and community among believers in both physical and virtual churches. For example, 1 Corinthians 12:13 states that all believers are baptised by one Spirit into one body. Based on this verse, communion and unity among believers can be achieved and maintained through the indwelling of the Holy Spirit among believers. This pneumatological understanding of communion and unity can be extended to virtual churches in the metaverse as believers gather, worship, and fellowship together in God's presence.

Power of the Holy Spirit

God's omni-attributes are inseparable. If God is omnipresent, he is also omnipotent. If God is present in the metaverse, it logically follows that his power can also be operated in the metaverse. It means that as the Holy Spirit is present and operates his power in physical spaces, the same holds true for virtual spaces. The power of the Holy Spirit for transformation, sanctification, impartation, and restoration is not constrained by the boundary between physical and virtual spaces. Then, how does the Holy Spirit operate his power in the metaverse, and where are the impacts of his power effectively and evidently demonstrated? We need to revisit the mediation theory by Don Ihde to find answers to these questions. The embodied relation between the human and the avatar provides a framework for understanding the spiritual interplay between the Holy Spirit and human beings through their avatars in the metaverse. The psychological and emotional intimacy between the human and the avatar can also be applicable to their spiritual interconnectedness. It means that the spiritual integration and unity between the human and the avatar are indivisible, as they are considered as one entity within the virtual environment, and are homogeneous, as there is a strong sense of alignment between the human's real identity and the anthropomorphic avatar, reflecting the human user's appearance, characteristics, and cultural behaviours in interactions with others in the metaverse. Due to this profound sense of inseparable and homogeneous interconnectivity, the power of the Holy Spirit can impact the lives of believers in physical spaces as they interact with him through their avatars in virtual spaces. It is important to be reminded that the ultimate purpose of the power of the Holy Spirit working in the metaverse by interacting with the avatars is to transform, sanctify, and restore individual believers to sincerely follow Christ as his disciples in the physical world.

Digital Pneumatology

Transformative Power for Regeneration

The Holy Spirit is the sole agent of salvation. In other words, without the inward work of the Holy Spirit, all the human efforts to save a soul can never be effective.[27] The ultimate purpose of the Father is to redeem us, and the Son has accomplished the Father's redemption plan for the fallen humanity. But this divine gift of salvation cannot be accomplished without the agency of the Holy Spirit. As salvation is not understood as an event but a process, the Holy Spirit plays several important roles in the process of salvation. Firstly, the Holy Spirit convinces individuals of their sinfulness and convinces them of the need for forgiveness through Christ. Secondly, the Holy Spirit brings a spiritual new birth to truly repentant individuals, which enables them to begin a personal relationship with God. Finally, the Holy Spirit indwells in believers' lives and seals them to secure their salvation as an eternal inheritance. Soto confirms that the Holy Spirit's transformative power for spiritual conviction, regeneration, and preservation works in the metaverse in the same way that it does in physical spaces.[28] The metaverse has become a new harvest field for modern missions as the digital natives who formerly experienced a deep sense of emptiness and even identified as atheists have testified that they encountered God and were saved by hearing the Gospel through the work of the Holy Spirit in virtual spaces.[29] In other words, biblically and theologically authentic conversion experience has happened to people in their physical lives while they participated in various activities of churches through their avatars in the metaverse. Through the embodied relation between the human and the avatar in the immersive virtual environment, the power of the Spirit of God works in the minds and hearts of human users for spiritual conviction of their sins and the need for forgiveness. This conversion experience through the immersive metaverse environment will continually impact their spiritual desire to grow as disciples of Christ in their daily life in the physical world.

Empowerment for Sanctification

The Holy Spirit empowers believers. Generally, the empowerment of the Holy Spirit is understood as receiving power for mission and evangelism.[30] Most Pentecostal scholars, especially Charles Finny, regard sanctification and

---

[27] Yuzo Adhinarta, *The Doctrine of the Holy Spirit in the Major Reformed Confessions and Catechisms of the Sixteenth and Seventeenth Centuries* (Carlisle: Lanham Monographs, 2012), 69.

[28] D. J. Soto, "4 Lessons from a Metaverse Pastor," *The Future of the Church is the Metaverse,* last modified 30 September 2022, https://vrchurch.substack.com/p/4-lessons-from-a-metaverse-pastor.

[29] Jeremy Lukens, "The Metaverse Is a New Harvest Field for Modern Missions," *Indigitous,* last modified 12 July 2023, https://indigitous.org/article/the-metaverse-is-a-new-harvest-field-for-modern-missions/.

[30] Amos Yong, *In the Days of Caesar: Pentecostalism and Political Theology* (Grand Rapids, MI: Eerdmans, 2010), 171.

empowerment as two separate results of the baptism of the Holy Spirit.[31] However, some of the early Pentecostal scholars, such as Donald Gee, who was a prominent British Pentecostal theologian in the early to mid-twentieth century, believed that the ultimate purpose of empowerment of the Holy Spirit was to sanctify believers to live a holy life.[32] Gee's Pentecostal theology always emphasised the importance of the empowerment of the Holy Spirit in light of sanctification. In this regard, the power of the Holy Spirit strengthens and enables believers to overcome the power of temptation and sin and to live consecrated lives to be progressively transformed into the likeness of Christ. If the metaverse is part of God's creation and God is present there, his Spirit must play a crucial role in empowering his believers to live holy and righteous lives in virtual spaces. Neal Stephenson wrote *Snow Crash*, in which he introduced the metaverse as a utopia.[33] After thirty years, his imagining of the metaverse has been realised through the convergence of digital technologies and the internet. However, the metaverse is far from the concept of utopia at present. In reality, all sorts of cyber-crimes take place in the metaverse, so there is an urgent need for meta-jurisdiction to create safe virtual environments.[34] This is the reason why the empowerment of the Holy Spirit for believers' sanctification in the metaverse is so significant to make the metaverse a safer and better place by demonstrating Christlike characters and attitudes.

Impartation for Service

God desires to impart not only his power but also his life, wisdom, and all the good gifts to his people. This nature of God's impartation is well demonstrated throughout the Bible, especially in the history of God's redemption. For example, the self-impartation of the Son in the incarnation and the cross to obey the Father's will effectively shows the divine desire to bestow his grace and love to restore the fallen humanity into his image. Ten days after the Son ascended to heaven, the Father and the Son imparted the Holy Spirit to believers who were fervently seeking power from above on the day of Pentecost. Afterward, the Holy Spirit imparts his gifts to believers, giving them spiritual abilities to fulfil their functions or callings for God's mission.[35] Jack Deere, a former professor at Dallas Theological Seminary, used to be a cessationist, but he has become a continuationist after personally experiencing the Holy Spirit imparting spiritual

---

[31] Bradley T. Noel, "From Wesley to Azusa: The Historical Journey of the 'Second Work' Doctrine," in Scott A. Dunham, ed., *Full of the Holy Spirit and Faith* (Wolfville, NS: Gaspereau Press, 1997), 52–53.

[32] Donald Gee, *Wind and Flame* (Southampton, UK: Revival Library, 2013), 32.

[33] Neal Stephenson, *Snow Crash* (New York: Bantam Books, 1992).

[34] Guichun Jun, "Mission in the Age of Digitalization: Metaverse, Metamodernism and Metanarratives," in Risto Jukko, ed., *Together in the Mission of God* (Geneva: WCC Publications, 2022), 244–45.

[35] Jim Wainscott, *Eleventh-Hour Overcomers: In Pursuit of the Ultimate Prize* (Bloomington, IN: Westbow Press, 2013), 205.

Digital Pneumatology   125

gifts unto him.[36] Gordon Fee affirms that the Holy Spirit works ceaselessly to impart his spiritual gifts to believers to serve God and his Kingdom.[37] This stimulates our theological speculation to understand whether this continual impartation of the Holy Spirit in the physical world is also available in the metaverse as believers seek spiritual gifts and power. If the transcendental nature of the presence and work of the Holy Spirit is possible in the metaverse, the digital impartation of the Holy Spirit is also possible because God cannot violate his divine nature of imparting all the good gifts to his people where he is present and operates his power, whether it is in physical spaces or virtual spaces. Furthermore, digital impartation may include the transmission of spiritual gifts or knowledge between believers willing to give and receive spiritual blessings from one another through the mediation of the Holy Spirit, in a similar way that Apostle Paul wanted to impart some spiritual gift to the church in Rome, as stated in Romans 1. This theological notion of digital impartation posits the crucial function of digital platforms in facilitating spiritual experiences and practices that foster a sense of community among believers and enable them to acquire the spiritual endowments of the Holy Spirit for their service to God in both physical and virtual worlds.

Healing for Restoration

Mediatisation has impacted various aspects of Christian ministries and missions to evangelise unbelievers and promote Christian faith. In particular, divine healing ministry has taken advantage of it for several decades.[38] Media-mediated divine healing raises the question of how the divine healing power of the Holy Spirit can interplay with human faith through media. Although media itself does not have the power of healing, it is certainly used as a channel of healing. God transmitted his power through objectives in the Bible, such as the mantle of Elijah to empower Elisha (2 Kings 2:13–14), the hem of Jesus' garment (Luke 8:40–48), and Apostle Paul's handkerchief or apron to heal the sick (Acts 19:12). Even Peter's shadow could be a divine means of healing for the sick (Acts 5:15–16). As technology has continually advanced, the trend of Christian ministries based on technology has shifted from mediatisation to digitalisation. Mobile applications for divine healing have been developed for believers, such as the Healing App,[39] which provides Bible verses concerning healing and the users' testimonies of healing. The metaverse is also used for various medical purposes, such as supporting patients with mental health issues or elderly people with

---

[36] Jack Deere, *Why I am Still Surprised by the Power of the Spirit: Discovering How God Speaks and Heals Today* (Grand Rapids: Zondervan, 2020).

[37] Gordon Fee, *God's Empowering Presence: The Holy Spirit in the Letters of Paul* (Grand Rapids: Baker Academic, 2011).

[38] Sonny E. Zaluchu, "The Impact of Mediatisation in the Healing Ministry of African Preachers," *Verbum et Ecclesia* 42:1 (2021).

[39] https://apps.apple.com/us/app/the-healing-app/id1293927143 [accessed on 14 August 2023].

cognitive decline.[40] Research shows that socially anxious individuals benefited substantially from social skills training sessions in the metaverse, since the programmes allowed them to engage and acquire skills in communication that boosted their self-esteem.[41] The metaverse has more than 400 million active users every month,[42] and behind 400 million avatars are real people with various kinds of pain in all dimensions. As believers participate in worship services or prayer meetings in the metaverse, the Spirit of God can heal their physical, emotional, and spiritual diseases through their embodied relations with their avatars. According to Asamoa-Gyadu, many modern Pentecostals believe that the Holy Spirit is present and active in virtual platforms, and they claim to have experienced divine healing of illnesses while participating in online spiritual activities, like healing services or the holy Communion.[43] Although divine healing is granted by the power of the Holy Spirit, it often takes place in communal settings as believers gather to support one another. The metaverse can provide opportunities to form support groups for people with various issues, such as mental health, grief, addiction, social phobia, or trauma. By creating a virtually safe environment, where people can share experiences and receive advice, fostering a culture of care and building a sense of belonging, these virtual support groups can contribute to healing and restoration through the presence and power of the Holy Spirit.

Conclusion

The emergence of the metaverse has opened up a new avenue for contemporary mission and church ministry. As Mark Zuckerberg said, "Metaverse isn't a thing a company builds. It's the next chapter of the internet overall."[44] Reimagining pneumatology and Pentecostal ministries in the age of digitalisation is not an option that Pentecostals may consider, but the necessary direction to be pursued with a professional understanding of technology and theology. All sectors of our society diligently explore opportunities to maximise the effectiveness of their

---

[40] Dominikus David Biondi Situmorang, "Will Metaverse Become a More Exciting Place to Listen to Music Streaming for Mental Health?" *Journal of Public Health* 45:2 (2023), 363–64 and Defu Zhou, Yi Jin and Ying Chen, "The Application Scenarios Study on the Intervention of Cognitive Decline in Elderly Population Using Metaverse Technology," *Chengdu: Sichuan Society for Biomedical Engineering* 40:3 (2023), 571.

[41] Suji Kim and Eunjoo Kim, "The Use of Virtual Reality in Psychiatry: A Review," *Journal of the Korean Academy of Child and Adolescent Psychiatry* 31:1 (2023), 26–32.

[42] Geri Mileva, "48 Metaverse Statistics: Market Size and Growth," *Influencer Marketing Hub* (2023). Last modified 20 July 2023, https://influencermarketinghub.com/metaverse-stats/.

[43] Kwabena Asamoa-Gyadu, "Locked Down but Not Locked Out: An African Perspective on Pentecostalism and Media in a Pandemic Era," in Heidi Campbell and John Dyer, eds., *Ecclesiology for a Digital Church: Theological Reflections on a New Normal* (London: SCM Press, 2022).

[44] Geri Mileva, "48 Metaverse Statistics: Market Size and Growth."

work in the metaverse. As aforementioned, the health sector has been developing programmes to reduce pain or cure disease using the metaverse's benefits. Education is another sector using the metaverse to overcome the failed promises of the current pedagogy taking place within the traditional classroom setting and to provide children with access to the relevant, creative, collaborative, and challenging learning environments they need to succeed.[45] There is no need for further noteworthy descriptions regarding the remarkable progression in the utilisation of the metaverse across the domains of gaming, entertainment, business, and social networking. It seems that various sectors in our society are giving serious consideration to the importance of reimagining their visions and missions in virtual spaces. This shift is necessary to overcome the limitations imposed by traditional concepts and practices that have been developed and maintained in physical spaces for a significant amount of time. Fortunately, there are discussions and writings in various fields of theology related to the metaverse. For example, *Ecclesiology for a Digital Church* is a book compiling articles on profound theological reflections on challenges and opportunities in the age of digitalisation.[46] It is a time for Pentecostal scholars and practitioners to delve deeper into theological discussions around developing digital pneumatology and ministry possibilities in the metaverse. As I theologically speculated and argued above, the presence and power of the Holy Spirit are not confined to physical spaces but permeate all corners of the created universe, including the metaverse. Religious phenomenology and sociology of religion have already embarked on research to explain human spiritual experiences in digital spaces and theorise them. In this significant transition time, digital pneumatology will play a crucial role not only in developing digital ministries for regeneration, transformation, impartation, and restoration in virtual spaces but also in laying the foundation of digital Pentecostalism to deepen and widen our understanding of the person and power of the Holy Spirit in this digital age.

---

[45] John D. Couch and Jason Towne, *Rewiring Education: How Technology Can Unlock Every Student's Potential* (Dallas, TX: BenBella Books, 2018).

[46] Campbell and Dyer, *Ecclesiology for a Digital Church.*

The Church as a Healing Community:
An African Perspective

Opoku Onyinah

Introduction

Over the last two decades, there has been a lot of attention paid to prayer/healing camps in Ghana and Africa, a lot of it appearing in press reports. A prayer camp is a place where a person goes with a problem to fast and pray with the aim of meeting God in a special way to answer his/her request. The camp is centred around a prophet/healer who plays the role of a spiritual consultant. The reports on these camps are depressing. Some of them are extremely lamentable. The reportage has shone a light in the very dark places of the abuses and the deplorable conditions in many of these camps and the neglect and lack of care and understanding by some of the healing prophets. Some of this has also been highlighted in the literature, including by practitioners in psychological services, psychiatry, and theology.[1] Their work underscores the burden placed on the respective churches and their prayer camps to correct these abuses. It is against this background that I proceed in the hope that the church in Ghana (and Africa as a whole), can become better equipped and hopefully represent the life and practices of a healing community that is a true imitator of Jesus Christ. I am very much aware of the intellectual debates – at least since the 1960s Africanist scholarship on the African continent – about what it means to use the term or label "African."[2] Therefore, I use the term "Africa" not as part of a generalisation or generic term – in terms of a homogenisation of cultures and practices. The same applies to my reference to Ghana. In both locales, cultures vary, with different segments or constituencies having their own idiosyncratic worldviews that inform their peculiar practices. Accordingly, I use the two terms from the perspective of shared human existential realities and experiences.

---

[1] Francis Ethelbert Kwabena Benyah, "Healing and Mental Illness in Ghana: Why Prayer Camps in Ghana are Sometimes Alternatives to Psychiatric Hospitals," *Nordic Journal for the Study of Religion Temenos* 59:1 (2023), 101–23; D. Arias, L. Taylor, A. Ofori–Atta, E. H. Bradley, "Prayer Camps and Biomedical Care in Ghana: Is Collaboration in Mental Health Care Possible?" *PLoS ONE 11* (2016), 9; Shantha Rau Barriga, "The (In)human Dimension of Ghana's Prayer Camps," *Human Rights Watch*, https://www.hrw.org/news/2014/10/10/inhuman-dimension-ghanas-prayer-camps, accessed 8 August 2023; Human Right Watch, "Like a Death Sentence: Abuses Against Persons with Mental Disabilities in Ghana" (2012).

[2] Chinua Achebe, *An Image of Africa; and the Trouble with Nigeria* (London: Penguin, 2010); Ali A. Mazrui, "On the Concept of 'We are all Africans,'" *American Political Science Review* 57:1 (1963), 88–97.

The prayer camp, as such, is not unique to African communities. There are precursors and forms of this in the Bible and in Christian history. Consequently, I begin by digging out for the antecedents of healing homes in the Bible and Christian history. Then, I shall continue by discussing the African Traditional healing communities and how they run through the African Christian healing communities. I then show how Jesus went about healing as compared to the then prevailing literature on demonology. I shall conclude by offering pastoral counselling.

Antecedents of Healing Camps

Over the years, the church has attempted to be a healing community within whatever environment it found itself. Th did not just happen. The church functions within the cultures that it exists. The people of God have always attempted to provide refuge for the hopeless, the neglected, and the vulnerable. In the Old Testament, Samuel set up a school of prophets where he trained people, worshipped, and prayed for God's wisdom and direction. During the time of Elijah, the school might have developed into two schools (2 Kings 2:3, 5). A Shunammite woman whose child died ran to Elisha's abode with the hope of Elisha praying for the dead child. Elisha sent one of the prophets in training, Gehazi, to restore the Shunammite woman's child who was dead (2 Kings 4:25–35). For the woman to run to where the prophet was suggests that the place was known as a place of refuge or power. This could be understood as an antecedent of the healing camps that were to develop in later times.

In the New Testament, there was the belief that a pool, stirred possibly by an angelic being, could heal people. Many people who were disabled (the blind, the lame, the paralysed) lay waiting by the pool hoping to be pushed into the stirred water to be healed. At this very place, Jesus healed a person who had been an invalid for thirty-eight years (John 5:1–9). This could be a foreshadowing of the various healing camps.

More recently, healing homes became quite popular in the mid-nineteenth century in Europe and America, for example. In the 1830s, Edward Irving, born in Scotland in 1792, was said to have organised people at Regent Square where he prayed for people to be healed, to speak in tongues and prophesy. In the 1850s, Dorothea Trudel of Switzerland is said to have established healing homes and prayed for people and anointed them with oil. In addition, she founded numerous faith-healing centres where she used the same method to heal people.

In 1864, Charles Culles of the USA, a physician, admitted people to his home. The home was used to treat people with tuberculosis who were homeless and hopeless and were dying. Later, it is said that he added three more homes, where in addition to medical care, he also prayed for the sick and had many successes of healing. In 1867, Otto Stockmayer, also of Switzerland, opened a home for healing, after he had been healed through the ministry of Samuel Zeller. Another home that became popular in 1882 was that of Carrie Judd-Montgomery of Buffalo in New York. She was said to be healed through the ministry of Sarah Mix after a fall which left her in excruciating pain. This infused faith in her that eventually led her to open a healing home called Faith Rest Cottage.

The Church as a Healing Community   131

Another interesting story is the healing home that was established in the early 1880s by Lucy Drake Osborn. Having been healed of tuberculosis and an incurable brain tumour through the ministry of Charles Culles in one of his healing homes, she decided to dedicate herself to healing by establishing a "Faith Home for Incurables" in Brooklyn in New York City, USA.

One of the most popular healing homes was that of John Alexander Dowie, of Chicago-Zion, USA. In the1880s, Dowie opened his own home for those who were coming to his healing meetings from great distances and had nowhere to stay. Then, later, two additional healing homes were founded to assist those who were coming for healing and needed accommodation. The beacon of twentieth-century Pentecostalism, Charles Parham, also started a healing home before starting his Bible College at Topeka, which eventually ignited the modern Pentecostal movement.[3]

These stories show that to some extent people have often sought to find a place where power is manifested in order to solve the existential fears that threaten their well-being. Similarly, in Africa, before the advent of Christianity, there were traditional shrines where people who were sick and suffering, who needed to find some meaning in their lives, went for help. These shrines and their practices did not completely stop after the advent of Christianity but mutated into Christian practices, since the indigenes saw traces of their traditions in the newly acquired Christian faith. Against this backdrop, I discuss the four healing communities in Ghana.

Traditional Healing Communities[4]

The first issue I want to address is the traditional healing community, which forms the basis for African healing beliefs and practices. Although this differs from one nation to another, there are some similarities among them. Formerly, in many African societies, every adult was expected to know the available herbs used for certain common ailments such as headache, stomach-ache, rheumatism, waist pain, and piles. If anyone felt ill, he would try one or another of these remedies. If this failed, his close relative would call in a "traditional healer."

The first task of the priest was to find out the cause of the disease. This was done through the priest's ability to divine or consult the deities, that which could

---

[3] For the development of healing movements and approaches to healing in Pentecostalism, see Kimberly Ervin Alexander, *Pentecostal Healing: Models in Theology and Practice* (Blandford Forum: Deo, 2006), 3–4, 8–27, 54–63; Paul Chappell, "Healing Movements," in Stanley Burgess and Gary B. McGee, eds., *Dictionary of Pentecostal and Charismatic Movements* (Grand Rapid: Regency Reference Library, 1988), 353–74; D. William Faupel, *The Everlasting Gospel: The Significance of Eschatology in The Development of Pentecostal Thought* (Sheffield: Sheffield Academic Press, 1996), 115–86; Donald W. Dayton, *Theological Roots of Pentecostalism* (Grand Rapids: Zondervan, 1987), 115–41.

[4] Much of the information in this section has been published in the German *Oekumenische Rundschau: Theologies und Naturwissenschaft* 69 (2020), 60–71.

be called divinatory consultation. The diagnosis of the priest was to search for the psychological or supernatural cause of the disease. Normally, it was perceived that if the disease had a natural cause, the administration of the herbs would have cured the person. The diagnoses often centred on the traditional priest's ability to neutralise spiritual powers behind the diseases to make the herbs effective.

Once the diagnosis was done, the priest would request the family to present a person from among themselves who would "stand behind" the patient; that is, the one who would support the patient to stay at the shrine (camp). A patient could spend up to two months at a shrine as the priest administered herbs until the patient was cured. The payment of the charge was the responsibility of the family.

In addition to the traditional deities who offered this type of healing, the anti-witchcraft shrine's priests performed rites that featured witch-hunting and claimed to quell social disturbances.[5] The rituals associated with the anti-witchcraft shrines produced many challenges. These challenges include witch-hunting, accusations of witchcraft, and the subsequent exorcism, which caused lots of problems such as dividing family members, accusing innocent victims, and placing people under stigmatisation.

Nevertheless, when it comes to the traditional healing priests, Margaret Field, an English ethno-psychiatrist in the mid-twentieth century, remarked that the traditional priest had the ability to cure disease.[6] The healing provided by the priest could be said to be both medical, as evidenced by the application of the herbs, and supernatural or magico-religious, as implied in the ritual and the process of divinatory consultation. This type of traditional healing includes admitting the patient into the camp for forms of Christian healing in sub-Saharan Africa.

Healing Communities of the African Initiated Churches

Another type of healing community in Africa is the kind offered by the Africa Initiated churches (AICs). Harold Turner, a missionary scholar who pioneered New Religious Movements Studies, observes in the whole continent of Africa, "they range from churches almost indistinguishable from the most westernized products of Christian missions, to cults that are a revival of traditional pagan religions with no more than a few Christian glosses."[7] A careful examination of

---

[5] Hans W. Debrunner, *Witchcraft in Ghana: A Study on the Belief in Destructive Witches and its Effects on the Akan Tribes* (Accra: Presbyterian Book Depot, 1961), 106.

[6] Margaret J. Field, *Religion and Medicine of the Ga People* (London: Oxford University Press, 1937), 160.

[7] Harold W. Turner, "The Significance of African Prophet Movements," *Hibbert Journal* 61 (1963), 2. For some reading on these churches, see also David B. Barrett, *Schism and Renewal in Africa* (Nairobi: Oxford University Press, 1968).

The Church as a Healing Community 133

their activities, nevertheless, reveals that the churches' claim to solve problems and heal various diseases is the main attraction.

The methods used in healing and exorcism differ from one church to another. However, there are some commonalities. Almost all of them have healing camps (also called gardens or centres), special days of prayer, prescribed fasting, and some diagnoses through dreams and visions. Turner notices in the whole of Africa that the majority of the use aids such as olive oil, crosses, incense, ritualistic baths, water, and Florida water,[8] but without any indigenous herbs.[9] However, in Ghana, others use these aids in addition to the native herbs or Western medicine.

The liturgy of healing in many of the African Independent Churches (AICs) differs from one church to another. However, there is a common process. There is a time of preaching and testimonies; thereafter, the congregation sings and claps to the drumming rhythm. As the atmosphere builds, the leader and his assistants begin to speak in different tongues, recite incantations, invoke spirits to come and assist, and then command the spirits behind the disease to leave. People begin to shake, jump, shout, crawl on the ground, or dance violently. These attract interrogation by the prophets or their assistants to find out the cause of the problem. Some prophets may anoint them with oil or sprinkle water on the clients to silence them. The response to this may last for a short period.

The rituals and healing of these churches, enhanced by the giving of aids, certainly strengthen the personality-spirit of those who are fearful of witchcraft and other threatening forces so that they can face life with little fear. In some cases, people can be healed here.

Pentecostal Healing Communities

The next healing community to be considered is the role played by the Pentecostals and Charismatics. For Pentecostals, just like the African Initiated Churches, healing and reconciliation are part of their tradition and necessarily part of the normal worship service. The service is cooperative and participatory, which involves both body and mind relationships. The Pentecostals sing, dance, and pray, spontaneously speaking in tongues and sometimes prophesying. It is believed that this type of corporate worship brings the blessing of healing and freedom in one's spirit and forms the basis of peace and reconciliation within oneself as well as unity among Christians. The opportunity to speak aloud or quietly, individually or collectively, with the hope that God will answer them as individuals, is of itself therapeutic. It enriches their spiritual lives, enabling them to face practical life situations with fortitude and hope.

---

[8] This is some sort of perfume which comes from the US. It is believed to have curative powers.

[9] Harold W. Turner, *Religious Innovation in Africa: Collected Essays on New Religious Movements* (Boston: G. K. Halls, 1979), 167.

Charismatic Healing Communities

The Charismatic renewal within Christianity in the latter part of the twentieth century brought another type of healing community within the Mainline churches and Pentecostal communities. There was a renewed awareness of demonology within African Christianity, that which I called "witchdemonology." This was the amalgamation of African Traditional beliefs and practices of witchcraft and the Western Christian concept of demonology. There was the general belief that demons were attached to various illnesses. Again, it was held that due to the idol worship of the ancestors of African people, there were curses following Africans, which exhibited themselves in illnesses, suffering, and poverty. Therefore, every African Christian needed deliverance. Certainly, there was a need for the churches to find groups/institutions which would cater to this group's needs. This was not a problem since the shrine of the deities and the AICs had already set the pace; consequently, the prayer camps and "prayer warriors" became the answers.[10]

Prayer Centres/Camps

These prayer warriors and the prayer camps serve as "safe havens" for the majority of society and address this so-called "urgent need for healing and deliverance."[11] Some of the camps are residential. The residential camps, just like the shrines, have residential facilities where people can stay and pray for a long period. In the non-residential camps, people, such as praying warriors, come to pray and go back to their residences.

All sorts of problems are represented at the camps. For example, in a survey I conducted in 1999, the responses from 807 people to the question concerning reasons for visiting the prayer camps broke down into four broad categories.[12] In 2017, as I visited some of these camps and inquired about why they had sent people there, I found that they still fell under these four broad categories with some variations. In November 2022, as I interviewed some participants in a prayer camp in Accra about what brought them to camps, the reasons still fell under the four broad categories. These categories included sickness, meditation and prayer, observation, and miscellaneous, such as unemployment, promotion at work, marital problems, love, desire to marry, and business success. Other miscellaneous reasons included release from addiction to drinking alcohol, smoking, sexual lust, and bad temper.

---

[10] Opoku Onyinah, *Pentecostalism Exorcism: Witchcraft and Demonology in Ghana* (Blandford Forum: Deo, 2012), 139–70.

[11] Finding a place for such prayer groups engaged the attention of church leaders, for example, see Chinonyelu Moses Ugwu, *Healing in the Nigerian Church: A Pastoral-Psychological Exploration* (Bern: Peter Lang, 1998).

[12] Out of the 1,201 people who filled in the forms, 347 (28%) did not state the reason why they went to the prayer camps. Thus, we were left with 807 people (71%) who responded to the question. The research was conducted in 1999.

The Church as a Healing Community   135

Healing and Deliverance Services

The services at the prayer camps vary from one place to another. However, they are similar to a Pentecostal type of healing prayer meeting and to that of the AICs. For this reason, I will analyse this and those of the AICs and, by that, bring out the difference between the two.

The deliverance sessions of the Pentecostal and Charismatic renewals clearly combine a wide range of practices, including traditional, African Initiated Churches and biblical practices. The approach of these churches – Pentecostals, Charismatics, and AICs – demonstrates a blend of Christian faith and traditional practices. Similar to the AICs, the Pentecostals/Charismatics type of healing and deliverance, which demands confessions of sins and includes drumming and singing, follows that of the traditional shrines. The prayer camps and special days are similar to those of the traditional day of consultation of the deities. The fasting, prayer, and command are the re-interpretation of some Scripture verses, especially those concerning Jesus' dealing with the demoniacs (e.g., Matt 17:21 (KJV); Mark 5:1–20). There is the indirect use of psychology in the various healing services. This is implied in the confession of witches and the repetition of songs that build up pressure on the people before deliverance is carried out. In addition to this, the techniques of hypnotherapy are applied indirectly; this is through the teaching about demons and deliverance. This is similar to divinatory consultation practised in the shrines. Here, the Pentecostals/Charismatics take it further than the AICs by using questionnaires and interviews, which makes the approach similar to those of professional psychoanalysts, who allow the patients to talk freely about personal experiences to extract information from them. Again, like the AICs, magical methodology is apparent in the repetition of the "prayer languages" during exorcism.

This notwithstanding, generally, healing within Pentecostals/Charismatics differs from those at both the shrines, where physical effigies represent the gods that are consulted, and at the AICs, where water, crosses, and crucifixes are almost always used. Thus, this paraphernalia appear to be absent in most of the Pentecostal and Charismatic churches. Nevertheless, as the study by the North American Pentecostal scholar Kimberly Ervin Alexander shows, "The Laying-on of hands, anointing with oil, use of anointed handkerchiefs and even the ceremonial giving of cold water in the name of the Lord have all emerged as important and regular practices within the [Pentecostal and Charismatic] movement."[13] Thus, Schomburg-Scheff's observation about the power of images is relevant here. Besides his recognition that specific images are stronger in certain cultures than others, he also feels that some "conceptions and actions ... seem to transcend historical, geographical, social, and cultural boundaries."[14] That is, for him, no matter how some people try to convince others that images

---

[13] Kimberly Ervin Alexander, *Pentecostal Healing: Models in Theology and Practice* (Blandford Forum: Deo, 2006), 227.

[14] Sylvia M. Schomburg-Scherff, "The Power of Images: New Approaches to the Anthropological Study of Images," *Anthropos* 95 (2000), 195.

136   *The Holy Spirit, Spirituality and Leadership*

are misconceptions, they will continue to have a strong impact on religion.[15] This concretisation's impact on people's psyches is significant.

The Challenge

A major challenge to the African healing communities is that which happens to be their strength – African religiosity. In African Traditional religions, the more deities a person has, the more powerful that person is. Thus, a person can have many deities. The tendency to have many deities makes flexibility easy for many African religious people, not excluding Christians. This is the picture that we have in the praying communities now – the adoption of some of the best practices of African Traditional religions as well as the dark sides. Some of the good sides may include the admission of suffering people to treat them until they are cured. The attention given to the vulnerable is another positive adoption of the African Traditional religions. However, the dark side includes the belief that diseases mainly have a supernatural origin and are the result of witchcraft, the chaining of so-called witches, and the violence which is done to them.[16] The establishment of many prayer camps within and outside both the Pentecostal/Charismatic and the Mainline churches indicates that the contemporary concept of healing is still strongly based on the African worldview. Although there are indications of abuses at these prayer camps, people still flock in – a signal that the camps are meeting the people at their worldview level.

Worldviews and Christian understandings are not consciously constructed but result from efforts to cope with the world. Worldviews are coping strategies that allow humans to make sense of otherwise meaningless worlds. A worldview cannot be enforced on another person, but a person could be guided to either enlarge his/her worldview or change it. The change has to come from within. The theologians, pastors, and missiologists have to concern themselves with this task. To address this task, the examples of Jesus and the apostles need to be examined.

Jesus as Compared to Selected Ancient Literature

Jesus healed many who were sick, but he did not heal all who were sick who came across his way. A typical example of this is his visit to the pool at Bethesda, where he healed a person who had been an invalid for thirty-eight years (John 5). Against this background, a few examples of Jesus' healing that are relevant to our purpose will be cited.

The first to consider here is the healing of the paralytic recorded in Mark 2:1–13 and Luke 5:17–26. In this episode, Jesus forgave the man's sins and later healed him. When Jesus pronounced the forgiveness of sin to the sick person, the

---

[15] See Margaret Mary Kelleher, "The Liturgical Body: Symbol and Ritual," in Bruce T. Morrill, ed, *Bodies of Worship: Exploration in Theory and Practice* (Collegeville: The Liturgical Press, 1999), 51–66.

[16] Human Rights Watch, "Like a Death Sentence," 1–10.

The Church as a Healing Community

bystanders felt he had blasphemed God. To this, Jesus replied, which one is more difficult to do, "Your sins are forgiven," or to say, "Get up, take your mat and walk" (Mark 2:9)? Jesus then healed the man. The story underscores the power of words to bring about an effect that is physically observable while, at the same time, focusing on something that is supposed to have been achieved without any immediate outwardly physical proof of the said action.

The observable prospect of the lame person rising up and walking is, humanly speaking, more difficult than the forensic claim that his sins are forgiven. Rising up and walking was a form of physical transformation. Jesus wished to do the more difficult one – the healing of the physical ailment – as proof that he could, in fact, do the hidden one as well, the saying of which is so easy. The paralytic needed both the forgiveness of his sins; that is, the ultimate redemption and deliverance, as well as the healing of his condition as a paralytic. Although the story clearly shows that Jesus, as the Son of God, had the power on earth to forgive sin, it also shows that no matter the condition of a person, his relationship with God is the most important aspect. This is a lesson that Jesus wanted to instil in people.

Yet, at the same time, Jesus appears to be responding partly to shared sensibilities, as we find in John 11 when a physical infirmity is linked to the sins not only of the disabled person but of his parents. In John 9:2, "His disciples asked him, 'Rabbi, who sinned, this man or his parents that he was born blind'" (NIV)? Jesus taught them the lesson that none of them sinned, not the parents nor the blind man. This was to indicate to them that sickness could result from natural causes. Thus, in the healing of the paralytic, Jesus confirmed their belief that sin could lead to sickness, and in the healing of the blind person, he taught them that not all sicknesses are the result of sin.

At the heart of all this is the demonstration of Jesus as the Son of God, the Messiah, who has the power to heal and set people free from all forms of bondage.

The next passage to consider is the woman with the issue of blood in Luke 8:42b–48. This passage is a story within a story. Luke 8:40–56 contains the story of Jairus, a synagogue leader, and his daughter. Within that story is the account of the woman bleeding for twelve years who touched Jesus and got healed (Luke 8:42b–48). This woman had visited many physicians, but she had not been cured. She had exhausted the medical knowledge and the therapies available to her then. She was at her limit and thus almost hopeless. The only hope left was Jesus.

There is a need to emphasise the idea of being at her limit. Why? Jairus, too, was at his limit. The daughter was dying, and in fact, she died before Jesus got there. These two came to Jesus because they had reached their limits. Mark's emphasis on the woman who was bleeding must not be overlooked, "She had suffered a great deal under the care of many doctors and had spent all she had, yet instead of getting better, she grew worse" (Mark 5:26, NIV). The woman had used all the available medical facilities at the time. Similarly, Jairus might have done the same; as a man of authority, he might have used all available medical resources. In both cases, when they approached Jesus, they received what they needed – Jesus healed the woman and brought Jairus' daughter back to life.

Although both had used all medical facilities available to them, Jesus did not link their conditions to either sin or evil spirits.

In many instances, some people flock to the prayer camps because they think going there is their last resort; they have reached their limits. Indeed, some people go there because they do not have money to benefit from the expensive medical facilities. However, often, both the rich and the poor go there because they link the origin of their problems to the demonic or supernatural. It is natural that people will go to wherever they think their problems can be solved.

Nonetheless, there is another important lesson that African Christians need to learn. The fact that this woman had spent much of her money on physicians shows that the ancient people seriously considered medicine. Some did not easily link sickness with the supernatural. They drew from both medication and the supernatural (prayer). The deuterocanonical book of The Wisdom of Jesus, Son of Sirach (also known as the Ecclesiasticus) offers this advice:

> Honor physicians for their services, for the Lord created them; for their gift of healing comes from the Most High, and they are rewarded by the king. The skill of physicians makes them distinguished, and in the presence of the great they are admired. The Lord created medicines out of the earth, and the sensible will not despise them … My child, when you are ill, do not delay, but pray to the Lord, and he will heal you. Give up your faults and direct your hands rightly, and cleanse your heart from all sin. Offer a sweet-smelling sacrifice, and a memorial portion of choice flour, and pour oil on your offering, as much as you can afford. Then give the physician his place, for the Lord created him; do not let him leave you, for you need him. There may come a time when recovery lies in the hands of physicians, for they too pray to the Lord that he grant them success in diagnosis and in healing, for the sake of preserving life. He who sins against his Maker, will be defiant toward the physician (38:1–15).

This text (Sirach 38:1–15) focuses on physicians and prayer or seeking God for supernatural help. The exhortation here is very sound, "When you are ill, do not delay but pray to the Lord and he will heal you" (13). This prayer is not supposed to oppose what the physicians can do. Rather, the prayer is to offer a sacrifice presumably for one's faults, not as a kind of exchange for physical healing. After the prayer, the sick person is also to seek help from the physician since "there may come a time when recovery lies in the hands of physicians" (13). The gift of the physician comes from God (2). Intriguingly, the call to prayer is buttressed by the claim that physicians, too, pray to God that they may be given success in their endeavours. The basic argument here is that physicians have an essential role to play. They cannot be displaced, nor can they be dismissed. The Lord has granted them their gift.

There is no appeal for incantations to dispel the disease. No formulas. This is similar to James, although with some nuances, who exhorted believers who are sick to call the elders to pray and anoint them with oil. The prayer offered in faith will make the sick person well, and upon confession, the Lord will forgive sins (James 5:13–16). James added the need to call the elders to pray. There was no mention of demons and exorcism.

The Dead Sea Scrolls offer a different view of things than Sirach and the New Testament. For example, in an essay on the discourses on demons in the Dead Sea Scrolls, Loren Stuckenbruck writes that the people of God at the time

The Church as a Healing Community   139

believed that afflictions, illnesses, and human sins could be effectively dealt with by various forms of piety, such as exorcism, prayer, and recitation of hymns.[17] Furthermore, Ida Fröhlich points out that most of the Qumran texts mention demons and reflect a relative dualism in which God has power over all of the demons. She shows how the book of I Enoch created a myth of the origin of evil and evil represented by evil demons, and how Jubilees absorbed various types of demons from the ancient Near Eastern tradition, originating from the fallen angels according to the Enochic tradition.[18] This indicates that before the arrival of Jesus on earth, a whole structure of demonology had been developed. However, Jesus did not follow this concept of demonology, and in fact, he did not endorse it.

The fact that Jesus omitted all these speculations and exaggerations in his ministry needs to be considered. Jesus only linked three cases of illness to demons (Mark 5:1–20; Matt 17:14–22; Luke 13:10–17). This suggests the possibility that some illnesses may originate from demons. But this was not the focus. The apostles, especially Peter and Paul, did not link illness with demons. The description of illness in the New Testament, apart from the three mentioned, is invariably that of common diseases or congenital physical impairments.

Concluding Remarks

From this perspective, therefore, pastors, prayer camp leaders, and Christian leaders in Africa need to consider the availability of modern technologies and knowledge and capabilities of physicians and hospitals. This does not eradicate the power of God through prayers. Rather, there should be collaboration. The research of Arias, Tylor, Ofori-Atta, and Bradley on the prayer camps indicated that some prayer camps were sometimes using medicine to tame mental health patients who were very difficult to control and that they needed collaboration. At the same time, there is a point of conflict and a challenge posed with respect to the differences in beliefs about causation and the origins of diseases and endorsed treatment practices. While the biomedical providers' interest was in reforming prayer camp conditions to handle complicated cases, this was not a priority for prayer camp leadership.[19]

The differences that exist concerning the very fundamental issue of the etiology of mental health illnesses and endorsed treatment practices from the biomedical sciences present one of the greatest challenges to the realisation of the church as a healing community as far as mental health is concerned. This is all the more concerning given how much mental health and unresolved health

---

[17] Loren Stuckenbruck, "The Demonic World of the Dead Sea Scrolls," in Ida Fröhlich and Erkki Koskonniemi, eds., *Evil and the Devil* (Crescent City: Bloomsbury, 2013), 51–70.

[18] Ida Fröhlich, "Evil and Second Temple Texts," in *Evil and the Devil*, 23–50.

[19] Arias, Taylor, Ofori-Atta, and Bradley, "Prayer Camps and Biomedical Care in Ghana," 12–14.

conditions continue to be under-appreciated as a major public health issue among the general population in the churches in Ghana.

Beyond that, I may also wish to redirect the attention of some African Christians towards a holistic ministry that seems lacking in so many areas of the church's life and practice. Jesus told his disciples, "Do not rejoice that the demons submit to you but rejoice that your names are written in heaven" (Luke 10:17). Thus, healing, deliverance from sin, or transformation of a sinner are absolutely important. Whatever we make of physical bodily healing, which is often needed, the body remains fragile until death swallows it up. Ultimately, it is resurrection hope that should be the focus of every Christian, even as he or she prays for healing or deliverance from bodily harm and psychological pain.

Consequently, the church needs to be reminded of the great potential God has given to serve the people. The Church has networks and is spread out in almost every community. The churches can help by mobilising their congregations and educating them in understanding the role of prayer and medicine. The church should collaborate with the health systems to improve the conditions in the prayer camps and employ the services of medical professionals to assist them in their operations. Thus, the ancient concept of prayer and medicine as cooperative enterprises needs to be seriously considered.

Pentecostal Glocal Ethics

Hanna Larracas

Introduction

As the first recipient of the Younghoon Lee Global Leadership Scholarship at Oral Roberts University, I am privileged to honour Dr. Younghoon Lee with this study. This research begins by defining glocalisation as it remains distinct from the process of globalisation. The definition of glocalisation is then applied to a brief overview of glocalisation within Pentecostalism's emergence and expansion. What follows is the task of resourcing Pentecostal theology to construct the framework and notion of glocal ethics situated within the Pentecostal imaginary. I suggest that the vision of Pentecostal adherents as glocal citizens, hence warranting the framework of Pentecostal glocal ethics, serves as a reflective and constructive framework in which to develop pneumatological ethics, especially in response to novel challenges to both the indigenisation and global expansion of the Pentecostal movement.

This research coins the term "glocal ethics" for Pentecostal theology as a subset of social ethics, making the context to which ethical values respond and in which they are constructed more explicit. Glocal, as the nominal derivative of glocalisation, situates the context of ethics between the local and the global. In addition, "Pentecostal" as an adjectival designation further texturises these local and global contexts by recognising particular communities demonstrating explicit commitments to the presence and action of the Holy Spirit. At this time, the notion of glocal ethics is a relatively under-researched concept; I argue that this concept carries significant potential contributions to Pentecostal social ethics in a glocalisation world. Recent trends in Pentecostal theology explore the implications of Pentecostal theological commitments for the political landscape, encompassing ethnic and religious relations and identities, demonstrated by Pentecostals in Indonesia, and sectarianism, demonstrated by Pentecostals in the United States in light of growing political polarisation.[1] In addition to providing a constructive framework for navigating a glocalising world, Pentecostal glocal ethics has the capacity to reflect current trends in the burgeoning discipline of Pentecostal political theology, attempting to grapple with the deleterious effects of Pentecostal theology and communities interfacing with the political landscape around the world.

---

[1] Steven M. Studebaker, "The Promise of American Pentecostal Political Theologies," *Pneuma* 44:3–4 (December 2022), 3–4.

Defining Glocalisation and Demonstrating
Glocalisation in Pentecostalism

This section explores how glocalisation emerged in the social sciences and how the term describes phenomena within the discipline. Sociologist Roland Robertson, upon introducing the term glocalisation into the English language from its original Japanese context, contends that the term captures particularising and universalising tendencies, reflecting important processes unfolding in the world and impacting the human experience.[2] In other words, global forces adapt in light of their local contexts. In glocalising, global processes that indigenise according to the local spaces in which they emerge demonstrate diversity (the formation of localised expressions) that remains tethered together (united through belonging to a global process). This stands in contrast with globalisation, which Robertson considers compresses the world, where horizons are shrinking between communities and cultures; for instance, through transportation and media.[3] Roudometof further reflects on this notion of globalisation and summarises that "globalization is about speed, and speed involves both spatial and temporal shifts."[4]

In providing an overview of the discourse around defining globalisation, Scheuerman identifies key foundational themes for a concept that otherwise lacks concrete consensus and remains subject to further nuance and definition.[5] He contends that in the most basic sense, globalisation corresponds with deterritorialisation, where "social activities take place irrespective of geographical location of participants."[6] Globalisation reflects how human activities, including ideas and experiences, are facilitated across territories with significant shifts in their temporal structures. The contours of social existence, shaped by spatial and temporal categories, are transformed through globalisation, albeit in varying ways and degrees. In the absence of a concrete consensus around globalisation, some scholars, such as Beyers, make the boundaries between globalisation and glocalisation porous and utilise both terms with a degree of interchangeability. However, I contest that texturising distinctions between these two terms, rather than conflating, is an effective tool for research.[7]

---

[2] Roland Robertson, "Glocalization: Time-Space and Homogeneity-Heterogeneity," in Mike Featherstone, Scott Lash, and Roland Robertson, eds., *Global Modernities* (London: SAGE Publications, 1997), 25.

[3] Victor Roudometof, "Glocal Religions: An Introduction," *Religions* 9:294 (2018), 10.

[4] Roudometof, "Glocal Religions," 10.

[5] William Scheuerman, "Globalization," in Edward N. Zalta and Uri Nodelman, eds., *The Standford Encyclopedia of Philosophy*, accessed 11 March 2023, https://plato.stanford.edu/archives/spr2023/entries/globalization/.

[6] Scheuerman, "Globalization."

[7] Peter Beyer, "Globalization and Glocalization," in James A. Beckford and Jay Demerath III, eds., *The SAGE Handbook of the Sociology of Religion* (Los Angeles: Sage, 2007), 98.

Pentecostal Glocal Ethics   143

After briefly presenting glocalisation within sociology, this section turns to Pentecostal scholarship to evaluate how the Pentecostal movement embodies glocalisation. Pentecostal scholars within the nexus of history and theology have grappled with the Pentecostal movement, which is identified as the "fastest-growing religious movement in the contemporary world."[8] Allan Anderson recognises Pentecostalism's explosive growth in the twentieth century, crediting the movement as a "missionary, polycentric, transnational religion."[9] Accounts of Pentecostalism's history at the beginning of the twentieth century demonstrate glocalising processes inherent to the movement. Blumhofer recognises the multiplicity of localities worldwide that facilitated revivals, recognising Azusa Street as "one of multiple sources of contemporary Pentecostalism."[10] Historians investigating early Pentecostalism recognise that "pentecostalism arose from multiple pockets of revival," which took on important elements of the culture surrounding the revivals.[11] Vondey concisely conveys the glocal nature of Pentecostalism. No notion of Pentecostalism as a monolithic entity exists. Rather, the Pentecostal movement unfolds and expands through "local roots or localized representations of what we term 'Pentecostal.'"[12]

Anderson's research into the origins of Pentecostalism recognises the movement's inherently plural and global character.[13] Due to the plurality of expressions of Pentecostalism within diverse communities worldwide, Anderson gives caution to attempts to define globalising processes undergirding Pentecostalism. He urges that "Pentecostalism's localness makes any attempt to understand the dynamics of its globalisation a hazardous exercise."[14] Jacobsen reflects this sentiment around the plurality of Pentecostalism; "there is no meta-model of Pentecostalism – no essence of Pentecostalism or normative archetype."[15] The particularity of Pentecostalism's expressions must exist in relationship with the movement's global features. For example, Anderson's account of Pentecostalism's emergence highlights the impact of transnational independent churches outside of North America on the movement.[16] The commitment to mission and evangelism, both of which can function as glocalising processes, latent within these communities contributed to Pentecostalism's widespread growth on a global scale.[17]

---

[8] Allan Heaton Anderson, *An Introduction to Pentecostalism: Global Charismatic Christianity*, 2nd ed. (Cambridge: Cambridge University Press, 2014), 1.

[9] Anderson, *An Introduction*, 1.

[10] Edith L. Blumhofer, "Revisiting the Azusa Street Blunder," *International Bulletin of Missionary Research* 30:2 (April 2006), 59.

[11] Joe Creech, "Visions of Glory: The Place of Azusa Street Revival in Pentecostal History," *Church History* 65:3 (September 1996), 406.

[12] Wolfgang Vondey, *Pentecostalism: A Guide for the Perplexed* (London: Bloomsbury, 2013), 25.

[13] Anderson, *An Introduction*, 1.

[14] Anderson, *An Introduction*, 5.

[15] Anderson, *An Introduction*, 5.

[16] Anderson, *An Introduction*, 37.

[17] Anderson, *An Introduction*, 37.

Attempting to provide a non-reductionist account of why Spirit-filled independent churches proliferated across the Global South, Anderson writes that these ecclesial communities emphasised the "proclamation of a message addressing communities' tangible needs, as a local response to the Bible."[18] Independent churches empower local communities to incarnate Scripture, Christ's life, and the Holy Spirit in contexts that affirm unique particularity. In other words, Pentecostalism has the capacity to pay attention to the granular and particular needs of communities, as indicated in the early phases of the movement's inception. [19] These dynamics demonstrate the simultaneity of embodied and spiritual realities within the Pentecostal worldview.

How can Pentecostalism be defined so that the definition does not misrepresent the phenomenon? Invoking Robert Mapes's definition, Anderson considers the term Pentecostalism to comprise of churches and movements that emphasise an "ecstatic *experience of the Spirit* and a tangible *practice of spiritual gifts.*"[20] This section contends that glocalisation unfolding within the Pentecostal movement functions as a site of reflection that can inform theological reflection for Pentecostal communities. After identifying these observations, what implications can be drawn from how the Holy Spirit is present in the world? What implications can inform how Pentecostals can best be present in the world? I posit that the discipline of social ethics is most adequately equipped to reflect on these questions meaningfully.

Ethical Methodology

This section explores Wariboko's ethical methodology as the prescribed methodology capable of bridging the gap between the observations of the reality of the Holy Spirit's presence globally and in local communities and what normative claims can be derived for Pentecostal communities to partner with God's work. Wariboko's work on ethical methodology originally extends to public theology, arguing that theology should not remain isolated within a community. He posits that theology has both the capacity and responsibility to inform and be informed by various contexts and communities.[21] While this current exploration into glocal ethics falls short of developing an outright public policy, the ethical methodology Wariboko sets provides parameters for translating or expressing Pentecostal commitments into a deeply interpersonal public context. This ethical methodology participates in constructing an ethical framework informed by theological commitments as well as a community's socio-cultural context and how God is present in both a community and their commitments.

---

[18] Anderson, *An Introduction*, 38.

[19] Anderson, *An Introduction*, 40.

[20] Anderson, *An Introduction*, 8. Italics are the author's.

[21] Nimi Wariboko, "Ethical Methodology: Between Public Theology and Public Policy," *Journal of Religions and Business Ethics* 1:1 (2010), 1.

Pentecostal Glocal Ethics   145

Wariboko presents ethics as concerned with "the determination of the proper ends, *teleoi*, of any human form of sociality," and is defined as "a process that unlocks the power of truth, justice, and harmony embodied in any form of human sociality."[22] Ethics is also creative, as this process participates in imagining orders and realities beyond what orders and realities currently exist. With reference to the work of ethics, Wariboko adds that faith in God invites Christians to the task of pursuing "something greater or better in the horizon and to always press on to it."[23] Ethics participates in the process of imagining new futures.

Wariboko demonstrates a pneumatologically leaning vision of "theological-ethical reasoning," which resources "creative principles at work in human coexistence and the larger cosmos" that "can be harnessed for human flourishing."[24] Pentecostalism recognises the Holy Spirit as the creative principle working within humanity and creation; in other words, the foundation for constructing ethical frameworks in pursuit of human flourishing, embodying truth, justice, and harmony in the community. In the context of Wariboko's ethical methodology, the Spirit-empowered ethical imagination for Pentecostals is oriented toward a "critical and constructive investigation of a social problem."[25] Problems identified are those which obscure God's promises, in terms of flourishing, for a community. Both the problem and solution are framed in relation to what a community considers to be the ultimate point of reference, this reference being God for Pentecostals.[26]

The partnering of the ethical imagination with an orientation towards theological frameworks, specifically Pentecostal theological frameworks, invokes the process of theological-ethical reasoning. Theological-ethical reasoning is

> a search for God and how God is revealed in humanity and in the struggles for human flourishing. Basically, to undertake theological ethics is to search for God in the midst of history and to relate a community's understanding of the nature of ultimate reality and its derived truth to the logic and dynamics of human sociality.[27]

Pentecostals participate in theological-ethical reasoning in searching for God's revelation in humanity and in humanity's pursuit of flourishing. The description of theological-ethical reasoning above can be succinctly summarised in the following three movements of Wariboko's ethical methodology.

a. Analysis of the problem
b. Relating the problem to the ultimate concern, ultimate reality, of the community
c. Offer suggestions for solutions that will strengthen the moral fabric of the community and move it closer to the principles of its ultimate concern.[28]

---

[22] Wariboko, "Ethical Methodology," 2.
[23] Wariboko, "Ethical Methodology," 6.
[24] Wariboko, "Ethical Methodology," 3.
[25] Wariboko, "Ethical Methodology," 5.
[26] Wariboko, "Ethical Methodology," 5.
[27] Wariboko, "Ethical Methodology," 5.
[28] Wariboko, "Ethical Methodology," 4.

After demonstrating Wariboko's ethical methodology as the prescribed methodology for first reflecting on glocalisation in Pentecostalism and subsequently constructing inroads to glocal ethics, this research progresses by analysing problems emerging within Pentecostalism's glocalisation. In other words, given the reality of glocalisation within the Pentecostal movement, what ethical challenges have emerged for Pentecostal communities?

Emerging Problems in Pentecostalism's Glocalisation

Although Pentecostalism emerged as a Spirit-filled polycentric movement that sought to respond to the needs of its local communities, Pentecostal scholarship identifies problematic themes of disconnection within the movement, specifically the disconnection of spiritual realities from material realities and consideration of localities apart from the global. These themes of disconnection deviate from the strengths showcased in Pentecostalism's glocalisation. Therefore, this research turns to Pentecostal political theology in two regions, the United States and Indonesia, as contexts to explore both issues of disconnection in glocalisation and to explore the possibilities of constructing Pentecostal glocal ethics. Both tasks of analysing problems and offering solutions in response to the analysed problems correspond with Wariboko's ethical methodology, and the latter work of constructing glocal ethics through theological-ethical reasoning will be taken up in a later section of the research.

Within Indonesian Pentecostalism, Soesilo reflects on the disconnection between the spiritual and the material for Indonesian Pentecostals, which is demonstrated by their hesitance to explore how theology can extend to public affairs.[29] Moreover, glocalisation is apparent in Indonesia due to the multi-religious and multi-ethnic identity expressions present within the country.[30] Soesilo examines how the current expression of theology remains limited to "dealing with spiritual matters and personal holiness," which is reflected in their eschatological commitments, culminating in millennial and apocalyptic views.[31] Emphasising the role of individual conversion to alleviate social problems demonstrates the lack of credence given to the impact of social structures towards social problems. These commitments are expressed in how Indonesian Pentecostals envision missions as limited to "winning the souls and personal repentance."[32] Soesilo observes the bifurcation of salvation into spiritual and material expressions, where evangelism and conversion are seen to compete with participating in social transformation and socio-political engagement. It is the case, then, that the multi-ethnic and religiously diverse landscape does not significantly influence expressions of Pentecostal commitments. While

---

[29] Yushak Soesilo, "From Mission to Doxology," *Journal of Pentecostal Theology* 31 (2022), 280.

[30] Soesilo, "From Mission to Doxology," 279.

[31] Soesilo, "From Mission to Doxology," 280.

[32] Soesilo, "From Mission to Doxology," 280.

Pentecostal Glocal Ethics   147

glocalisation affects the ethnic and religious diversity of Indonesia, this reality is not integrated into Pentecostalism's theology and practice. Whereas missions are believed to be empowered by the Holy Spirit, it is not the case that the Holy Spirit is believed to empower participation in social transformation and socio-political engagement. Soesilo's observation identifies these themes of disconnection.

> The sharp separation between the spiritual and the physical, of course, feels odd to the nature of the pneumatology work as the foundation of Pentecostal theology. On the one hand, Pentecostals believe that the Holy Spirit is an entity that works dynamically, but in praxis, the work of the Holy Spirit is to be understood as limited, namely, only working within the scope of ecclesiastical ministry.[33]

In other words, Pentecostal praxis strongly contrasts the theological foundations of Pentecostalism that contain the capacity for transformation in a physical and material sense. Along the lines of Soesilo's observations, glocal ethics, as this research seeks to construct in a later section, will aim to reflect the emerging task of Pentecostal political theology, which inquires how the theological dynamism of the Holy Spirit can be reflected or become reconnected with Pentecostal praxis more comprehensively within the context of communities.

Moving on to the context of the United States, Studebaker reflects on contemporary culture wars and political strife unfolding in the United States and identifies the absence of a particular Pentecostal political theology, cautioning that "if Pentecostals do not consider and discern the implications of their experience of the Holy Spirit for their lives, they run the danger of political capture and manipulation by public leaders."[34] The highlighted issues for Pentecostalism in the United States are apparent in both the disconnection of the spiritual from the material and the disconnection of the local from the global. For instance, the identified culture wars perhaps reflect sectarian attitudes of disconnection from the broader Pentecostal community worldwide. The widespread acceptance of the prosperity gospel is also indicative of wider systemic issues within Pentecostalism, where Pentecostalism is ill-equipped to respond to structures of oppression in the community.[35]

At the beginning of the twentieth century, classical Pentecostalism in the United States demonstrated a lack of distinctive qualities, besides initial evidence of Spirit baptism identified in speaking in tongues, that adequately separated classical Pentecostal commitments from those of early twentieth-century conservative Evangelicals embodying Christian Fundamentalism.[36] Pentecostal eschatology, borrowed from conservative Evangelicalism, withheld empowerment from Pentecostals to address injustice operative in social realities.[37] Studebaker writes, "Pentecostal eschatology offers little to no

---

[33] Soesilo, "From Mission to Doxology," 280.

[34] Studebaker, "The Promise of American Pentecostal Political Theologies," 327–28.

[35] Studebaker, "The Promise," 334.

[36] Studebaker, "The Promise," 329.

[37] Studebaker, "The Promise," 329.

foundation for engaging in the world of politics. It regards the world outside the church and Christian spirituality as a distraction at best and as sinful and satanic at worst."[38] The other-worldly orientation of Pentecostal spirituality, where the Christian life goal is oriented towards heaven and "life on earth is a short-term pilgrimage," according to Studebaker, disincentivises the formation of a Pentecostal political theology.[39] Studebaker gives reasons for the apolitical temperament of Pentecostals. Pentecostals prioritised defining doctrines of Spirit baptism, including glossolalia and gifts of the spirit, and a dispensational eschatology. Pentecostals were also excluded from mainstream and Mainline Evangelical and Protestant communities during their formal arrival on the religious scene.[40]

Beginning in the 1980s, Pentecostals have increasingly become affiliated with conservativism and the Christian Right.[41] This trend has continued, even intensified, into the present political environment when observing the turnout of Pentecostal support for Trump, even if out of a resistance to an ideology Pentecostals disagree with, believing Trump will "halt the progress of the progressive Left and even win some battles in the culture wars."[42] Noticing this shift in attitude towards engagement with the political, Studebaker noted how the Pentecostal support of the Moral Majority and later conservative Christian Right groups and movements is a departure from previous Pentecostal attitudes towards political engagements."[43]

Similar to Soesilo's observations of Pentecostalism in an Indonesian context, Studebaker's reflection on Pentecostalism in the United States identifies a strong disconnect between the latent implications for political activity within Pentecostal eschatology and spirituality (or what a political theology for Pentecostals could be) and the absence of political praxis in Pentecostal communities.[44] In addition, an underdeveloped Pentecostal political theology is affected by a low theology of creation, which emphasises the sinfulness and evil of the material world, claiming that Satan rules the domain of the earth. A negative view of the world as sinful, while considering the Kingdom of God and the spirituality life of the community as incommensurate, deprioritized the reflection and construction of pneumatologically informed Pentecostal political theology. This attitude creates disconnections between the spiritual and the material, and the local from the global.

---

[38] Studebaker, "The Promise," 329.

[39] Studebaker, "The Promise," 330.

[40] Studebaker, "The Promise," 337.

[41] Studebaker, "The Promise," 337.

[42] Studebaker, "The Promise," 340.

[43] Studebaker, "The Promise," 338.

[44] Studebaker, "The Promise," 330.

Glocal Ethics as an Ethical Paradigm

The following questions arise, as this paper's task is to think ethically about glocalisation. Why is thinking ethically about glocalisation important? What are the concerns, and what is at stake if we don't think ethically about glocalisation? What seems to be at stake is perhaps the failure to recognise the Holy Spirit's presence and action in other communities, or even within one's own community, as indicated in scenarios presented in the United States and Indonesia, in ways that can inspire creating spaciousness within a particular community to engage with that which is unfamiliar. Or perhaps the failure to recognise the capacity for expressions of Pentecostalism and practices that resonate with and are informed by culture. In addition, the other extreme is intense sectarianism, which reflects, to a degree, the culture wars which Pentecostalism in the US is experiencing. The framework that glocal ethics aims to facilitate is the task of reconnecting the spiritual with the material and the local with the global as commensurate contexts and realities for Pentecostal theology.

Pentecostal glocal ethics, as a framework, brings to the forefront of theological-ethical reasoning the importance of navigating diverse operative contexts for reflecting and acting both ethically and theologically. Engaging political theology in a discussion of glocal ethics is reasonable given that political theology is concerned with factors that affect how Pentecostals participate in public spaces. This participation by Pentecostals ultimately shapes values that contribute to the common good. Glocal ethics reflects current trends in Pentecostal political theology, navigating Pentecostalism as a glocalising movement.

Another consideration is raised regarding the necessity of glocal ethics if the framework is a rehearsal of affirming multiculturalism. Is this task necessarily an ethical exploration, though, if what will come of glocal ethics is an affirmation of multiculturalism? To this end, glocal ethics can facilitate more than affirming multiculturalism. It is a recognition of the reality of particularity and difference in community brought into an explicitly Pentecostal theological reflection. Glocal ethics as an ethical paradigm and framework recognises that Pentecostals remain tethered to a locality with particularities while at the same time belonging to a broader Spirit-empowered network and movement.

Soesilo demonstrates glocal ethical reasoning when reflecting on the capacity of Isaiah 41:1–9 to function as a programmatic text to inform Pentecostal political theology for Indonesian Pentecostals. [45] Contrary to Indonesian Pentecostal beliefs around mission and socio-political engagement, the Holy Spirit equally empowers both works. Soesilo resources Scripture in challenging the perspective of placing socio-political engagement as secondary to mission or viewing socio-political engagements as tasks that ultimately serve the work of missions. Activities comprising socio-political engagement are regarded as co-equal in importance with missions traditionally understood as concerned with evangelism and salvation.

---

[45] Soesilo, "From Mission to Doxology," 290.

How might glocal ethics respond to issues raised regarding Pentecostal eschatology, which disconnects the spiritual from the material? The foundations of constructing glocal Pentecostal political theology are recognised when reflecting on embodied expressions of Pentecostalism, including expectations for the Holy Spirit to transform the lives of adherents in the present.[46] "The Holy Spirit renews embodied life in all its dimensions and, therefore, political implications are intrinsic to Pentecostal renewal." [47] Scripture reflects the movement of God as one that draws close to humanity and that God comes to creation.[48] The theological significance of Christ coming to the world and the Spirit coming to the world affirms the significance of both the spiritual and the material. Pentecost descended upon humanity rather than bringing humans out of the world and bringing people out of their communities.

This world- and human-ward move responds to sectarian attitudes upheld by Pentecostals, for example, those in the United States, by affirming that the same Holy Spirit present in their personal lives and communities facilitates grace in wildly disparate Pentecostal communities in cultures elsewhere. Studebaker demonstrates the capacity for glocal ethics to construct a Pentecostal political theology by referencing how Pentecostal communities outside of the United States (via Miller's and Yamamori's research) can influence the theologies and practice of Pentecostalism in the United States.[49] As no one singular vision of Pentecostalism exists, no monolithic vision of Pentecostal political theology can exist. The inroads of glocal ethics into political theology is evidenced when recognising that the diversity of Pentecostal identities and expressions warrants a diversity of possible and potential political theologies. [50] Recognising the diversity of expressions and practices of Pentecostalism as a glocal enterprise keeps in mind that various practices of Pentecostalism in other localities are equally "Pentecostal" expressions as are other iterations of Pentecostalism that feel more familiar.

Glocal ethics is a viable framework for the Pentecostals in the United States, in that observing the work and presence of Pentecostalism in other cultures and communities would inform Pentecostal practices in the US. Glocal ethics is a viable framework for Indonesian Pentecostals attempting to navigate the confluence of various ethnic identities and religious communities within a national border, to which the Pentecostal community can best respond by expanding what the community considers as Spirit-empowered work. It is apparent that the promises of glocalisation are not without their dangers, as demonstrated earlier in this research. However, at the same time, glocal realities function as strengths for Pentecostalism with regard to shaping ethical life.

---

[46] Studebaker, "The Promise of American Pentecostal Political Theologies," 330.

[47] Studebaker, "The Promise," 333.

[48] Studebaker, "The Promise," 334.

[49] Studebaker, "The Promise," 330.

[50] Studebaker, "The Promise," 328.

Community Engagement After Pentecost:
Apostolic Forays Then and Now

Amos Yong

I begin with a few introductory comments about the title of this chapter.[1] The *community engagement* at the beginning relates to what I understand to be central to the Whitelands seminar initiative. The notion of "after Pentecost" has been foregrounded especially in my more recent work, as those familiar with such will recognise.[2] While it is known that I have been doing work as a theologian in the pentecostal tradition or movement for most of my theological career,[3] in the last decade or so, this "after Pentecost" theme has emerged to the forefront. As should be clear to theological students, especially, Pentecost belongs not to any particular group or movement, not even those who are part of the pentecostal community. Rather, it is a New Testament event, recorded in Luke's book of Acts and, in that respect, belongs to the entire Christian *oecumene*. So, even as I do not apologise for my reflections as a pentecostal theologian, I bid all of us, those within pentecostal communities and churches, or otherwise included in the wider body of Jesus Christ, to consider how Pentecost – or the Pentecost narrative, or the arc of the Pentecost event and its aftermath – may have implications for all Christian practice, discipleship, and theologising. In that sense, our focus here is to consider community engagement in this "after Pentecost" mode.

And that also leads us to the subtitle of this essay. As we know, the Pentecost event in the book of Acts is at the beginning of Luke's account of the apostolic

---

[1] Thanks for how this essay emerged is due in three directions: first, to the volume editors for inviting my contribution to this book; second, to Caroline Polly Ueriraisa Tjihenuna, the Dean's Fellow for the College of Theology & Ministry at Oral Roberts University, for help with transcription of the audio recording of a Zoom-mediated lecture I prepared for the Whitelands Centre for Pentecostalism and Community Engagement at the University of Roehampton, presented 5 June 2023; and third to Prof. Richard Burgess at the Whitelands Centre for inviting my talk and to Prof. David Clark for facilitating the recording. I have further edited the transcribed version, retained some (not all) of the oral elements, and added especially notes and references (with a bit of an embarrassed forewarning needed here about the many self-references included). I take responsibility, however, for all errors of fact or interpretation.

[2] E.g., Amos Yong, *Mission after Pentecost: The Witness of the Spirit from Genesis to Revelation*, Mission in Global Community (Grand Rapids: Baker Academic, 2019) and *Renewing the Church by the Spirit: Theological Education after Pentecost*, Theological Education Between the Times series (Grand Rapids: Eerdmans, 2020).

[3] Here, as elsewhere in my writings, I do not capitalise *pentecostal* when used adjectivally, only when in titles or with reference to proper nouns.

experience and the early Christian and messianic movement. Hence, we look at this notion of community engagement through this apostolic lens in the Third Evangelist's sequel to his Gospel account and then explore and inquire about the implications of specific readings of this narrative after (the Day of) Pentecost for this task, both in terms of the apostolic experience of such and then also in terms of our own engagements with our communities today.[4]

Before we begin, however, let me add a paragraph that connects the original form of this essay to the purposes of this Festschrift by recognising the achievements of its honoree, Rev. Dr. Younghoon Lee. It is indeed remarkable that here we have a leading pentecostal scholar-practitioner, one who has emerged at the vanguard of a maturing Korean pentecostal academy on the one hand,[5] and yet also who has had the responsibility of being the chief shepherd of both Yoido Full Gospel Church and of the Assemblies of God of South Korea on the other hand. And with regard to the thematic focus of this essay, it is particularly important to recognise how Yoido Full Gospel Church, beginning with Lee's predecessor but continued since under Lee's guidance, has also been exemplary as a pentecostal ecclesial community in engaging with the broader society, impacting its local communities, and having a public witness and impact.[6] In these various respects, consider the following reflections, inspired in

---

[4] As we shall see, my own approach is less on apostolicity as understood in its traditional historical and ecclesiological senses than a hermeneutical one, wherein the adjectival *apostolic* points to attempts to retrieve the New Testament more generally and the book of Acts more specifically for contemporary theological purposes; see, for instance, other essays of mine adopting similar interpretive strategies for present endeavours such as Yong, "Jubilee, Liberation, and Pentecost: The Preferential Option of the Poor on the Apostolic Way," in Elise Mae Cannon and Andrea Smith, eds., *Evangelical Theologies of Liberation* (Downers Grove: IVP Academic, 2019), 306–24 and "Understanding and Living the Apostolic Way: Oral Culturality and Hermeneutics after Pentecost," in Raphael Madu, Marco Moerschbaher, and Augustine Asogwa, eds., *International Conference on the Catholic Church and Pentecostalism: Challenges in the Nigerian Context – Proceedings, Presentations and Final Report* (Abuja, Nigeria: Catholic Secretariat of Nigeria, 2016), 87–103.

[5] I know only of Dr. Lee's English-language academic works, e.g., Younghoon Lee, *The Holy Spirit Movement in Korea: Its Historical and Theological Development* (London: Regnum, 2009) and Younghoon Lee, Wonsuk Ma, and Kuewon Lee, eds., *Pentecostal Mission and Global Christianity: An Edinburgh Centenary Reader* (Oxford: Regnum, 2012).

[6] I discuss some of these developments and contributions in my articles, "Glocalization and the Gift-Giving Spirit: Informality and Shalom beyond the Political Economy of Exchange," *Journal of Youngsan Theology* 25 (2012), 7–29 and "Salvation, Society, and the Spirit: Pentecostal Contextualization and Political Theology from Cleveland to Birmingham, from Springfield to Seoul," *Pax Pneuma: The Journal of Pentecostals & Charismatics for Peace & Justice* 5:2 (2009), 22–34, reprinted in Mun Hong Choi, ed., *The Spirituality of Fourth Dimension and Social Salvation: Studies on Dr. Yonggi Cho's Theology*, Journal of Youngsan Theology Supplement Series 1 (Gunpo, S. Korea:

Community Engagement After Pentecost

part by Yoido's role in inviting and urging pentecostal churches around the world to open up to their communities. Perhaps also in the process, our discussion might further inspire such efforts both theologically and on the ground wherever pentecostal disciples and churches meet and serve with others.

From Faith-Rooted Community Organising to Faith-Rooted Community Engagement

I will start by introducing us to a work that needs to get more attention globally, which is a book by two colleagues: Alexia Salvatierra, who is a professor of Global Transformation and Missional Engagement at Fuller Seminary, and a mutual friend, Dr. Peter Heltzel. I like to highlight a few elements that I have gleaned from my reading of their *Faith-Rooted Organizing: Mobilizing the Church in Service of the World*, especially how they commend faith-rooted community organising.[7] Salvatierra has spent many decades working as a practical theologian and community organiser, and Heltzel has long been a theological advocate for marginalised communities.[8] Here are some basic interlocking and interrelated principles they present that those wanting to engage in/with and organise a community from a faith-rooted perspective should consider.

They urge us first to ask, what kind of goals we are looking for on the other side of whatever community organising we might be envisioning? Then, we need to assess the initiative in light of those objectives; for instance, where do we start? What are the obstacles? What are the resources at our disposal? These considerations involve the situation of the community that we want to organise, mobilise, or engage with, as well as our own situatedness *vis-à-vis* that community. Third, then, includes developing some strategic pathways into and within that community. How do we get from "here" to "there," particularly in light of our goals, the present situation, and the existing set of circumstances? Fourth, recruitment. How do we galvanise the body of Christ in particular, but maybe also adjacent groups or persons, to achieve whatever community-organisational goals we might be committed to?

But the focus of Salvatierra and Heltzel is on the body of Christ in any particular community. How do we motivate, recruit, and then empower disciples of Jesus to serve their community and to achieve strategic purposes? And any notion of empowering the body of Christ involves developing and orientating leaders, equipping and enabling the analysis, implementation and adjustment of the strategy toward those goals, and mobilising resources. The process sometimes includes a launching of the organisational endeavour and then

---

Hansei University Press, 2012), 163–88.

[7] Alexia Salvatierra and Peter G. Heltzel, *Faith Rooted Organizing: Mobilizing the Church in Service of the World* (Downers Grove: IVP, 2014).

[8] I write about and reflect on my personal experiences with the advocacy dimension of Peter's work in my article, "Liberating and Diversifying Theological Education: A Subversive or Empowering Aspiration?" *CrossCurrents* 69:1 (2019), 10–17.

reiterative assessment – interaction that may require adjustments in all kinds of respects, maybe even adjustments of some of the goals. In being attentive to the process of community organisation itself, we need to be flexible rather than rigid with our aspirations, since some challenges that might come up in the meanwhile may be of the sort that call for and even require redirection.[9]

Finally, Salvatierra and Heltzel name the sustainability indices of this community-organisational initiative, particularly as they relate to the specifics of the set or types of interfaces anticipated. How are leaders flourishing or thriving – being sustained – through this process? Then and also, how are "followers," those doing the work of community organisation, doing? How is the community collectively and in its various parts responding to the witness of the body of Christ, and how is the ecclesial community and the wider social and public community thriving in the short, mid-, and longer-term? So again, depending on the community's organisational goals and its time frames – e.g., is this a one-year, two-year, or three-year project? – and as we are being attentive to the developments, resourcing the leaders, and empowering the members, how do we ensure the initiative is flourishing and thriving? Is what is envisioned sustainable? This should be an ongoing question, in the shorter, mid-, and longer terms. As such, any community-organisational strategy has to be reiterative.[10] Some of the goals may be revised as we go forward. That leads to differentiated ongoing assessment, and then maybe further adjustments of strategies. As we know, the vagaries of life intrude; e.g., members of the community come and go, and others join in the initiative. But how do we maintain a certain degree of stability from a leadership perspective and advance this vision and strategy in a sustainable and more-or-less coherent manner?

Salvatierra and Heltzel invite us to consider, and then participate in and contribute to, community organising initiatives from a Christian or a faith-rooted perspective. Our focus on community engagement maps onto their community organising proposals and both parallels and also grows out of the latter. In other words, any community engagement enterprise seeks to accomplish some or other set of objectives in relationship to that community, and, in that respect, presumes and, at some point, has to enact, the sort of community-organising practices presented by our colleagues. Both community organisation and community engagement ultimately, in the broadest sense, are intended to foster Christian service in and to the wider world. Perhaps not every point I have summarised from their contribution will be relevant to diverse global and local contexts. And surely, every one will also need to be adapted when implemented in various sites.

---

[9] I expect that some if not most of these principles will be manifest and further exemplified in Salvatierra's more recent (collaborative) work, e.g., with Brad Christerson, Robert Chao Romero, and Nancy Wang Yuen, *God's Resistance: Mobilizing Faith to Defend Immigrants* (New York: New York University Press, 2023).

[10] In his earlier book devoted to articulating a practical theology addressing racism and poverty, Heltzel proposes an improvisational methodology that reappears as this flexible and dynamic praxis for *Faith Rooted Organizing*; see Peter Goodwin Heltzel, *Resurrection City: A Theology of Improvisation* (Grand Rapids: Eerdmans, 2012).

Community Engagement After Pentecost 155

Nevertheless, as an orientation to our search for a relevant theological praxis for community engagement, I begin with this helpful resource.

What Did/Would the Apostles Do?

Now, then, *What did or what would the apostles do?* That is our play on the popular slogan, WWJD (*What would Jesus do?*). I take us on a hermeneutical detour now from what we have just discussed before diving into the heart of the matter. I am keenly attuned to the possibility that some among us may presume a sharp contrast between what we might call *exegesis* and what we might call *eisegesis*. The former might be understood generally as how we hermeneutically and appropriately retrieve what the biblical text says, while the latter, less prominently in use but still present in at least some theological circles as a pejorative practice, involves less appropriate impositions brought by readers on the scriptural text. So, plainly said, for some of our hermeneutic seminars or hermeneutical schools, what is good *exegesis* is presumed to be readings controlled by the biblical authors, and what is not so good *eisegesis* is when we bring too many of our presuppositions or preferences and read them into the Bible.[11] Although I recognise these perspectives, I also think it is impossible to insist on too hard and fast of a distinction between the horizon of the biblical authors on the one hand and that of any contemporary generation of readers on the other hand.[12] Without saying, therefore, that we want to neglect completely what the text says, I also believe that any interpreter of Scripture involves various dynamic commitments. So, as a theologian, I approach Scripture with a set of emergent and provisional theological perspectives, one that presumes, in this two-horizons sense, that our present world and experiences of such and the past worlds of Scripture meet unpredictably in any act of reading. Hence, we cannot avoid bringing our assumptions, experiences, and present realities to the Scripture. Yet also, as we read Scripture, we wait on the Holy Spirit to bring that scriptural message to challenge and interrogate our present experiences and assumptions as well. There is the *then* horizon and the *now* horizon, and we always want to be careful both that we are not presuming too much about how our present horizon might construe the past horizon of Scripture, and yet, at the same time, we also realise that as embodied, situated, and historically informed creatures, none of us ever approaches the scriptural (or any other textual) horizon only and absolutely on its terms. What is at stake, then, is an ongoing navigation of these two horizons.[13]

---

[11] Some of the arguments in these directions are in D. A. Carson, *Exegetical Fallacies*, 2nd ed. (Grand Rapids: Baker Academic, 1996); attentive readers of Carson's text will discern I would not agree with all of his presuppositions.

[12] I go back here a generation ago to Anthony C. Thiselton, *The Two Horizons: New Testament Hermeneutics and Philosophical Description* (Grand Rapids: Eerdmans, 1980).

[13] My summary statement here is more elaborately articulated in chapter 1 of *Learning Theology: Tracking the Spirit of Christian Faith* (Louisville: Westminster John Knox

And in that respect, what I like to provide in the following is a pentecostal response, or an after-Pentecost perspective, where we revisit the apostolic witness, in part, although not necessarily only, for understanding the goals, assessment strategies, recruitment, leadership development, and sustainability elements that Salvatierra and Heltzel have asked us to consider. So, I want us to go back to the book of Acts and look at some of the passages there and ask ourselves whether or not some of these contemporary faith-rooted organisational notions that have been introduced for community engagement purposes may or may not be applicable or illuminative of our reading and understanding of the apostolic experience. What we are doing, then, is traversing the terrain between normative sets of theological and theoretical commitments – theologically as understood in the apostolic legacy and theoretically as informed by our community-organisational colleagues – and the ecclesial practices of actual community engagement. To navigate these two horizons, I want to look through five windows into the apostolic community-organising and engagement world. I realise mine is the perspective of a non-community organiser, meaning I have not had decades of experience in participating in community organisations, as have my colleagues. Yet, what I intend to do is conduct a thought experiment in which we revisit the apostolic narrative, or at least five snapshots of that account, from this community-engagement posture, and then observe how the readings might unfold.[14]

Window 1: Community Engagement after Pentecost (Acts 2:42–47)

Here we go. The first apostolic community emerged on the day of Pentecost. In a familiar passage, Acts 2:42–47, we observe the first interactions of these messianists with their community: "They devoted themselves to the apostles' teaching and fellowship, to the breaking of bread and the prayers. Awe came upon everyone, because the apostles were doing many wonders and signs. All who believed were together and had all things in common; they would sell their possessions and goods and distribute the proceeds to all, as any had need. Day by day, as they spent much time together in the temple, they broke bread at home and ate their food with glad and generous hearts, praising God and having the

---

Press, 2018): "Scripture: The Word and Breath of God," where I discuss the world behind the text, the world of the text, and the world in front of the text.

[14] Elsewhere I have attempted an identical hermeneutical strategy for constructive missiological and theological (respectively vis-à-vis the next two references) purposes, e.g., Amos Yong, "Apostolic Evangelism in the Postcolony: Opportunities and Challenges," *Mission Studies* 34:2 (2017), 147–67 and "The Spirit, the Common Good, and the Public Sphere: The 21st Century Public Intellectual in Apostolic Perspective," in Todd C. Ream, Jerry Pattengale, and Christopher J. Devers, eds., *Public Intellectuals and the Common Good: Christian Thinking for Human Flourishing* (Downers Grove: IVP Academic, 2021), 21–41. Those interested can consult and compare how this overall method might be performing when applied across various realms of theological praxis.

Community Engagement After Pentecost 157

goodwill of all the people. And day by day the Lord added to their number those who were being saved."[15]

A few things to highlight here from some of the community engagement tools we have been provided with. First, what was the nature of the community engagement? A number of the previously mentioned elements are at least phenomenologically observable, including, on the one hand, the selling of possessions and goods and then a redistribution of the proceeds to all. Now, the *all* refers to probably the community of 3,000 or so recorded as responding to Peter's day of Pentecost sermon (Acts 2:41). But the selling of possessions and goods would involve interfaces with the broader Jerusalem community, and it is within that wider geopolitical community that this fledgling apostolic group bubbled up.

Then, in verse 47, there is another intimation of the sort of blurring of the lines between this apostolic band and its surrounding community, where it says that "they spend much time together in the temple breaking bread at home, eating the food with glad and generous hearts," thus trafficking (maybe not the best word) and travelling between home and temple. Amidst this movement, members of this embryonic apostolic community were also "praising God and having the goodwill of all the people." The "goodwill of all the people" includes those of the surrounding community. So, it's this apostolic community of 3,000, living in these various homes around the temple community, that gains "the goodwill" and estimation of those in the wider public space. And the result Luke narrates is that: "day by day, the Lord added to the number of those who were being saved."[16]

So, goodwill was being fostered by the apostolic band, and that goodwill also produced additions to the community. Hence, we are not surprised when, between Acts chapter 2 and chapter 4, the number of 3,000 initially baptised had increased to about 5,000 (4:4). This window thus invites observation of a variety of community engagement forms "after Pentecost." Neither individually nor cumulatively does what we see in these early chapters of the book of Acts fit completely the criteria for understanding community organising and engagement that we saw in the Salvatierra and Heltzel volume. However, as we bring those insights into these passages, we can hopefully appreciate more deeply Luke's sketched account.

So, this is a case in which there are communal relationships, there is goodwill being generated, and there is movement – literal, economic, ideological, etc. – in

---

[15] These (and all later) scriptural passages are simply the transcriptions of the audio recording (even as my scriptural recitations relied on the New Revised Standard Version); I have not gone back to correct any misreadings and have retained instead the transcribed renditions.

[16] Biblical scholarship might be more focused on attempting to assess the historicity of the Lukan narrative but ours is first and foremost a theologically informed hermeneutical approach; see also the introductory chapter to Amos Yong, *The Hermeneutical Spirit: Theological Interpretation and the Scriptural Imagination for the 21st Century* (Eugene, OR: Cascade Books, 2017).

multiple directions. There is addition to and growth of the apostolic community. More importantly for our purposes, there is an openness of exchange, in terms both of the selling and buying of possessions and of the interactive space sharing between homes and temple, that facilitates the interpersonal give-and-take of apostolic disciples and those in the wider community.[17]

Window 2: Signs and Wonders in Community Engagement (Acts 3–4)

Another window, an extension of the first, comes in Acts 3 and 4, which begins with the day Peter and John were going up to the temple at the hour of prayer at three o'clock in the afternoon. For healing the lame man on the Sabbath, they were arrested and put in custody until the next day. Then, Luke records further encounters with the religious leaders and community leaders.

We read about one form of the early apostolic posture and approach to the wider community at the end of Acts 4: "They went to their friends and reported what the chief priest and elders had said to them when they heard it, they raised their voices together to God … And when they had prayed, the place in which they had gathered together was shaken, and they all filled with Holy Spirit and spoke the word of God with boldness" (4:24–25, 31).[18] The rest of the passage also records Peter and John saying to the religious leaders that if it was between being submissive to God and listening to the authorities, that they would be obedient to God instead (4:19–20). Their convictions were predicated in part on their allegiances: "For there's no other name under heaven by which human beings would be saved" (4:12).

It is in this context that I want us to consider the manifestation of healings, signs, and wonders (4:30) as part of this early apostolic community engagement experience.[19] This is replicated in Acts 5, when Peter's shadow was healing

---

[17] For more on especially the economic aspects of this nascent apostolic group's engagement with the broader community, see part 3 of Amos Yong, "Pentecostal Health and Wealth: A Theology of Economics," in Paul Oslington, Paul S. Williams, and Mary Hirschfeld, eds., *Recent Developments in the Economics of Religion*, The International Library of Critical Writings in Economics 341 (Cheltenham, UK, and Northampton, MA: Edward Elgar Publishing, 2018), which is a reprint from my *In the Days of Caesar: Pentecostalism and Political Theology* (Grand Rapids: Eerdmans, 2010), 295–303.

[18] I once preached on this Acts 4:23–31 prayer passage; see my "Praying with the Apostles: Then and Tomorrow," chapter 8 in my *The Kerygmatic Spirit: Apostolic Preaching in the 21st Century*, edited by Josh Samuel, commentary and afterword by Tony Richie (Eugene, OR: Cascade Books, 2018), 107–19.

[19] This is not an essay on signs and wonders, so I do not want to be detracted on the plausibility or veracity of this Lukan account; yet those interested to hear more from me about signs, wonders, and miracles can consult Amos Yong, "Theological and Scientific Perspectives on Signs, Wonders, and Miracles: Toward a Full(er) Gospel Account," in Simo Frestadius, ed., *Signs, Wonders, and Miracles: Pentecostal and Scientific Reflections* (Cleveland, TN: CPT, 2023), forthcoming.

Community Engagement After Pentecost   159

people and people from the countryside were joining the apostolic community (5:12–16), and also in Samaria in the story of Simon Magus and his dealings with Philip and his ministry (8:4–25). We see thereby different forms of community engagement with various experiences of prayer, worship, and signs and wonders that prompt, catalyse, and present opportunities for interacting with the broader community. We see the disciples in their prayer time at the end of chapter 4 include an assessment of their situation and the next steps in their engagement. Prayer and worship are thus part and parcel of their process of discernment. In that respect, community engagement assessments can involve a variety of ecclesial practices, not least that of prayer and worship.[20]

And now, on the sustainability front, obviously, getting incarcerated isn't at the top of the list of anyone's community engagement strategy. And, again, it wasn't necessarily the case that as Peter and John were going up to the temple and then healing this man, they expected to land in the local jail. But there were indications in the Gospel of Luke of similar actions of Jesus leading to his apprehension and final execution. In that respect, the disciples might have anticipated that healing acts on the Sabbath might be incendiary. This window thus urges us to see apostolic engagements with the early Judean community in their broader context and how those might have evolved over time as well.

Window 3: Community Engagement Challenges (Acts 6:1–7)

A third window I want to open is Acts chapter 6, "During those days when the disciples were increasing the number, Hellenists complained against the Hebrews because their widows were being neglected in the daily distribution of food" (6:1).[21] This is an ongoing unfolding of the very dynamic early messianic community that included Judean and Jerusalemite locals as well as those gathered from every nation under heaven (2:5), and all those visiting back and forth, maybe with their families. And we can see that the 3,000 who were baptised included Hellenists as well, and both party segments continued to grow. This fluid dual-language community had to respond to the needs of locals as well as those who may have had some broader Mediterranean cultural roots and other kinds of backgrounds, and both groups were now called to grow community in and between their homes and the temple, including intermingling with other locals. Exceeding 5,000 and growing, centred loosely around the temple, and also with ongoing exchanges with the wider community, the question intensified

---

[20] I have some short articles on worship that are suggestive, in light of our focus here, on how what is otherwise an intra-Christian practice can have wider (public and social) implications; see Amos Yong, "Worship in Many Tongues: The Power of Praise in the Vernacular," *Worship Leader* 122 (May–June 2015): 14–17 and "The Power of Language: The Implications of Pentecost for Global Worship," *Reformed Worship* 119 (March 2016), 28–33, https://www.reformedworship.org/article/march-2016/power-language, accessed 7 April 2023.

[21] For more on the contexts surrounding this passage, see parts II–III of my book *Who is the Holy Spirit? A Walk with the Apostles* (Brewster, MA: Paraclete Press, 2011).

over time: how is the daily distribution of food to be managed in light of the fact that apostolic believers were already involved in a great deal of buying and selling to meet its communal needs?

The twelve called together the whole group of disciples and said, "It's not right that we should neglect the word of God in order to wait at tables. Therefore, friends select from among yourselves seven men of God, good standing full of the spirit and wisdom, whom we may appoint to this task" (6:2–3). Here, we see not only the mobilisation of the community that we saw in Salvatierra and Heltzel, but also the appointment of leadership. "'While we, for our part, will devote ourselves to prayer and to serving the word.' What they said pleased the whole community, and they chose Stephen, a man full of faith and the Holy Spirit, together with Philip, Prochorus, Nicanor, Timon, Parmenas, and Nicolaus, a proselyte of Antioch. They had these men stand before the apostles, who prayed and laid their hands on them. The word of God continued to spread; the number of the disciples increased greatly in Jerusalem, and a great many of the priests became obedient to the faith" (6:4–7).[22]

In this passage, the goals were in part to continue to meet the needs of those within the community. There was ongoing recruitment and leadership development, and in many respects, this enlargement of the circle of community leadership came about precisely as a result of growing sustainability capacities in and for the community. In doing so, the apostolic leadership community drew from those with broader "global" (wider Mediterranean) experiences and ties. So, in this instance, we see the apostolic community continue to engage with the broader community in differentiated respects.

Window 4: Communal Dialogue and Disputation (Acts 17–19)

I want to fast forward now to Acts 17–19 for a different window, with multiple frames even, into community engagement.[23] "While Paul was waiting for them in Athens, he was deeply distressed to see the city was full of idols. So he argued in the synagogue with the Jews and the devout persons, and also in the marketplace every day with those who happen to be there" (17:16–17). There is so much to unpack in every one of these passages, but I want to look through

---

[22] For more on this passage, see Young Lee Hertig, "Cross-Cultural Mediation: From Exclusion to Inclusion," in Robert L. Gallagher and Paul Hertig., eds., *Mission in Acts: Ancient Narratives in Contemporary Contexts* (Maryknoll: Orbis, 2004), 59–72.

[23] My reflections in "From Demonization to Kin-domization: The Witness of the Spirit and the Renewal of Missions in a Pluralistic World," in Amos Yong and Clifton Clarke, eds., *Global Renewal, Religious Pluralism, and the Great Commission: Toward a Renewal Theology of Mission and Interreligious Encounter*, Asbury Theological Seminary Series in World Christian Revitalization Movements in Pentecostal/Charismatic Studies 4 (Lexington, KY: Emeth Press, 2011), 157–74, provide further discussion of a number of the "windows" of chapters discussed here, including Acts 6, what we now turn to here at the Areopagus, and what we discuss later at Ephesus and Malta.

Community Engagement After Pentecost

these windows into how the apostle engaged with the broader community. Here, we see a sense that St. Paul was discerning, assessing the local situation. And his response was to engage first in the synagogue, and then that engagement with the synagogue opened up to engagement in and with the marketplace. We can well imagine how these marketplace exchanges extended and stimulated further dimensions of community engagement as he was assessing and responding to the developments, next landing him in the Areopagus (17:22). Now, obviously, in these instances, community engagements came out of his own apostolic mandate or were derived from his apostolic commitments to be a purveyor of the good news of Jesus Christ and to establish local bodies of messianic believers. Community engagement was hence central to this apostolic vocation.

In Corinth, Paul "left the synagogue and went to the house of a man named Titius Justus, a worshipper of God; his house was next door to the synagogue. Crispus, the official of the synagogue, became a believer in the Lord, together with all his household; and many of the Corinthians who heard Paul became believers and were baptized" (18:7–8). Here, we can see some of the dynamics of how the local synagogue might have been considered to be a centre of the believing community, and the house next door, belonging to Titius Justus, again, replicated the early apostolic experience in Acts 2–4 where we saw the believing community navigating the spaces of the broader community between homes and temple. And now, at Corinth, the synagogue was a site that had both some insider status to Paul and his ministry, but also some outsider dimensions as well, as the space wherein Paul the Apostle engaged with other Corinthians. For apostolic and evangelistic purposes, Paul's community engagement modality deployed dialogical and disputational forms: "Every sabbath he would argue in the synagogue and would try to convince Jews and Greeks" (18:4).[24]

Lastly, refracting Acts 17–19 as a kind of rotating or multi-lensed/framed window (to extend our window metaphor), Paul "entered the synagogue and for three months spoke out boldly, and argued persuasively about the Kingdom of God. When some stubbornly refused to believe and spoke evil of the Way before the congregation, he left them, taking the disciples with him, and argued daily in the lecture hall of Tyrannus. This continued for two years, so that all the residents of Asia, both Jews and Greeks, heard the word of the Lord" (19:8–10). Note the ongoing navigation of Paul between the synagogue and the lecture hall, particularly the latter as a site and locus of community engagement. This was a space of community discussion, dialogue, and disputation, so to speak. As Luke tells us, these engagements transpired over two years and even longer. What we have is a more extended set of apostolic contacts with the surrounding community. In that sense, we can appreciate many aspects and dimensions of what Salvatierra and Heltzel shared with us, especially if we had more time to read between the lines of the text and explore the world behind these texts. We might be able to name better the goals, assessments, recruitment, pathways, resourcings, and sustainability elements in Athens (the Areopagus), Corinth

---

[24] For more on my dialogical method and approach, see Amos Yong, *The Dialogical Spirit: Christian Reason and Theological Method for the Third Millennium* (Eugene, OR: Cascade Books, 2014).

162   *The Holy Spirit, Spirituality and Leadership*

(note Priscilla and Aquila, and the adding of Apollo as part of the mobilised group of both members and leaders to engage in the Corinthian community), and Ephesus. In the latter context, to stay on this point for a moment, there is a lot happening, including the seven sons of Sceva, the ensuing (after some time) riot, the communications with the town clerk, and how the town clerk attempted to calm down those who felt that the spirit of the Gospel threatened the worship of Artemis, the sales of the Artemesian artefacts in the Ephesian community, etc.[25] Unpacking further Paul's efforts in Athens, Corinth, and Ephesus (really, everywhere throughout Paul's travels) from our community organising perspective will shed further light on contemporary community engagement after Pentecost.

Window 5: Indigenous Community Engagement (Acts 28:1–10)

I want to close briefly by looking at Malta, in which the natives – the Greek refers to *barbaroi*, transliterated *barbarians*, so to speak (28:2) – and the indigenous population of the island showed unusual kindness to Paul and his companions. This is after the shipwreck of Acts 27, in which Paul and Luke and others find themselves as castaways. Later in the account, we read: "Now in the neighborhood of that place were lands belonging to the leading man of the island, named Publius, who received us and entertained us hospitably for three days" (28:7). Here we find community engagement simply to be no more or less than the receiving of hospitality from others. Then we discover: "It so happened that the father of Publius lay sick in bed with fever and dysentery. Paul visited him and cured him by praying and putting his hands on him. After this happened, the rest of the people on the island who had diseases also came and were cured" (28:8–9). Here we see indigenous community engagement as it happens, not planned, through developing circumstances that were beyond apostolic control, the aftermath of "acts of God," so to speak, in which the community engagement on the island comes through faithful dependence upon God and prayer, with the ministry of prayer to those who are sick extended beyond any arbitrary border that might be erected between "us" and "them."

But attend carefully to the fact that the apostolic reception of hospitality is given by those like "barbarians," whom historically we (as Jesus-followers) have not considered to be communities worthy of engagement, even. "They bestowed many honors on us, and when we were about to sail, they put on board all the provisions we needed" (28:10). This window reflects a bright and even burning set of rays inviting our willingness to receive from otherwise dismissed communities for our benefit and even salvation (Paul and his companions

---

[25] My Zoom-mediated lecture, "Where Did the Holy Spirit Go? Pneumatology for a Post-Secular Age," presented to the "Church with Spirit, in our Secular Age" Conference organised by the Danish StudieCenter Menighedsbaseret Teology [Study Centre for Church Based Theology], 11 May 2023 [available at http://scmt.dk/ressourcer/], focuses on Acts 19 and elaborates further some of the themes I have introduced here.

literally saved out of the storm). So here is a mode of community engagement that we stumble upon and wherein we realise that it is not so much what we might bring to the community, but how we can and must receive from those in places we find ourselves who are in a position to bless us.[26]

Reconsideration: Community Engagement after Pentecost

Goals: A few summary remarks, gleaned from the above, of apostolic engagement after Pentecost goals. Primarily, we see heralding the reign of God as a priority, and doing so through many tongues. Again, many opportunities, many locations, many cultures, many ethnicities, and many nationalities (usually the form *ethnos* in the New Testament), occur all throughout the book of Acts. So, in that respect, the many tongues of Pentecost are the many languages and peoples through whom the Gospel is resounded, and to whom also the Gospel is declared.[27]

Assessment: Assessment involves understanding the present state of the local ecclesial community, that of its wider community, and the community resources and needs. In fact, the windows we have peered through indicate that there were many needs even within the early apostolic community. So, the community engagements of the apostolic narrative involve engagements of those wider communities but sometimes for the benefit of the body of Christ, as we've seen in Acts 2, Acts 4, Acts 6, and then Acts 28. Thus, the apostolic brothers and sisters were beneficiaries of that broader community engagement. So, the assessment goes both ways: both of who we are as a malleable body of Christ, but also of the wider communities within which we are situated and find ourselves. Sometimes, we should acknowledge being at the mercy of others, like, for instance, in the Maltese example.

Strategies: The many tongues of Pentecost, I suggest, is an effective metaphorical pointer that directs our attentiveness to the many modalities through which we collaborate toward the common good, including the good of the apostolic community. The modalities of engagement could involve, as we have seen, signs and wonders, dialogue and disputation, and the giving and

---

[26] The final chapter of my *Who is the Holy Spirit? A Walk with the Apostles* is titled, "Barbarians, Believers, and the Spirit of Hospitality" (185–88); see further Amos Yong, "Guests, Hosts, and the Holy Ghost: Pneumatological Theology and Christian Practices in a World of Many Faiths," in David H. Jensen, ed., *Lord and Giver of Life: Perspectives on Constructive Pneumatology* (Louisville: Westminster John Knox Press, 2008), 71–86 and 172–74.

[27] See Amos Yong, "Many Tongues, Many Practices: Pentecost and Theology of Mission at 2010," in Ogbu U. Kalu, Edmund Kee-Fook Chia, and Peter Vethanayagamony, eds., *Mission after Christendom: Emergent Themes in Contemporary Mission* (Louisville, KY: Westminster John Knox Press, 2010), 43–58, 160–63.

receiving of hospitality. So, we could say many tongues and many forms of community engagement practices.[28]

Recruitment: The Holy Spirit enlarges our relational capacity and even our relational capital by bringing us into the broader community. The Spirit empowers and equips us who are on the margins of society, if you will, and in that respect, also privileges others who are marginalised communities in other respects, like Hellenists in the first-century Mediterranean world. The Spirit also brings us into some adversarial relationships with the broader community, although even in and through such adversarial relationships – like between the apostolic believers and the religious leaders of Acts 3–5 – further community engagement opportunities evolve. Again, Paul's public appearances are at times conversational and at times disputational and argumentative; not merely dialogical but also apologetically combative. Yet these diverse modalities of rhetorical persuasiveness open up into a variety of relational dimensions that not only grow the body of Christ, but also recruit, empower, equip, and transform the ecclesial community as new members get added.

Leadership: Leadership development includes discipleship across many cultures, as we see throughout the Acts narrative, beginning in Jerusalem, expanding into Judea and Samaria, and arriving to the ends of the earth, as seen in Acts 28.[29]

Sustainability: This final element involves the many practices of giving, sharing, and embracing all things in common as we see laid out in the apostolic narrative.

Time constraints prevent more from being said, even as every one of these passages we peered into and through could have been read in much more depth. We might also have spent a lot more time unpacking and critically applying the Salvatierrean/Heltzelian categories in light of the apostolic experience. But I hope there is enough here to at least prompt further consideration and conversation regarding not just the apostolic experience, but also our best theological frames for and practical approaches to community engagement in the present time.

---

[28] Consistent with what I articulate elsewhere for other purposes: Amos Yong, "Pentecostal Christianities and Their Political Lives: Many Tongues, Many Political Practices," in Leandro L. B. Fontana and Markus Luber, eds., *Politischer Pentekostalismus: Transformation des globalen Christentums im Spiegel theologischer Motive und pluraler Normativität*, Weltkirche und Mission 18 (Regensburg: Verlag Friedrich Pustet, 2023), 183–96.

[29] Amos Yong, "Missional Renewal: Pentecostal Perspectives to and from the Ends of the Earth," *Quadrum: Journal of the Foursquare Scholars Fellowship* 1:2 (2018), 133–56.

Divine Healing as a Characteristic of the Holy Spirit Movement[1] in Korea

Jun Kim

Introduction

The Pentecostal movement, gaining momentum as a formidable catalyst for church growth, stands out as one of the "fastest-growing components of Christianity."[2] This exceptional proliferation of Pentecostal churches is deeply rooted in their theological emphasis on the intrinsic relationship between the baptism of the Holy Spirit and the subsequent spiritual empowerment, which fuels effective evangelism. While a multitude of factors can be credited for the impressive rise of Pentecostalism, the role of divine healing often comes under scrutiny due to its potential implications in missions. In this spectrum, Donald A. McGavran has undertaken a significant exploration, identifying a correlation between church growth and divine healing,[3] an association that is particularly evident in parts of Asia.[4]

---

[1] In *The Holy Spirit Movement in Korea: Its Historical and Theological Development* (Oxford: Regnum Books International, 2009), Korean Pentecostal scholar Younghoon Lee strategically employs the term "Holy Spirit Movement." This choice serves to emphasise the dynamic, Spirit-empowered events within the annals of Korean church history. Lee's preference for this terminology over "Pentecostal/Charismatic" is to circumvent the specific denominational connotations often associated with groups, such as classical Pentecostals and Catholics. Through the adoption of "Holy Spirit Movement," Lee aspires to capture a more inclusive spectrum of denominations. In a parallel vein, I utilise this term in my scholarly discourse on the divine healing phenomena observed among Korean Christians, underscoring their shared belief in spiritual gifts, supernatural miracles, signs and wonders, irrespective of denominational affiliations.

[2] W. W. Menzies and R. P. Menzies, *Spirit and Power: Foundations of Pentecostal Experience* (Grand Rapids, MI: Zondervan, 2000), 9; E. L. Hyatt, *2000 Years of Charismatic Christianity: A 21st Century Look at Church History from a Pentecostal/Charismatic Perspective* (Lake Mary: Charisma House, 2002), 3; K. Warrington, *Pentecostal Theology: A Theology of Encounter* (Edinburgh: T.& T. Clark, 2008), 1.

[3] D. A. McGavran, *Understanding Church Growth* (Grand Rapids, MI: Eerdmans, 1990), 133–34.

[4] W. W. Menzies, "Frontiers in Theology: Issues at the Close of the First Pentecostal Century" (a study presented at the International Forum for Non-Western Pentecostalism: Asian Issues on Pentecostalism, Seoul, Korea, Sept 1998), 25; V. Synan, "Roots of

Not merely acting as a catalyst for church expansion, divine healing epitomises the essence of Pentecostalism. As noted by Donald Dayton, divine healing is perhaps even more representative of Pentecostalism than the central doctrine of the baptism of the Holy Spirit.[5] In this light, divine healing emerges as both a theological tenet and a phenomenological hallmark of Pentecostalism. This assertion gains credibility as Pentecostals have been instrumental in advancing the belief in *charismata*, especially at a time when the majority of Protestant churches were swayed by cessationist perspectives, particularly since the Reformation era.

Consequently, the divine healing movements of the twentieth century are frequently viewed as affiliated with Pentecostalism. Yet, delineating the origins of global healing movements warrants meticulous analysis. Allan Anderson's investigative work illuminates the existence of indigenous Pentecostal groups that evolved independently, without the influence of the mainstream Pentecostal movement from the Global North.[6] Corroborating Anderson's findings, Younghoon Lee's research on the Holy Spirit Movement in Korea elucidates the distinctive origin of Pentecostal phenomena that predated the inaugural arrival of the first Pentecostal missionary in Korea.

To gain a nuanced understanding of the Korean healing movement, one must first rigorously examine its formative phases and the distinct Korean contexts that influenced the theological orientations of native Korean healing practitioners. Elements such as local religious paradigms, engagements with Western theological perspectives, missionary impact, socio-economic backdrops, and personal accounts of healing have collectively informed its trajectory. In this regard, this research endeavours to probe the lives, ministries, and practices of seminal Korean healing figures – Ikdu Kim, Seongbong Lee, and Yonggi Cho. Each of these luminaries epitomises distinct eras in the Korean church's annals. By critically appraising these individuals within their respective socio-politico-economic-religious milieus, this study aims to present a comprehensive perspective on divine healing as an intrinsic element of the Holy Spirit movement in Korea.

Indigenous Origin

To comprehend the historical development of the divine healing movement in Korea, it is crucial to first address its indigenous origins. Notably, the early practices of divine healing in the Korean church predated the arrival of Western missionaries who later promoted and supported the doctrine of divine healing. Beginning in 1907, the teachings of the Holiness Church began to take hold in

---

Yong-gi Cho's Theology of Healing," in Young San Theological Institute, ed., *Dr. Yonggi Cho's Ministry & Theology* I (Seoul: Hansei University Logos, 2008), 284.

[5] F. D. Macchia, "The Struggle for Global Witness: Shifting Paradigms in Pentecostal Theology," in M. W. Dempster, et al., eds., *Globalization of Pentecostalism: A Religion made to Travel* (Oxford: Regnum Books International, 1999), 23.

[6] A. H. Anderson, *An Introduction to Pentecostalism: Global Charismatic Christianity* (Cambridge: Cambridge University Press, 2004).

Divine Healing as a Characteristic of the Holy Spirit Movement in Korea 167

the Korean spiritual landscape, owing to the significant efforts of figures like Sangjun Kim (1881–1933) and Bin Jeong (1873–1940). These individuals laid the foundation for what would later evolve into a more widespread movement. In addition, critical milestones in the dissemination of the message of divine healing included the appointment of John Thomas (1868–1940) as the Korean missions overseer in 1910 and the establishment of the Bible school in 1911,[7] both of which emphasised divine healing as a foundational belief of the Holiness tradition.

Simultaneously, another denomination rooted in the 1906 Azusa Street Revival in Los Angeles, USA, made its way to Korea. This occurred when Mary C. Rumsey, a missionary associated with this classical Pentecostal group, arrived in Incheon in 1928.[8] Her presence in Korea and the subsequent establishment of the Seobinggo Church in 1932, the first Pentecostal church in the country, contributed to a more active propagation of the message of divine healing.[9] However, it is important to note that the ministries of both denominations primarily operated after 1907, and their influence remained limited within their respective groups until the Korean War. Therefore, it becomes essential to focus on the records of divine healing that appeared in the Korean church around the turn of the twentieth century when exploring the early formation of the Korean healing movement.

The dynamics of early Korean Protestant missionaries from 1884 to 1910 offer valuable insights into this complex history. Principal constituents included key denominations from the United States, such as the Northern Presbyterian Church (33.1%), the Northern Methodist Church (22.9%), the Southern Presbyterian Church (12.4%), and the Southern Methodist Church (9.2%).[10] Additionally, contributions from the Australian Presbyterian Church, the Canadian Presbyterian Church, and the British Bible Society should not be overlooked. During this early period, the Korean church's primary understanding of the work of the Holy Spirit focused on regeneration and sanctification, rather than spiritual gifts.

When the healing movement emerged from various places in the world, the anti-Pentecostal perception on *charismata* was concretised in the North

---

[7] The Academy of Korean Studies, "기독교 대한 성결 교회" [Korea Evangelical Holiness church], *Encyclopedia of Korean Culture*, at https://encykorea.aks.ac.kr/Article/E0008162, assessed 7 August 2023.

[8] Younghoon Lee, "한국 오순절 운동과 신유" [Korean Pentecostal Movement and Divine Healing], *The Holiness Church and Theology* 11 (2004), 173.

[9] The Compilation Committee of the Fifty-Year History of the Korea Assemblies of God, *기독교 대한 하나님의 성회 50 년사: 역사편 1953–2004* [The 50th History of the Korea Assemblies of God: 1953–2004] (Seoul: Creation, 2005), 293–94.

[10] Yunkeum Chang, "The Needs of Digital Archive Development for the Records of Early Foreign Missionaries in Korea (1800–1910)," *Journal of the Korean Society for Information Management* 30 (2013), 268.

American context,[11] and was circulated in other areas of the Global South with the growing roles of the North American cessationist missionaries in the mission fields. Most of the early Korean missionaries also held negative views about ministries of divine healing and exorcism within this historical context. Although records of divine healing did occasionally appear in the mission reports of Western missionaries, and evidence shows some missionaries engaging in divine healing ministries, including exorcism, it was the Korean ministers who played central roles in these ministries.[12] This underlines the indigenous character of divine healing within the Korean church, indicating that its roots were deeply associated with local spiritual worldviews and practices.

The biblical accounts of Jesus casting out demons and healing the sick were undoubtedly intriguing and astonishing to Koreans, whose society was already steeped in an indigenous understanding of a spiritual world. This worldview was reflected in the widespread use of the term *byeongma* to refer to illness. Interestingly, this term has two different meanings: 1) serious "sickness," "illness," or "disease," and 2) "the demon of ill health," "the curse of a disease,"[13] or "sickness as demon, in a metaphorical sense."[14] The primal understanding of sickness has a spiritual connotation, as if sicknesses are demons or caused by them. This concept naturally influenced other religions such as Buddhism, Taoism, and Confucianism. This spiritualised understanding of illness was firmly established within the collective Korean consciousness long before Christianity's advent in the region.

The story of Ikdu Kim (1874–1950), a Presbyterian healing evangelist, provides a vivid portrayal of the initial characteristics of the divine healing movement in the Korean church. Initially, Kim, in line with the teachings of his denomination, believed that divine healing was exclusively for prophets or apostles in the Bible. However, driven by his religious worldview, he began to explore the feasibility of divine healing based on the notion of the unchanging omnipotence of God. Eventually, after graduating from seminary, he initiated his ministry in 1911, which centred on the words of Mark 9:23, "All things are possible to him who believes," leading to the establishment of the divine healing

---

[11] Cessationism was believed to be presented by "the Reformed and the dispensational segments of evangelism" while being taught at Westminster Seminary, Dallas Seminary, and The Master's Seminary. See Wayne A. Grudem, *Are Miraculous Gifts for Today?* (Grand Rapid, MI: Zondervan, 1996), 10–11.

[12] The perspective of Western missionaries on evil spirits and miracles formerly occupied by their "modern rational, and scientific" view was transformed as they testified to "numerous cases of demon possessions." See Sungdeuk Oak, "Healing and Exorcism: Christian Encounters with Shamanism in Early Modern Korea," *Asian Ethnology* 69 (2010), 113.

[13] *교회 용어 사전* [Church Glossary], "병마" [disease], http://terms.naver.com/entry.nhn?docId=2380561&ref=y&cid=50762&categoryId=51371, accessed April 2016.

[14] *표준 국어 사전* [Standard Korean Language Dictionary], "병마" [disease], http://stdweb2.korean.go.kr/search/View.jsp, accessed March 2016.

Divine Healing as a Characteristic of the Holy Spirit Movement in Korea 169

ministry. Kim's vibrant ministry led to a significant revival in the Korean church, particularly after he became the ninth moderator of the Korean Presbyterian Church in 1920.[15] His meetings attracted large numbers of attendees, with numerous sick individuals receiving healing and leading to mass conversions in their villages.[16]

Kim's healing ministry was controversial within his denomination, leading to the formation of a special team called the Miracle Witness Committee[17] to investigate Kim's healing ministry for nearly two years. Taekgwon Im, a key figure in this committee, submitted a positive report in 1923,[18] and Ikdu Kim went a step further by proposing a modification of the denomination's doctrine to acknowledge that the gifts of the Holy Spirit had not ceased.[19] Although this proposal was ultimately rejected in 1924 due to opposition from Western missionaries,[20] it highlighted the significant impact of Kim's divine healing ministry on the Korean church as an indigenous movement. In this regard, the formation process of the divine healing movement in Korea holds special significance as a contextualisation of the Gospel resulting from the Korean spiritual worldview.

Kim's theological perspective on healing was deeply shaped by his long-standing monotheistic devotion to *Haneul*,[21] the supreme deity. This reverence for *Haneul* predated his conversion to Christianity, as evidenced by his ritual of seeking solace in the mountains to invoke the deity's presence during challenging times.[22] Such practices are rooted in a venerable tradition that acknowledges a transcendent being's intricate involvement in pivotal human experiences, encompassing events such as birth, death, matrimony, and illness.

---

[15] Yonggyu Park, *안악 산골: 한국 교회 부흥 목사 김익두 전집* [The Backwoods of Anag: The Biography of Korean Revivalist Rev. Ikdu Kim] (Seoul: Christian Sinmunsa, 1968), 90.

[16] H. A. Rhodes, "Some Results of the Kim Ik Tu Revival Meeting in Seoul," *The Korea Mission Field* (June 1921), 113–14.

[17] The committee primarily consisted of twenty-six members of pastors, elders, and doctors, centred around Taekgwon Im, from 1919 to 1921.

[18] Taekkwon Im, *Ijeok Myeongjeung* [A Testament of Miracles in the Joseon Jesus Church], edited by KIATS and translated by Deberniere J. Torrey (Seoul: KIATS Press, 2008).

[19] Doekju Lee, *새로 쓴 한국 그리스도인의 교회 이야기* [Revision of the Conversion Stories of Korean Christians] (Seoul: Institute of the History of Christianity, 2003), 426.

[20] Gyeongbae Min, *대한 예수교 장로회 백년사* [A Centennial History of the Presbyterian Church in Korea] (Seoul: General Assembly of the Presbyterian Church in Korea, 1984), 354.

[21] According to Sungwook Hong, *Naming God in Korea: The Case of Protestant Christianity* (Oxford: Regnum Books International, 2009), 55, *Haneul* is a "realistic being who plays a very important role in aspects of human life, like birth, death, marriage and disease."

[22] Inseo Kim, *김익두 목사 소전* [A Short Biography of Rev. Ik-du Kim] (Seoul: Sinmangaesa, 1976), 136.

This belief influenced Kim's healing theology, which centred on the notion that everything, including life and death, is under the control of God, the Creator.[23]

While it is critical to acknowledge that the Korean healing movement did not emerge as a syncretic outcome of blended elements from Korea's indigenous religion, its spiritual worldview indeed enabled Korean Christians to grasp the authenticity of divine healing. This was especially true in understanding spiritual entities as the root of both healing and illness. Thus, in exploring the genesis of the Korean healing movement, it is pivotal to recognise that divine healing was not birthed from a specific denominational doctrine. Instead, it was a distinct and native phenomenon that can be presented as our spiritual heritage within the Korean churches from the outset.

Encounter with Western Perspectives

The Korean healing movement underwent systematic organisation under the influence of established concepts from churches in the Global North. While Kim's perspective on healing was primarily rooted in a religious belief system that recognised the monotheistic God as the Creator and Sustainer of the universe, the theological education and denominational beliefs greatly influenced the views of Seongbong Lee and Yonggi Cho.

While Lee (1900–1965) deeply revered Kim as his spiritual guide, his theological foundation was firmly rooted in the doctrine of the Holiness Church. Whereas Kim emphasised God's omnipotence as a central tenet of his healing theology, Lee's viewpoint was deeply aligned with the redemptive acts of Jesus Christ. Lee's profound affiliation with the Holiness Church and its consequential impact on his revival endeavours, especially in divine healing, underscores the institution's significant influence. Scholars highlight that the intentions, strategies, techniques, and essence of Lee's ministry are markedly imbued with the hallmarks of the Holiness Church.[24] Lee, in his own explicit declarations, also ascribes the success of his ministries to his tenure at the Holiness Church Bible School, as he was resolute in his belief that divine healing could be witnessed by "receiving, relying on, experiencing, and proclaiming it [divine healing] as an integral component of the four-fold Gospel of the Holiness Church."[25] Within the four-fold gospel of the Holiness Church, Lee confessed Jesus as the Saviour, sanctifier, healer, and the second coming king. Consequently, for Lee, the redemption of Jesus Christ was not solely to eliminate the sins of humanity, but it also encompassed the healing of physical diseases.

---

[23] Jun Kim, "A Historical and Theological Investigation of the Healing Movement in Korea: With Special Reference to Ik-du Kim, Seon-bong Lee, and Yong-gi Cho" (Ph.D. diss., Middlesex University/Oxford Centre for Mission Studies, 2021), 39–40.

[24] Geunhwan Kang, "이성봉 목사의 부흥사역" [The Revival Ministry of Seong-bong Lee], in the Commemoration Committee of the 100th Anniversary of Lee Seong-Bong's Birth, ed., 이성봉 목사의 부흥운동 조명 [The Examination of Seong-bong Lee's Revival Movement] (Seoul: Lifebook, 2000), 137.

[25] Seongbong Lee, 말로 못하면 죽음으로 [If You Cannot Preach in Words, Preach by Death] (Seoul: Lifebook, 1993), 100.

Divine Healing as a Characteristic of the Holy Spirit Movement in Korea 171

In essence, the theological development between Kim and Lee can be seen as an additional emphasis on Christology, viewing Jesus as a divine healer under the influence of the theological legacy of A. B. Simpson within the Holiness Church.

While the viewpoint of Yonggi Cho (1936–2021) differs from Lee's, it is distinguished by the integration of a pneumatological understanding into the Christological foundation. This perspective, rooted in Acts 1:8, crystallises the theological connection between the baptism of the Holy Spirit and the spiritual empowerment to become compelling witnesses of Jesus.[26] Although Cho was influenced by some world-renowned healing practitioners like Oral Roberts and T. L. Osborn,[27] historical records affirm the considerable influence of the US Assemblies of God (USAG) on Cho, a factor that should not be overlooked. Min's observations suggest that the decade from 1964 to 1974 was pivotal in the evolution of Cho's healing theology and pneumatology.[28] This period implies that Cho's theology of healing was not fully formulated until his interactions with USAG missionaries and his tutelage at an Assemblies of God Bible school. Cho's reflections on his 1964 illness reveal a struggle to strengthen his faith in healing and an admission of deficient biblical understanding concerning divine healing.[29] This hardship instigated the development of Cho's healing theology and the publication of his first book on the topic, despite his healing of multiple individuals beforehand.[30] This defining moment validates that Cho's systematic understanding of healing theology was not established until 1964. Consequently, the role of the USAG is crucial to understanding Cho's theological journey, considering his significant affiliation with the USAG during the foundational stage of his healing theology.

The question arises about the extent of the USAG's theological influence on Cho. Synan argues that Cho's interpretation of healing as part of the atonement, a doctrine prevalent in classical Pentecostalism, was acquired at an AG Bible school in Seoul after his conversion to Christianity.[31] Menzies and Park concur with Synan, highlighting the influence of USAG missionaries during Cho's

---

[26] Euncheol Kim, *하나님의 성회 교리* [Doctrine of the Assemblies of God] (Suwon, Korea: Moses Publisher, 2011), 79.

[27] Jun Kim, "A Historical and Theological Investigation of the Healing Movement in Korea," 165–69.

[28] According to Min, Cho's theology was not clear before 1961. Gyeongbae Min, "조용기 목사의 성령신학과 한국 교회" [The Theology of Holy Spirit of Rev. Yong-gi Cho and the Korean Church: An Historical Approach], in Panho Kim, ed., *영산의 목회와 신학* 2 [The Ministry and Theology of Cho 2] (Gunpo, Korea: Hansei University Press, 2008), 39–40.

[29] Yonggi Cho, *희망 목회 45 년* [45 Years of Hope Ministry] (Seoul: Institute for Church Growth, 2004), 72.

[30] Cho, *45 Years of Hope Ministry*, 64.

[31] V. Synan, "Roots of Yong-gi Cho's Theology of Healing," in Young San Theological Institute, ed., *Dr. Yonggi Cho's Ministry and Theology* I (Seoul: Hansei University Logos, 2008), 15.

formative years.[32] Ryu's research singles out John Stetz,[33] R. L. Johnston,[34] and John Hurston[35] as the most impactful missionaries, given that their influence was evident in Cho's interpretive work for them.[36] In this context, it is widely argued that Cho's healing theology aligns closely with the classical Pentecostal position concerning 1) healing in the atonement,[37] 2) healing as an indispensable part of the Gospel,[38] and 3) healing as the spiritual empowerment given through the baptism in the Holy Spirit.[39]

Distinctive Development of Korean Healing Theology

The development of Korean healing theology is not merely an adaptation of Western Pentecostal theology. Although the pneumatological perspective of Korean healing theology saw substantial evolution influenced by Pentecostal theology, particularly through the significant contributions of Yonggi Cho, it would be a misrepresentation to contend that a pneumatological comprehension

---

[32] W. W. Menzies, "Cho's Theology of the Fullness of the Spirit," *Journal of Youngsan Theology* 1 (2004), 30; Myeong-Su Park, "David Yong-gi Cho and International Pentecostal/Charismatic Movements," *2002 Youngsan International Theological Symposium* (Gunpo: Hansei University Press, 2002), 107–28.

[33] Stetz, distinguished as the inaugural USAG missionary to Korea (1954–1977), undertook a multifaceted role: he served as the president of the Korean Assemblies of God [KAG] Bible school, engaged in welfare initiatives, led an orphanage ministry, and championed evangelism efforts for prisoners. Furthermore, he held esteemed positions within the KAG, serving both as its general superintendent and mission director. *The 50-Year History of the Korea Assemblies of God: 1953–2004*, 314.

[34] Before arriving in Korea in 1957, Johnston served as a missionary in Japan. He then took on the role of general superintendent consecutively in 1957 and 1958. His ministry in Korea encompassed teaching at the Bible school, establishing new churches, and conducting Bible studies for stationed American soldiers. Tragically, Johnston passed away in 1960 as he was preparing for his return to the USA. During this time, Cho resided in Johnston's residence while contemplating his move to the States for advanced studies. *The 50-Year History of the Korea Assemblies of God*, 315 and Cho, *45 Years of Hope Ministry*, 22.

[35] Cho acknowledged Hurston's significant contribution to his ministry, especially in his early ministry until Hurston departed for Vietnam in 1969. See Cho, *45 Years of Hope Ministry*, 144.

[36] Donghee Ryoo, "영산 조용기 목사의 목회사상에 대한 신학적 조명" [Theological Study on the Philosophy of Cho's ministry] (Ph.D. Diss, Hansei University, 2008), 62.

[37] J. Wright, "The Profiles of Divine Healing," *Asian Journal of Pentecostal Studies* 5:2 (2002), 286.

[38] W. W. Menzies, *오순절 성경교리* [Doctrine of Pentecostalism], trans. The General Council Administration Office (Seoul: Korea Assemblies of God, 1994), 235.

[39] W. W. Menzies, "Yong-gi Cho's Theology of the Fullness of the Spirit: A Pentecostal Perspective," 16.

Divine Healing as a Characteristic of the Holy Spirit Movement in Korea 173

of divine healing is scarcely present in the theologies of Ikdu Kim and Seongbong Lee, which are conventionally deemed non-Pentecostal.

For instance, Kim understood divine healing as the work of the Holy Spirit, and the primary purpose of his healing ministry was to lead many people to the Lord. [40] In essence, divine healing was emphasised as an evangelistic tool bestowed by the Holy Spirit. Whenever Kim heard people testifying to miraculous works in his healing services, he prayed for "more power of the Holy Spirit."[41] Similarly, Seongbong Lee acknowledged that healing occurred through the baptism in the Holy Spirit as a powerful tool "to spread the gospel."[42] Though not employing the systematic terminology of Pentecostalism directly, both Kim and Lee had pneumatological concepts within their divine healing theologies. In this regard, one should know that the pneumatological understanding of Korean healing theology is not a mere copy of Cho's Pentecostal denomination's doctrine. In fact, the primitive understanding of divine healing by Kim and Lee intersected with Pentecostal perspectives and was subsequently articulated with more systematised terminology through Cho, building upon their established beliefs. As a result, while Korean healing theology demonstrates piggybacking on global Pentecostal theology, it also exhibits the development of distinctive theological concepts influenced by the unique socio-politico-economic-religious contexts of the Korean church.

The development of healing theology within the Korean church took place through a process of contextualisation, wherein the spiritual worldview played a positive role, but not all choices made were necessary. A clear example of this is the notion of spiritual warfare, where disease was usually attributed to spiritual causes. While this perspective allowed the healing movement to take deep root in churches previously entrenched in cessationism, it also presented a stumbling block in some instances. For Ikdu Kim, sin was seen as the primary cause of disease, and the reasons for relapses after healing were sought within the context of sin.[43] Preceding Kim's prayers for the sick, a simple inquiry was posed: "Do you believe in God and do you acknowledge your sins?"[44] This confessional process is recognised as a characteristic hallmark of Kim's healing practice. Seongbong Lee viewed the healing ministry as spiritual warfare, referring to the disease as Satan's weapon to impede the expansion of God's Kingdom. He used military metaphors to describe revival meetings, depicting spiritual renewal as

---

[40] This perspective is epitomised in his sermon "Let's serve the Lord by receiving the Baptism of the Holy Spirit," where he construed the Spirit baptism as a critical tool for disseminating the gospel. See Ik-du Kim, *김익두 목사 설교 및 약전집* [Sermons and A Short Biography of Rev. Ik-du Kim], edited by Seong-ho Lee (Seoul: Hyemunsa, 1977), 62–63.

[41] Yonggyu Park, *The Backwoods of Anag*, 88.

[42] Seongbong Lee, *사랑의 강단* [The Pulpit of Love] (Seoul: Word of Life Books, 1993), 65.

[43] Taekkwon Im, *조선 예수교 이적 명증* [Proof of Miracles in the Joseon Jesus Church] (Korea: The Christian Literature Society of Korea, 1921), 31, 137, and 114.

[44] Yonggyu Park, *The Backwoods of Anag*, 173.

"rearmament" and his revival ministry as a "hand-to-hand fight" against the "large forces of Satan."[45] This emphasis on spiritual warfare was influenced significantly by the context of the war-torn Korean church during that period.[46] Likewise, Yonggi Cho's healing theology also emphasised sin and Satan as the main cause and transmitter of disease, as he said that the devil "ceaselessly infuses illness with life and strength, leading to an incessant loss of life through pain and suffering" through sin.[47] Consequently, prayers for healing often included proclamations against evil spirits, believed to be the source of disease. However, it is crucial to exercise caution against overly spiritual interpretations. It is worth noting that Jesus' healing ministry, as documented in the Bible, did not invariably necessitate a process of sin forgiveness or spiritual combat against Satan. Consequently, the proposition that all or most diseases originate from spiritual causes is not universally tenable.

Another distinctive feature of the Korean healing movement is its emphasis on the personhood of the Holy Spirit. Kim and Lee underscored the perils of over-emphasising the functional dimension of the Holy Spirit. Instead of concentrating exclusively on phenomenological experiences or manifestations resulting from Spirit baptism, they construed the Holy Spirit as an autonomous entity guiding Christian lives.[48] In their view, the Holy Spirit was not merely conceptualised as an instrumental force, but rather as the central agent facilitating miracles, inclusive of healing. While global Pentecostal healing theology accentuates the operational nature of the Holy Spirit in missionary work, Korean healing theology underscores its relational dimension. This approach reframes the healing ministry, directing its focus towards cultivating a deep connection with the source of healing power, rather than merely seeking the power in and of itself.

Cho's healing theology has evolved significantly, with an augmented emphasis on the principles of "fellowship" and "partnership" with the Holy Spirit.[49] During the early stages of his spiritual development, Cho's pneumatological views seemed predominantly influenced by the USAG doctrine, especially during his academic period at an Assemblies of God Bible

---

[45] Seongbong Lee, *If You Cannot Preach in Words*, 125.

[46] Lee did not use the military terms to describe the nature of his healing ministries until the Korean War.

[47] Yonggi Cho, *Suffering, Why Me?* (Gainesville, FL: Bridge-Logos, 1987), 13, and Dawkmahn Bae, "Healing Jesus: A Study on Young San's Christology Focusing on Jesus Christ as a Healer," *Journal of Youngsan Theology* 5 (2005), 118–19.

[48] Kim underscored the Holy Spirit as the Supreme Entity, from whom ultimate authorisation for healing should be sought. See The Korea Institute for Advanced Theological Studies, ed., *Kim Ik-du: The D.L. Moody of Korea*, trans., Woong G. Kim (Seoul: KIATS Press, 2008), 116–17. Moreover, Lee also perceived the Holy Spirit as a guiding Person in his spiritual life. See Seongbong Lee, *If You Cannot Preach in Words*, 65.

[49] Yonggi Cho, *나의 교회 성장 이야기* [My Church Growth Stories] (Seoul: Seoul Logos, 2006), 60–67.

Divine Healing as a Characteristic of the Holy Spirit Movement in Korea 175

school. This engagement with the USAG doctrine led him to underscore spiritual empowerment for ministry, a sentiment encapsulated by the quintessential Pentecostal tenet: "the Holy Spirit comes in power." Consequently, at the outset of his ministry, Cho largely interpreted the baptism of the Holy Spirit as a mechanism for spiritual empowerment rather than an intimate union with the Holy Spirit as a person. Yet, as he realised the Holy Spirit's unique personhood and independent intent to heal the sick, Cho's healing ministry transitioned toward fostering a closer relationship with the Holy Spirit rather than solely seeking the healing power. Cho believed this theological paradigm shift led his ministry to another level, with about 18,000 members by 1973, when his church growth had stopped with 3,000 members in 1964.[50]

Another notable feature of the Korean healing movement is the intensified degree of fervent prayer. Amid the oppression under Japanese colonial rule and the agony of the Korean War, the church had consistently sought miracles as symbols of God's comfort and hope. Kim, who served during the Japanese colonial era, witnessed a significant revival in the midst of the hardship inflicted on the church following the failure of the Korean independence movement in 1919. This period, characterised by profound despair and viewed as a "crisis" for the Korean church,[51] culminated in Kim's revival meetings in 1920. These gatherings swept Korean society and were marked by the believers' tears and prayers of lamentation,[52] accompanied by testimonials of liberation from deep oppression and suffering.[53] Similarly, Lee began intensive nationwide revival meetings to rebuild the Korean church after it had been devastated by Japanese rule and the Korean War.[54] Cho's response to witnessing agonising death in the slums after the Korean War was to develop a passion for the spiritual gift of healing as he said, "I have felt I need the gifts of healing while seeing people dying."[55] In his view, healing ministry was an absolute necessity, not a mere choice, with fervent prayers of seeking and crying out serving to express this urgent need.

The emphasis on fervent prayer for healing was seen in various prayer forms, such as mountain, fasting, dawn, and night vigil prayers. Following Kim's healing service, congregants would continue praying on the mountain until dawn, uninterrupted.[56] Kim further intensified his supplication by resorting to fasting prayers when his healing prayers were unanswered.[57] Likewise, Lee

---

[50] Yonggi Cho, *My Church Growth Stories*, 74–75.

[51] Seongho Lee, *Sermons and A Short Biography*, 123.

[52] Gyeongbae Min, 일제하의 한국 기독교 민족 신앙 운동사 [The History of Korean Christian Beliefs under Japanese Colonisation] (Seoul: Christian Literature Society of Korea, 1991), 307.

[53] Janghyun Ryu, 한국의 성령운동과 영성 [The Holy Spirit Movement and Spirituality in Korea] (Seoul: Preaching Academy, 2004), 95.

[54] Seongbong Lee, *If You Cannot Preach in Words*, 112.

[55] Yonggi Cho, *My Church Growth Stories*, 74.

[56] Taekkwon Im, *A Testament of Miracles* (1921), 93.

[57] Taekkwon Im, *A Testament of Miracles* (1921), 4–5.

incorporated fasting prayers before significant healing ministries,[58] and Cho established a prayer centre specialising in fasting and praying for the sick.[59] A unifying thread among these leaders was their unwavering dedication to prayer. Their ministries teemed with fervour and consistency in prayer – a spirituality deeply rooted in the Korean church's history. Though these diverse prayer traditions were not initially devised for the healing movement, they evolved to serve as potent vehicles for conveying the Korean church's earnest desire for healing.

In the Korean healing movement, repentance is underscored as a foundational element for divine healing, associating numerous ailments within the framework of sin. Nonetheless, the nexus between repentance and healing transcends the simple correlation of addressing illnesses stemming from sin. It is posited as an avenue to bolster the potency of prayers, underlining the efficacy of a righteous individual's prayer, as articulated in James 5:16–18.[60] Kim, Lee, and Cho have enriched this emphasis by drawing from a wider range of biblical texts. Yet, the heart of their theology stands on God, not the act of prayer itself. Repentance is perceived not merely as a mechanism to elevate the sanctity of the supplicant but as an essential precursor to fostering an appropriate relationship with the divine Healer. Building on the theological foundations laid by Kim and Lee, Cho's theology, in alignment with Matthew 15:21–28, posits that repentance facilitates the believer's ability to earnestly seek God for divine healing in the capacity of a child of God.[61] Consequently, within this movement, repentance is championed not merely as an instrument for divine healing but, more crucially, as a conduit for re-establishing a rightful rapport with the supreme Healer.

Moreover, another vital aspect of the Korean healing movement is its holistic view of healing, encompassing not just the physical body but also the wounded mind. To understand the concept of emotional healing within the Korean context, it's necessary to explore the term *han*, representing the suffering souls filled with anger, bitterness, and resentment due to unjust death. As defined by Adams, *han* is "an accumulation of suppression" and "condensed experiences of oppression."[62] Though some similar concepts may be found in other cultures, its recent experience on a national scale makes it distinctively Korean. In this

---

[58] Lee believed that fasting prayer amplified the innate urgency embedded within passionate prayer. See Taekkwon Im, *A Testament of Miracles* (1921), 4–5; Deukhyeon Kim, "평신도로써 내가 본 이성봉 목사" [Rev. Seong-bong Lee Whom I have Met as a Layperson], in The Commemoration Committee of the 100th Anniversary of Lee Seong-Bong's Birth, ed., *이성봉 목사의 부흥 운동 조명* [The Examination of Seong-bong Lee's Revival Movement] (Seoul: Lifebook, 2000), 30.

[59] Yonggi Cho, *위대한 소명: 희망 목회 50 년* [Great Calling: 50-Year Ministry of Hope] (Seoul: Yoido Full Gospel Church, 2008), 125.

[60] See Ikdu Kim, "기도의 종교" [Religion of Prayer], in SeongHo Lee, *The Sermons and Biography*, 17; Seongbong Lee, *임마누엘 강단* [The Pulpit of Immanuel] (Seoul: Word of Life Books, 1993), 60; and Yonggi Cho, *How Can I Be Healed?* 59.

[61] Yonggi Cho, *신유론* [Healing Theology] (Seoul: Seoul Logos, 2001), 230.

[62] D. J. Adams, *Christ and Culture in Asia* (Quezon, Philippines: New Day, 2002), 97.

Divine Healing as a Characteristic of the Holy Spirit Movement in Korea   177

cultural context, Kim's healing movement provided physical, mental, and spiritual relief to the broken-hearted who had lost hope. Similar emotional healing was observed in Lee's revival meetings, bringing joy and comfort, and in Cho's ministry, which emphasised a message of hope rather than simple divine healing. These movements expanded the scope of the healing ministries as a holistic restoration to every aspect of human beings, both physical and psychological.

As the pioneering work of Kim and Lee established a foundation for holistic healing that addresses both physical and emotional ailments, the Korean healing movement has broadened its scope to societal dimensions. This shift became evident when Yoido Full Gospel Church (YFGC) emerged as the world's largest church by 1981, boasting approximately 200,000 members. As the church grew, Cho's perspective evolved to meet the increasing demands for the church's involvement in societal matters. This change was emphasised around the turn of the twenty-first century, although Cho was already involved in various social activities to take care of the marginalised and the poor. In this regard, Younghoon Lee, Cho's successor and a Korean Pentecostal historian, noted:

> YFGC must broaden its interests to include wider social concern and social reformation. Previous Holy Spirit movements have been more concerned with personal salvation and church growth, and the YFGC will have to make a critical choice for its future.[63]

Lee subtly indicates that societal matters have consistently been secondary to individual issues. In a confession in 2005, Cho also stated:

> I recently began to realize some shortcomings of my 47-year ministries. The Bible clearly says that God so loved the world that he gave his one and only Son. It does not say that God gave his Son for God so loved the man ... My evangelistic ministries have been man-centred without including the world.[64]

Cho's admission emphasises the importance of extending the Gospel to all of society and even the ecosystem. This was a significant shift, viewing every creature as a potential recipient of divine healing, since the Fall impacted relationships between God, humanity, and the natural environment. The pursuit of holistic restoration extended to every facet of creation became a significant hallmark of the Korean healing movement under the influence of the YFGC.

Conclusion

The Korean healing movement originated indigenously, predating the arrival of the first Pentecostal missionary in Korea in 1928. This underlines the unique roots of the Holy Spirit movement in Korea, which broadens its scope to be more inclusive of non-Pentecostals. Notably, the Korean healing movement represents

---

[63] Younghoon Lee, "Life and Ministry of David Yong-gi Cho," in Wonsuk Ma, et al. eds., *David Yonggi Cho: A Close Look at His Theology and Ministry* (Baguio, Philippines: APTS Press, 2004), 22–23.

[64] Hyeonggeun Lim, 조용기 목사 일대기: 여의도의 목회자 [The Life Story of Rev. Yonggi Cho: A Pastor of Yoido] (Seoul: Seoul Logos, 2008), 563.

a long-standing legacy of the Korean church, forged and developed within the distinctive socio-cultural contexts of Korea. The interplay of cultural and religious factors has significantly contributed to creating a fertile ground for the reception and substantial growth of the Korean healing movement and the affirmation of the validity of spiritual healing gifts.

The spiritual worldview of the Korean church inspired indigenous leaders to question the imported doctrine of cessationism, which originated from the early Protestant church in the Global North. In these cultural–religious contexts, shamanistic beliefs and faith in the high god, *Haneul*, served as fundamental tools in validating the relevance of healing ministries in contemporary churches. Subsequently, spiritual warfare was established as a central tenet of the healing practice, leading to an extreme belief that most, if not all, diseases are spiritually rooted, with sickness often attributed to sins and malevolent spirits.

The significant influence of the Global North's Pentecostal movement in systematising and energising Korean healing theology cannot be overlooked. The theological education received by Korean healing practitioners allowed them to systematically frame their primal understanding of divine healing, as embodied in the healing practices of the Korean church. Notably, the relational aspect of the baptism in the Holy Spirit emerged as a unique theological component of the Korean healing movement, while healing was generally emphasised by Pentecostals as a spiritual gift bestowed upon believers for powerful witness.

The political and economic turmoil during the Japanese occupation and the Korean War shaped a firm belief that healing is both a physical and psychological process for marginalised and suffering individuals. Healing emerged as a divine act, reminding Korean Christians of God's enduring love and hope. Mountain prayer, early morning prayer, fasting prayer, and overnight prayer were coupled with the healing movement to express the urgency and persistence of the earnest prayer of the Korean church. Repentance is also considered a prerequisite, not only for ailments caused by sins but also for the effective prayers of righteous people. The most significant distinctiveness of the Korean healing movement is the pneumatological emphasis on the personhood of the Holy Spirit, not on the power of the Holy Spirit. Lastly, the Korean healing movement evolved into a more comprehensive model aimed at bringing holistic restoration to individuals, society, and even the ecosystem. Nonetheless, the Korean healing movement is expected to adapt to newly emerging needs, since healing is a practice that must be continually reinterpreted and regenerated within its unique, shifting contexts.

Contending for the Faith: Pentecostalism and the Reshaping of World Christianity

J. Kwabena Asamoah-Gyadu

Peter Hocken, the late Catholic Charismatic priest and Spirit-empowered theologian, talks about the rise of Pentecostalism as constituting a series of surprises in world Christianity. The fundamental surprise, he notes, is that the Spirit of God was poured out in a way that gave rise to an identifiable move of God's power across the world.[1] The result of the outpouring of the Spirit of God is the rise of the Pentecostal/Charismatic movement and its move from the margins to the centre of world Christianity within a century. That the world's largest churches are Pentecostal, and most of these Christian communities are in non-Western contexts, could not have been predicted at the beginning of the twentieth century.

My thesis in this chapter is that by a process of reclamation and restoration, the Pentecostal movement is "contending for the faith once for all delivered to the saints" (Jude 3). Pentecostalism, as a worldwide movement, contends for a return to the "full gospel" of Jesus Christ. This means, among other things, that the movement preaches salvation as regeneration, holiness or sanctification as a critical outflow of regeneration or new birth, baptism in the Holy Spirit, with speaking in tongues as the initial evidence of being with the Spirit, the reality and manifestations of spiritual gifts, including the power to heal, deliver, exorcise, and empower believers, all in the name of Jesus and the power of the Holy Spirit. Pentecostals contend for the faith through their functional pneumatology, which is seen in testimonies of transformations wrought by God in the name of Jesus and by the power of the Holy Spirit.

To take one well-known example, many will have heard of the mega-size ministry of David Yonggi Cho's Yoido Full Gospel Church in Seoul, South Korea. It is as much a mega-sized Pentecostal church as a site and ministry of religious tourism and pilgrimage for many worldwide. The work and ministry of the founders and leaders of Yoido Full Gospel Church in Seoul needs to be celebrated for hosting the single largest Christian congregation in the world and for its outreaches to other parts of the globe. The prayer mountain of the church is a place where many encounter the interventions of God and the sort of pneumatic presence that Pentecostals preach and testify to in ministry. The Spirit of the Lord has been on the move in many of these churches. Speaking to Nicodemus about the move of the Spirit, Jesus said:

> The wind blows where it chooses, and you hear the sound of it, but you do not know where it goes..." (John 3:8a).

---

[1] Peter Hocken, *The Glory and the Shame: Reflections on the 20th Century Outpouring of the Holy Spirit* (Surrey, UK: Eagle Publications, 1994), 16.

Today, we hear of the "sound" of the Spirit in the rise of waves of Pentecostal/Charismatic movements through whose ministries God is reviving his church across the world. Many visit Yoido Full Gospel Church simply to be inspired to replicate some of the processes they see at work in that initiative in their own parts of the world. What is said of Yoido Full Gospel Church in terms of global influence could be said of Matthew Ashimolowo's Kingsway International Christian Centre in East London, Enoch A. Adeboye's Redeemed Christian Church of God in Nigeria, T. D. Jakes' Potter's House, and Joel Osteen's Lakewood Church, both in Texas, USA.

Pentecostalism in World Christianity

The rise of Pentecostal/Charismatic Christianity is the divinely inspired surprise element in world Christianity today. God is certainly doing something new with global Christian mission that has the renewing presence of the Holy Spirit at the heart of it. Nations formerly belonging to the margins of Christianity – Africa, Asia, and Latin America – are now part of the Christian rising. As Southern Christianities continue to expand and mature, Philip Jenkins surmised, they will churn out a "wider theological spectrum" than at present and this spectrum, he notes, will encompass a Christianity that is traditionalist, orthodox, and supernatural.[2] The reference to the "supernatural" is important because, as Walter Wink notes, the "dominant materialist worldview" of secular Western society seems to have no place for angels, demons, spirits, principalities, and powers. In Wink's words,

> These archaic relics of a superstitious past are unspeakable because modern secularism has no categories, no vocabulary, no presuppositions by which to discern what it was in the actual experiences of people that brought these words to speech.[3]

According to Rudolf Bultmann, Pentecostalism emerged precisely to counter the reductionist approach to the supernatural element of faith that had characterised much of Western Christianity following its Enlightenment worldview and the demythologisation of the miraculous. Jenkins notes that the new Christianity emerging as a corrective to secularism and ecclesiastical routinisation of church life preaches deep personal faith and is Puritan.[4] It is a faith with a Charismatic orientation in which the experience of the Spirit and the manifestations of his gifts loom. That is a key characteristic of Africa's new Christianity. It takes the experience of the Holy Spirit seriously, even when it does not identify itself as Pentecostal/Charismatic.

In global religious discourses, the world is constantly talking about Pentecostalism because, as this chapter seeks to argue, it has become the world's most significant stream of Christianity today. Hocken summarises the meaning of the outpouring of the Holy Spirit, which serves as a theological identity marker of the worldwide Pentecostal movement. He describes the baptism of the

---

[2] Philip Jenkins, *The Next Christendom: The Coming of Global Christianity* (Oxford: Oxford University Press, 2011), 11.

[3] Walter Wink, *Collected Readings* (Minneapolis, MN: Fortress Press, 2013), 64.

[4] Jenkins, *Nex Christendom*, 10.

Contending for the Faith   181

Holy Spirit as a sovereign outpouring of the Spirit of God by the risen and ascended Jesus upon the people of God. It is through that experience that the Lord equips the church to fulfil its mission in the world by restoring those elements in the work of the Spirit that have been ignored by the historic churches.[5]

Mark Cartledge also points to how early Pentecostal revivals, the most popular of them being the 1906 Azusa Street Revival, inspired the global spread of this pneumatic wave of Christianity:

> These centers of Pentecostal revival were gradually mirrored in other countries around the world. From these revivals developed a global movement and classical Pentecostal denominations began to emerge that enshrined key beliefs and practices: powerful personal experiences of the Spirit especially in the context of worship, holiness of life, missionary endeavor, signs and wonders, *charismata*, and an expectation of the soon-coming return of Jesus Christ. It was this final expectation that motivated mission, and the outpouring of the Spirit in the revivals was regarded as the "latter rain" in preparation for the harvest of souls that would usher in the return of Christ.[6]

The world has witnessed the significance of the Pentecostal movement through many developments, as Hocken and Cartledge point out. These include numerical growth, the mainstreaming of Charismatic experiences in worship, the increasing prominence of Pentecostal pastors in public life, the academic study of Pentecostalism within world Christianity, and the saturation of the media space with Pentecostal religion. In the past three decades, conferences on Pentecostalism have taken centre stage in the study of world Christianity. The John Templeton Foundation of the USA has in the last two decades, for example, also sponsored major studies on Pentecostalism, with millions of dollars disbursed across the globe. These studies have assessed the continuing impact of the Holy Spirit-inspired, empowered, and driven movement within Christianity from multidisciplinary perspectives.

Contending for the Faith in Functional Pneumatology

Pentecostalism emerged as a critique of historic mission Christianity because its appeal lies in the belief that the power of the Holy Spirit, once poured out at Pentecost, can be experienced in the church today. The person and work of the Holy Spirit, Pentecostals contend, must not simply be confessed as an article in the historic creed of the church. The Spirit, who proceeds from the Father and the Son, and who is the Lord and the giver of life, must be encountered and experienced. If Pentecostalism has changed the face of world Christianity, it is because, wherever it has emerged, it has drawn attention to the importance of the work of the Spirit in the church.

We must, therefore, confront the following question: "In what ways are Pentecostal Christians, churches, movements, and ministries contending for the

---

[5] Hocken, *Glory and Shame*, 61.

[6] Mark Cartledge, *Testimony in the Spirit: Rescripting Ordinary Pentecostal Theology* (Surrey, UK: Ashgate Publishing, 2010), 2.

faith that was once and for all delivered to the saints?" The passage on which this question is based is found in Jude, who describes himself as "a servant of Jesus Christ" and writes "to those who are called, who are beloved in God the Father and kept safe for Jesus Christ" (v. 1). He had set out to write to the recipients of his letter about their shared salvation. Still, he then found it rather necessary to write and appeal to them to "contend for the faith that was once for all entrusted to the saints" (v. 3). The observation is clearer in Frank D. Macchia's work: "Luke focuses on Jesus' anointing 'with the Holy Spirit and with power' to heal the sick and otherwise deliver those oppressed of the devil because Luke sees Pentecost as the empowerment of God's people for analogous ministry in their time. Pentecostals are convinced that the same is true today."[7]

Pentecostals claim their legitimacy by appealing to certain aspects of the faith delivered to the saints, which they often argue lie neglected in the lives and ministries of non-Pentecostal churches, and to which the Pentecostal movement serves as a religious and theological corrective. What are these neglected areas of Christian faith, and how have Pentecostals repositioned themselves to contend for them? In this essay, I first discuss the distinctive nature of Pentecostalism and identify some of the salient areas in which the movement has sought to make a difference in world Christianity. I then interrogate the identified areas of Pentecostal influence and how they can legitimately claim to have impacted world Christianity.

In this exercise, we discover how conventional systematic theological writings have, for example, failed to account for the experiential dimensions of the Holy Spirit that give Pentecostalism its distinctive character. We know about the Holy Spirit as a person and his character and attributes through the works of some of the finest theologians in the world. However, the question of how the Holy Spirit makes his presence and power felt in the church is not something that traditional systematic theological writings have often accounted for in the literature.

Pentecostalism as a Divine Initiative

Pentecostalism is a stream of Christianity that values, affirms, and consciously promotes the experience of the Holy Spirit as normative to the church's life. In the church's historic creeds, the expression "I believe in the Holy Spirit" has been constantly confessed since the formulation of the Apostles' and Nicene Creeds. The challenge of the Pentecostal movement to the confessional churches lies in the distinction that the latter makes between "belief" and "experience" when it comes to the Holy Spirit. The two may be related for most Pentecostals, but not the same. Pentecostals contend that the church ought to function as an empowered and Charismatic community, and as Arnold Bittlinger would have it, the church of the New Testament was Charismatic. The spread of

---

[7] Frank D. Macchia, *Baptized in the Spirit: A Global Pentecostal Theology* (Grand Rapids, MI: Zondervan, 2006), 76.

Contending for the Faith

Pentecostal/Charismatic Christianity, Bittlinger explains, is due to a three-fold longing in the hearts of people, their faith, and the church:

1. The longing for a truly spiritual life in reaction to and against an over-cerebral Christianity.
2. The longing for real fellowship (one in which the gifts of the individual are taken seriously) in reaction against a Christianity that reduced church members to minor supernumeraries.
3. The longing for strength in reaction to and against a Christianity that denied or explained away the miracles and mighty works attested in the New Testament.[8]

When believers long for, hunger, and thirst for righteousness and spiritual fulfilment and nourishment, when they desire to function in the power of the Spirit, and they experience it, the next logical pursuit is to contend for those Charismatic experiences in the quest for renewal of others and the community.
In the rest of this chapter, although by no means all, we consider some of the specific ways in which Pentecostal/Charismatic Christianity contends that the Charismatic aspects of the faith seem marginalised in historic Christianity. Firstly, the most important contribution of Pentecostalism to world Christianity is its contention that the promise of the outpouring of the Holy Spirit by Joel (Joel 2:28ff.), and fulfilled on the day of Pentecost, can be experienced by the church today. I refer to this as the normalisation of Charismatic experiences in church life. On the day of Pentecost, Peter laid the foundation for the reclamation of the foundations of the Christian heritage as laid by Jesus Christ when he referred to the outpouring of the Holy Spirit as fulfilling God's promise.

In other words, Pentecostalism is not simply a humanly crafted denominationalised religious phenomenon. We cannot explain away the testimonies of Spirit empowerment of millions of people worldwide as fake and nonsensical. With all its rough edges, failures, and vulnerabilities, Pentecostalism is the modern testament to something that Peter confessed when the Gentile household of Cornelius was baptised in the Holy Spirit: "...I truly understand that God shows no partiality, but in every nation anyone who fears him and does what is right is acceptable to him" (Acts 10:34–35). Pentecostals will say that their movement is a divinely orchestrated initiative in which the Holy Spirit, poured out on all flesh as in the day of Pentecost, is now available to all who believe, repent, and convert to Christ. Amos Yong will argue that this Pentecostal vision of original Christianity is animated by the conviction that the accounts of the Spirit in Luke-Acts "are not merely of historical interest but an invitation to participate in the ongoing work of the Holy Spirit."[9]

Secondly, for most Pentecostals, the single most important signifier of this new religious phenomenon is being baptised in the Holy Spirit, with speaking in tongues as the initial evidence of the experience through which one is also an

---

[8] Arnold Bittlinger, *The Church Is Charismatic* (Geneva: WCC, 1982), 9.

[9] Amos Yong, *The Spirit Poured Out on All Flesh: Pentecostalism and the Possibility of Global Theology* (Grand Rapids, MI: Baker Academic, 2005), 27.

empowered Christian. This empowerment begins with regeneration, followed by the infilling of the Holy Spirit. This process makes what it means to be Christian clearer than the denominationalised understandings in which the historic mission denominations operate. There is some merit in the Pentecostal argument that Christianisation through infant baptisms and confirmations accounts for the high levels of nominalisation in historic church traditions. The quest for renewal must, therefore, relate to something a bit different: a functional pneumatology in which the power of the Spirit is not simply a theological idea but a manifestation of the presence of God to be encountered by people and the community of believers.

John the Baptist contended for the faith when he presented Jesus as the one who baptises with the Holy Spirit and with fire. Peter did the same when he connected Joel's prophecy and the events at Pentecost. Paul contends for the faith when he writes to the Colossians: "See to it that no one takes you captive through philosophy and empty deceit, according to human tradition, according to the elemental spirits of the universe, and not according to Christ" (Colossians 2:8). Jude provides the context within which he also invites believers to "contend for the faith." This is stated in verse 4 as follows:

> For certain intruders have stolen in among you, people who long ago were designated for his condemnation as ungodly, who pervert the grace of our God into licentiousness and deny our only Master and Lord, Jesus Christ.

In contrast to the denial of the lordship of Jesus Christ among the recipients of the letter, which in today's world translates into theological liberalism and permissive Christianity, Pentecostals contend differently.

Pentecostals contend that Jesus, who was crucified, was raised by God in the resurrection. When he had been exalted and received the Holy Spirit as the promise of the Father, he poured this Spirit at Pentecost (Acts 2:32–33). The promise of the Father is the promise of the Spirit, who transforms and empowers. Testimonies abound among Pentecostals on the transformative power of the Gospel of Jesus Christ, in which people are delivered not just from the ways of the world and born-again in Christ but also delivered from lives being destroyed by the devil through wrongful moral choices and lives lived in disobedience to God. Those who were once not a people now testify to becoming "the people of God," having been called out of darkness into his marvellous light (1 Peter 2:9–10). In other words, Pentecostals contend for the fact that not only is salvation available in Jesus Christ, but also the baptism of the Holy Spirit and speaking in tongues are legitimate biblical experiences that the Christian must desire, hunger, and thirst for as a sign of our belongingness in Christ.

Thirdly, one of the most important contexts in which to encounter the notion of Pentecostalism as a critique of the historic mission of Christianity is in the context of worship. Pentecostal corporate worship services are contexts for putting into action what Paul says in Colossians 3:16, "Let the word of Christ dwell in you richly; teach and admonish one another in all wisdom; and with gratitude in your hearts sing psalms, hymns, and spiritual songs to God." In the context of worship, praying and singing in tongues, prophesying, declaring words of knowledge, healing, and exercising other gifts of the Spirit often occur. It is through its expressive, exuberant, dynamic, emotional, and affective forms of corporate worship that Pentecostals have changed the face of world

Contending for the Faith   185

Christianity. I refer to this as the functional pneumatology of the Pentecostalism movement; that is, bringing together the belief and experience of the Holy Spirit in ways that affirm what the Bible teaches about his ministry among the people of God.

The Doctrine of the Holy Spirit in Systematic Theology

To appreciate the significance of the functional pneumatology associated with Pentecostalism, it is important to observe that virtually none of the traditional systematic theology books handle the doctrine of the Holy Spirit in a way that accounts for his experiential role in the lives of believers. Consider the case of Charles C. Ryrie. In a 1965 publication titled *The Holy Spirit*, he writes that the baptising work of the Holy Spirit was particular to the age of the Bible.[10] Ryrie acknowledges the baptising work of the Holy Spirit, such as in the house of Cornelius (Acts 10:46); nevertheless, he argues, "a believer is baptized only once, and that at his conversion."[11] Ryrie's reference to the baptism of the Holy Spirit as being "nonexperiential" is very instructive:

> ... the baptizing work of the Spirit is not based upon or derived from experience. It happens whether or not the believer is conscious of it. It is not implied, however, that no resultant experience flows from this ministry. Many experiences in the believer's life are the result of being placed in the Body of Christ through the baptising work of the Spirit, but the baptism itself is nonexperiential.[12]

In his 1964 publication, *The Doctrine of the Holy Spirit*, Hendrikus Berkhof also writes with veracity that the church cannot expect renewal without an awareness and necessity of the Holy Spirit. We cannot be aware of this necessity without knowing about his nature, promises, actions, and gifts.[13] The expression "vitality" with respect to the work of the Spirit seems to be key to Berkhof's understanding of the work of the Spirit. "Spirit," he says, means that "God is a vital God, who grants vitality to his creation."[14] Similarly, Berkhof notes that Ezekiel sees that in the last days, God will perform a new creative act like he did to Adam. He will grant a new vitality to people who are dead through trespass and sins.[15]

This paucity of discussions on functional pneumatology in classic systematic theology texts and discourses brings us to a fourth way Pentecostals contend for the faith. The number of texts on renewal theology that have come out in the last three decades is staggering, not simply in number but also in the very conscious attempt to engage with functional pneumatology, in which the gifts of the Spirit as experienced among Pentecostals are discussed. One is Amos Yong's

---

[10] Charles C. Ryrie, *The Holy Spirit* (Chicago: Moody Press, 1965).

[11] Ryrie, *Holy Spirit*, 77.

[12] Ryrie, *Holy Spirit*, 77.

[13] Hendrikus Berkhof, *The Doctrine of the Holy Spirit* (Atlanta: John Knox Press, 1964), 12.

[14] Berkhof, *Holy Spirit*, 14.

[15] Berkhof, *Holy Spirit*, 15.

Renewing Theology: Systematics for a Global Christianity. In that work, Yong writes that the Spirit not only inspires the polyphonic testimony of the human encounter with the Triune God but also illuminates this witness to many others near and far off. The Spirit, Amos avers, brings Scripture alive with the message of Christ to people who are ready to receive this faith.[16]

Pentecostal/Charismatic Christians make direct connections between the work of the Spirit, as described by Yong in his work on renewal theology, and what they experience from day to day. They understand the vitality of the Spirit too, but beyond its application to creation and the cleansing of sin, the Spirit's vitality is understood and apprehended in the sense of revivalism and renewal through which Paul's *charismata pneumatika*, gifts of the Spirit, become evident in the lives and individuals and the church in a functional manner. The church and its mission are both at the disposal of the Spirit, Berkhof argues, and Pentecostal understandings of the Spirit as the custodian of mission and the church would not be doubted.[17]

However, as we have sought to point out from the works of Spirit-empowered theologians, when Pentecostals conceive of the work of the Spirit in mission and the church, it normally has more to do with a demonstrable pneumatology or acts of power attributed to the Spirit, including evidential tongues, healings, miracles and signs of wonders, and other acts of supernatural interventionism that bring deliverance to people in the face of the threats of evil. In his book, Berkhof places Pentecostals under the subtitle "Truth and Untruth in the Churches and the Sects," accusing them of neglecting the "less sensational gifts" that Paul talks about and preferring to pay attention to the speaking of unknown tongues. Although Berkhof recognises that Pentecostalism is "God's judgment upon a church which lost its inner growth and its outward extension," he still argues that "the church cannot accept the Pentecostal presentation of the work of the Spirit."[18]

The Spirit and Conservative Evangelical Thought

There are three other outstanding conservative Evangelical theologians of the twentieth century who also dealt with the work of the Spirit in the lives of believers and the church. They are John W. Stott, James I. Packer, and the popular American evangelist Billy Graham. Stott's *Baptism and Fullness: The Work of the Holy Spirit Today* was first published in 1964.[19] It is in the preface to the second edition that it becomes clear that Stott, in some way, responds to the Pentecostal/Charismatic understandings of the work of the Spirit. Like Berkhof, Stott affirms the Pentecostal/Charismatic movement as "a healthy

---

[16] Yong, *Renewing Christian Theology*, 350.

[17] Berkhof, *Holy Spirit*, 38.

[18] Berkhof, *Holy Spirit*, 92, 93.

[19] John Stott, *Baptism and Fullness: The Work of the Holy Spirit Today* (Downers Grove, Illinois: Intervarsity Press, 1964, 1975, 2005).

Contending for the Faith

challenge to all mediocre Christian living and all stuffy church life." [20] Pentecostals share with other Christians the notion that "every Christian believer has an experience of the Spirit" because "the Christian life begins with the new birth, and the new birth is a birth of the Spirit (John 3:3–8).[21] At the new birth, Stott asserts, the Holy Spirit "comes himself to dwell within us, and the indwelling of the Spirit is the common possession of all God's children."[22]

James I. Packer writes that Pentecost has to do with the work of the Spirit as he empowers, enables, purges, and leads generation after generation of sinners to face the reality of God.[23] Pentecostal/Charismatic Christians do not dispute any of these. Pentecostals contend that the indwelling of the Spirit and his work of sanctification when we come to Jesus Christ and accept him as Lord and Saviour is just one side of the equation. Following regeneration by the Spirit, Christians ought to experience a second blessing: baptism of/in the Holy Spirit, an experience that is expected to manifest in speaking in tongues. That will be the Pentecostal understanding of "indwelling" by the Holy Spirit – he regenerates individuals when they accept Christ. However, when the Spirit comes to indwell the believer, he manifests his presence in other ways apart from the born-again experience of regeneration. We have mentioned this as constituting the Pentecostal theology of initial evidence or subsequence. The Pentecostals largely contend that this experience be normalised as a standard for believers. Still, conservative Evangelists and Evangelical authors, including Graham, Stott, and Packer, argue against the experience as valid but not normative for the believer.

According to Stott, the principal works of the Spirit are regeneration and sanctification. In his words,

> Once [the Spirit] has come to us and taken up his residence within us, making our body his temple ... his work of sanctification begins ... his ministry is both to reveal Christ to us and to form Christ in us, so that we grow steadily in our knowledge of Christ and in our likeness to Christ.[24]

In Stott's understanding, believers bury their old natures by the power of the indwelling Spirit and cultivate and produce "the good fruit of Christian character."[25] Suppose this is considered the standard conservative Evangelical position on the indwelling function of the Holy Spirit. In that case, we see how it falls short of the sort of pneumatology of experience that Pentecostals contend for. Pentecostals contend for an experience of the Spirit that recognises a further confirmable experience that signifies that a person is not just "born of the Spirit" but is also "indwelled by the same Spirit." According to Stott, to be "baptized in the Spirit" is synonymous with "receiving the Spirit": "baptism of the Spirit is

---

[20] Stott, *Baptism and Fullness*, 13.

[21] Stott, *Baptism and Fullness*, 25.

[22] Stott, *Baptism and Fullness*, 25.

[23] James I. Packer, *Keep in Step with the Spirit: Finding Fullness in Our Walk with God* (Grand Rapids, MI: Baker Books, 2005), 42.

[24] Stott, *Baptism and Fullness*, 27.

[25] Stott, *Baptism and Fullness*, 27.

188   *The Holy Spirit, Spirituality and Leadership*

the same as the promise or gift of the Spirit and is as much integral part of the gospel of salvation as is the remission of sins."[26]

John W. Stott's position as a conservative Evangelical theologian is shared by his contemporaries, James I. Packer and Billy Graham. Billy Graham talks about how he had been made to believe that, unless he had the experience of baptism in the Holy Spirit with speaking in tongues, his Christianity was virtually incomplete:

> [In] my own study of the Scriptures through the years I have become convinced that there is only one baptism with the Holy Spirit in the life of every believer, and that takes place at the moment of conversion. This baptism with the Holy Spirit was initiated at Pentecost, and all who come to know Jesus Christ as Savior thus share in that experience and are baptized with the Spirit the moment they are regenerated ... The important thing is the great central truth – when I come to Christ, God gives His Spirit to me.[27]

Billy Graham is adamant that Christians are baptised into the body of Christ by the Spirit at conversion, with this being the only Spirit baptism that the Bible testifies to: "I do not see from Scripture that this filling by the Holy Spirit constitutes a second baptism nor do I see that speaking in tongues is a necessary accompaniment of being filled with the Spirit."[28] Interestingly, in support of his position that Spirit baptism with speaking in tongues is not part of the biblical mandate to believers, Billy Graham quotes the position of John Stott on the matter.[29]

Contending Differently

These conservative Evangelicals are not necessarily alone in their position that Spirit baptism with speaking in tongues is not necessarily designed by God for all believers. Many Pentecostals, including scholars like Gordon Fee and Max Turner, take a similar position. The difference between the conservative Evangelicals and Pentecostal/Charismatic leaders on this matter is that, whereas Pentecostals like Fee and Turner have the experience, the conservative Evangelicals do not. In other words, the Pentecostal/Charismatic contention that baptism of the Spirit with speaking in tongues is a reality that must be embraced is not necessarily based on a theoretical understanding of the Scriptural passages. It is based on the experiences these Pentecostal academics have been through, but which they do not think must be "forced" on others who may not have the experience. Contending for the validity of Spirit baptism with speaking in tongues, even in Pentecostal/Charismatic scholarship, is therefore based not simply on exegeting scriptural passages on the matter but on the experiences of those who write about it.

---

[26] Stott, *Baptism and Fullness*, 34.

[27] Billy Graham, *The Holy Spirit* (New York: Inspirational Press, 1988), 367, 368.

[28] Graham, *Holy Spirit*, 369.

[29] Graham, *Holy Spirit*, 371.

Contending for the Faith   189

Fifthly, Pentecostals contend for the validity of Spirit-empowered scholarship. The representatives of this bridge between scholarship and Spirit-empowered Christianity include such names as the following: Gordon D. Fee, Frank D. Macchia, Amos Yong, Craig S. Keener, Cecil Mel Robeck, Juan Sepúlveda, Allan Anderson, Amos Yong, and Nimi Wariboko. These are highly accomplished biblical scholars, church historians, and theologians who are very accomplished in their fields of study and contend that there is such a thing as Spirit-empowered Christian scholarship. In the preface to his *Renewing Christian Theology*, cited earlier, Yong just wrote the book on the fact that "the vanguard of world Christianity is itself increasingly shaped by renewalism, if not becoming renewalist in orientation."[30] The impact of these Spirit-empowered scholars on world Christianity is evident in their contributions to Pentecostal history, theology, and mission, which marks a shift from what has come from traditional theological writings that do not account for the functional pneumatology that we encounter in Luke-Acts and in Pauline thought.

In the introduction to his Spirit-empowered work on systematic theology, *Renewing Christian Theology,* Amos Yong argues that the "recent explosion" of Pentecostal/Charismatic churches and movements "has shaped Christianity as a world religion."[31] The impact of the Pentecostal movement on world Christianity, Amos avers, occurred through the missionary zeal of its early participants in the early twentieth century. Many of these movements were of indigenous origin. They worked within local geographical contexts, but those from the Azusa Street Revival travelled to the ends of the earth as they engaged in intense world evangelisation.[32] Additionally, Charismatic forms of Christianity have developed worldwide as a direct result of the impact of Pentecostalism, and this has occurred as a direct result of the deployment of media for Pentecostal activity. As Yong argues, "pentecostal and charismatic types of spirituality are renewing existing churches and charting new frontiers" around the world.[33]

To cite two other examples in Spirit-empowered scholarship, Frank D. Macchia writes that what is distinctive about Pentecostal theology is the understanding of Spirit baptism as an empowerment for ministry distinct from regeneration or initiation into Christ.[34] Spirit baptism, Macchia avers, implies "a baptism in or with the breath or Spirit of God, indicating a participatory metaphor of our relationship with God that is to have a significant experiential effect."[35] The critical observation for our purposes is Macchia's reference to the experiential effect of Spirit baptism. In the context of scholarship, Pentecostal theology accounts for the experience of the Spirit in a way that we do not

---

[30] Amos Yong, *Renewing Christian Theology: Systematics for a Global Christianity* (Waco, Texas: Baylor Universities), xviii.

[31] Yong, *Renewing Christian Theology*, 5.

[32] Yong, *Renewing Christian Theology*, 5.

[33] Yong, *Renewing Christian Theology*, 6.

[34] Macchia, *Baptized in the Spirit*, 20.

[35] Macchia, *Baptized in the Spirit*, 32.

encounter in some of the otherwise very important traditional works on the Holy Spirit or pneumatology. Macchia's emphasis on experience draws attention to the issue of empowerment of Christians for vibrant witness in the everyday lives of Christians. This means the experiential effect of Spirit baptism also influences the way participants work, including how we understand and interpret the Bible.

Pentecostal spirituality bridges the chasms others create between confession and experience, and between rational articulations of faith and experiential theology. Pentecostal experiences have one theological principle at their core: the disruptive grace of God that transforms lives and empowers believers. The experience of the Spirit testifies to the enabling power of divine, disruptive grace. This grace brought people to Christ on the day of Pentecost and disrupted the flow of Paul's life when he encountered the risen Jesus on the road to Damascus. Every Pentecostal testimony is woven around God's disruptive grace, and Pentecostals contend that it is a reality that the world cannot do without. God's grace, Nimi Wariboko says,

> ... radically challenges and unsettles our human presumptions of self-sufficiency and self-complacency, and warmly embraces and *settles* us in salvation, service, our identification with Christ, and as beings indwelled by the Holy Spirit.[36]

In other words, as Wariboko argues elsewhere, for Pentecostal/Charismatic Christians, the experience of God in his powerful acts and signs and wonders may not make sense, but they make spirit. This is because in the reckoning of Pentecostals, "true knowledge does not exist independent of the experience ... of the knower."[37] Wariboko explains that the common understanding of it-makes-spirit is that it is a Pentecostal shorthand for fundamentally grounding knowledge in spiritual reflection and consciousness or religious faith.[38]

Finally, Pentecostal theologians contend for the critical role of the Holy Spirit in biblical hermeneutics. Perhaps the most important Pentecostal/Charismatic theologian who makes the strongest case for this approach to biblical interpretation is Craig S. Keener. He does so through his monumental work, *Spirit Hermeneutics: Reading Scripture in Light of Pentecost*.[39] Incidentally, the foreword to Keener's work was written by another advocate of Spirit hermeneutics, Amos Yong. We have already referred to Yong's thesis that Pentecostalism as a worldwide movement provides an "emerging theological tradition" that enables the exploration of the possibilities and challenges confronting Christian theology today.[40]

Amos Yong contends that *Spirit Hermeneutics* helps to emancipate Pentecostal voices, moving them from the margins to the centre of the "present

---

[36] Nimi Wariboko, *The Pentecostal Principle: Ethical Methodology in New Spirit* (Grand Rapids, MI: William B. Eerdmans, 2012), 2.

[37] Nimi Wariboko, *The Pentecostal Hypothesis: Christ Talks, They Decide* (Eugene, Oregon: Cascade Books, 2020), xiv.

[38] Wariboko, *Hypothesis,* 6.

[39] Craig S. Keener, *Spirit Hermeneutics: Reading Scripture in the Light of Pentecost* (Grand Rapids, MI: William B. Eerdmans, 2016).

[40] Yong, *Spirit Poured Out*, 18.

Contending for the Faith

ferment in *theological interpretation of Scripture*."[41] According to Keener, Spirit hermeneutics demonstrates interest in biblical texts not simply for their historical value, important as that may be, "but because we expect to share the kind of spiritual experience and relationship with God that we discover in Scripture."[42] The historical–critical methods of biblical interpretation demystified the Bible and stripped it of its sacred awe. Spirit hermeneutics is a corrective to this demystification of Scripture in order to restore it in the lives of believers, the church, and Christian theology as the "living and active" Word of God (Hebrews 4:12). Many traditional approaches to biblical interpretation, Keener observes, fail to do justice to the internal witness of Scripture itself. Spirit hermeneutics, on the other hand, helps us appreciate that biblical patterns of supernatural interventionism can also be experienced today because they are empowered by the God who made them happen in biblical times.[43]

Conclusion

In this chapter, we have pointed out that the Pentecostal/Charismatic churches are reshaping world Christianity through their impactful spirituality in several areas of the life of the church. The whole movement contends for a different kind of relational spirituality that is Charismatic. Pentecostal/Charismatic Christianity contends that certain fundamental biblical truths such as regeneration, sanctification, and baptism in the Holy Spirit are not marginal but rather central to biblical thought and must be so for Christians today as well. To that end, Pentecostal/Charismatic Christians continue to influence world Christianity through their Spirit-empowered worship services and theological interventionism by which the power of God is made manifest in healing, deliverance, exorcism, the prophetic, and other such pneumatic phenomena. A new generation of Spirit-empowered theologians have emerged who, using Spirit hermeneutics, contend that it is possible to pursue Christian scholarship careers as people who themselves have been touched and influenced by the Spirit of God. Thus, Pentecostalism is no longer the pariah of Christianity but an important player in the future shape of the faith, especially in non-Western contexts that have emerged as the new heartlands of Christianity in the twenty-first century.

---

[41] Amos, Foreword in Keener, *Spirit Hermeneutics,* xviii.

[42] Keener, *Spirit Hermeneutics*, 5.

[43] Keener, *Spirit Hermeneutics*, 5.

Revival in the Borneo Jungles

Hwa Yung

Introduction

The theme of this book centres primarily on what is now commonly called Pentecostal/Charismatic Christianity.[1] In the past, there had been a tendency to speak of this form of Christianity as it originated from the Azusa Street Revival that began in 1906 and spread from there to the rest of the world. But increasingly, it is now perceived as a movement that "began at the beginning of the twentieth century by a series of revivals in four continents – Asia, Europe, North America and Latin America – almost simultaneously."[2] Today, it is manifested in classical Pentecostalism and Charismatic movements in traditional denominations, as well as in independent and indigenous churches throughout the globe.

However, even this characterisation is somewhat over-simplistic because there is abundant evidence that such forms of Christianity never died out in 2,000 years of church history. For our purposes here, I will simply give two examples. The first is found in the faulty historical reading of John Calvin, who has been classified as a cessationist, largely because he repudiated the Catholic claims to apostolic authority based on their miracles.[3] But this cannot be correct because, in his address to the King of France in the same *Institutes*, he plainly states that the Reformers are "not entirely lacking in miracles, and that these very certain and not subject to mockery."[4]

A second example comes from the Methodism in which I grew up. In the mid-twentieth century, most books that dealt with John Wesley hardly mention the Charismatic dimension in the eighteenth-century Methodist revival. All the supernatural manifestations of those years were excised from the records because they were part and parcel of the "enthusiasm" (the contemporary word for "Charismatic" expressions) from which all rational religion must be freed. However, it is heartening to note that scholarly writings in the past few decades have begun to do justice to the supernatural dimension of early Methodism under

---

[1] This term is used, for example, in Todd M. Johnson and Gina A. Zurlo, eds., *World Christian Encyclopedia*, 3rd ed. (Edinburgh: Edinburgh University Press, 2020), 26.

[2] Johnson and Zurlo, *World Christian Encyclopedia*, 26.

[3] John Calvin, *Institutes of the Christian Religion*, ed. John T. McNeill, The Library of Christian Classics, Vol. XX & Vol. XXI (Philadelphia, PA: Westminster, 1960), Books 4.19.6 & 4.19.18, 1454 & 1467.

[4] John Calvin, "Prefatory Address to King Francis I of France," in Calvin, *Institutes*, 9–31, here 17.

Wesley, the most notable being Robert Webster's Oxford dissertation, published as *Methodism and the Miraculous*.[5]

The above two examples are drawn from an abundance of historical evidence to show that Pentecostal/Charismatic Christianity did not begin in the twentieth century. It has always been in the church but repeatedly pushed underground. This is because, too often, church leaders and scholars prefer, for whatever reasons, rationalistic readings of history, especially since the dawn of the European Enlightenment. However, in the twentieth century, this Pentecostal form of Christianity exploded all over the Majority World or non-Western world. Indigenous believers in Africa, Asia, Latin America, and the Middle East and North Africa (MENA), unshackled by Enlightenment thinking, simply read the Bible and put its teachings into practice. Hence, almost everywhere in the Majority World, where the church is growing rapidly, the supernatural is taken for granted.

This chapter tells the story of one such indigenous church among the Lun Bawang people in a place called Ba'Kelalan,[6] a cluster of ten villages in the mountainous jungles of the state of Sarawak, Malaysia. The Lun Bawang are one of the indigenous people groups in Sarawak and used to be found largely in the Trusan Valley but are now more dispersed. They were Christianised in the 1930s and are part of the Borneo Evangelical Mission (BEM) Church or Sidang Injil Borneo (SIB). I will use BEM/SIB church to designate this denomination for our purposes. This chapter tells how the Lun Bawang came to Christ and describes the supernatural encounters in the revivals they experienced. If some stories seem far-fetched to modern ears, they are nevertheless based on proper historical documentation and interviews with eyewitnesses.[7]

It should be noted that there are other revivals in the BEM/SIB church, either linked or parallel, in the same period in Bario, Sarawak, and around Taginambur

---

[5] Robert Webster, *Methodism and the Miraculous: John Wesley's Idea of the Supernatural and the Identification of Methodists in the Eighteenth Century* (Lexington, KY: Emeth Press, 2013).

[6] Ba'Kelalan is easily found on Google Maps. There used to be twelve villages but only ten are inhabited now, with two abandoned due to migration. The whole region is about 1,000 meters above sea-level and located near Mount Murud, the highest mountain in Sarawak at 2,424 meters (7,946 feet).

[7] This paper is based on the work done on a much fuller account of the same story published as Michelle Chan and Hwa Yung, *Revival in Ba'Kelalan: Discerning God's Purposes for Today* (Petaling Jaya, Malaysia: Canaanland, 2023). Because the present author was involved in the writing and editing of the book, similarities in wordings may be noted in some accounts. The details in both the book and this paper are based on written records, in so far as they are available, and on personal interviews with eye-witnesses of the revivals. The former includes Roland Satu Ukab, *The Ba'Kelalan Revival* (unpublished manuscript, 1985), which was written down at the time of the events of the 1984–86 revival or almost immediately thereafter.

Revival in the Borneo Jungles 195

in the adjacent state of Sabah.[8] For the purpose of this chapter, I will only discuss the events in Ba'Kelalan and, briefly, those in Bario, within Sarawak.

The Beginnings

The Borneo Evangelical Mission[9] was inaugurated in Melbourne, Australia, on 31 August 1928, and shortly thereafter sent out three graduates of the Melbourne Bible Institute as missionaries to Sarawak on 5 October. Sarawak was then under the rule of the family of "Raja" James Brooke, a British adventurer, which had begun in 1842. It is located in the northwestern sector of Borneo, the largest island in Southeast Asia, and today is part of Malaysia.

The first missionaries were directed by the Brooke administration to work in the Limbang Valley, which is near the coast. They arrived there in February 1929 and established their base at Sungai Pranga. From there, they fanned out into other areas and soon came into contact with various tribal groups. They were eager to go further inland to reach those living in the mountains, including particularly the Murut people, known today as the Lun Bawang. However, when the administration's chief secretary visited them in August 1930, he made it clear that "the work of the Mission must be confined to the Limbang valley and not pressed too far inland, not at all into the mountains."[10]

This was unsurprising, given the geographical difficulties in reaching the indigenous tribes in the innermost interior and their unpredictable response towards outsiders. At this point, the Lun Bawang, then numbering some 3,000 – 4,000, were plagued by a high mortality rate caused by rampant alcoholism, violence, and widespread diseases. Shirley Lees describes the situation in *Drunk Before Dawn* as follows:

> The Lun Bawang were drunk one hundred days out of every 365, according to the *Sarawak Gazette*. They were dying out. In the past they had been both prosperous and numerous, but as headhunting was abolished by law under the rule of the White Rajah these former warriors had time on their hands. The Lun Bawang men no longer had to guard their farms while the women worked. Always hospitable, they entertained even more lavishly and at every marriage, death, festival and other celebration they drank jar after jar of rice beer. The celebrations would last for days and even small children would take part. In fact, only the dogs were sober.[11]

Or, as Edward Banks, the then curator of the Sarawak Museum, commented, "The upriver Murut was more often drunk than not, his house indescribably

---

[8] For details of the revival in Bario, see Solomon Bulan and Lilian Bulan-Dorai, *The Bario Revival* (Kuala Lumpur: Home Matters Network, 2004) and the revised version, Lilian Bulan-Dorai, Solomon Bulan with Crescentia Morias, *Rushing Wind: The Bario Revival, A Malaysian Story* (Puncak Jalil: Word Matters Services, 2023). On Taginambur, see the brief account in Peter Elliot, *Asang: The Story of Trevor White and the Dusuns of Sabah* (Cleveland, Queensland: Delia Wilson, 1997), 91–99, 104–112.

[9] Since 1975, the BEM has become part of OMF International.

[10] Cited in Shirley Lees, *Drunk Before Dawn* (Sevenoaks, Kent: OMF Books, 1979), 37.

[11] Lees, *Drunk Before Dawn*, 43.

filthy, covered in soot and cobwebs, the floor showing traces of recent debauches, dogs everywhere, pigs under the house in a general 'lavatory after a gale of wind effect.'"[12]

In fact, the Brooke administration's policy was to minimise contact between the Murut people and other tribal groups, leave them to die out, and allow other tribal groups eventually to take over their lands. This was the main reason for the refusal of permission for the missionaries to move further inland, apart from the concern for their physical safety.

Nevertheless, by 1933, the Gospel had reached the Muruts through the Christian & Missionary Alliance missionaries working from across the Dutch side of the border in Borneo. This sparked a deep hunger for God, which resulted in a mass movement and the conversion of the whole tribe, leading to a complete change in the lifestyle of the Muruts. But because the Brooke administration took time to be convinced, permission to move further inland into the Upper Trusan area and work among the Muruts was only finally given in October 1937.

The new, fledgling Lun Bawang church was hungry for *Tuhan Isa* (Lord Jesus) and for teaching, preaching, and discipleship. They threw away the charms and amulets of their old pagan religion and grew rapidly in their newfound faith. As well as nurturing their spiritual lives, the missionaries also taught them hygiene and communal health, and provided basic medical care. Overall, the living conditions of the Lun Bawang improved drastically, and their filthy dwellings soon became transformed into neat and well-kept longhouses.

In 1939, a government party, which included Banks, the museum curator, visited the area to investigate the stories about the dramatic changes among the Lun Bawang. Arriving in one village, Long Semadoh, Banks was absolutely astonished and asked C. Hudson Southwell, one of the missionaries: "What have you done to this people? The last time I was here, the house was rickety and filthy. Pigs were scavenging under the house, and there were drunken people everywhere. Now, they have a new house, quite clean, no *borak* (rice wine), and you can walk anywhere under the house! What has happened?"

To this, Southwell responded, "I have not changed them … God has changed their hearts. They have simply heard and believed the message recorded in the Bible. Jesus Christ's teaching to the world is so clear that they recognized it met their need, and they believed and acted upon it."[13]

Eventually, Banks, who had earlier denounced the extreme drunken stupor of the tribe in the *Sarawak Gazette*, grudgingly penned another article in the same publication describing them as a changed people.[14] He even jested that one no longer needed an aspirin for a bad hangover when visiting them, but a Moody and Sankey hymnbook instead.[15]

---

[12] Cited in Lees, *Drunk Before Dawn*, 43.

[13] Conversation related in C. Hudson Southwell, *Uncharted Waters* (Calgary: Astana Publishing, 1999), 96.

[14] Edward Banks, "Murut Morons," *Sarawak Gazette*, 1030 (1 July 1939).

[15] Southwell, *Uncharted Waters*, 96–97.

Revival in the Borneo Jungles

For our purposes, we will skip over the World War II years, the handover of Sarawak by the Brooke family to the British government as a Crown Colony in 1946, and Sarawak's subsequent independence as part of Malaysia's sovereign state. Instead, we will look at the two revivals that impacted the Lun Bawang in Ba'Kelalan in 1973–74 and 1984–86.[16]

The 1973–74 Revival

The 1973–74 revival in Ba'Kelalan was part of a move of the Spirit in at least three centres in the two states of Malaysia in Borneo, namely Sarawak and Sabah. It appears that the one person that God used to prepare the ground for revival was Petrus Octavianus, the Indonesian evangelist who played a major role in the Indonesian revival of 1964 to 1970. This revival swept through many islands and impacted a number of churches, resulting in some two million new converts.[17] From 1971 onwards, he began preaching at a number of meetings of the BEM/SIB church in both Sabah and Sarawak. Octavianus was a no-nonsense and hard-hitting preacher and his sharing on the work of the Spirit in the Indonesian revival helped prepare many for the Spirit's move in 1973. We will now look at what happened in Bario and Ba'Kelalan in the state of Sarawak.

Bario, Sarawak, from 4 October 1973

The place where the revival began was Bario, a cluster of twelve villages of another tribal group, the Kelabit.[18] It is also located in the Borneo highlands, within two days' walking distance from Ba'Kelalan and on the other side of Mount Murud. It began on 4 October 1973, at a meeting of the school of Christian fellowship attended by Solomon Bulan, the teacher in charge, and a group of students in the second and third years of secondary school. Bulan, overcome by a sense of sin, openly confessed his failures before his students. Bulan's humility led to an outpouring of the Spirit among them and to repentance and open confession by everyone present. Soon, an unprecedented spirit of prayer and hunger for holiness in the school impacted the whole community and surrounding region. Repentance, reconciliation, changed lives, and a new enthusiasm for God were reported, along with stories of signs and wonders, and various manifestations of spiritual gifts, including prophetic utterances by school kids. Many travelled on foot for hours just to attend the revival meetings, which went on for some weeks. Unable to keep the revival to themselves, the Kelabit

---

[16] On the BEM/SIB church from its beginnings to the 1970s, see Lees, *Drunk Before Dawn*, Southwell, *Uncharted Waters*, and Jin Huat Tan, *Planting an Indigenous Church: The Case of the Borneo Evangelical Mission* (Oxford: Regnum, 2011).

[17] Kurt Koch, *The Revival in Indonesia* (Berghausen Bd., W. Germany: Evangelization Publishers, 1972); Avery T. Willis, *Indonesian Revival: Why Two Million Came to Christ* (Pasadena, CA: William Carey, 1977).

[18] For details, see Bulan and Bulan-Dorai, *The Bario Revival* and Bulan-Dorai, Bulan with Morias, *Rushing Wind: The Bario Revival, A Malaysian Story.*

Christians sent preaching teams out to other parts of Sarawak, including Ba'Kelalan.

Ba'Kelalan, Sarawak, from 9 November 1973

The first night on which the Bario team[19] preached was 9 November. Nothing extraordinary happened. The team then preached on the second night at another church, that at Long Langai, the oldest in Ba'Kelalan, built in 1947. It was here that the Holy Spirit was poured out in power upon the people. Some started weeping non-stop in repentance, confessing their sins under the conviction of the Spirit. Others went around seeking forgiveness from their families, relatives, and neighbours. Many fell to the floor in a swoon, overcome by the Spirit. People seemed to lose track of time and did not want to leave the church. There was such a hunger and desire for the presence of God that nothing else seemed to matter. When one group stopped their weeping and lengthy prayers, another would start. With the ceaseless waves of prayers and repentance going on, some started to prophesy, and others received visions. Many started praying in unknown tongues, and others received the gift of interpretation of strange languages. The scene was one of continuous but joyful chaos. Nothing like this had happened before and the church leadership was at a total loss as to how to manage it.

Among those present were two younger women, Tusi Agung and Maria Gugkang. That evening, they were overcome by the Spirit for almost twenty-four and forty-eight hours, respectively. Tusi Agung only regained consciousness in the mid-afternoon of the second day. During the time when she was overcome by the Spirit, she had various visions and angelic encounters through which she was rebuked for her many sins. In particular, she was rebuked for the several abortions that had been carried out because of tribal taboos that predated their Christian conversion. The other woman, Maria Gugkang, was sitting on a bench when she collapsed onto the floor and only recovered consciousness on the afternoon of the third day. During that time, she had numerous visions and encounters with God and his angels that led to deep-seated repentance and repeated confessions. Although she appeared totally unconscious to others, much of what she experienced during those long hours is still vivid in her memory. As a result of these powerful encounters in the Spirit, both women emerged as two of the key intercessors in the Ba'Kelalan church over the next fifty years.

Although God's presence was powerfully and spectacularly manifested during this time, even more impactful was his call to repentance. For example, apart from Maria Gugkang and Tusi Agung, many others fell under the power of the Holy Spirit. However, when they gradually recovered consciousness, many were not able to get up, as if pinned to the ground by some unseen force. Others

---

[19] The Bario team who came to Ba'Kelalan included the pastor and six others, one of whom was Ramy Bulan, then a seventeen-year-old schoolgirl, who eventually became the associate professor of Law at the University of Malaya and who was among those interviewed for this story.

had to be sent to various villages to bring back relatives, neighbours, and friends whom they had wronged or quarrelled or fought with. Only after apologies were made, mutual forgiveness offered, and reconciliation effected could they get up and return home that night!

The revival service ran continuously for three days and nights and is now regarded as a watershed moment for the entire community. By this time, news of the outpouring in the Long Langai church had spread throughout Ba'Kelalan, and people from other villages had thronged to the place to witness the work of the Spirit unfolding there. After three days, the Bario team returned to the Buduk Nur church, where they had preached on the first night. This time, the Spirit fell in power there as well. The manifestations spread like wildfire around the villages and continued for a period of time.

Not everything went smoothly. After all, this was something entirely new and unprecedented, even for the BEM missionaries. In the initial period, worship and prayer meetings at times became disorderly, and, further, some people caught up in the excitement of the revival did not even stop to eat or sleep. Eventually, wise leadership prevailed, and the situation stabilised.

The decade that followed the initial outbreak of revival was relatively quiet, but it was also a period during which there was much emphasis on repentance, prayer, holy living, and outreach. Like the stories coming from the Korean revivals of the twentieth century, prayer was a central feature of the life of the churches there, with numerous prayer groups formed.

Although there were a number of pastors who gave leadership to the Ba'Kelalan churches in that period, the one person who emerged as the key leader there was Agong Bangau, more commonly called Pak Agong. He had formerly worked as a pastor but had moved back in 1967 to his parental village to care for his aged parents. He was a man of prayer and much accustomed to hearing God's voice as he spent hours and even nights alone in the mountains and jungles to pray. In 1974, he moved to Buduk Nur, the administrative centre of Ba'Kelalan. And in the years that followed, he was the person who gave the needed spiritual oversight to the whole revival movement, especially in 1984–86.

The Fire Spreads to the Rest of Sarawak

From the above two centres, the revival spread to other parts of Sarawak. Jin Huat Tan, in his doctoral dissertation, *Planting an Indigenous Church*, gives multiple references to the reports of the spreading revival in the *BEM Newsletters* of that period.[20] Within a few years, the revival had reached far and wide. Tan describes the spread, beginning from Bario, as follows:

> Various preaching teams, comprising school teachers, young people, church deacons, district and village chiefs, were formed and began to disperse in different directions, one going to Ba Kelalan, another to Long Lellang, another to Long Peluan and Lio Mato and down the Baram, another to Long Bemang, Long Atip and Long Bedian and others reaching Marudi, Miri, Kuching, Lawas and Limbang.

---

[20] See Tan, *Planting an Indigenous Church*, 225–43.

By August 1974, the "reviving work of the Holy Spirit had touched churches from the extreme north to Kuching at the other end of the country."[21]

Further, Tan also argues that the revival bore many of the marks of historical revivals throughout church history. The general pattern that emerged was:

Church services became unusually long with many people confessing their sins publicly, dramatic conversions among "die-hard sinners," backsliders restored, old addictive habits discarded, and marital relationships restored. Further, many pending court cases were settled amicably, people apologized to one another for wrongs done and sought forgiveness, which effected reconciliation and, in some cases, sick people were healed immediately.[22]

It was as if many parts of Sarawak were suddenly being hit by a series of spiritual tsunamis! From these two epicentres, the spiritual awakening would spread, especially among the indigenous peoples, throughout Sarawak and beyond. Moreover, these revival fires would also prepare the way for the next phase of the revival that took place in Ba'Kelalan in 1984–86.

The 1984–86 Revival

Most people outside the BEM/SIB churches first came to hear about the next movement of the Spirit that began in 1984 through a write-up in December 1985 over two days in the *New Straits Times*, then the main English daily in the country. Titled "Sarawak Sightings,"[23] these reports told of strange happenings in the Borneo highlands in Ba'Kelalan, Sarawak, including the miraculous transformation of rice and water into flour and oil and of supernatural lights appearing in the sky. These accounts were supported by photographs of actual people involved in the revivals and some of the happenings, thus heightening the reader's interest.

The writer of the articles, James Ritchie, a journalist, even suggested that what was being reported had the "Makings of a Classic Movie."[24] As if to prove the point, years later when a researcher went looking for the two articles in one newspaper office, they could only be located after the archivist looked under "UFO" in the index.

The 1980s was a time of much excitement over the Charismatic movement hitting the church big time in Malaysia. Within the church, reports and claims about the miraculous were plentiful, or, as the English would say, "two a penny." Many were no doubt genuine accounts of the work of the Holy Spirit in healing, prophecies, and the like; others were doubtful and exaggerated claims. Against

---

[21] Tan, *Planting an Indigenous Church*, 235. The statement in quotation marks is from *BEM Newsletter* (August 1974), 1.

[22] Tan, *Planting an Indigenous Church*, 239.

[23] James Ritchie, "Sarawak Sightings – Villagers Witness 'Miracles,'" *New Straits Times, Times Two* (2 December 1985), 1, 16; and "Sarawak Sightings – Holding the Key to the 'Miracles,'" *New Straits Times, Times Two* (3 December 1985), 1, 5, 8, 9.

[24] Ritchie, "Sarawak Sightings," (3 December 1985), 5.

Revival in the Borneo Jungles   201

this background, I simply wrote off the articles as another example of the extreme Charismatic claims flying around then.

But that view was not to last. Apart from Shirley Lees' book, *Drunk Before Dawn*, other reports and books about the amazing breakthroughs and rapid growth of the church in different parts of Sabah and Sarawak had gradually come into circulation. These confirmed reports that God had indeed been moving in some extraordinary ways in these two states of Malaysia.[25] Subsequently, from 2011 onwards, I made a number of personal visits to Ba'Kelalan and attended twice the Mount Murud Prayer Conferences, hosted by the church there. During these visits I met a number of eyewitnesses of the 1973–74 and also the 1984–86 revivals, and was able to hear from them first-hand concerning many of the details of the revivals.

What follows is a summary of the main events.[26]

The Events Centered in and around Ba'Kelalan

To begin with, all the events took place in and around Ba'Kelalan. Whereas the 1973–74 revival began in Bario and spilled over to Ba'Kelalan, this time round, the Bario Christians were not the major players, although some took part. Furthermore, unlike earlier revival movements, wherein outsiders played important roles, this time the initiative and leadership came entirely from the Ba'Kelalan folks, including Tagal Paran, Musa Sigar, Maria Gugkang, and, especially, Agong Bangau or Pak Agong.

The First Sign: Rice Grains and Water Miraculously Changed into Flour, Sugar, and Cooking Oil; Bukit Tudal, 20 September 1984

During one of his prayer escapades in the mountains, Pak Agong was instructed through an angelic encounter in mid-1983 to get the people of Ba'Kelalan to make a specific kind of uniform in preparation for the next phase of God's work. Little did they know what a divine surprise was in store for them. On 19 September 1984, at a prayer meeting held in Maria Gugkang's home, Pak Agong announced that God would reveal his glory at a prayer service the next day on Bukit Tudal, a nearby mountain peak. The next morning, thirty-six persons dutifully went up the mountain, led by Pak Agong. The latter instructed the party to bring along the following:

- Two plastic bags, each filled with a small tin (ca. 400 ml) of uncooked rice
- One 15-litre tin with a small amount of water
- Three small tins (ca. 400 ml), each with water filled to about 2.5 cm deep
- One small glass bottle (ca. 750 ml)
- One wok (frying pan)

---

[25] On the growth of the BEM/SIB churches in the latter half of the twentieth century, apart from references already given in the footnotes, see also Ray Cunningham, *Longhouses Open Doors: God's Glory in Borneo* (Ormond, Vic: Hudson Press, 2002) and Christopher Choo, *The Ba Kelalan Revival of East Malaysia* (Petaling Jaya: El Shaddai, 1994).

[26] For details, see Chan and Hwa, *Revival in Ba'Kelalan*, 67–118.

After waiting on God in prayer the whole morning and much of the afternoon, they witnessed a miraculous transformation first-hand. The rice in the plastic bags was changed into flour, the water in the bottle and one of the small tins was changed into cooking oil, the water in the other two small tins transformed into sugar, and the water in the large 15-litre tin became a drink that looked like black tea. With these the party produced something similar to *you tiao* (Chinese fried dough sticks), enough to feed the whole party up on the mountain and another two hundred persons at the church, upon their descent from the mountain. And there were still leftovers for the students in the boarding school nearby.

Pic 1: Ba'Kelalan villagers displaying the flour and cooking oil miraculously transformed from rice and water, with Agong Bangau on the left; 20 September 1984. Photo credit: Musa Sigar.

On being asked how was it that there was so much food for so many when they had brought so little up the mountain, those present could not explain. All they could say was that the food seemed to have been multiplied in the process of preparation and cooking. It appears similar to what happened at the feeding of the 5,000 in the Gospels.

More Signs and Wonders: Fire in the Sky

Over the next year, 1985, on four separate occasions, 9 April, 9 May, 15 July and 25 September, under instructions from Pak Agong, members of the church gathered in different locations to witness fireballs moving through the night sky. Perhaps the clearest was that on the night of 15 July, which was captured on a time-lapse photograph. On that night, the uniforms which they had been instructed to make were finally ready. More than 1,000 worshippers from the Ba'Kelalan villages and the surrounding areas, even as far as Lawas, gathered at the football field in Buduk Nur. Then suddenly, in the midst of the darkness, the fireball appeared and stayed for about forty-five minutes in the sky. When the photograph was developed, it appears that the fireball had traced out a gigantic angelic figure in the night sky.

Revival in the Borneo Jungles

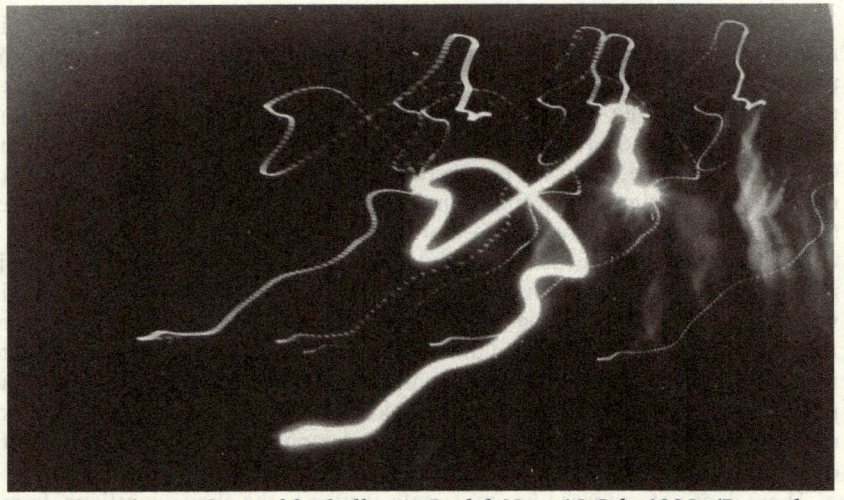

Pic 2: Time-lapse photo of fireball over Buduk Nur; 15 July 1985. (Reproduced in James Ritchie, "Sarawak Sightings – Villagers Witness 'Miracles,'" New Straits Times, Times Two [2 December 1985], 1.) Photographer unknown.

Mount Murud and the Miracle of Water-soaked Moss on Fire; 20–21 July 1985

In between the sighting of fireballs in the sky, Pak Agong also led a group of six hundred and thirty people, which included some one hundred persons from Bario, on a five-day climb up Mount Murud. On the evening of 20 July, the people were ready for a prayer service which went from 6 pm to 6 am the next morning. During that service, Pak Agong instructed one of those present to pour water repeatedly onto some moss found on the mountain. He then proceeded to put a match to the water-soaked moss, which exploded into flames like a petrol bomb, just like what happened on Mount Carmel when Elijah confronted the prophets of Baal!

The above is a brief and abbreviated account of some of the divine encounters experienced by the Ba'Kelalan folks. There were also other manifestations of God's glory and power during this period, including reports of angelic singing[27] on at least one occasion, the climb up Mount Belingi' for a prayer service on 25 May 1985. Space limitation prohibits further discussion here.

---

[27] The phenomenon of angelic singing being heard is nothing strange or new, having been reported in various records of revivals. For example, one account of the Welsh revival of 1817 describes what happened at Beddgelert as follows: "An unusual phenomenon in this revival was the 'singing in the air' which many reliable witnesses had heard. The sound of heavenly, angelic voices, sweetly and softly joined in harmony, without any apparent melody, was overpowering." Eifion Evans, *Revival Comes to Wales – The Story of the 1859 Revival in Wales*, 3rd ed. (Bridgend, Evangelical Press of Wales, 1986), 15.

To sum up, the 1973–74 revival brought about deep-seated repentance in many lives, a new spirit of prayer, a fresh emphasis on holy living, and a genuine passion to reach out and share the amazing power of God in the revival. In similar manner, the 1984–86 revival also brought a powerful sense of God's awesome holiness, gave rise to a renewed intensity of prayer and a passion to proclaim the Gospel far and wide. Nevertheless, there appears to be a difference. The powerful manifestation of signs and wonders in the second revival brought about a deeper awareness and an even greater sense of God's awesome majesty and glory.

The question that needs asking is why did God manifest himself in this manner? Unlike the 5,000 in the Gospel story, the people up on the mountain were not exactly hungry. What, then, is the point of the miraculous provision of food? What about the fireballs in the sky? Is God a mere exhibitionist seeking to impress some poor humble country bumpkins of his incomparable majesty and power? And why the burning of water-soaked moss up on a mountain top when, unlike in Elijah's case, there was no need to demonstrate Yahweh's superiority over pagan gods like Baal?

There does not appear to be any simple answer to the above questions. In my conversations with the people of Ba'Kelalan, they do not seem to have grappled with these questions at all. Could this be an issue that the church as a whole in Sarawak and the nation, moving forward, must wrestle with?

The Impact of the Revivals

As has already been noted, the events of 1973–74 in Bario and Ba'Kelalan led to the fires of revival spreading across the whole state of Sarawak and beyond. The 1984–86 revival in Ba'Kelalan accentuated the impact of the earlier revival further. Together, they brought new life to many churches and God's gracious outpouring of spiritual gifts upon many indigenous Christians in Sarawak. In seeking to assess the long-term impact of these revivals, at least three things need to be said.

First, at the local level in some BEM/SIB churches in the Sarawak interior, and often among the poorest and most marginalised peoples such as the Penans, revivals are ongoing today. The Spirit's signs and wonders are still being seen, daily 5 am prayer meetings are still being held, and lives are still being transformed.

Second, the strong impact of the revivals continues to be felt at the personal level by individuals, as the following story shows. A friend of mine, Randy Singkee, runs Wawasan Penabur, the largest Malay-language Christian publisher catering primarily to the indigenous churches. In 1990, he was offered a place to do a Master's degree in computerised mapping at the University of Edinburgh, with the promise of a scholarship from his sponsoring institution. But as the date of departure drew near, the confirmation letter for the scholarship still had not come. In a state of desperation, he went to a prayer meeting where a group had come from Ba'Kelalan to speak about the revival there.

At the end of the meeting, Singkee sought prayer. A woman prayed for him and to his great surprise, she started praying in tongues – in Mandarin Chinese, to be exact. Now this was a woman with barely any formal education, from the

Revival in the Borneo Jungles

Borneo jungles, who only spoke her own mother tongue, Lun Bawang, and Malay. She did not know what she was saying as she prayed in tongues. But Singkee, also an indigenous person, had gone to a Chinese primary school and understood exactly what God was saying to him through her prophetically. He was thereby given a powerful assurance that God would provide fully for his needs.

To cut a long story short, Singkee flew to Edinburgh the very next day and, shortly after he arrived, was told by his institution that the scholarship would not be forthcoming. The university, understanding his very difficult situation, encouraged him to continue with his studies and helped him in whatever ways possible. Throughout that one year, Randy worked at restaurants in the evenings and during vacations and wonderfully earned enough for his fees and all other expenses to complete his Master's degree. Years later, in 2015, during a visit to Ba'Kelalan, and after careful checking, Singkee found that the woman who had prayed for him was Maria Gugkang, the woman who had been overcome by the Spirit for 48 hours in the 1973–74 revival. Over the years, she has emerged as the one with the strongest prophetic gifting in Ba'Kelalan.

Finally, how did the revivals impact the church in Sarawak? Official government statistics indicate that from 1970 to 2020, the church grew from 19.3% of the state population to 50.1%[28] in fifty years, with an increase of just over a million. This makes Sarawak the only majority-Christian state in Malaysia, wherein Christians comprise only 9.1% of the population.[29] And God is still at work!

---

[28] Jabatan Perangkaan Malaysia, *Penemuan Utama Banci Penduduk dan Perumahan Malaysia, Key Findings Population and Housing Census of Malaysia* (Putrajaya: Jabatan Perangkaan Malaysia, 2022), 46.

[29] Jabatan Perangkaan Malaysia, *Penemuan Utama Banci Penduduk dan Perumahan Malaysia*, 33.

Part 2

THE HOLY SPIRIT AND LEADERSHIP

Megachurches in Global/World Christianity:
North and South

Philip Jenkins

Introduction

Numbers can dazzle, but they do not tell the full story. In the case of global/world Christianity, Westerners interested in the global spread of the faith often have some awareness of Yoido Full Gospel Church, with its astonishing congregation size. But in its general character and approach, that church is by no means unique. Most of those observers miss the larger role of such institutions in the present and future mappings of the Christian faith on a global or world scale. As I will show, a considerable gulf of understanding and sympathy separates many of those academic experts from the realities they are describing and perhaps from appreciating the real significance of these institutions. Nor do such observers appreciate that any realistic consideration of such a phenomenon demands a vocabulary that is somewhat unfamiliar: we have for some years been at a quantitative level far above those "megachurches," as they were originally defined.

I will focus on how the rise of megachurches responds directly to new conditions and social circumstances that were little dreamed of before quite modern times – conditions that include, for instance, urbanisation, globalisation, and modernisation, but also critical demographic transitions worldwide. All have occurred, and are occurring, at a breakneck pace. Not only will those circumstances continue to apply for the foreseeable future, but they will surely accelerate. However, the fact that the context offers such opportunities does not mean that such churches would automatically have arisen and flourished as they have. We see some instances that have conspicuously failed. In order to succeed, such congregations needed leaders who were both visionaries and administrators, those who could read the signs of the times, and a remarkable number of such pivotal individuals could be identified. As I will argue repeatedly, the stories of modern giant churches thus illustrate the conjunction of opportunities with human direction and leadership, and we can debate the exact significance of each part of the equation. What is undeniable is that these churches have played, and will continue to play, a leading role in the making of a truly worldwide Christianity that speaks to all societies and all sorts and conditions of people.

Megachurches

The term "megachurch" is usually dated to 1966, and it originally referred to US-based congregations that attracted at least 2,000 worshippers weekly. The term was especially associated with newer churches in the US Sunbelt, usually from roots that were what the World Christian Database terms "ECP," which is to say, Evangelical, Charismatic, and Pentecostal. In 1980, US researchers identified some fifty such churches, rising to almost nine hundred in 2006: by the time of the pandemic in 2020, there were some 1600 nationwide, and an elite cohort of ninety of those had 10,000 or more worshippers. The largest concentrations were found in four Sunbelt states, namely Texas, California, Florida, and Georgia. As such, they were closely identified not just with the Evangelical upsurge, but (often) with the politically and socially conservative variants of that movement. (That picture must of course be tempered by the substantial number of churches aimed at African American or Latino constituencies.)[1]

In fact, as David Eagle shows, the megachurch phenomenon is much older than that, dating back as it does to great nineteenth-century urban churches such as London's Metropolitan Tabernacle, founded in 1861 during the era of the celebrity Baptist preacher Charles H. Spurgeon. Both in terms of its scale and achievements and the criticisms levied against it, the Metropolitan Tabernacle is, in a sense, the near ancestor of all modern megachurches. Another famous example was the Angelus Temple founded by the brilliant religious entrepreneur Aimee Semple McPherson in the 1920s, which pioneered so many of the features that attract both the admiration and hostility of more modern critics. The Angelus Temple, in particular, deserves note not just for the nature of its services and outreach but for the social niche it occupied in a new and rapidly expanding city, which foreshadows many of the later institutions that would arise in Global South communities. Then, as now, megachurches were intimately bound up with migration, modernisation, urbanisation, and the creation of whole new forms of urban and suburban life. They appealed especially to the aspirational, often to those who had achieved a moderate degree of success and status, but in ways that appeared tenuous. They appealed to restless societies.[2]

---

[1] "Database of Megachurches in the US," http://hirr.hartsem.edu/megachurch/database.html [accessed 6 August 2024]. Anne C. Loveland and Otis B. Wheeler, *From Meetinghouse to Megachurch: A Material and Cultural History* (Columbia: University of Missouri Press, 2003); Scott Thumma and Dave Travis, *Beyond Megachurch Myths: What We Can Learn from America's Largest Churches* (San Francisco: Jossey-Bass, 2007); Stephen Ellingson, *The Megachurch and The Mainline: Remaking Religious Tradition in the Twenty-First Century* (Chicago: University of Chicago Press, 2007); Omri Elisha, *Moral Ambition: Mobilization and Social Outreach in Evangelical Megachurches* (Berkeley: University of California Press, 2011); Tamelyn N. Tucker-Wongs, *The Black Megachurch: Theology, Gender, and the Politics of Public Engagement* (Waco, TX: Baylor University Press, 2011); Sam Hey, *Megachurches: Origins, Ministry, and Prospects* (Eugene, OR: Wipf & Stock, 2013); James Wellman Jr., Katie Corcoran, and Kate Stockly, *High on God: How Megachurches Won the Heart of America* (Oxford: Oxford University Press, 2020).

[2] David E. Eagle, "Historicizing the Megachurch," *Journal of Social History* 48:3 (2015), 589–604, http://people.duke.edu/~dee4/articles/Eagle_Hist_Megachurch.pdf [accessed 6 August 2024].

Megachurches in Global/World Christianity

The New Scale of Institution

Identifying megachurches with a particular size of congregation soon proved quite inadequate, as congregations swelled to far larger proportions, both within the United States and especially on the Global/World stage. By 2007, some thirty-six US churches were already drawing congregations of 10,000 weekly, leading to the coining of the still more ambitious term "gigachurch," which has not yet really entered popular parlance.[3]

But even that terminology seems over-modest when set alongside global developments. From the 1960s, very large churches began to proliferate around the world, in regions far removed from the traditional centres of Euro-American faith. Seoul's Yoido Full Gospel Church was founded in 1958 by David Yonggi Cho, and already, by 1977, it had claimed some 50,000 members, a number that soon climbed steadily. Since 2008, the senior pastor has been Younghoon Lee. In many cases, consciously following that precedent, other congregations emerged across Asia, Africa, and Latin America. In Table 1, I present a working list of the world's largest churches as of today, which raises many significant questions of definition. (I say immediately that actual numbers here are very difficult to determine, and these figures should properly be classified as guesstimates).[4]

TABLE 1 The world's largest churches by average attendance		
Yoido Full Gospel Church	South Korea	480,000
Church of Signs and Wonders	India	400,000
Calvary Temple	India	350,000
Jotabeche Methodist Pentecostal	Chile	150,000
Graha Bethany Nginden	Indonesia	140,000
New Life Fellowship Association	India	70,000
Deeper Life Bible Church	Nigeria	65,000
Victory	Philippines	65,000
Christ's Commission Fellowship	Philippines	55,000
Lakewood Church	USA	55,000

The first point is the sheer scale of congregation size, showing the existence of major churches with 50 or 100,000 followers, or more – far more in the case of Yoido Full Gospel, but also some other competitors. I do not propose to join

---

[3] Alicia Budich, "From Megachurch to 'Gigachurch,'" *CBS News*, 6 April 2012, https://www.cbsnews.com/news/from-megachurch-to-gigachurch/ [accessed 6 August 2024].

[4] Jonathan D. James, ed., *A Moving Faith: Mega Churches Go South* (Thousand Oaks, CA: Sage Publications, 2015); Wonsuk Ma, "Megachurches in Asia and the Dissenting Movement: The Case of Yoido Full Gospel Church," in Jehu H. Hanciles, ed., *The Oxford History of Protestant Dissenting Traditions*, vol. 4 (Oxford: Oxford University Press, 2019), 108–9.

a competition to devise new terms here, but clearly, the simple language of megachurch is quite inadequate. For what it is worth, in the world of information technology, the next level above "giga" is usually "tera." Here, I will use the somewhat less technical generic term of "superchurches."

A New World Map

Also striking is the sheer geographical spread, and how enormously the South now outpaces the North. That in itself has to be a central element of our story, that the global superchurch phenomenon has now become so decisively and irrevocably Southern. Of the world's ten largest churches, only one – Lakewood in Houston, Texas – stands in the United States. Moving our lens slightly to churches with 40,000 or more known or claimed believers, we find seventeen examples, divided as follows:

TABLE 2
The world's largest churches by regions

Asia	8	India	4
		Philippines	2
		Indonesia	1
		South Korea	1
Africa	3	Nigeria	3
Latin America	4	Brazil	1
		Chile	1
		El Salvador	1
		Peru	1
Other	2	United States	2

All fall in the general category of "ECP." Some are strictly non-denominational, but all, to some extent, follow those broad outlines.[5]

Were we to shift our vision more broadly, to take in, say, "gigachurches" with ten or 20,000 followers, we would assuredly find many other examples, but the overall geographical picture would not be too different. More examples would occur in Africa, say, in Nigeria, Ethiopia, and Kenya. In those nations, we find, for instance, Kenya's Nairobi Chapel, the subject of a fine study by Wanjiru Gitau. Ethiopia is home to the thriving but diffuse Mulu Wongel (Full Gospel) Church: its main congregation in Addis Ababa is one of Africa's largest megachurches. Also, as we move to this slightly smaller level, we find other churches from the Catholic tradition.[6]

---

[5] Cecil M. Robeck, Jr. and Amos Yong, eds., *The Cambridge Companion to Pentecostalism* (Cambridge University Press, 2014).

[6] Philip Jenkins, *The Next Christendom: The Rise of Global Christianity,* 3rd edition (New York: Oxford University Press, 2011); Wanjiru M. Gitau, *Megachurch Christianity Reconsidered: Millennials and Social Change in African Perspective*

Other Asian examples (both mega and giga) certainly come to mind, in Indonesia, Singapore, and elsewhere. Since the late 1980s, booming congregations such as Singapore's City Harvest have become very prominent in the city's landscape. New Creation Church has over 30,000 members, Faith Community Baptist has 12,000, and other booming congregations include Victory Family Centre and the Covenant Evangelical Free Church. As the names suggest, such churches would strike an immediate chord with anyone familiar with the structure and worship style of Charismatic or Evangelical groups in North America or around the Pacific Rim. They combine prosperity teachings with lively, vibrant services, all to the tune of cutting-edge contemporary music. With its superstar pastor, Joseph Prince, the fast-growing New Creation fits every stereotype of the expanding megachurch. It offers a wide range of media activities and is deeply involved in commercial and entrepreneurial investments. Immensely strengthened by the practice of tithing, these churches have become a huge economic force. New Creation's main sanctuary, with its spaceship architecture, proclaims success and glitzy modernity.[7]

Indonesia offers a similar picture. By far, the largest single church is Graha Bethany Nginden (Bethany Church of God), which was founded in 1977 by Pastor Abraham Alex Tanuseputra in Surabaya, the country's second city. Within a decade, the church officially qualified as a megachurch, with 2,000 worshippers, but that number then exploded to the claimed 140,000. In 2000, the church built a facility intended to seat up to 35,000. Another visible Christian entrepreneur is Stephen Tong, founder of the Indonesian Reformed Evangelical Church, which has much in common with the Pentecostal worship style, although in its theology, it diverges quite widely from that pattern. In 2008, the church opened its Messiah Cathedral in Jakarta, a classic megachurch seating 6,000, and a grandiose structure that would not look out of place in Seoul or Singapore.

Although it is by no means the largest example of its kind, for sheer ambition, it would be hard to surpass one overwhelming recent structure; namely, the Temple of Solomon, in São Paulo, Brazil. Opened in 2014, the Temple is the work of the Universal Church of the Kingdom of God (*Igreja Universal do Reino de Deus*), a Pentecostal body for whom it serves as a denominational headquarters. By global standards, its seating capacity is almost modest – a "mere" 10,000 – but the edifice is literally a reconstruction of that ancient Temple, as described so precisely in the Bible. The main difference is that it is

---

(Downers Grove, IL: IVP Academic, 2018); Asonzeh Ukah, "Sacred Surplus and Pentecostal Too-Muchness: The Salvation Economy of African Megachurches," in Stephen Hunt, ed., *Handbook of Megachurches* (Leiden: Koninklijke Brill NV. 2020), 323–44.

[7] Francis Khek Gee Lim, ed., *Mediating Piety: Technology and Religion in Contemporary Asia* (Leiden; Boston: Brill, 2009); Terence Chong, ed., *Pentecostal Megachurches in Southeast Asia: Negotiating Class, Consumption and the Nation* (Singapore: ISEAS Publishing, 2018); Vivien K. G. Lim, Thompson S. H. Teo, Neha Tripathi, and Sherry Aw, *Faith or Blind Faith: Ethical Breakdown at City Harvest Church* (London: SAGE Business Cases Originals, 2021).

substantially scaled up from that holy original, which stood a mere forty feet high. Among many other details, the Temple building includes a precise replica of the Ark of the Covenant, as well as massive menorahs, and materials were imported from Israel.[8]

For anyone accustomed to traditional maps of the Christian world, such a representation is multiply surprising. Roughly half of what we might call the superchurches are found in Asia: who would have suspected that India would have had the largest single contingent?

The Newness of Faith

In most cases, the churches are found in regions where the Christian faith is new, at least in the particular forms that we find it. Obviously, that is an oversimplification. Christianity has had some kind of presence in Korea or the Philippines since the sixteenth century, but in its distinctive "ECP" forms, this is a novelty, mainly dating to the 1950s or afterward, and enjoying its greatest success from the 1980s. The same is clearly true of Brazil and other parts of Latin America, where the presumed normality until the mid-twentieth century was Catholic, and later Protestant, and *evangélico* forms are far more recent. The superchurches thus represent what we might call the cutting edge of a new or newly defined faith.

Even so, it is highly debatable whether the superchurches should be seen as part of a wider movement towards Christianity, as opposed to vital and attractive institutions in their own right. Arguably, they represent distinctive islands of activism, rather than what we might call the visible peaks of much wider religious movements or enterprises. This is in contrast to the United States, where we find churches of every possible size and scale, and a few hundred happen to occur at the peak of the pyramid. To use another analogy, they stand at one end of a natural distribution curve. The same is true of South Korea, or Nigeria and Kenya, but elsewhere, it is evidently not true. In India, in contrast, the megachurches stand and flourish without any necessary sense that they are the forerunners of mass conversion, either in the nation as a whole or even in particular regions. Even by the most optimistic estimates, it is unlikely that Christian numbers overall will rise significantly from a (perhaps) 3% share of the population, where other faiths, both Hindu and Muslim, overwhelmingly predominate. Nor are we contemplating any kind of mass turn to Christianity in Indonesia or Singapore. The success of superchurches must, therefore, be explained on their own terms.

The Economic Context

To begin with the Asian context, the geography alone further suggests that the superchurches are a product of Asia's sensational economic and technological expansion from the mid-twentieth century. Looking today at the futuristic

---

[8] Philip Jenkins, "The Temple in Brazil," *Christian Century* (1 July 2020), 44–45.

Megachurches in Global/World Christianity   215

skylines of cities like Singapore or Seoul or Hong Kong, it is easy to forget how recently they gained that prosperity and separated themselves from other non-Western nations that have progressed much more slowly. Measured crudely by GDP per capita, South Korea in the 1960s was a poorer country than Egypt or Ghana. Matters then changed very quickly indeed, as several nations developed ferociously successful export-led economies and joined the club of high-income nations. The pioneers were the Four Tigers of South Korea, Hong Kong, Singapore, and Taiwan. That drive to growth, in turn, spilled over into other countries on the Pacific Rim, so that with varying degrees of plausibility, we speak of the Tiger Cubs – Indonesia, Malaysia, the Philippines, Thailand, and Vietnam. Progress there has been uneven, and the late 1990s witnessed a gruelling economic downturn, but conditions soon improved. In the new century, the colossal growth of China further accelerated growth in East and Southeast Asia. A separate dynamic drove the immense growth of India, above all in the more prosperous centres of innovation in the country's south, in the very regions that are now marked by those booming urban churches.

India offers multiple examples of this close association with growth, development, and rapid modernisation. The Christian presence is apparent in Hyderabad (in Telangana), with its mighty pharmaceutical and biotech industries. Hyderabad is the home of Calvary Temple, which (according to the source one chooses) proclaims itself the world's second- or third-largest Evangelical megachurch. Calvary boasts an astonishing record of growth that is wholly concentrated in the present century, from a few dozen followers at its inception in 2005 to over 300,000 today. In 2020, the church managed to accommodate 50,000 worshippers at a single service. As always in such cases, we can quibble about exact numbers, as different churches vary in how they define members, and how they collect statistics. But beyond argument, Calvary has been a phenomenal success, largely due to the energy of its charismatic founder, Satish Kumar.[9]

If Calvary stands out for its enormous scale, megachurches are a well-known feature of southern India's religious landscape. Chennai (which locals generally still call Madras) also has its great churches of recent mushroom growth. The New Life Assemblies of God church was founded in 1973 by David Mohan, and it is currently home to 40,000 members. Bangalore/Bengaluru (in Karnataka) is home to impressive megachurches of that same Assemblies of God denomination, respectively Full Gospel and Bethel. Each claims a membership of around 20,000. Both Chennai and Bangalore also count other Pentecostal-inclined megachurches, although each has "only" a few thousand followers apiece.[10]

---

[9] Jonathan D. James, "Global, 'Glocal' and Local Dynamics in Calvary Temple: India's Fastest Growing Megachurch," in Stephen Hunt, ed., *Handbook of Megachurches* (Leiden: Koninklijke Brill NV, 2020).

[10] Jonathan D. James, *McDonaldisation, Masala McGospel and Om Economics: Televangelism in Contemporary India* (London: SAGE Publications, 2010).

However, we see a similar correlation elsewhere and in surprising settings. Despite its endemic problems with religious conflict, Nigeria has enjoyed impressive development since the 1980s, and urbanisation has, of course, been very marked. It presently jostles alongside South Africa to claim the title of the continent's largest economy. But this country was not alone. Particularly during the 2010s, some of the world's most remarkable growth occurred in African nations. To quote the *Economist*'s John O'Sullivan, writing in 2013, "In the past decade, only the bloc of developing Asian economies, led by China, has grown faster than Africa ...four of the world's six fastest-growing economies in 2014 will be in sub-Saharan Africa."[11] Suddenly, Ethiopia's economy was a model to be envied – a development that has sadly been reversed following the violence and civil conflict of recent years – but for a few precious years, "Africa's Lions" reproduced the Asian Tigers and Dragons. It was these years that saw the sharpest growth in the African megachurches in Nigeria, Ethiopia, and elsewhere.

Uprooting and Aspiration

In whatever region, the economic context had and has many implications, which we may not immediately think to relate to religious matters. Of course, we are speaking of headlong urbanisation, which often occurs very swiftly. Although this point could be illustrated from any number of examples, we might look at the former Madras, which in 1950 had a population of 1.5 million: today, under the name of Chennai, the population is approaching twelve million. The population of the Manila area grew from 1.5 million in 1950 to 15 million today. Lagos's story is still more explosive, growing as it has from a near-bucolic 300,000 in 1950 to at least 16 million today, and many would put the present-day figure still higher.

Such developments drive mass migrations to cities that have recently enjoyed mushroom growth, and which have attracted hundreds of thousands of people from rural communities rooted in traditional ways of religious belief. That move has detached people from those older ways, which were commonly based on particular landscapes and ritual years intimately bound up with the cycles of nature. None of those guideposts still stand in the new urban setting. Looking at the urban growth of modern Evangelical and Pentecostal churches around the world, many observers, including myself, point to the ways in which those churches meet people's most basic needs of education, health, and welfare. Migrants newly arrived from rural or village settings desperately need to find ways of coping in a hostile metropolis where the government offers little or no assistance. Churches offer a way of achieving instant community.

Having said this, megachurches assuredly cater to constituencies far higher on the social scale, to distinctly middle-class and aspiring groups. Were we to

---

[11] John O'Sullivan is quoted from
https://www.economist.com/news/2013/11/18/digging-deeper [accessed 6 August 2024].

Megachurches in Global/World Christianity

identify India's largest and most globalised urban communities, the booming high-tech centres of Bangalore, Hyderabad, and Chennai would all rank at or near the top, and as we have seen, they are home to the most ostentatiously booming churches. Such economic growth and modernisation have obvious consequences, including a shift from agriculture and industry to service sectors and technology, with a proliferation of professional, managerial, and administrative positions. The change also demands a very substantial growth of workers at lesser and middling positions, which opens the way to women's employment on an unprecedented scale. That change also correlated with a huge upsurge in higher education, again with women very well represented. Such a change – a social revolution – could not fail to have sweeping effects on aspirations and self-definitions.

As more women work outside the home, that further undermines traditional concepts of home and family obligations and is commonly reflected in a precipitous decline in fertility rates and family size, which was most acutely evident in such economic vanguards as South Korea, Taiwan, and Singapore. Increasingly, then, both men and women find themselves in search of new ways of finding and defining community, outside older and seemingly inevitable family structures. To a surprising extent, a neat correlation can clearly be traced between the upsurge of superchurches and the decline of fertility rates in particular regions.[12]

Although stemming from very different backgrounds, those aspirational groups are just as detached as those newly arriving peasants from the older ways of rural society. In particular, they are very accustomed to technological modernity and identify easily with communities that offer and reinforce such a package of ideas and symbolism. Although those ideas might have originated in North America, they have subsequently spread very widely and represent what we might call a global style of international religious modernity. That certainly includes mass media and an expectation of familiarity with social media in advertising and communication.[13]

The growth of very large churches thus reflects social, economic, and demographic trends, which together create a market for a new and innovative institution, an opportunity for a visionary church planter. However, those "demand" factors alone can never be sufficient to stand in isolation. Two countries may have exactly the same conditions that give rise to superchurches, but whether such an institution develops in one rather than the other depends on factors beyond the market. Not only must a marketplace exist, but the legal and political environment must be suitable and accommodating. To take an obvious

---

[12] Philip Jenkins, *Fertility and Faith: The Demographic Revolution that is Transforming all the World's Religions* (Waco, TX: Baylor University Press, 2020).

[13] Prema A. Kurien, *Ethnic Church Meets Megachurch: Indian American Christianity in Motion* (New York: New York University Press, 2017); Kathryn Joyce, "Deliver Us, Lord, From the Startup Life," *Wired*, 18 February 2020, https://www.wired.com/story/midwest-christian-entrepreneurs-startup-life/ [accessed 6 August 2024].

example, megachurches face a very difficult challenge in communist countries such as China or Vietnam, which have such an embedded hostility to civil society and organisations beyond party control.

Absolutely all the factors that underlie the success of superchurches in Indonesia or India should theoretically apply to Chinese boom cities, and we do indeed find some very large congregations in awe-inspiring new buildings, as at Tianhe Church in Guangzhou, or Chongyi Church in Hangzhou, which with seating for 5,500 is an indisputable candidate for a megachurch. But so also was the Golden Lampstand Church, in Shanxi Province, which communist authorities literally dynamited in 2018, as part of a general purge of unlicensed and unapproved buildings. Beijing's very sizeable Shouwang Church was closed in the following year. Such acts were widely condemned, but the horror caused precisely served the interests of the authorities, who were and remain anxious to underline the draconian limitations that would befall any church if its numbers appeared to be growing out of hand, or if those churches ventured into anything like the same range of activities as their counterparts in neighbouring societies.[14]

In other regions, religious rivalries play a role, and even normally tolerant countries such as Indonesia and Malaysia would be reluctant to allow too much of a very public Christian efflorescence. The fact that superchurches are so well represented in India, say, reflects the attitudes of local and state governments, and not the fact that India is any more "Christian" than China. Superchurches happen not just where demand exists, but where they are allowed.

Exporting the Megachurch

Of their nature, the Global South societies that support superchurches are very well connected with larger patterns of migration and trade, which unite them with the Global North. It is not, then, surprising to see those very characteristic institutions faithfully reproduced in settings within the landscapes of traditional Euro-American Christendom.

In the British context, one of the major demographic trends in recent years has been the influx of African migrants, especially from countries where very large megachurches are deeply familiar institutions. One spectacular manifestation of the new churches on British soil would be London's Kingsway International Christian Centre (KICC), founded by Nigerian pastor Matthew Ashimolowo. He began in 1992 with only three hundred members, and now the KICC seats 5,000 worshippers at its main facility, the Miracle Centre, as well as several satellite churches. The KICC is claimed as the largest church to be created in Britain since the Metropolitan Tabernacle in 1861, and the Miracle Centre's auditorium offers double the capacity of Westminster Abbey or St.

---

[14] Russell Goldman, "Chinese Police Dynamite Christian Megachurch," *New York Times* (12 January 2018); Massimo Introvigne, "Shouwang Church: The Rise and Fall of Beijing's Largest Megachurch," *Bitter Winter* (March 2019), https://bitterwinter.org/the-rise-and-fall-of-beijings-largest-megachurch/ [accessed 6 August 2024].

Paul's Cathedral. Although the church has been hit by financial scandals, the ministry continues to be a powerful force in Britain and beyond. Matthew Ashimolowo uses cable television and radio to speak to a wider audience in the United Kingdom and beyond – in Nigeria, Ghana, South Africa, Malawi, Uganda, Sierra Leone, and the Anglophone Caribbean. His programmes also reach much of Europe.[15]

Another very successful planter of churches of all sizes is Nigeria's Redeemed Christian Church of God, founded in 1952, and which developed a global mission outreach of extraordinary scope. Among its thousands of churches and "parishes" we find places like London's Jesus House of All Nations, founded in 1994, with some 3,000 worshippers. Of Britain's four largest megachurches, all have African pastors. Pastors from Francophone Africa also dominate such large congregations in France and Belgium.

Others from the Global South play a visible role in contemporary European churches, but recent political developments have sharply constrained their activities and achievements. For many years, scholars of global/world Christianity were fascinated by the work of Nigerian Sunday Adelaja, who founded a flourishing church in Kyiv, Ukraine, the Embassy of the Blessed Kingdom of God for all Nations. Adelaja was one of many bright African and Asian students brought to the Soviet Union to receive an education and ideally to become a future advocate of pro-Soviet views. Within a couple of years, the Soviet Union itself dissolved, and in 1994 Adelaja founded a Pentecostal congregation in the new Ukrainian republic. From seven founding members, the church soon claimed 30,000 adherents, overwhelmingly white, and some very powerful indeed. At its height, in the early 2010s, over twenty services were held every Sunday in various auditoriums, and fifty daughter churches function in the larger region. The church's Christian television and radio programmes reached some eight million people. Pastor Adelaja faced several legal and political challenges, which could probably have been withstood, but of course the recent war in Ukraine has profoundly disrupted all aspects of civil society, and the future of this ministry remains highly uncertain.[16]

There is little point in enumerating every example of such migrant megachurches, but one in particular does demand our attention. In recent decades, the Arab Gulf nations have attracted many migrants from India, including a good number of Christians following the ancient churches of that land. Dubai is now home to St. Thomas's Orthodox Cathedral, with its 3,500 parishioners, which technically qualifies it as a megachurch. Having said that, this is not part of the familiar "ECP" story, as the cathedral is part of the

---

[15] Philip Jenkins, *God's Continent: Christianity, Islam and Europe's Religious* Crisis (New York: Oxford University Press, 2007); Mark J. Cartledge, Sarah L. B. Dunlop, Heather Buckingham, and Sophie Bremner, *Megachurches and Social Engagement: Public Theology in Practice* (Leiden: Brill, 2019); Katharine Stockland, *African Pentecostalism in Britain: Migration, Inclusion, and The Prosperity Gospel* (New York: Routledge, 2022).

[16] Jenkins, *God's Continent.*

Malankara Orthodox Syrian Church, which traces its origins to Christian missions in southern India during the first or second centuries AD. In modern times, the Malankara Church is strongest in the province of Kerala, from which throngs of migrants travelled to the Gulf.

Attacks and Advantages

In understanding the appeal of mega (and larger) churches, we can actually learn a great deal by considering the highly negative criticisms of such institutions launched by their foes. This does not mean that we should take such attacks as necessarily correct or truthful, but some actually contain some worthwhile insights that are more positive than they might have intended.

When the megachurch phenomenon was first identified in the 1960s (or rather, rediscovered), scholars and journalists alike tended to be highly critical, and even scornful. Throughout, the point of comparison was with the familiar Mainline churches, which were then at the height of their prestige and popularity. The presumed normality of religious life was of established small or midsize congregations in cities or suburban areas, which followed well-established practices and organisational methods. They were sober (in every sense), respectable, and eschewed outward displays of religious passion or enthusiasm. Above all, this vision assumed settled and stable communities where congregants were well integrated into local structures. It also assumed a stable family structure, and a rigid division of gender roles in the labour market.

In contrast, megachurches fascinated and amazed because they departed so far from this vision in so many ways, appealing as they did to very new communities arising in whole new suburbs or exurbs, developed on a far larger geographical scale. That detachment from older assumptions and class perspectives made the new churches open to innovative kinds of presentation, as well as music and devotional practices. From a hostile perspective, the suggestion was, and often is, that megachurches represented a spectator sport, a kind of passive entertainment, where a person lost in a vast auditorium watched a stage act of professional musicians, flanking a showman preacher. The megachurches seemed to offer little direct human contact when compared with the highly integrated and face-to-face settings of the Mainline. The recurrent themes in the critique are those of the congregation's passivity and shallowness and an utter lack of spiritual or intellectual depth, all of which open the door to predatory pastors out for their own profit. It is, at best, cheap grace, and the spirituality of such churches is – in this grim view – barely skin deep. Not coincidentally, critics of the Mainline deployed ideas very similar to those then being deployed against the mass media in which Americans were believed to be saturated. It was in 1961 that we first find the famous description of television as "a vast wasteland of junk."

The classic example of such a critique was Sinclair Lewis's *Elmer Gantry* (1927), a sweeping satire of Evangelical abuses in that era, culminating in a thinly veiled parody of Aimee Semple Macpherson and the Angelus Temple, with what was alleged to be its vulgar showmanship. Lewis's suggestion is that the vast majority of such celebrity preachers were fakes or confidence tricksters,

Megachurches in Global/World Christianity   221

while the book's fictionalised version of Sister Aimee is in fact a crypto-pagan planning to restore the worship of a Mother Goddess. Putting aside that extreme charge, most of the other elements of the Elmer Gantry critique remain very much alive, and are reinforced by later scandals involving televangelists and megachurch pastors.[17]

Responses and Realities

The responses to such an indictment are many, but the most significant is that the megachurches – from Spurgeon's time onward – were making a genuine effort to reach out to the masses, especially within urban settings, where one could no longer assume the prosperous and stable structures of Baby Boom families. Very significantly, the great majority of the Mainline denominations that were used as the point of comparison were already beginning a precipitous decline, which by the end of the century could become near-terminal. In contrast, the megachurches were beginning their remarkable upward ascent.

Throughout the critique of that older era, we cannot fail to be struck by the overwhelming class prejudice and the blinkered vision that this provoked in observers. To take a specific point of controversy, we look at the question of authentic spirituality in this so-called "wasteland," which in reality is no such thing. The experience of an ordinary megachurch believer is not confined to the auditorium spectaculars that fit so easily into segments on television news and documentaries. Of course, most or all such churches combine that communal experience with a great many other forms of participation, especially in small group settings and networks, in which so much of the actual spiritual development occurs. To take one of the most famous examples, Yoido Full Gospel Church has been spectacularly successful in its use of "cells" to promote both community and spirituality and to localise the works of the Spirit. The heritage of Pietism and the small group extends far more widely than we might easily assume.

Moreover, the new and large churches practise distinctive forms of Spirit-based devotion that are, in fact, deeply rooted in the Christian tradition, above all, the ministry of healing, which was so central a fact of the earliest church and its evangelism. Again, that kind of activity often appalled conservative critics, who freely cited "Elmer Gantry," but the global appeal is unquestionable and quite central. Particularly hard to convey to liberal critics in the Global North is the very wide concept of healing in such churches: healing of the body, yes, but also of the mind, the spirit, the community, and of society as a whole. It is an impressive vision.[18]

---

[17] Mark T. Mulder and Gerardo Marti, *The Glass Church: Robert H. Schuller, the Crystal Cathedral, and the Strain of Megachurch Ministry* (New Brunswick: Rutgers University Press, 2020).

[18] Paul Gifford, *Ghana's New Christianity* (Bloomington, IN: Indiana University Press, 2004) and also *Christianity, Development and Modernity in Africa* (New York: Oxford University Press, 2016). Candy Gunther Brown, ed., *Global Pentecostal and*

Prosperity

It is in this context that we must read the critiques of the prosperity teachings that are so commonplace in the superchurches, in the ministry of such figures as Nigeria's David Oyedepo, of the Faith Tabernacle mentioned earlier, which seats some 50,000 worshippers. Bishop Oyedepo is usually cited as one of the country's wealthiest pastors, who commands a wide range of enterprises in media and education, including his own university. Across Africa, prosperity teachings are central to the ubiquitous culture of revivals and miracle crusades, so much so that they overwhelm more traditional Charismatic or Pentecostal doctrines. In London, Matthew Ashimolowo's church teaches that poverty and unemployment are manifestations of sin, against which Christians must struggle. However heartless this may sound at first hearing, the actual consequences are very different. In practice, this means that the faithful should relieve other members of the congregation by giving them jobs, while the church sternly teaches habits of thrift and sobriety. Viewed correctly, prosperity too is a form of healing.[19]

Most prosperity churches not only condemn poverty, they teach invaluable ways of avoiding it, like learning not to fall into debt, and actually saving up in order to buy material goods. Debt is a demon to be defeated. Few communities in the world could fail to benefit from such a lesson, but it is vital for people moving suddenly from a rural setting into an overwhelming African metropolis, with all the consumerist blandishments offered to the poor. In such a setting, being a member of a church offers life-saving access to social networks of mutual aid and support, which teach essential survival skills. Meanwhile, peer pressure (especially in small group settings) helps believers avoid the snares of substance abuse. If the faithful do not actually receive blessings that are too rich to count, at least their membership in a church vastly enriches their life chances. Bishop Oyedepo has reasonably said that the prosperity promise only makes sense in the context of enriching the wider community far beyond the narrow confines of the church.[20] Once again, we must be conscious of the sources of the critiques so regularly offered of such teachings, coming as they do from people in prosperous societies which can reliably assume the provision of basic necessities. Such advantages cannot safely be assumed in Nigeria, say, or India, where it seems highly appropriate to make them the subjects of prayer.

Charismatic Healing (Oxford: Oxford University Press, 2011); Kate Bowler, *Blessed: A History of The American Prosperity Gospel* (New York: Oxford University Press, 2013).

[19] Philip Jenkins, *The New Faces of Christianity: Believing the Bible in the Global South* (New York: Oxford University Press, 2006); Jenkins, *God's Continent.*

[20] David Maxwell, "Delivered from the Spirit of Poverty," *Journal of Religion in Africa* 28:3 (1998), 350–73.

Opportunity and Response

In summary, the very large churches foster the creation of whole new forms of community that are ideal for "people in motion," for migrants both domestic and international, and individuals in search of a larger context. The new institutions are ideally suited for those who aspire to better lives, and who seek strictly practical means of achieving those goals, against obstacles that can appear quite overwhelming. Moreover, the megachurch setting is perfect for people who no longer fit into nuclear family structures: besides the families who obviously do attend, the setting also appeals to young adults of both sexes, to singles and the divorced, and to the aged. At every point, these churches fulfil those roles far better than the now fading Mainline.

But if they are so well fitted for a new and emerging world, any account of those churches must pay full credit to the individuals and teams who sparked them, who saw those opportunities and built upon them.

Christianity Moving South – Walter Hollenweger's Propositions Revisited: A Conversation

Casely B. Essamuah and Jean-Daniel Plüss

Introduction[1]

Recent studies on global Christianity have stressed the fact that the centre of Christian faith is moving south.[2] For centuries, the heart of Christendom was in Europe, which had a Christian population, universities, spiritual centres, and missionary agencies. The situation was still predominantly Western as adherents of Jesus moved to the Americas. However, a shift set in when the number of converts to Christ began to grow rapidly on the Asian and African continents. Today, we can surmise that the typical average Christian in sub-Saharan Africa is male and is about 24 years old. This starkly contrasts with what can be observed in the West, where congregations are greying, and young people are increasingly less religious.

Concurrently, one hundred years ago, Pentecostalism as a movement had just begun to exist and was considered by representatives of other churches as the "new kid on the block."[3] Now, Pentecostalism is considered the fastest-growing religion in the world.[4] It has been estimated that one out of every twelve people alive in the world today is Pentecostal or Charismatic in their orientation. In other words, one out of four Christians consider the concrete guidance and experience of the Holy Spirit essential to their faith.[5]

One may wonder why these developments have taken place and what role Spirit-empowered faith may play. Walter J. Hollenweger (1927–2016), an influential scholar on Pentecostalism and an intercultural theologian, gave five reasons why he believed Pentecostals have an important role to play in the context of world Christianity. He claimed that they were influenced by the black oral roots of that movement. The reasons he gave are:

---

[1] The introduction, the context to the questions, and the material on the ecumenical roots of Pentecostalism have been written by J-D. Plüss.

[2] Gina A. Zurlo, *Global Christianity: A Guide to the World's Largest Religion from Afghanistan to Zimbabwe* (Grand Rapids, MI: Zondervan Academic, 2022) and Wesley Granberg-Michaelson, *Future Faith: Ten Challenges Reshaping the Practice of Christianity* (Minneapolis, MN: Fortress Press, 2018).

[3] Wonsuk Ma, "Pentecostalism: A New but Big Kid on the Global Christian Block," *Pentecostal Education* 7:1 (2022), 73–91.

[4] Cf. HolyBlog, "Mind-Blowing Statistics About Christianity You Need to Know," https://www.holyart.com/blog/mind-blowing-statistics-christianity-need-know/, accessed 1 March 2023.

[5] Granberg-Michaelson, *Future Faith*, 88; Zurlo, *Global Christianity*, 30.

1. Pentecostals are primarily oral in their liturgies;
2. they are basically narrative in their theology and witness;
3. Pentecostal services are geared to maximum participation;
4. dreams and visions are part of personal and communal life, and finally,
5. they are open to holistic solutions, thereby overcoming the dichotomy between body and mind.

Hollenweger elaborated these criteria in the 1980s, and since then, many significant events have occurred. We may raise the question: how are these claims looked at today? And, more specifically, if they still hold, what could they mean for global Christianity?

In an attempt to illuminate the subject, five questions have been raised to Dr. Casely Essamuah, the current secretary of the Global Christian Forum (GCF). He is a Ghanaian-born Methodist minister well-acquainted with Christianity in the Majority World. Later in the text, another root of Pentecostalism will be addressed. According to Walter Hollenweger, a strong ecumenical conviction characterises Pentecostal thought and praxis. In order to exemplify this "ecumenical root," in an interview led by Dr. Plüss, Dr. Casely Essamuah will be looking at the ministry of Yoido Full Gospel Church in Seoul, Korea, which is currently led by Rev. Dr. Younghoon Lee.

Orality in Worship

The Western mind is often described as analytical in nature and preoccupied with written statements. Similarly, many Christians in the North worship with set liturgies. Does it hold true that people in the Global South tend to communicate within a framework that is shared orally? Is that, in your opinion, a blessing? If so, what would it take for Western people to appreciate an oral way of celebrating their faith and interpreting life?

Casely Essamuah answers:

In an article of this length, we can only reflect on generalities and paint with broad strokes, but it is true that the non-Western mind, generally found in the Global South, tends to be more orally engaged than with written orientation. Part of these trends have to do with the church traditions that have grown in different regions. For example, Catholic and Orthodox churches in the Global South will still use their traditional liturgies, while many Protestant churches in the Global North do not follow a text-based liturgy. The difference occurs when many historical Protestant traditions are planted in the soil of the Global South, and they no longer follow the same written liturgies, or they proceed to add significant non-textual elements. This helps to include local ways of thinking and interpreting the world in the spiritual lives of the church members.

However, just because the Global South prioritises orality does not mean that they do not value written literature. The volume of new literature produced by Global South Pentecostals, for example, is quite staggering. These books tend to be more popular than academic ones, seeking to build up the faith of local congregations rather than engaging in scholarly conversation with the academic guild.

This being said, it is also important to remember that the significant inequities in access to higher education and publishing resources also result in fewer academic

Christianity Moving South

works from these communities and regions. Could it be the case that since the majority of scholarly Christian output in the Global North is geared to the academy, this may as well explain some of the decline in active Christianity in the Global North?

Western Christians are learning about the value of orality, especially due to the influence of social media. People are taking in an increasing amount of content every day through audio-visual means, whereas previously they relied more on texts. The rise in social media and its influence on society, including on faith formation in local congregations, shows the power of oral forms of thinking and expressing faith.

Narrative Theology and Witness

The well-known Roman Catholic liturgist James D. Crichton once wrote that the ground pattern of all Christian worship is a "response in faith which issues into praise, thanksgiving, and supplication ... This response is also promoted by the Holy Spirit (Rom 8:27) so that through Christ in the Spirit we respond to the Father's love."[6] It seems that many Christians in the Majority World do exactly that by telling stories of how they have found faith in Jesus Christ. They have reasons for thanksgiving because they are witnesses to the grace and goodness of God personally experienced. Furthermore, they wrap their supplications into real-life narratives of suffering and struggle. Based on these interactions, Hollenweger would argue, these mostly young Christians develop their faith and their theological convictions in this way. How have you experienced the impact of sharing faith stories on world Christianity?

Casely Essamuah answers:

It is true that Christians in the Majority World often turn to stories when thinking about their faith. However, it is easier for us to understand the value of stories when we remember how frequently the Bible uses stories to talk about God and God's people. The Israelites were told to recount stories of God delivering them from Egypt and other saving works. The early church spread the good news by telling stories about Jesus.

Christians today read these biblical stories and expect to receive the same works of grace that previous generations of God's people received. For Global South Christians, the stories in the Bible are not for analysis but to reinforce the belief and expectation that these miracles may be repeated in their lives as well. At the interpersonal level, people share testimonies with the hope that they inspire faith in hearers (Romans 10:17). If God did something miraculous for my neighbour, what stops me from expecting a similar miracle in my own life? Stories are also used as a worshipful response to these acts of God. Narrative theology is a common way for Christians to process their experiences and share them with each other according to a biblical pattern.

The Global Christian Forum uses the sharing of faith stories, not necessarily for the sake of exhortation or worship, but because that is the way that Christians use stories to share the beginnings of their faith journey with Jesus Christ. Even when

---

[6] J. D. Crichton, "A Theology of Worship," in Cheslyn Jones, Geoffrey Wainwright, Edwad Yarnold, eds., *The Study of Liturgy* (London: SPCK, 1978), 9.

communities use stories for different purposes, the inclusion of these differences within the Forum lets participants understand more easily the diversity that exists within and between churches. Forums encourage unity and communication using a model of dialogue that local Christian communities already employ.

One way we describe what we do in the GCF is that we seek to discover "Christ in each other and each other in Christ" and, by so doing, break down barriers that have divided us and build bridges for closer cooperation or, at the very least, better understanding. Not set up as a formal organisation or an institution, we use our network to serve as an incubator for many significant theological dialogues that are initially conceived through encounters at GCF tables.

Our mantra, "who is missing at the table," also enables us to keep our circumference nimble to engage with others outside our fold, for whom Jesus Christ is acknowledged as perfect in His divinity and His humanity.

Maximum Participation

In many Mainline churches, the participants expect the priest, pastor, or layperson to lead in worship, and the believers follow more or less passively. Even in younger churches, where so-called worship bands play popular songs of worship, one often notices an active/passive divide. Some people perform, and others listen. It seems that not only Pentecostals, but African Christians in general are much more involved in worship. How do you see the importance of the communal dimension in celebration and commitment? Can Christians in the North learn from their brothers and sisters in the South?

Casely Essamuah answers:

The communal dimension of Christian worship is because of Christians gathering for worship. Again, we see this pattern in Scripture where the whole of the body of Christ is built into a spiritual house and holy priesthood. In the Hebrew Scriptures, Moses wishes that all of God's people were prophets, with the Spirit of the Lord falling on them as well (Numbers 11:29). The priesthood and prophethood of believers shape Christian worship. Priests and prophets, after all, are not passive bystanders in the service of God.

Another undeniable factor is that most Global North communities operate out of an individualistic worldview, whereas most Global South communities tend to operate out of a communal worldview. That worldview determines one's sense of freedom as well as restriction in any given space.

The global church in worship usually incorporates elements that embody significant physical movements beyond standing and sitting. Several churches in the Global South, particularly in sub-Saharan Africa, have lengthy offertory times when the congregation dances to the front to present their tithes and offerings. To an outsider who is used to a sedate and predicate form of worship, this maximum participation of all could be an interesting dimension of worship.

Another aspect of communal participation has been propagated by promoting small group meetings during the week. Pastor Yonggi Cho, the founder of Yoido Full Gospel Church in Seoul, Korea, has been a primary force in advancing such cell groups where believers and interested people gather in small groups to worship, share their faith, and study the teachings of the Bible. Dr. Younghoon Lee, Pastor Cho's successor, has continued this essential element of church life and thus has contributed to the adoption of this model of Christian discipleship across the world.

Christianity Moving South 229

This way of being together has found positive resonance within the various branches of Christianity during the past decades. This aspect of practising one's faith is very much in line with communal values and lifestyle found in the Majority Word.

Transrational Phenomena

Walter Hollenweger used to tell how he learned to take the stories of his African and Asian students more seriously when he realised how intertwined their belief in spiritual powers was with the daily realities they faced. In the 1970s, he had to convince his fellow university professors in the West that there was more than intellectual argument shaped by the Enlightenment.[7] Fifty years later, we find many churches, especially in the Global South, that have incorporated deliverance ministries and prayers for healing in their worship. Are these developments significant? Do we need a more holistic approach to understanding a life of faith?

Casely Essamuah answers:

It is worth remembering that Christian liturgies were first developed in cultures where struggles against spiritual powers were a normal part of social life. However, over time, some parts of Christianity decided that parts of the Bible were no longer operational and thus limited in its day-to-day usefulness in the realities of life.

Christians in the global world, and of all denominational backgrounds, have done much in reintroducing these concerns into communal worship settings. The presence of "signs and wonders" during services is also seen as an attractional model of mission and evangelism. The demonstration of God's power among his people is seen as a confirmation of the Gospel proclamation of the church. Christians in the Global South care more about the effectiveness of the Gospel message than what I would term "prepositional or philosophical truthfulness." After all, of what use is something if it is considered true but ineffective?

However, this understanding of evangelism does have dangers. Jesus often criticised people for seeking signs or following him because he provided food. Even today, Christians in some parts of the world are more concerned with whether a religious system works rather than if it is true. It is tempting for churches to draw crowds through Charismatic manifestations without preaching the fullness of the Gospel message.

Some preachers unfortunately take advantage of the hopeless situation in which their congregations find themselves. J. Kwabena Asamoah-Gyadu argues that since Africa struggles with a litany of problems ranging from "endemic poverty, corruption at the highest level of governance, and broken medical and economic systems," the peoples' faith in God becomes an irreplaceable anchor in this stormy sea. It is rather unfortunate; he goes on to argue that "some preachers exploit the same vulnerable people with principles of sowing and reaping that many have practiced for years without the expected results, keeping the cycle of poverty

---

[7] Walter J. Hollenweger, *Geist und Materie, Interkulturelle Theologie 3* (München: Chr. Kaiser Verlag, 1988).

running by blaming insufficient tithes and offerings and demons for the unworkable principles that they are taught."[8]

Overcoming Dichotomies

As a follow-up to the last question, we could say that many Christians in the South do not live with a spirit/body dichotomy and that the Charismatic emphasis on healing can be understood in a wider context. Walter Hollenweger, therefore, emphasised the significance of Spirit-empowered Christianity for ecumenical endeavours.[9] How have you, as secretary of the Global Christian Forum, experienced the potential for healing and reconciliation among Christians? Again, can the churches of the North learn something from the churches of the South?

Casely Essamuah answers:

Here, let me reference one of my mentors. The late Professor Kwesi Dickson taught me at the University of Ghana, Legon, and later served as head of the Methodist Church Ghana and in the ecumenical world as president of the All Africa Conference of Churches. He used to share with us that the predilection that Africans had for the Old Testament arose out of four categories: 1) the lack of a distinction between secular and spiritual realms; 2) the use of rites of passage into different phases of life; 3) the numerous ways of honouring the ancestors/dead; and lastly 4) the presence of themes of justice and emancipation among African Christians akin to the Israelite experience.

These four commonalities between the world of the Old Testament and the social world of African Christianity dominate the concerns of African churches. Healing and reconciliation are areas where the secular/spiritual divide is overcome. In a biological sense, healing is a physical act caused by the supervening act of the Spirit. In a more metaphorical sense, healing and reconciliation are both acts that concern the ordinary, daily, observable world, and yet they are acts of God.

The Global Christian Forum tries to overcome this same divide by showing that the spiritual unity of Christians should not be separate from the concrete, physical nature of the church in its organisational structures and practices. What churches do cannot be held separate from the theological claims we make about their unity. The contribution of Spirit-empowered Christianity to the ecumenical movement is another manifestation that overcomes this false dichotomy within global Christianity.

On Hollenweger's Ecumenical Root of Pentecostalism

It is almost a contradiction in terms to refer to the Pentecostal movement as being basically ecumenical in outlook. Has not the rise of Pentecostal churches led to a proliferation of denominations and independent ecclesial bodies across the globe? The Center for the Study of Global Christianity counted in 2019 45,000

---

[8] J. Kwabena Asamoah-Gyadu, "Your Miracle is on the Way: Oral Roberts and Mediated Pentecostalism in Africa," *Spiritus: ORU Journal of Theology* 3:1 (2018), 5–26.

[9] Hollenweger, *Pentecostalism*, 334–88.

Christianity Moving South   231

Christian denominations worldwide.[10] Many of these are considered to belong to the classical Pentecostal renewal movement and the independent Charismatic churches and networks. So how can Pentecostal churches be claimed to have the potential to be an instrument towards greater unity in Christ? Walter Hollenweger has argued that the Pentecostal renewal movement had ecumenical beginnings.[11] He mentioned the German Lutheran minister Jonathan A. A. B. Paul (1853–1931), the French Reformed pastor Louis Dallière (1887–1976), the British Anglican priest Alexander. A. Boddy (1854–1930), and the Dutch officer of the Salvation Army, Gerrit R. Polman (1868–1932).[12] All of these had diverse ecclesial backgrounds and doctrinal convictions. Yet they had two points in common. They could witness to a personal relationship with the risen Christ, and they had experienced a life-changing encounter with the Holy Spirit. These points of convergence weighed heavier than differences in sacramental practice or ecclesial structure. To give an example, Pentecostal pastors in Switzerland wrote an open letter in 1913 emphasising that they understood their ministry as one that would want to maintain unity in the Spirit because God's children could be found in all denominations.[13]

Dr. Hollenweger detected four developments towards ecumenical attitudes within Western Pentecostalism. In the first phase, Pentecostalism began as an ecumenical renewal movement breaking through many conventional barriers. "[Pentecostalism] sees in the experience of the Holy Spirit the one important force which sweeps away all denominational, racial, educational, and social divides."[14] During a second period, early Pentecostals organised themselves into local congregations and were heavily influenced by Evangelicalism. In the third phase, Pentecostals in the West were no longer part of a renewal movement. Their churches instead developed into highly clericalised denominations. Hollenweger then argued that, in a fourth phase, Pentecostals began to return to their ecumenical root by starting dialogues with mainline denominations like the Roman Catholic Church (1972–), the World Communion of Reformed Churches (1996–), the Lutheran World Federation (2004–2010, 2016–) and other bodies.[15]

The question arises: is this ecumenical disposition visible more concretely than exclusively on the level of international conversations? How far can it be

---

[10] https://www.gordonconwell.edu/center-for-global-christianity/research/quick-facts/ accessed 13 December 2023.

[11] Hollenweger, *Pentecostalism*, 334–47.

[12] Others could be added, like Thomas Ball Barratt (1862–1940), the Norwegian Methodist pastor, and Lewi Pethrus (1884–1974) from Sweden, who was a Baptist minister.

[13] Jean-Daniel Plüss, *Vom Geist bewegt. Die Geschichte der Schweizerischen Pfingstmission* (Kreuzlingen: Asaph Verlag, 2015), 38, 216.

[14] Hollenweger, *Pentecostalism*, 355.

[15] When Walter Hollenweger wrote his second major book on Pentecostalism in the mid-1990s he mentioned the Catholic–Pentecostal dialogue and the involvement of Pentecostals with the World Council of Churches. Since then, the dialogues with the Reformed, Lutherans, and Anglicans have also been significant.

noticed on a regional and local level? Is this ecumenical development noticeable in the Global South? And if we want to look at a local context, how does this disposition, for example, manifest itself in the world's largest Pentecostal congregation, Yoido Full Gospel Church in Seoul, Korea?

Casely Essamuah answers:

Cecil (Mel) Robeck, in an article in this book, spells out some of the ecumenical engagements of Yoido Gospel Church and the role played by the honoree of this Festschrift, Dr. Younghoon Lee.

Armed with a terminal theological degree from an outstanding Christian university in the United States and firmly grounded in the Korean Pentecostal heritage, Dr. Lee has served as a bridge-builder in interpreting the global Christian community, first to Pentecostalism and then to Korean Pentecostalism. By so doing, he has shown that the worldview shared by Pentecostals (and, dare I say, of most Global South Christians) is much closer to the Scriptures than the "desacralized, post-Enlightenment and scientific worldview" in the Global North.[16]

The world needs more and more church leaders of the calibre of Dr. Younghoon Lee, who have studied in the best that the Western world can offer and hold significant leadership positions in their home countries, [and] who can serve as bridge-builders in a world that is increasingly divisive.

Conclusion by Casely Essamuah

In his farewell lecture, Hollenweger said that one of the greatest forces of multiculturalism in the church was the ministry of Christians from the Global South serving in the Global North, especially those who serve beyond their ethnic or national enclaves. In a very telling quotation, cited below, he states,

It is very important that some *Third World theologians help us in the West to develop our congregational life and theology.* They should not be recruited for service to their own so-called ethnic minorities only, i.e., Chinese for the Chinese in California, Caribbeans for the Caribbeans in England, Africans for the Africans in France. The *native* western congregations and the western faculties of theology should have representations of another type of Christianity. When an Indian baptizes a little Swiss girl, when a Caribbean celebrates a white English marriage, when a German congregation receives communion from the black hands of an African, this does more to help us see and overcome our monoculturalism than many learned articles. After all, we will still send Europeans and Americans into all the world to teach the gospel – even if these missionaries have sometimes only a flimsy knowledge of local culture and languages. So why should we not have the experience from the other side and accept pastors and teachers who have to wrestle with the culture and language of Switzerland, France or Germany?[17]

I first read these words of Hollenweger as a graduate student at Harvard, and I was immediately struck by them, and so I always kept a copy of the article in my files. More than thirty years later, I can see that, as far as my ministerial

---

[16] See Cecil M. Robeck's "Yoido Full Gospel Church and Ecumenism" in this book.

[17] Walter J. Hollenweger, "The Discipline of Thought and Action in Mission," *International Review of Mission* 80:317 (1991), 103–4.

Christianity Moving South

career is concerned, Hollenweger was a prophet. As a Ghanaian Methodist, I have had the privilege of serving two significant majority-white congregations in Boston (Park Street Church) and Annapolis, MD (Bay Area Community Church). For both churches, I was the only non-white, non-American-born minister. My daily assignment was to oversee their large global missions programmes by liaising with the sent missionaries and mobilising for their requests for prayer and material support. I visited them as often as necessary. In addition to that, I was serving as a minister or pastor and so officiated at baptisms, weddings, funerals, and all other ministerial duties that were assigned.

I hope that my three decades in ministry of serving as a Global Southerner in majority-white churches have positively impacted the understanding of each other as followers of Christ. Hollenweger prophesied it and I lived it unwittingly.

Theology in the Global South is conceived and lived in practical terms. Its goal is to ensure the faithfulness of the called to a lifestyle of discipleship modelling Jesus Christ. Dr. Younghoon Lee, serving one of the largest churches in today's world, models for us what a bridge-building ministry can be.

The Significance of the Voice of the Spirit in Pentecostal Spirituality and Leadership in the Malaysian Assemblies of God

Eva Wong Suk Kyun

Introduction

Pentecostal spirituality is often contextualised from the main beliefs and practices described in the two fundamental texts, Joel 2 and Acts 2. These texts shape the understanding of traditional Pentecostal theology and practice. [1] Baptism in the Holy Spirit (BHS) is the primary Pentecostal experience and doctrine from which other key Pentecostal distinctives are derived. BHS, glossolalia, and missions are stated in the Tenets of Faith of the Assemblies of God (AG), while prophecies, dreams, and visions (PDV) or "Voice of the Spirit" in Pentecostal parlance, is an implicit theology and practice shaped by Joel 2:28–29 and its fulfilment in Acts 2. The parlance "Voice of the Spirit" (VoS)[2] has

---

[1] Some earlier Pentecostal scholars and systematic theologians on the espoused Pentecostal theology includes: Donald Gee, *The Fruit of the Spirit: A Practical Approach to the Fruit of the Spirit by a Renown Charismatic Leader* (Springfield, MO: Gospel Publishing House, 1928); Donald Gee, *A New Discovery (Formerly Published as Pentecost)* (Springfield, MO: Gospel Publishing House, 1932); Donald Gee, *Pentecost* (Springfield, MO: Gospel Publishing House, 1932); Donald Gee, *The Pentecostal Movement: Including the Story of the War Years (1940-1947)*, rev. and enl. Edn (London: Elim Publishing Company Limited, 1941); Donald Gee, *Concerning Spiritual Gifts*, A Series of Bible Studies, rev. and enl. Edn (Springfield, MO: Gospel Publishing House, 1947); Donald Gee, *Upon All Flesh: A Pentecostal World Tour*, rev. edn (Springfield, MO: Gospel Publishing House, 1947); Ernest Swing Williams, *Systematic Theology: Pneumatology, Ecclesiology, Eschatology* (Springfield, MO: Gospel Publishing House, 1953); Donald Gee, *All With One Accord* (Springfield, MO: Gospel Publishing House, 1961); Donald Gee, *Fruitful or Barren?: Studies in the Fruit of the Spirit* (Springfield, MO: Gospel Publishing House, 1961); Donald Gee, *Spiritual Gifts in the Work of the Ministry Today* (Springfield, MO: Gospel Publishing House, 1963); Peter Christopher Nelson, *Bible Doctrines: A Series of Studies Based on the Statement of Fundamental Beliefs of the Assemblies of God* (Springfield, MO: Gospel Publishing House, 1981); Stanley M. Horton, *The Book of Acts* (Springfield, MO: Gospel Publishing House, 1981); Myer Pearlman, *Knowing the Doctrines of the Bible*, rev. edn (Springfield, MO: Gospel Publishing House, 1981); William W. Menzies and Stanley M. Horton, *Bible Doctrines: A Pentecostal Perspective* (Springfield, MO: Gospel Publishing House, 1993).

[2] Pentecostal parlance "VoS" and PDV are used interchangeably in this essay. This essay is an extract and adaptation of a section in my Ph.D. dissertation of 2022 entitled

been used since the beginning of the modern Pentecostal movement in the early 1900s. Donald Gee, an AG minister and theologian, used the term in the early 1930s to describe divine revelations and messages inspired by the Holy Spirit in the various forms of prophecies, visions, and dreams, audible voice of God, and inward witness.[3] The VoS has been a significant distinctive of Pentecostal spirituality and leadership since the early church in the book of Acts and early revivals like the Azusa Street Revival and the worldwide Pentecostal missions movement of the last century. In the more classical Pentecostal view, Roger Stronstad and Robert P. Menzies view the Spirit poured out on the day of Pentecost as the Spirit of prophecy and as empowerment for service based on Luke-Acts pneumatology. The Holy Spirit comes upon all flesh as the inauguration of the prophethood of all believers, where every person will be able to prophesy.[4] Menzies interprets it as the "restoration of the Spirit of prophecy," where the Spirit grants inspired speech, prophetic inspiration, and special revelations (prophecy, vision),[5] and emphasises that Luke sees the believers' reception of the Pentecostal gift or BHS as the means by which the prophetic community is empowered for missions.[6] There are broader views of BHS among contemporary Pentecostal scholarships which will not be discussed here.

This study examines the role of the VoS in the Pentecostal leadership and Pentecostal spirituality in Assemblies of God (Malaysia) AGM, and aims to discover how God's revelation through prophecies, dreams, and visions impacts the Pentecostal movement both individually and corporately. This empirical study on the VoS involves surveys and interviews among AGM leadership, pioneers, church planters, pastors, missionaries, church workers, and Bible College full-time residential students. Spirit-baptised believers are sensitive to God's revelation and communication, particularly in receiving God's call to full-time service and the Holy Spirit's guidance in missions, church, and ministry.

"Contextualised Pentecostalism from a Classical Pentecostal Movement to a Contemporary Pentecostal Church Movement: A Study of the Assemblies of God of Malaysia with Special Reference to Joel 2:28–32," Oxford Centre for Mission Studies/Middlesex University, UK.

[3] Gee, *Pentecost*, 52–65.

[4] Roger Stronstad, *Prophethood of All Believers: A Study in Luke's Charismatic Theology* (Sheffield: Sheffield Academic Press, 2004), 66–68.

[5] Robert P. Menzies, "Spirit-Baptism and Spiritual Gifts," in Wonsuk Ma, William W. Menzies, and Robert P. Menzies, eds., *Pentecostalism in Context: Essays in Honour of William W. Menzies*, Journal of Pentecostal Theology Supplement Series 11 (Sheffield: Sheffield Academic Press, 1997), 55–56.

[6] Robert P. Menzies, "Luke's Understanding of Baptism in the Holy Spirit: A Pentecostal Dialogues with the Reformed Tradition," *Journal of Pentecostal Theology* 16 (2008), 100.

The Significance of VoS in the Calling of Ministers

The empirical study reveals most Pentecostal ministers receive God's call to full-time ministry by hearing the VoS through Scripture, prophecies, dreams, visions, an audible voice, and impressions. Testimonies from senior and junior ministers revealed that they experienced spiritual encounters through different modes of hearing the VoS when God called them. The consistency of the testimonies affirmed that firstly, the call of God is always personal and received personally through a spiritual encounter with God. Secondly, the call of God is often revealed by the Holy Spirit to a third party, particularly to a preacher, leader, or pastor who will release prophetic words in order to confirm that the future minister is being led by the Holy Spirit, with some even experiencing visions or dreams about the call of others to the ministry. All these spiritual encounters bring about personal conviction and a strong desire to serve God, and most of the ministers expressed a deep stirring and burden in their hearts. It is noteworthy that a few began full-time ministry simply out of a desire to serve God in response to the needs in God's Kingdom where "the harvest is plentiful, but the laborers are few" (Matt 9:37; Luke 10:2). Some ministers hear God's call progressively and on many different occasions, through prophetic words, dreams, visions, sermons, and Scripture. Some receive only one very distinct and clear call into Christian ministry.

Occasions and places have been important for ministers in hearing and processing God's call to serve Him in a full-time capacity. There can be no doubt regarding the importance of camps, especially youth camps and revival meetings, in the process of receiving and responding to God's call. Two-thirds of the respondents answered God's call as a result of hearing a sermon or in response to an altar call at one of these meetings. Only one-third of those who participated in the interviews heard God's call during their personal devotional, worship, and prayer times.

Below are a few testimonies that illustrate the significant role VoS has played in the calling of Christians into Pentecostal ministry. The late Tan Sri Datuk Rev. Dr. Prince Guneratnam, an early pioneer and the first Malaysian Assemblies of God general superintendent from 1974 to 2000, graduated from the Bible Institute of Malaya in 1966 and immediately began full-time ministry. He received his call at the age of twelve, at a three-night series of revival meetings in Penang, led by Rev. Luther Sezto from Hong Kong. The revival meetings were followed by what are known as Tarrying Meetings for those seeking the baptism of the Holy Spirit, and in each of the Tarrying Meetings, Guneratnam received dramatic visions of Jesus Christ. On the first night, he saw a vision of Christ, more as it were an impression that stimulated his desire to seek Christ more. On the second night, in a vision, he was travelling on a steep road to the top of a hill when he saw a bright light on one side and, curious, desired to discover what it was. As he reached the top, he saw Jesus, but the bright light blinded him and physically affected his vision. On the third night, he had a vision of Jesus, who handed him a Bible.

Although Guneratnam regained his eyesight after being prayed for by the evangelist, he doubted his calling in his teenage years, when he was drawn away by the worldly influence of teenage friends. Yet, during those years, and remembering the visions of Christ and his call, he would envision himself preaching to huge crowds as he stood on the veranda of his father's house. At the age of sixteen or seventeen, he received a prophetic word from a preacher during some "spiritual emphasis" meetings and was convicted of his call once again. The prophetic word was so personal that he felt he was the only one in that room and that God was speaking to him directly about his love and his will; it was also accompanied by words of confirmation from an elderly uncle whom he accompanied to the meeting: "I know God spoke to you. You go back to do what God has told you to do." Guneratnam broke down, wept before God, and prayed. That was his turning point, and soon after, he enrolled in the Bible school and began his ministerial journey. In Guneratnam's own words:

> So what was his voice like? There was no voice spoken. It's an understanding and you just have it. And it cannot be the devil. The devil will not ask you to do things like that. It cannot be an evil spirit, it cannot be demonic. It cannot be human, because the human will never want to do what is spiritual because it's carnal. So, who else can it be? It has to be the Holy Spirit. And from that point on, I began my journey in serving God.[7]

Rev. Ng Kok Kee, pioneer, former AGM general secretary, and former president of Bible College of Malaysia (BCM), received God's call in 1971 during a church service: through the message preached, he felt that God spoke to his heart to serve him. It was simply a sense of "What are you going to do with your life? Serve God." After that call, he also saw a vision of Christ: "I saw Christ dying on the cross and saying to me, 'I did this for you. Why are you still resisting?' That was the call. I saw Jesus dying on the cross, and he spoke, 'I died for you; I gave my life for you. What would you give for me?'"[8]

Rev. Dr. Vincent Leoh, pioneer, former AGM general superintendent, and former senior pastor of Glad Tidings Assembly of God, Petaling Jaya, received his call in June 1975, when he received the baptism of the Holy Spirit and was immediately filled with passion and tears for the lost. God called him by means of a vision and spoke to him in an audible voice as he was cycling to church. In his own words:

> Suddenly, I saw a vision of just three birds. And the characteristics of these three birds were looking up to heaven with their mouths open, waiting for the mother bird to drop in the worm or food. And then later on, as I cycled further, the birds turned into the faces of three people, three men, and then after that, as I cycled on further, they turned into, as far as my eyes could see, the faces of human beings. All were looking up to heaven with their mouths open. So, I just didn't understand. I asked the Lord, "Lord, what is this?" And then the word of the Lord came to me.

---

[7] Interview with the late Tan Sri Datuk Rev. Dr. Prince Guneratnam on 4 May 2017. Guneratnam was the first Malaysian AGM general superintendent for twenty-six years from 1974 to 2000. He was pioneer of Glad Tidings Assembly of God, Klang (1967) and pioneer/senior pastor of Calvary Church (Assemblies of God), Kuala Lumpur (1972), the largest AGM church.

[8] Interview with Rev. Ng Kok Kee on 24 April 2017.

The Significance of the Voice of the Spirit　　　　　　　　　　239

And the word said, "They are hungry. Feed them." So, it was just five words, "They are hungry. Feed them." At that time, I knew that God had called me.[9]

Rev. Philip Mathius, pioneer and senior pastor of Shekinah Assembly of God Taiping, received Christ in 1971, began serving in his local church, and, in 1973, received God's call after a church service. He went home deeply burdened in his spirit, prayed, and went to sleep. When still not fully asleep and fully aware of his surroundings, he received a vision of Christ and heard Jesus' audible voice:

> Suddenly, there was a vision that came so real that I saw myself right at Calvary's cross … the blood of Jesus flowing, and I was trembling at the sight of it. And then the voice just came, "I shed this blood not only for you but also for others. And therefore you need to take the gospel and preach the gospel." And it was so sudden, I just woke up in a cold sweat.[10]

According to Mathius, he told the Lord that he felt inadequate for the task. Notwithstanding, the Lord instructed him to go preach the Gospel to his neighbour immediately. He obeyed, and his young teenage hearer received Christ, a clear confirmation that the Lord had called Mathius. He struggled two more years with his call until he finally resigned from his job, and experienced great peace as he obeyed the Lord's call and enrolled in the Bible school.[11]

Rev. Fiona Mathius-Lee Saik Eiang, pioneer and associate pastor in the pioneering period, testified that, although her Christian commitment meant that she faced rejection and was, in fact, disowned by her family, she grew strong in the Lord, evangelised from door to door, and started helping out in an AG church. In 1975–76, she dreamed that she was among stars in the heavenly places, and that the Lord spoke to her, saying; "Go, ye into the world and preach the gospel." She knew it was God's call and had many subsequent dreams of preaching to large crowds. At a National Youth Camp in 1975, she saw many visions of blood, fires, and the silhouette shadows of people walking and falling into a pit; as though blinded, something like a magnet was dragging multitudes down into a pit of burning fire. So, she told the Lord, "Send me to warn them," and she responded to God's call to full-time ministry during an altar call at the camp.[12]

So, when God called Guneratnam, Ng, Leoh, Mathius, and Fiona, through visions, dreams, and words, there was such deep conviction and the call was so clear, there could be no doubt about it. And once they obeyed God's call, there was no turning back.

Among full-time Bible college students who participated in the survey, most of them also had spiritual encounters in hearing the VoS in PDV, when they received God's call. For example, Student A, while fasting and praying, had a dream and visions of Jesus accompanied by an audible voice of God calling his name very clearly and assuring him that he would bless him and his family when he answered God's call. He shared what took place: "In a dream, I saw Jesus laying his hands on me and he was holding a sheep and he walked facing me and

---

[9] Interview with Rev. Dr. Vincent Leoh on 18 April 2017.

[10] Interview with Rev. Philip Mathius on 27 April 2017.

[11] Rev. Mathius.

[12] Interview with Rev. Fiona Mathius-Lee Saik Eiang on 27 April 2017.

I knelt before him. I saw him pouring oil on me. In a vision, I saw Jesus and he asked me to preach his word." He also received personal prophecies of God's affirmation, comfort, and assurance.[13]

Student B dreamed that he was preaching and that God spoke to him in an audible voice: it was the verse of Scripture, "Unlike so many, we do not peddle the word of God for profit. On the contrary, in Christ we speak before God with sincerity, like men, sent from God" (2 Cor 2:17, NIV). His call was confirmed by his parents and church pastor.[14]

Student C had a dream: "I was standing in front of many people, and I saw the place was very dark, but I prayed and preached to them. Suddenly I felt the power from God upon me and all the people fell down and I saw a very bright [light]." Then, God spoke to her about his call as she was reading Isaiah 42:6–7, verses which still "burn in her heart," "I am the LORD; I have called you in righteousness; I will take you by the hand and keep you; I will give you as a covenant for the people, a light for the nations, to open the eyes that are blind, to bring out the prisoners from the dungeon, from the prison those who sit in darkness." A church leader who heard from God also prophesied over her, "Next year you will become a full-time minister."[15]

One significant aspect arising from the analysis of the testimonies about the call of God to full-time ministry is that, even though manifested and experienced in many different ways, as the Holy Spirit chose, they all display only one specific purpose: God calls individuals to be part of his redemptive mission so that the world may know him. This is evident in the conviction that a desire, vision, dream, and word received for full-time ministry is about the lost, the harvest, the mission field, preaching the Gospel and fulfilling God's Kingdom purposes.

Spirit-Led Missions

The early pioneers and church planters were led by the Holy Spirit through impressions, promptings, prophecies, dreams, visions, and burdens, and their unanimous conclusion is that hearing the VoS is fundamental in God's guidance and direction for missions and the growth of the AGM movement and churches. There are many testimonies, including Rev. Terrence Sinnadurai, who pioneered and, through raising young pastors, planted twenty churches in the early period.[16] Rev. Christopher and Rev. Marianne Mun pioneered churches in East Malaysia, then in Seremban. He testified, "A few pastors and leaders prophesied over me, and also, four of the leaders had a vision of me serving God full-time."[17] Rev. Phillip Wee testified about receiving clear direction from the voice of the Holy Spirit and a call to commit and to obey, which led him in his pioneering and

---

[13] Survey on 4 May 2017.

[14] Survey on 4 May 2017.

[15] Survey on 5 May 2017.

[16] Interview with Rev. Terrence Sinnadurai on 28 March 2017.

[17] Interview with Rev. Christopher and Rev. Marianne Mun on 26 April 2017.

The Significance of the Voice of the Spirit   241

church planting in Southern, Central, and East Malaysia districts.[18] Rev. Chee
Siew Tai was led in her mission work through prophecies.[19] Rev. Isaac Chan
received a prophetic word of confirmation from a minister from overseas one
year after embarking on a ten-year church planting and expansion project.[20]

Rev. Lawrence Yap, senior pastor of Charis Christian Centre and current
AGM general secretary, having been led by words dropped into his heart or a
prompting of the Holy Spirit, pioneered the church's social work, and,
encouraged by the prophetic dream of a church member, ventured into
purchasing land for new church and ministry facilities. He testified:

> At Charis Christian Centre, we have started various ministries, we are strong in
> community services. We have started things like a dialysis centre since '97, we
> have started [an] orphanage since '89, we have started six other ministries; for
> example, reaching out to the refugee children, to the marginalised children, to the
> exploited women including sex workers down in China Town, Petaling Street and
> medical clinics and all that. And all these I would say were guided by the Holy
> Spirit. Take for instance, why we started the dialysis centre in '97? It was because
> God enabled us to purchase five shop lots in a row. The Lord just dropped into my
> heart, "The five shop lots are not just going to be utilised on Sunday." It was a very
> clear conviction that the Lord brought into my heart ... the Lord guided me to the
> need of the kidney patients, "They are growing, you know, every year by
> percentage." ... We are the first to start this dialysis charity centre in 1997. And
> when I look back, it was definitely divinely inspired by this circumstantial
> providence and secondly what the Lord dropped into my heart ... all the ministries
> which we have set up were Spirit-inspired and Spirit-led. And, one thing we can
> proudly say, that God has helped us to become a church without walls, meaning,
> we are building bridges towards the community, and connecting with them, so that
> we can show them the way to the Kingdom of God.

> Another good example will be one of my members who had a dream of seeing our
> new church building. He saw the land. So he came to me and of course I was
> sceptical, and I said, "Well, good for you ... go and look for the land which the
> Lord has given to you." And months later, because of his conviction that this is a
> dream from God, he went to the Land Office, and by divine guidance, he pointed
> to a place, and then the search was done. The result of a land title was brought to
> my attention ... the land is available ... And when I saw it, I got a shock. This guy
> is a new born again believer, in his late 60s, and the Holy Spirit used a dream to
> bring about a revelation, that I wasn't even aware of. And as I am speaking right
> now, we are at the verge of signing the letter of offer and entering into a Sales and
> Purchase Agreement for this piece of land, which will potentially become a place
> where we are going to build our facilities ... measuring about 2.75 acres.[21]

Rev. Dr. Samuel Ng, AGM Executive Committee and senior pastor of Faith
City Church (A/G), Subang Jaya, read a newspaper report of a tragedy in the
interior of the country and on the following day heard the voice of the Spirit
saying, "Go there." He obeyed immediately, and soon met a man who became

---

[18] Interview with Rev. Phillip Wee on 11 April 2017.
[19] Interview with Rev. Chee Siew Tai on 21 March 2017.
[20] Interview with Rev. Isaac Chan on 19 April 2017.
[21] Interview with Rev. Lawrence Yap on 20 April 2017.

242   *The Holy Spirit, Spirituality and Leadership*

the first native to graduate from BCM and who now serves in national leadership. His testimony goes:

> The second very distinct one was the Pos Dipang Tragedy '96, the landslide in the Orang Asli camp. I was sitting at home, and this voice that I heard just said, "Go, go." ... Yeah, I was reading the newspaper, there was a tragedy, you remember that time there was no social media, so the fastest news you get was through *Star* newspaper. The front page reported the tragedy in Pos Dipang ... Then I remembered Pastor Joshua Lau, he was involved with Orang Asli work, I called him. He also said he had the prompting of the Holy Spirit to go. So, both of us went without knowing what to do. I mean, it was so dramatic. I drove all the way to Pos Dipang, then we were standing by the road side, because the police blocked the place, they barricaded the place. So, we were standing there and we looked at each other, and we whispered to each other, we prayed, "God, you asked us to come but we are stuck here." The police won't let us in but amazingly the police chief came, and because we were the two weirdest that stood out from the crowd, so the policeman asked, "What are you doing here?" So, I told him the story, I said, "I was at home, I heard God speak to me, I drove here, and I want to go in." And he just asked us to hop into his police truck, so we went in, and because of that we met up with Samoan and Sanusi, and (now) together they are Orang Asli pastors. So that's one very distinct, prophecy, voice of God, and all of us remember. They were also wondering what we were doing there ... then they came out, they went to Bible school, they became our first trained Orang Asli pastors, trained in Bible school, and today they are running a very successful Orang Asli ministry.[22]

Rev. Connie Chan shared how the Holy Spirit gave her the vision to start a Church Social Responsibility, a tuition ministry, and to reach out to neighbours:

> Basically, we do help, share, and give to the orphanages, but having the manpower going on the ground to do it, has never been the strength of our church. But at the end of 2015, God stirred our hearts to spend more time with him, in prayer and worship like in Acts 2, spending time with him, waiting on him and ministering to him, so we have this "harp and bowl worship" session in the church, where we just spent time worshipping, and just waiting on him, basically worship and intercession ... One day, the Lord just put in our hearts while we were really enjoying the worship, being in his presence, "Are we not aware of the people around here so in need? They don't even know anything about God?" ... I don't know whether it is a vision or just an impression but we were just facing that side [pointing out the window] ... within sight ... 500 metres away, there is this low-cost flat around our area here ... So, it's an amazing thing actually and these are the people whom we would not have been in contact with if we didn't take the step of faith according to the prompting of the Spirit. So, God birthed that in us, because of the time of waiting, and I'm always amazed by that.[23]

A church member received his call as a missionary during personal devotional and prayer time and was led by the prompting of the Holy Spirit in the direction of missionary work. He testified, "I was praying and felt God speaking to pack

---

[22] Interview with Rev. Dr. Samuel Ng on 23 May 2017. Pos Dipang is an Orang Asli (native) settlement located in Kampar, in the state of Perak, West Malaysia. The landslide and mud flood tragedy happened in the evening of 29 August 1996. Rev. Sanusi a/l Bah Sahak currently serves on the AGM Executive Committee.

[23] Interview with Rev. Connie Chan on 23 May 2017.

The Significance of the Voice of the Spirit 243

our bags to go to the mission field. It wasn't a clear audible voice. It was a prompting and strong desire." His missionary call was confirmed by the message brought by a visiting preacher. Both he and his wife felt that the message was aimed directly at them. They served in a foreign country for a while, and upon return, they helped start social work in a farming industry, which empowered the native villagers in efforts to help improve their economy in the interior of East Malaysia.[24]

A high proportion, 70% of ministers, responded that the VoS, by means of PDV, has been fundamental to the guidance and direction for missions and the growth of AGM churches over the decades. Alongside that, almost one-third of the respondents come to a broader and more holistic perception of missionary needs through research, networking, the considered opinions of a "man of peace,"[25] detecting open doors, and meeting social needs. God not only leads through supernatural means but also through natural ways. As such, missions and church planting are ultimately guided by God-given passion and desires[26] and the inner witness of the Holy Spirit's direction.[27] And, when God has spoken, ministers experience boldness and confidence, and God brings to fulfilment his word, which never returns to him void but accomplishes what he purposes (Isa 55:11). Prophecies from God always come with his providence and grace.

Holy Spirit's Guidance in Church Growth

The AGM was established by foreign missionaries and began with only three or four churches. However, this small beginning produced explosive growth in the 1970s and 1980s, when over 300 churches were added to the movement. At the same time, this new phase focused more on erecting church buildings and establishing organisational structures, departments, and ministries to deal with the numerical growth in membership.

In this new phase, churches have continued to focus on the spiritual growth and needs of the members but perhaps in more holistic ways: pioneering workers and senior pastors have continued to depend on the leading of the Holy Spirit through PDV in their church planning and practice. These ministers typically share the visions they receive from God not now so much in the form of imagery but in the form of words, insights, ideas, desires, burdens, inner promptings, and plans. This opens up a new understanding of the fulfilment of Joel's prophecy regarding dreams and visions as experienced by AGM ministers; today, these are received more in non-image forms, especially in words, desires, and inner witness. The late Tan Sri Guneratnam testified to the leading of the Holy Spirit through God-given desires and plans, and on seeing them fulfilled for the good of God's Kingdom and for glorifying his name. One great example is the

---

[24] Survey on 16 May 2017.

[25] Rev. Dr. Vincent Leoh refers to the Gospels: mission is to go to where they are being received and welcomed (Matt 10:11–14; Mark 6:10–11; and Luke 9:4–5).

[26] Tan Sri Guneratnam.

[27] Interview with Rev. Ong Sek Leang on 7 April 2017.

building of the Calvary Convention Centre (CCC) with an auditorium for 5,000 as a testimony to God. He shared:

> Moving here to CCC is a big step. The Lord gave me the faith and confidence, and showed me that this is what he would like me to do. When I began to share it with my leaders, they were 100 per cent with me ... That's very important because when God deals with you and when the people you work with reaffirm, it becomes a very clear indication that is what God wants you to do ... When God speaks and moves, it is on the basis of your relationship. He sees your heart and desire. That's why desires are very important. See, the Bible says, "He grants you the desires of your heart." So, how do you know what's your desire? If you have a desire, you know it can't be from the enemy. It has to be from God. The devil will never give you a desire to plant churches. He'll never give you such desire. So where is it coming from? Now isn't that God's way of speaking with you? Leading you? See, it's your desire. See, the desire is within you and that's the open door for you, to help you. When you have that kind of desire, when you have that kind of openness, He then plants those desires within you to know that it is what it is. Same with this building. I can tell you what struggle I had to have this building when the Lord desired us to move out, to grow, and to establish this building as a testimony. The challenge to have it, I said to myself, "Can this desire be selfish? ... Who wants to come into a building like this that costs RM225 million? But [if] God puts [the desire] in you ... then God makes it happen." See, so this business of "What is God's voice? How does he speak to you? How do you know his leading?" They're alright questions but it's no secret. If you really desire and you really want to know, he will show you. It all depends on your relationship, how open, and willing you are.[28]

Rev. Marcus Tan, senior pastor of Penang First Assembly of God; Rev. Ronnie Chin, AGM assistant general superintendent and senior pastor of Revival Centre (Assemblies of God), Ampang, and his wife, Rev. Lisa Chin in Kuala Lumpur, received very specific prophecies in a prophetic conference by Cindy Jacobs in 2012 that God would give them new church buildings in Penang and Ampang; the prophecy was accompanied by detailed descriptions of the projects and, within a few years, the prophecies were fulfilled. They moved into their new multi-storey church buildings in June 2015 and September 2016, respectively, and so were equipped for greater growth and expansion. Rev. Ronnie Chin testified:

> We had been praying for a new property for quite a while. We struggled and asked, "Lord, what's happening? Why so long?" I remember two speakers' prophecies. In a meeting, Cindy Jacobs called us [both he and his wife] up, and prophesied, "God is going to give you a building" and she described some of the features ... We took it to heart as it was an encouragement to our prayers. And then, another speaker who came to our church also prophesied that God is going to give us a building and he has already prepared it for us. So that was an encouragement that there is already a prepared place, and he described two or three different features of the building. Finally, God just opened the door and we looked at this place [in the new premises]. As we remembered those prophecies, it was very much like what was described when we actually saw the building, i.e. what the hall and the ceiling look like, the

---

[28] Tan Sri Guneratnam. He shared his vision of Calvary Church of 5,000-seater capacity in mid-1980s. The land was purchased in 2003, building project initiated in 2004 and completed in 2013. *Calvary Church 40th Anniversary Magazine, 1968–2008*, 60.

The Significance of the Voice of the Spirit   245

surrounding area of a busy highway, and that it looks like a multi-purpose building, unlike a normal kind of church building.[29]

Rev. Marcus Tan, on showing me his new church in Penang as prophesied by Cindy Jacobs, said: "We moved here just about one and a half years ago, so this hall is ready, this sanctuary can sit 2,000."[30]

The Ministering of the Holy Spirit

The VoS leads to widely varying ministerial practices in AGM churches, especially in prayer and intercession, preaching, altar calls, and general ministering to people. The most common practice is the use of a word of knowledge, a prophetic word, visions, and so-called "prompting." For example, Rev. Michael Ho shared that he often receives prophetic promptings while praying for church members. He testified that there was one incident when doctors had given up hope on an HIV patient, who was one of his Chinese pastors. The doctor called the family to prepare for his death. As he was praying in tongues for the patient, his tears just flowed, and he knew it was the anointing of the Holy Spirit. The Lord added to the patient's life. In another case, as he was praying for an elderly church member who was also dying, the family members had gathered at the hospital to prepare for his death. He prayed as tears flowed, and later, the elderly man woke up and lived a while longer.[31]

Rev. Ronnie Chin often receives impressions of the Holy Spirit's leading through pictures or a vision, especially during altar calls:

> In a service during worship and altar call time, I would think of how to close the service and very often I will get a vision of something and the interpretation, which would be my key point in making the altar call. More of pictures, mental pictures … static pictures. Others talk about how they see things moving, but that has not been my privilege. I would ask the Lord, "How to interpret this? What does it mean?" I think it strikes a chord when I say in the altar call, this is what I see. This is what God is saying and how we should respond.

And Rev. Lisa Chin, his wife, would receive prophetic words and knowledge during an inner healing ministry:

> For me, very often God gives a prophetic word or I see the imagery … I'm a very visual person, so I can see a lot of pictures … Having been a minister for so long, I think that God has developed maturity in me. More often, it would be the impression, rather than a vision. When I minister to people, prophetic revelations come very easily for me.[32]

Most often in their ministerial practice, ministers receive and release prophetic words for the people they pray for and minister to; these can be words of confirmation, edification, comfort, healing, assurance, or a simple Scripture.

---

[29] Interview with Rev. Marcus Tan on 28 April 2017. Interview with Rev. Ronnie Chin and Rev. Lisa Chin on 26 May 2017.

[30] Rev. Marcus Tan.

[31] Interview with Rev. Michael Ho on 18 April 2017.

[32] Rev. Ronnie and Rev. Lisa Chin.

When the Holy Spirit speaks in this manner, it is common for the minister not to know anything about the person's situation or condition, the Spirit-given words being released through the leader as the temple of the Holy Spirit (1 Cor 6:19–20) and God's vessel in and through whom the Holy Spirit flows. Thus, the church and its members are edified.

The PDV from Vivid Imagery to Enigmatic

One conspicuous change in the interpretation of PDV in AGM over time is the form of literal imagery and words received by early Pentecostals and pioneers of AGM. But nowadays, VoS is not necessarily in imagery form but more commonly in the form of inner witness, burden, prompting, desire or conceptual ideas, impressions, personal prophecies, and praying over people with instant revelations, which is a new phenomenon where these new kinds of PDV are enigmatic.

A very significant change occurred in PDV over time in Guneratnam's case. When he was twelve years old in 1957, he received a vision of Christ on his call in vivid imagery, which was quite typical for Pentecostals. Later, in the mid-1980s, his new kind of visualisation in the form of a "desire" with "faith" to build the Calvary Convention Centre[33] was realised in 2013, knowing that God gives the desires and answers the "prayer of faith."[34] This shows a shift in perception and the nature of vision.

I see that the language reveals a different ethos between a classical Pentecostal practice and a new concept of PDV, which is somewhat similar to that of Cho's concept of vision in "desire" and praying. However, Cho's contextualisation and pneumatology were elaborated much more in relation to the primal religious worldview and context. Cho related the vision in "desire" as "instruments of the fourth dimension," "a spiritual plane" to "envision the future," "imagination" being the "soul of the vision and dream," and "ability to see and dream." Cho described, "I liken the heart of man to a painter's canvas. What a man dreams and envisions is the paint. If the Christian takes the brush of faith and begins to paint on the canvas of his heart the pictures that God has revealed to him, those revelations become reality."[35] "Faith-incubation" in the spiritual realm of the "fourth dimension" encompasses envisioning, desiring, praying, and speaking

---

[33] Tan Sri Guneratnam.

[34] Michael Fackerell, "The Prayer of Faith – by Prince Guneratnam," *Christian-Faith*, https://www.christian-faith.com/the-prayer-of-faith-by-prince-guneratnam/, accessed 22 June 2020. This article was reproduced from Dr Yonggi Cho's "Church Growth" magazine and Church Growth International, where Guneratnam served on the board of directors for Church Growth International (CGI).

[35] Yonggi Cho and R. Whitney Manzano, *The Fourth Dimension: More Secrets for a Successful Life*, vol. 2 (Plainfield: Bridge Publishing, 1983), 50–55.

The Significance of the Voice of the Spirit

the word, and it will become a reality in the physical realm; particularly, miraculous healing and blessings from God.[36]

According to Kay, Cho understood the Holy Spirit to give dreams and visions by which God's work is led forward.[37] Cho observed, "In Sokagakkai, they drew a picture of prosperity, repeating phrases over and over, trying to develop the human spiritual fourth dimension; and these people are creating something ... Sokagakkai has applied the law of the fourth dimension and has performed miracles ..." Cho believed that the Bible, God, and the Holy Spirit realm are all in the "fourth dimension." Thus, when we apply a similar "fourth dimension" technique for Christian visioning, we can dream and vision, pray in faith and create.[38] Here, we can see that within the Pentecostal/Charismatic and Christian traditions, there are different views on the practice and forms of PDV. More than that, a different worldview is in operation in the process of contextualisation!

From the 1980s on, there has been a stronger focus on the VoS in the widely varying ministerial practices in AGM churches, especially in prayer and intercession, preaching, altar calls, and general ministering to people. The most common practice is the use of a word of knowledge, a prophetic word, visions, and so-called "prompting." Given the change of meaning over time, a prophetic word can mean God's word and message given through the written Word of God, thoughts, impressions, or prompting by the Holy Spirit for his specific purpose, which will be fulfilled.

The Third Wave's prophetic movement has introduced many new kinds of PDV and new parlance; namely, "personal prophecy," "confirmation," "releasing" prophetic word, and "inner vision." "Specific prophecies" given in prophetic conferences have become a new kind of prophetic movement and a popular contemporary feature. All these have been made popular practices in the prophetic movement but were rare in early Pentecostalism. This new apostolic and prophetic movement is initiated and propagated by the late Peter Wagner, Cindy Jacobs, Bill Hamon, and many more in a global network of "prophets."[39]

---

[36] Cho, *The Fourth Dimension*. See Hwa Yung, "Mission and Evangelism: Evangelical and Pentecostal Theologies in Asia," in Sebastian C. H. Kim, ed., *Christian Theology in Asia* (Cambridge: Cambridge University Press, 2008), 262–63.

[37] William K. Kay and Anne E. Dyer, eds., *Pentecostal and Charismatic Studies: A Reader* (London: SCM Press, 2004), 83, introduction by Kay. See Cho, *The Fourth Dimension: Discovering a New World of Answered Prayer,* Special combined edition – volume one and two (Alachua: Bridge Logos, 2017), 45–46.

[38] For Cho's pneumatology, see George Canty, *Hallmarks of Pentecost: Discerning the True Spiritual Gifts* (London: Marshall Pickering, 1989), 171–73; Allan Anderson, "The Contextual Pentecostal Theology of David Yonggi Cho," in Wonsuk Ma, William W. Menzies and Bae Hyeon-Sung, eds., *David Yonggi Cho: A Close Look at His Theology and Ministry*, AJPS Series, 1 (Baguio: APTS Press, 2004), 145–46; and Simon Chan, "The Pneumatology of David Yonggi Cho," in Ma, Menzies and Bae, eds., *David Yonggi Cho*, 97.

[39] See Bill Hamon, *Prophets and Personal Prophecies* (Shippensburg: Destiny Image, 1987); C. Peter Wagner, *The Third Wave of the Holy Spirit: Encountering the Power of*

Their teachings and practices are prominent among the Charismatic circle, which has infiltrated the Pentecostal movement, resulting in a blend of practices among the Pentecostal/Charismatic churches in the USA and their global network in other nations. This new kind of prophecy is very different from prophecy practised by earlier Pentecostals, who usually reference 1 Corinthians 12 to 14. Their practices have permeated Pentecostal circles. While these new views have encouraged more common expression of spiritual gifts, the underlying theology is not the same as classical Pentecostal theology.

Conclusion

The significance of the VoS is evident in the AGM history, whether in the call of ministers to full-time service or in the theological, missiological, ecclesiological, and ministerial aspects of the Pentecostal movement, as testified and documented. The experience of God speaking through the Holy Spirit in PDV is evidence that the power of Spirit baptism brings about a greater sensitivity to the supernatural dimension and VoS. The work of the Holy Spirit in empowerment for witness, as well as guidance in evangelism and missions, has formed a vital part of Pentecostal spirituality and leadership. It has impacted the growth of AGM from the early years to the present time.

However, I would offer a word of caution at this point. There is a danger in the new, more enigmatic kind of visioning increasingly practised in Pentecostal circles. If the prophetic gifting is exercised by less mature believers lacking in biblical-theological foundations and sensitivity to the Holy Spirit, this kind of enigmatic "vision" may result in misrepresentations, misinterpretation, and ultimately, in believers being misled. Scripture is the ultimate authority, the Word of God upon which the biblical-theological foundation of faith is built. Hearing God's voice and sensitivity to the VoS come naturally from an intimate relationship with the Triune God.

Pentecostals need to use the PDV gifting to be the prophetic voice in the church, society, and nation. Believers need to stand up and speak for justice, righteousness, and truth, especially in the public square and marketplace. AGM ministers ought to be sensitive to the VoS to bring God's word of truth and life to the community and to bring God's love and hope to the world. The leading of the Holy Spirit through VoS is crucial in the preaching of God's word and being prompted and guided in ministry, in missions, in God's calling, and in life.

Signs and Wonders Today (Ann Arbor: Servant, 1988); Bill Hamon, *Prophets and the Prophetic Movement: God's Prophetic Move Today, Paul Thigpen, ed* (Shippensburg: Destiny Image, 1990); Cindy Jacobs, *Voice of God* (Ventura: Regal Books, 1995); C. Peter Wagner, *Apostles and Prophets: The Foundation of the Church* (Ventura: Regal Books, 2000); Cindy Jacobs, *The Supernatural Life* (Ventura: Regal Books, 2005); Peter Wagner, *Dominion! How Kingdom Action Can Change the World* (Grand Rapids: Chosen Books, 2008); Cindy Jacobs, *The Reformation Manifesto: Your Part in God's Plan to Change Nations Today* (Minneapolis: Bethany House, 2008).

Asian Pentecostalism as a Growth Engine for Global Christianity: Potentials and Challenges[1]

Wonsuk Ma

Introduction

In my decades of study on global Christianity, the unique role of Pentecostalism has grown in significance. This has led to focused research on the future role of Yoido Full Gospel Church, which had empowered churches toward numerical growth.[2] This study zooms out to take in the whole region of East and Southeast Asia, to probe the global role of its Christianity.

Baselines and Observations

Based on the latest statistical studies of global Christianity, the following baselines lay a foundation for the discussion developed in this study. The first is the growth trajectory of Islam, posing as the number-one missionary competitor to Christianity. According to the third edition of the *World Christian Encyclopedia*, Islam is outgrowing Christianity. In 2020, Islam accounted for 24.3% of the world population, while Christianity claimed 32.3%. By 2050, the numbers will change to 28.7% versus 35.0%. Islam's annual growth rate is particularly alarming, as it grew at 1.88% each year in the twentieth century, while Christianity recorded 1.28%. The growth gap in the 2000–2020 period widened to 1.93% vs. 1.19%.[3]

The second baseline is another fast-growing segment, that of atheists and agnostics (or "nones"). In the global picture, this category ranks number four (11.3% in 2020) after Christianity, Islam, and Hinduism. The nones are particularly challenging for the West (or the Global North), where much of the "conversions" are suspected to occur from Christianity. Although its global picture is complex, this religious category is relevant to the region.[4]

The third baseline is the significant growth of Pentecostal/Charismatic Christianity since the last century. Although to be elaborated on more below, two sets of numbers will illustrate this point. It grew from 0.1% of the world's population in 1910 to 8.3% in 2020, and it is expected to reach 10.3% by 2050.

---

[1] The first version of this study was presented to the 2023 William Menzies Annual Lectureship of the Asia Pacific Theological Seminary, Baguio, Philippines in February 2023.

[2] Wonsuk Ma, "The Future Growth of Global Christianity and Yoido Full Gospel Church: Its Potential Role in the New Context," *Great Commission Research Journal* 10.1 (Fall 2018), 8–29.

[3] Todd M. Johnson and Gina A. Zurlo, eds., *World Christian Encyclopedia*, 3rd ed. (Edinburgh: Edinburgh University Press, 2019), 6. Henceforth *WCE*, 3rd ed.

[4] *WCE*, 3rd ed., 6.

Also, its annual growth rate has been the highest among Christian families. In the twentieth century, it recorded 6.30%, while the Christian average was 1.28%.[5] Pentecostal/Charismatic churches grew more than five times faster than all the other churches.

The last observation is the steady growth of global Christianity toward one-third of the world's population (as seen in the graph),[6] while its recent shift is staggering. Todd Johnson creatively identified the centre of gravity of global Christianity in each century.[7] The most glaring is the southward move of global Christianity. In 1900, 82.4% of world Christians were found in the Global North and only 17.6% in the South.[8] In 2020, the North claimed only 33.1% and the South 66.9% of the world's Christians. And this gap is expected to grow further. As the centres of gravity have made a three-quarter circle, the acceleration of the speed of change is also unmistakable, further widening the North–South gap.[9]

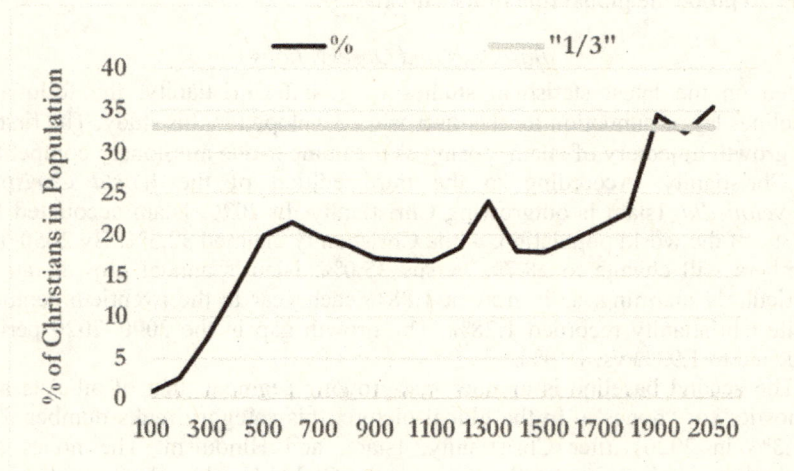

Figure 1: Percentage of Christians in the Global Population, from AD 0 – 2020

This Essay

The thesis I will build towards is that Christianity in the East and Southeast holds a crucial key to the continuing growth of global Christianity, and at the centre is Pentecostalism. To establish this possibility, I will engage with Islam and the nones, the two religious groups that pose the most severe challenge to the continuing growth of global Christianity. With regard to Islam, I plan to commit

---

[5] *WCE*, 3rd ed., 6.

[6] © Wonsuk Ma, 2016.

[7] Todd M. Johnson and Kenneth R. Ross, eds., *Atlas of Global Christianity* (Edinburgh: Edinburgh University Press, 2009), 53.

[8] *WCE*, 3rd ed., 4.

[9] Wonsuk Ma, "Global Christianity: Where Are We and How Did We Get Here?" *Pentecostal Education* 6.1 (Spring 2021), 37–38.

to an extensive discussion to identify possibilities by drawing from historical lessons. In so doing, I will anchor my thoughts on Andrew Walls' theory of the Christian movement. Then, I will argue from the region's "growth room" vis-à-vis two other southern continents. The last element is the Pentecostal growth trajectory compared to other Christian traditions and continents. My study concludes with issues facing Asian Christianity in fulfilling this historical potential.

Christianity and Islam

Islam has spread since the seventh century to become the second-largest world religion. It also claims close to one-third of the world's population: 24.3% in 2020 and 28.7% in 2050.[10] Its recent growth rate threatens to unseat Christianity from its number-one title in the global religious scene. Also, Figure 1 illustrates the impact of Islam on global Christianity, as Islam caused the first two significant setbacks to Christian growth. The first was around its birth, which stopped the Christian growth trajectory. It took over five centuries before Christianity finally recovered from this devastating impact. During this period, most of the Middle East and North African ancient Christian centres became Muslim territories. The second setback occurred during the rise and expansion of the Ottoman Empire from the fourteenth century. It practically cancelled the recovered Christian growth for another three centuries. Thus, its rise and expansion have significant implications for global Christianity.

Serial vs. Progressive Movement

Comparing the life cycle of Christianity and Islam, the prominent mission historian Andrew Walls proposed in 2005 a rather disturbing observation.[11] Initially published in a Swedish mission journal, a summary also appeared in *Atlas of Global Christianity*.[12] He concludes that Christianity advances serially, based on his historical analysis of the first millennium of Christian history and the twentieth-century shifts in global Christianity. A Christian centre with strength, such as Northern Africa in the early Christian centuries, eventually withered, while the margins began to blossom.[13] This serial move can be likened to a life cycle: starting with birth, advancing to growth, maturity, and reproduction, and then ageing and even death. The receding centre, however, reproduces itself in new territories before the Christian centre runs through the life cycle. In contrast, according to Walls, Islam advances progressively: once a Muslim territory, it remains Muslim permanently. At the outset, Christianity appears lacking resilience as compared to Islam. Indeed, since the seventh

---

[10] *WCE*, 3rd ed., 6.

[11] Andrew F. Walls, "Mission History as the Substructure of Mission Theology," *Swedish Missiological Themes* 93.3 (2005), 367–78.

[12] Andrew F. Walls, "Christianity across Twenty Centuries," in *Atlas of Global Christianity*, 48–49.

[13] Walls, "Mission History," 368.

century, most of church history has seen the repeated pattern of Islam taking over Christian territories. Christianity was pushed to new areas in order to establish a Christian presence. Walls' generalisation is disturbingly plausible despite minute exceptions, as he provides ample cases from early to recent times. Yet, I still would like to search for clues for exceptions to this historical "rule."

Exceptions

The first to look at is Africa. Three prominent religious blocks in sub-Saharan Africa have been Traditional African Religions, Islam, and Christianity (in the order of existence). As illustrated by the Pew graph,[14] in 1900, more than three-quarters of Africans belonged to Traditional African Religions (76%), followed by Islam (14%), and then Christianity (9%). As Christianity grew exponentially in the twentieth century (to 57% of the sub-Saharan population), Islam continued its steady growth (20%) but lagged behind Christianity. The most notable change was the shrinking of Traditional African Religions (to 13%). Its loss (by 63%) was divided among Christianity (by a 48% addition) and Islam (15%) – the exact number! Although transfer conversion between Christianity and Islam may have occurred, the majority of the gains by these two were the believers of the Traditional African Religions. Today, only a tiny population is left in the Indigenous religions (to be reduced to 5.4% by 2050 for the entire African continent). The most relevant fact is that Christianity took deep root in Africa and outgrew Islam, whose presence predated the Christian faith. Equally significant is the faster growth rate of Christianity than that of Islam. For the entire African continent, the annual growth rate of Christianity in the past century was 3.75%, vs. Islam's 2.32%. The pattern continued for the first two decades of the current century: 2.82% for Christianity vs. 2.45% for Islam.[15]

The second clue to look at is Central Asia, one of the most challenging Islamic heartlands for Christian witnessing. This region of the five "stans" – Kazakhstan, Uzbekistan, Turkmenistan, Kyrgyzstan, and Tajikistan – claimed only 8% of its population was Christian in 2015. However, the real challenge is its growth or decline rate: Christianity lost one-third of its share of the population in less than half a century. Thus, it is hard to imagine that this barren region was saturated with Christians, not just once but twice! This is illustrated in a beautifully crafted video, *The Spread of the Gospel*, by GospelMap.com.[16] Beginning in the third century, Christianity made an eastward expansion through the Silk Road, and by the sixth century, the region was fully Christianised. This Christian era lasted for more than eight centuries through the rise and fall of the Mongols. But the Christian presence had disappeared by the mid-fifteenth century, even before

---

[14] Pew Research Center, "Tolerance and Tension: Islam and Christianity in Sub-Saharan Africa" (Washington, DC: Pew Research Center, 2010), i,
https://www.pewresearch.org/religion/2010/04/15/executive-summary-islam-and-christianity-in-sub-saharan-africa/, accessed 2 December 2022.
[15] *WCE*, 3rd ed., 8.
[16] https://vimeo.com/113801439?embedded=true&source=video_title&owner=2978961, accessed 30 November 2022.

Islam occupied the "stan" lands. After four centuries of total absence, Christianity was reintroduced at the turn of the nineteenth century. Then, the region was overwhelmed by communist dominance, a devastating blow to the (second-time) new Christian faith.

These two cases provide several valuable observations, challenging Walls' observation. First, while the first period of Christian presence in Central Asia ran its life cycle (serial move), Christianity was reintroduced many centuries later. This is a serial move in a complete cycle. Second, Christianity is not always on the run while Islam chases after it, as noticed in Africa. Islam predates Christianity by eleven centuries (except in Northern Africa), but today Christianity is the dominant religion. Third, Christianity can outgrow Islam, and Africa has brilliantly demonstrated this possibility, as discussed above with specific numbers. However, it is imperative to remember that an organised religion poses more challenges for the missional front than unorganised or Indigenous religions. Also, the rise and fall of a religion in a given time is complex. For example, an empire could support or suppress Christianity. It took an imperial force (Russia) to impose Christianity over Central Asia for the second time.

The Nones and Other "Low-Hanging Fruits"

In this section, I will look into the nones and other religious groups for the continuing growth of Christianity in the region.

Different Nones

Both in North America and Latin America, the nones (combining atheists and agnostics) are the fastest-growing "religion"! In the first two decades of this century, it recorded a 3.37% annual growth rate in North America and 1.93% in Latin America. In Europe, the nones remain the second-largest religious group. It recorded the fastest annual growth rate of 4.29% among all the continents in the past century. Its sudden drop in the growth rate to -0.05% in 2000–2020 requires further study.

In East and Southeast Asia, the nones claim to be the largest religious group (Figure 2). In 1970, the combination of agnostics and atheists reached 41.1% (and 26.4% in 2020)! Zurlo contends that many of the nones are due to the state's control of religious affairs, such as communism.[17] Understandably, the most substantial number of nones are found in China (453 million out of 503 million agnostics in the region in 2020). We are talking about quite different nones in this region than elsewhere. The growth of Chinese Christianity may provide an encouraging mission implication. While Christianity grew at an annual rate of 1.42% between 2000 and 2020, the highest among all the categories, nones recorded a mere 0.17% increase.

---

[17] Gina A. Zurlo, "A Demographic Profile of Christianity in East and Southeast Asia," in Kenneth R. Ross, Francis D. Alvarez SJ, and Todd M. Johnson, eds., *Christianity in East and Southeast Asia* (Edinburgh: Edinburgh University Press, 2020), 5.

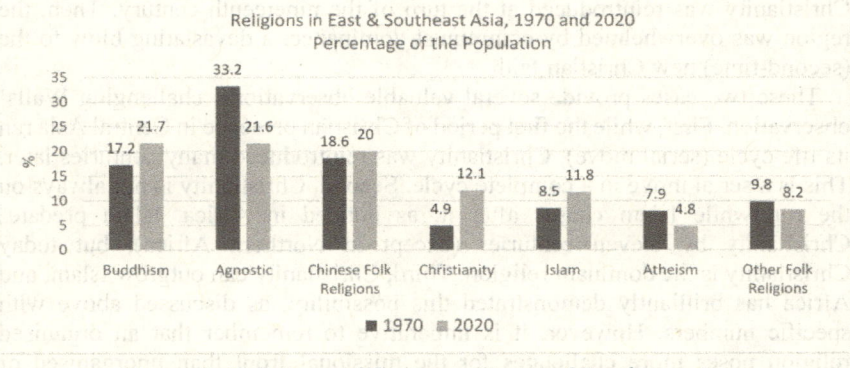

Figure 2: Religious Affiliation in East and Southeast Asia

Different State of Islam

To understand the presence of Islam, which is different from the rest of Asia, a historical overview will be helpful. Islam had steadily and consistently advanced eastward from the Middle East to South Asia (including modern-day Afghanistan, Pakistan, and India) and followed the coastal states, such as today's Malaysia, Brunei, and Indonesia. As expected, it reached Mindanao, the southern island of the Philippines, and was going to the north through the Philippine archipelago. That was when Ferdinand Magellan and his crew landed on a Visayan island in the middle of the Philippines in March 1521. Since the Spanish priests "Christianised" the islanders, the nation became a Spanish colony and has remained the only Christian nation in Asia (except East Timor, which gained its final independence from Indonesian occupation in 2002). This Christianisation by an imperial presence has also blocked the northward advance of Islam. Otherwise, following the pattern of Islamic spread throughout the coasts in East Africa and Southeast Asia, it would have continued its move to the coastal areas of China, Taiwan, Korea, and Japan. Therefore, the region has a relatively weak presence of Islam. Islam in 2020 claimed 11.8% of the region's 2.33 billion population, the fifth largest after Buddhism, agnostics, Chinese folk religions, and Christianity (12.1%).[18] For the whole of Asia, by comparison, Islam topped the list (27.4%), followed by Hinduism, Buddhism, Chinese folk religions, and Christianity (8.2%).[19] It lagged significantly behind Christianity in its growth trajectory.

In addition to the historical aspect, Islam in the region tends to be less fundamental than in West Asia. The result is often a legal provision for various religions to coexist. For instance, Indonesia, the largest Muslim country in the world, constitutionally allows Protestantism and Catholicism among the six recognised religions. Christianity is ranked as the second-largest religious group,

---

[18] Zurlo, "A Demographic Profile of Christianity in East and Southeast Asia," 3.

[19] *WCE*, 3rd ed., 10.

with 12.2%.[20] The visibility of Christianity in the country is also seen in large churches. The 2023 list of global megachurches includes three Indonesian churches among the top thirty-five: Gereja Bethany (with 140,000 members), Gereja Bethel Indonesia (30,000), and Mawar Sharon Church (30,000).[21] This is a significant achievement, as almost all others are from countries with full or relative religious liberty. On the contrary, the share of Islam remains constant in this century: 79.1% of the population in 2000, 79.5% in 2020, and 79.0% in 2050.[22] Although other Muslim-majority countries claim to have protective measures provided for other religious groups in the rest of Asia, many Christians feel threatened if they practise their faith. It is also observed that many Muslims in this region tend to incorporate their folk religious elements. This may also explain why all three Indonesian megachurches are Pentecostal and Charismatic, where supernatural experiences, including healings, are preached and experienced.

Folk Religions

In East and Southeast Asia, combining Chinese folk religion and other folk religions accounted for 28.4% of the total population in 1970. In fifty years, it slightly decreased to 20.2% by 2020. Thus, much of the Christian gain in recent decades may have come from the nones. While this will remain a primary mission target, the folk religionists may also be the low-hanging mission fruit. The African experience provides critical insight.

As seen in Figure 3,[23] the explosive Christian growth in Africa was due to the mission success among ethno-religions or African Indigenous religions. In 1900, this category was the largest, with 57.9% of the population, followed by Islam (32.5%), and Christianity (with a meagre 8.9%). By 2020, African Indigenous religion had shrunk to the smallest (7.9%), while Islam and Christianity grew significantly.[24] While the Indigenous religion lost by 50%, Christianity gained by 40.4% and Islam by 9.0%. The gain of the two latter (and missionary) religions corresponds to the loss of the former. This proves that Christianity in East and Southeast Asia is standing before a massive harvest field, and 46.6% (the combinations of the nones and folk religions in 2020) of the population are considered "soft" missionary targets!

---

[20] *WCE*, 3rd ed., 394.

[21] Warren Bird, "Global Megachurches: World's Largest Churches" (Leadership Network, https://leadnet.org/world/), accessed 1 August 2023.

[22] *WCE*, 3rd ed., 394.

[23] © Wonsuk Ma, 2023.

[24] *WCE*, 3rd ed., 8.

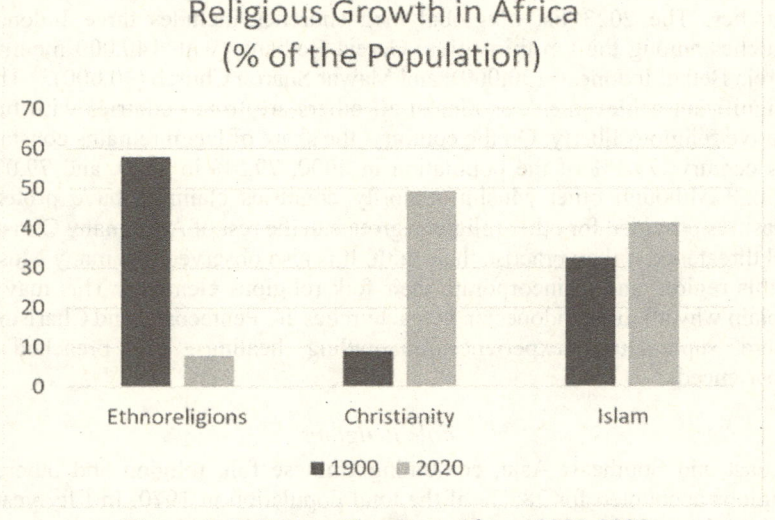

Figure 3: Religious Change in Africa, 1900-2020

Growth Potential

Decades ago, I published a study with an audacious claim that the only limit for Asian Pentecostalism is the sky.[25] Although now almost two decades old, my argument stands for Asian Christianity in general and Pentecostalism in particular. East and Southeast Asia held about half (2.33 billion) of the continent's population (4.62 billion in 2020). Having investigated the religious scene of the region, I will probe the growth potential of Christianity from several angles.

Growth Room Factor

My claim may sound ridiculous for Asian Christianity, which claimed only 8.2% in 2020 and is projected to reach 10.2% by 2050. How can it be a "growth engine" for global Christianity? This amounts to only about a quarter of the world's average (32.3% in 2020). However, a comparison with two other Southern continents will prove my point.

Latin America has maxed out any growth room, with 95.2% of the population claiming to be Christian in 1900. Once you have reached the "sky," the only move left is either staying up or coming down. Unfortunately, Latin American Christianity has steadily lost its share in the population: 92.1% in 2020 and 90.2% in 2050. Its annual growth rate of 1.16% between 2000 and 2020 is below the population growth of 1.18%. Christianity is shrinking because there is no more room to grow! Even the phenomenal growth of Independents (2.38%),

---

[25] Wonsuk Ma, "Asian Pentecostalism: A Religion Whose Only Limit Is the Sky," *Journal of Beliefs and Values* 25.2 (Aug 2004), 191–204.

Asian Pentecostalism as a Growth Engine for Global Christianity 257

Protestants (1.80%), Evangelicals (1.71%), Unaffiliated (1.49%), and Pentecostal/Charismatics (1.43%) cannot offset the substantial and steady loss of Catholics (0.72%).[26] Most of the "growth" takes place through transfers between Christian traditions. When Christianity is saturated, the best scenario is the rise of a missionary movement, as seen in the Western church. For this reason, the world is delighted with the growing missionary presence from this Christian continent. But this will not serve as the leading force of growth for global Christianity.

African Christianity is the next to examine. The Christian expansion in this region in the twentieth century was the marvel of Christian mission, transforming the whole continent into becoming Christian. In 1900, only 8.9% of Africa was Christian, but it grew to 49.3% in 2020. With 41.5% Muslims, less than 10% of Africa remains for missionary expansion of the two competing religions. Yes, proselytising Muslims is the next option available, which will be harder to accomplish and often bloody. As the Christian growth rate topped (at 2.82%) that of Islam (2.45%) between 2000 and 2020, it is expected to reach 52.4% of Africa, while Islam slightly shrinks to 41.0% by 2025. Again, there is small room for growth in the continent.[27] Like Latin America, we expect African churches to be mobilised for mission. With African Christian migrants spreading throughout the world, their dynamic spirituality impacts the churches of the host nations. Nonetheless, Christianity in homeland Africa has dwindling room for growth. These two cases make Asia the continent with the most growth potential.

Christian Growth

Also notable is the Christian growth rate of the region. In 2000, 11.9% of the population was Christian, which grew to 12.2% in 2020, and is estimated to reach 13.3% by 2050. Christianity recorded the fastest annual growth rate of 3.1% among all the major religions, from 62.2 million believers to 281.9 million in 2020. That means, in the rest of Asia (South Asia, Central Asia, and West Asia), less than 4% claimed to be Christian in 2020. In other words, East and Southeast Asian Christianity was more than three times larger than in the rest of Asia. The Christian annual growth rate (3.1% between 1970 and 2020) in the region was two times higher than that of the whole of Asia (1.52% between 2000 and 2020). These two statistical sets prove that Christianity in East and Southeast Asia leads the Christian growth in Asia and beyond.

As an example, Chinese Christianity grew significantly. Although the exact numbers are difficult to secure, the *World Christian Encyclopedia* reports that Christianity multiplied from 6.2% (or 80 million) in 2000 to 7.4% (or 106 million) in 2020 and is expected to continue its growth to 14.7% (or 200 million) by 2050.[28] After Chinese folk religions (28.2% in 2050) and Buddhism (19.5%), Christianity is the third-largest organised religion! Second, its annual growth rate between 2000 and 2020 was the highest at 1.42%, compared with Buddhism

---

[26] Statistics from *WCE*, 3rd ed., 14.

[27] *WCE*, 3rd ed., 32.

[28] Data from *WCE*, 3rd ed., 195.

(1.3%). Although the pressure and restrictions of the authorities over Christianity, especially the unregistered churches, have increased in recent years, its crucial role in Asian Christianity cannot be ignored, both in its numbers and dynamism.

Missionary Movement

Among the top ten missionary-sending countries, according to the *World Christian Encyclopedia* (which includes the Catholic Church), three are in this region. South Korea was ranked third with 35,000 missionaries in 2020, the Philippines ranked fourth with 25,000, and China ranked sixth with 15,000. The combined number of missionaries from these three countries was 75,000, estimating the number of missionaries from the region to be about 80,000. To place this number in context, the total number of missionaries from the whole of Asia in 2020 was 91,200. Then, about 88% of Asian missionaries came from this region. Also, this region ranked as the second-largest missionary-sending place after North America.

The missionary ratio to the Christian population is also encouraging. In 2020, East and Southeast Asia sent 283.8 cross-cultural missionaries per million Christians; and this is compared with 240.8 for the whole of Asia, 143 for Europe, 134 for Latin America, and 103 for Africa. The missionary commitment of the region is the highest among the Global South and only second to North America (563) in the world. For reference, the world average was 168 per million.[29]

Perhaps two snapshots may illustrate the rising missionary zeal and commitment of the churches in this region. The first is the large "creative" group of mission workers, defying the traditional definition of a missionary. For example, mission watchers have understood migration as part of God's missional move. Many studies argue that Christian immigrants to Western nations impact the declining host churches with zeal and commitment. Christian migrant workers in the Middle East radically changed the Christian landscape of hard-to-reach places.[30] The other is a surprise missionary movement of the Chinese churches, primarily house churches. Its missionary impetus has been popularly expressed in the Back-to-Jerusalem movement. Initially spread among rural house churches, the idea received a significant boost as urban house churches inherited and developed it. One of its leaders published a biblical argument for the movement,[31] while the urban churches organised annual Mission China 2030 conferences between 2015 and 2018.[32] However, the increasing government

---

[29] The ratios are calculated using the statistics found in *WCE*, 3rd ed., 5 and 32.

[30] Heartwarming stories are found in Miriam Adeney and Sadiri Joy Tira, *Wealth, Women & God: How to Flourish Spiritually and Economically in Tough Places* (Pasadena, CA: William Carey Library, 2016).

[31] For an insider's rationale, see Mingri Jin, *Back to Jerusalem with All Nations: A Biblical Foundation* (Oxford: Regnum Books, 2016).

[32] David Ro, "Mainland China (House Churches)," in *Christianity in East and Southeast Asia*, 71–73; David L. Ro, "A Study of an Emerging Missions Movement in Urban

restrictions prevented the urban house churches and their missions programmes from developing, but the commitment to the Back-to-Jerusalem missionary vision has persisted.

Although the church in this region has always faced challenges, especially from dominant religions, it has the most significant potential to lead the growth of global Christianity. However, one question remains: weren't all these growth potentials, except the mission development, in the past? If so, why is the Christian presence in Asia less than a quarter of the world's rate? Even if East and Southeast Asian churches have performed better than the rest of Asia, isn't it about a third of the world's rate? If the church remains in the same context, why can we believe it will be different in the future? I propose Pentecostal Christianity is a new and positive component to respond to these profound questions.

Asian Pentecostalism

In this section, I need to begin with a disclaimer: as with all other church traditions, Pentecostalism, in its wide variety, comes with its unique promises and challenges. The best gifts it may bring are 1) its rapid growth in its brief history and its spread among and renewal impact on different church traditions,[33] and 2) its unique missional pneumatology that undergirds the growth.

Growth

For the global picture, Pentecostalism (644.3 million in 2020) in all three subsets has become the second-largest Christian family after Catholicism (1,239.9 million). It is expected to grow to 1,031.5 million by 2050, or one in every ten persons globally (10.3%). Staggering, however, were its annual growth rates: 6.30% between 1900 and 2000, compared with the Christian growth (1.28%) and the population growth (1.34%). In the first two decades of this century, it recorded the highest growth rate (1.89%) among Christian groups (an average of 1.19% per annum). It was followed by Evangelicals (1.80%) and Independents (1.61%). For comparison, the world population grew at the annual rate of 1.20% during the period, thus making any group with a lower rate than the population's decline. They include Catholics (at 0.96%) and Orthodox (0.63%), lowering the net Christian annual growth rate to 1.19%, slightly lower than the population growth in 2000–2020. These statistics also beg the question, which is relevant to Pentecostal Christianity, why did its splendid growth not stop the steady decline of global Christianity? Was its growth primarily through the proselytisation of Christians from other groups? It is understandable in the Christianised places such as Latin America that the Pentecostal growth largely owes to transfers and conversions. However, in Asia, this question requires thoughtful consideration.

China: Fron the Perspective of Four Beijing Pastors" (Oxford and London: Oxford Centre for Mission Studies/Middlesex University, 2023).

[33] For a useful overview, see Wonsuk Ma, "Pentecostalism: A New but Big Kid on the Global Christian Block," *Pentecostal Education* 7.1 (Spring 2022), 73–91.

How does Pentecostalism fare in East and Southeast Asia? Between 1970 and 2020, Pentecostals/Charismatics grew from 4.6 million to 90.9 million: almost twenty times (Figure 4)! This growth translates from 0.4% of its population in 1970 to 3.9% in 2020.[34] This makes Pentecostal/Charismatics the fastest growing among all the religions!

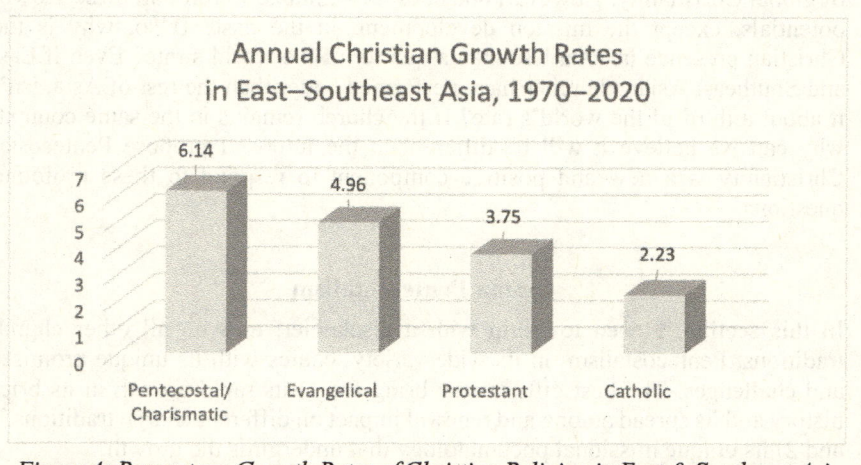

Figure 4: Percentage Growth Rates of Christian Religion in East & Southeast Asia

After checking the numbers, let's revisit two places in the region: Indonesia and China. In Indonesia, the annual growth rate of Pentecostals/Charismatics between 2000 and 2020 was 2.31%, almost two times faster than Islam (1.30%) and the population (1.27%). All the Christian traditions grew faster than the population (except Catholics at the par) and Islam (again, except Catholics). Thus, the proportion of Pentecostal/Charismatic believers in the population grew impressively from 1.9% in 1970 to 3.3% in 2000 and 4.0% in 2020 and is expected to reach 6.2% by 2050. The growth is more pronounced by looking at the actual numbers: from 2.2 million in 1970 to 11 million in 2020. Following this growth bud, Evangelicals also grew fast (at 2.28% in 2000–2020), and so did Independents (1.75%) and Protestants (1.68%).[35] All the megachurches I mentioned earlier are of the Pentecostal and Charismatic nature.

The growth of Christianity in China from the third quarter of the previous century has triggered studies. For example, Global Chinese Pentecostal and Charismatic Christianity[36] provides helpful reflections, casting an encouraging

---

[34] Julie Ma, "Pentecostals and Charismatics," in *Christianity in East and Southeast Asia*, 336–38.

[35] *WCE*, 3rd ed., 394. Also, Sulistyowati Irianto, "Indonesia," in *Christianity in East and Southeast Asia*, 201.

[36] Fenggang Yang, Joy K. C. Tong, and Allan H. Anderson, eds., *Global Chinese Pentecostal and Charismatic Christianity*, Global Pentecostal and Charismatic Studies 22 (Leiden, Netherlands: E. J. Brill, 2017). Equally useful was Brent Fulton, *China's*

Asian Pentecostalism as a Growth Engine for Global Christianity   261

future. Among the Christian blocks, understandably, the Independents lead in number (4.4% of the population in 2020), although its 2000–2020 annual growth was only 0.83%. Pentecostal/Charismatics were the next largest (2.6%) with a yearly growth rate of 0.68%. Surprisingly, the third-highest growth rate was recorded by historic Protestants at 2.4%, the fourth largest body after Evangelicals. How one categorises Chinese Christians is complex. Most house churches prefer Protestant to Independent or Pentecostal/Charismatic for several reasons. David Ro observes theological fault lines between rural and urban house churches. According to him, rural house churches widely embraced Charismatic and Holiness beliefs and their practices are widespread among rural house churches.[37] And the overlap between Pentecostal/Charismatic and Independents has been well acknowledged.

Before ending this discussion, I must point out that the demarcation between Pentecostal/Charismatics and Independents is complex, with much overlap.[38] One may argue that the majority of African Independent or Initiated churches are believed to practise a Pentecostal/Charismatic ethos. The Independents are the second-largest group in this region, with 103 million in 2020. It also grew second fastest (4.3% per year) after the Pentecostals/Charismatics. And the largest Independents are Chinese house churches, some of which are classified as Pentecostal/Charismatic. However, some scholars argue that more Independents should be counted among Pentecostals/Charismatics.[39]

Two Theological and Spiritual Dynamics[40]

Pentecostal pneumatology is missional in its nature. Although every Christian tradition affirms the person and work of the Holy Spirit, Pentecostalism has distinguished itself through its dynamic pneumatic beliefs and practices. Two distinctives deserve our attention: the Spirit's empowerment and the "prophethood of all believers," based on the belief in the baptism in the Holy Spirit.

First, divine empowerment through the Spirit of God is a long-established tradition. Spirit empowerment assumes a divine call and God's commissioning for a specific task. Christ's promise of the Holy Spirit, thus, continues this pattern: "But you will receive power when the Holy Spirit comes on you; and you will be my witnesses in Jerusalem, and in all Judea and Samaria, and to the

---

Urban Christians: A Light That Cannot Be Hidden (Eugene, Oregon: Pickwick Publications, 2015).

[37] David Ro, "Mainland China (House Churches)," in *Christianity in East and Southeast Asia*, 67.

[38] E.g., Zurlo, "A Demographic Profile of Christianity in East and Southeast Asia," 14.

[39] Luke Wesley, *The Church in China: Persecuted, Pentecostal and Powerful* (Baguio, Philippines: AJPS Books, 2004).

[40] This is a summary of Wonsuk Ma, "Pentecostal Theological Formation: Serving the Future of Global Christianity and the Movement (sec 1)," *Pentecostal Education* 7.2 (Fall 2022), 261–73.

ends of the earth" (Acts 1:8, NIV). The key is "receiving (divine) power" (or "empowerment") through the Holy Spirit. The task is to become Christ's witnesses to the ends of the earth. The book of Acts can be called the Acts of the Holy Spirit as his empowered witnesses scatter everywhere. Spirit-empowered witnessing has several common elements. They boldly proclaimed the lordship of Christ, as seen in Stephen's public proclamation in Acts 7. Also, their ministries were frequently accompanied by signs and wonders through the power of the Holy Spirit, such as healing and breaking prison doors. The newborn church met every day, breaking bread, praising the Lord, and even sharing their possessions with the needy. As a result, the "Lord added to their number daily those who were being saved" (Acts 2:44–47). And this Spirit-empowered ministry is patterned after Jesus' ministry: "... how God anointed Jesus of Nazareth with the Holy Spirit and power, and how he went around doing good and healing all who were under the power of the devil because God was with him" (Acts 10:38). This is repeated in modern-day Pentecostal Christianity. Spirit empowerment is the central dynamic causing the dramatic growth of Pentecostal and Charismatic Christianity.

Second, this highly focused experience of empowerment was radically "democratised." The exclusive presence of God's Spirit upon a small number of selected individuals now applied to all 120 on the day of Pentecost. To the puzzled audience in Jerusalem from many parts of the known world, Peter rightly chose the Joel 2 passage to explain the coming of the Holy Spirit:

> These people are not drunk, as you suppose. It's only nine in the morning! No, this is what was spoken by the prophet Joel: "In the last days, God says, I will pour out my Spirit on all people. Your sons and daughters will prophesy, your young men will see visions, your old men will dream dreams. Even on my servants, both men and women, I will pour out my Spirit in those days, and they will prophesy" (Acts 2:15–18).

The cataloguing of diverse community members, including the marginalised, creates a clear impression that everyone (or "all people") is included. The advent of the Holy Spirit on the day of Pentecost fulfilled this promise of radical democratisation. The book of Acts, again, demonstrates the witnessing of the good news by Spirit-empowered "everyone." Acts 11 records that "some" who fled persecution in Jerusalem reached various parts of the region, "spreading the word" initially among Jews (v. 19) but eventually to the Greeks (v. 20). They were the church planters in Syrian Antioch. Acts 19 is another example: Paul's ministry in Ephesus began with the coming of the Holy Spirit (v. 6). While he and his companions continued their daily teaching in Tyrannus (v. 9) accompanied by "extraordinary miracles" (v. 11), in two years, "all the Jews and Greeks who lived in the province of Asia heard the word of the Lord" (v. 10). It is the new converts in Ephesus who scattered to different parts of Asia, the democratised, Spirit-empowered witnesses.

If we borrow the law of physics, the more concentrated, the more power you can produce. The same rule reverses the strength of energy as the focus is spread. The Pentecostal logic defies this scientific rule. Yes, the infinite amount of energy in the source will maintain the same power strength even if the scope is indefinitely expanded.

Asian Pentecostalism as a Growth Engine for Global Christianity   263

Equally encouraging is the missionary movement among the churches in the region. Three top-ten missionary countries are in the religion: South Korea (ranked third with 35,000 cross-cultural missionaries), the Philippines (fourth with 25,000), and China (sixth with 15,000). Outside of this region, but still in Asia, India is ranked eighth with 10,000. And as the fastest-growing segment of Christianity, Pentecostal/Charismatic (along with Independent) churches hold the key to the future expansion of the world's Christianity!

Conclusion

This study has presented an audacious claim that Pentecostal Christianity in East and Southeast Asia is poised to play a pivotal role in the growth of Asian and global Christianity. The basis for the thesis is the region's Christian engagement with two prime religious competitors, Islam and "nones," its growth potential and performance, and the unique possibility of Pentecostalism. As the stage is divinely set, a human agency determines the outcome of the growth potential. This is where Yoido Full Gospel Church (YFGC) finds its unique call.

The church has been the bastion of the Asian Pentecostal movement and its growth. It has become the epitome of church growth through Pentecostal beliefs, spirituality, and creativity. Indeed, the church is viewed as the forerunner of the church growth movement. For almost three decades, the church has maintained the prized title of "the largest church in the world," even after a dozen campuses were released to become autonomous congregations. This feat was achieved in fast-changing social and cultural environments, often posing formidable challenges to the church. The Pentecostal message from this church has proven to be resilient, agilely positioning the church to respond to the changes and creatively reframing the message to empower its people. As a result, the church has never lost its growth momentum.

At the same time, the church took the leadership mantle for church growth. For example, its legendary cell group system has been widely propagated through its Church Growth International conferences, giving birth to contextually modified versions, such as the G12 Movement. The extensive national and international evangelistic events of the church always include extensive church growth training for church leaders.

The leadership succession of the church was a process that the whole Christian world observed. Lee's leadership began in the context of radical social changes in Korea. He has skilfully maintained the balance between continuity and creativity, solidifying the foundation for the next generation. This study, thus, celebrates his spirituality and leadership.

Korean Pentecostalism, Shamanism, and Intercultural Theology

Allan H. Anderson

Introduction

Korean Pentecostalism, like Christianity as a whole, is deeply influenced by its culture, including its religious past. I have spent my academic life exploring the relationship between the Christian message and culture, and especially the so-called "traditional" religions. I put the word "traditional" in quotation marks because the word implies some static and historical phenomenon. Ancient and foundational religions in any society constantly move and adapt to a changing world. This paper will examine how Korean shamanism fits into Pentecostal practices and whether the encounter can be considered a continuity or discontinuity. In doing this, I will draw on the writings of Walter Hollenweger, my predecessor at the University of Birmingham, and his concept of "intercultural theology." I first met Dr. Younghoon Lee as a speaker at a conference on Asian Pentecostalism in Birmingham in 2001, where he addressed the subject of the Korean Holy Spirit movement, later published in an edited collection. His contribution was also the subject of his doctoral dissertation, the Holy Spirit movement in Korea in the early twentieth century and its relationship to Korean Pentecostalism.[1] As the second senior pastor of the famous Yoido Full Gospel Church and an ecumenical leader who participated in the Busan Assembly of the World Council of Churches, Lee commands great respect. Apart from the insights of Hollenweger, my thoughts on Korean Pentecostalism are based on the research Lee and others have done, as well as my own personal observations during visits I have made to South Korea.

One of the issues that had long been a personal concern for me was what has been called "contextual theology," where theology becomes influenced by and relevant to its socio-political context. Hollenweger preferred to use the term "intercultural theology."[2] Although I first encountered Hollenweger's intercultural theology during my initial studies into African Pentecostalism in the 1970s and 1980s, the concept was by no means confined to African Pentecostalism. Korean Pentecostalism can also be discussed. During the years, I have attempted to tie intercultural theology to my work on Pentecostalism. Hollenweger's writings were monumental and pioneering. When the rest of the Christian world considered Pentecostalism a strange, misguided fundamentalist

---

[1] Young-Hoon Lee, "The Korean Holy Spirit Movement in Relation to Pentecostalism," in Allan Anderson and Edmond Tang, eds., *Asian and Pentecostal: The Charismatic Face of Christianity in Asia,* 2nd ed. (Oxford: Regnum Books, 2011), 430–44.

[2] Allan H. Anderson, "The Intercultural Theology of Walter J. Hollenweger," *Journal of the European Pentecostal Theological Association* 41:1 (2021), 35–51.

sect (at best) and academia was interested only in its most exotic and so-called "syncretistic" fringes, Hollenweger raised important questions and made observations that make the study of this movement the growing and creative activity it is today.

While I was deeply immersed in a pastoral and teaching ministry to Africans during my graduate studies in South Africa, I learned to appreciate the riches of African religious and cultural heritages and the need for Western scholars like me to be sensitive to these when doing theology in Africa. Arriving in Birmingham in 1995, I began to explore potential resources in Pentecostalism worldwide for an intercultural theology. Through invitations to visit South Korea, Korean Pentecostalism, particularly the ministry of Yonggi Cho, became my first case study outside Africa. I discovered that Korean Pentecostalism had its own characteristics, deeply influenced by the religious and social cultures in which it was formed. We begin here with a brief introduction to "intercultural theology" as envisaged by Hollenweger and how he and others have applied this to Korean Pentecostalism, particularly in relating it to shamanism. I reflect on how misunderstandings easily arise and how Korean Pentecostalism has contributed to our understanding of Pentecostalism. Finally, I discuss how the tension between continuity and discontinuity is played out in Korean Pentecostalism.[3]

Intercultural Theology

Pentecostalism has managed for well over a century to adapt itself to different cultures worldwide in a seemingly effortless fashion. Hollenweger, a former Pentecostal pastor, first encountered African Pentecostalism during his years with the World Council of Churches in the 1960s. It was there that he first began to promote the need for an intercultural theology. From the 1970s onwards, Hollenweger applied the concept of intercultural theology to studies of Pentecostalism, including the movement in Korea. He expressed his understanding during a theological conference in Zürich in 1984, where he stated that "A truly universal and ecumenical theology must be intercultural" because "all theologies are culturally conditioned."[4] In a newly globalised world with faster communications and increasing migration into Europe of people from the "Third World," Hollenweger challenged contemporary theologians about the need to acknowledge the relativity and ideologically conditioned nature of their precious "traditional" theology and, therefore, to be prepared for change. Most of Hollenweger's life and work were devoted to presenting to the Western theological world the voices of the universal people of God, especially those who

---

[3] Some of what follows is based on earlier research, and in particular, I have adapted ideas from my most recent book: Allan Heaton Anderson, *Spirit-Filled World: Religious Dis/Continuity in African Pentecostalism* (Cham, Switzerland: Palgrave Macmillan, 2018).

[4] Walter J. Hollenweger, "Intercultural Theology," *Theology Today* 43:1 (January 1986), 28.

had been marginalised by Western dominance. All his writings on Pentecostalism can be seen in this light. For him, Pentecostalism was the prime example of intercultural theology in practice. He repeatedly stated that theology was more than a written text – in Pentecostalism, it came to life in the practices, liturgies, prayers, dances, and testimonies of Pentecostal believers.

I have studied Pentecostalism in Africa in detail, including the independent "Spirit" churches found throughout the continent. These churches have practices that reflect the background of African "traditional" or popular religion. For example, consulting the traditional healer is replaced by visiting healing "prophets" for prayers and, sometimes, for instructions on what to do to solve a problem. Western analysts have been tempted to say that the traditional healer continues in the person of the prophet. However, once these *forms* (which are similar) are distinguished from their *meaning* (which is very different), the revelations of the Spirit point to a realistic encounter and confrontation between the new Christian faith and the old pre-Christian beliefs. So, Christianity gets an "intercultural" character by penetrating the old in continuity with the past and creating the new in discontinuity. Questions about what "true" Christianity is and what it is not are also often questions about who has the power to decide. The Pentecostal pastors, bishops, or prophets who exorcise demons, lay hands on the sick, and lead their congregations in rituals of worship are enacting their intercultural theology. Hollenweger's concern in advocating an intercultural theology was that it was liberating not only for non-Western churches but also for Western Christianity itself.[5]

Theology as a human response to God should be intercultural, contextual, and expressive of everyday life or be in danger of being irrelevant. Korean Pentecostals, like others throughout our world, have made creative adaptations to their Christian faith that amount to a comprehensive contextual theology as well as a liturgical transformation. They have been able, by these various means, to re-evaluate their Korean culture and religion. Korean Pentecostals take seriously both their religious, social, and cultural context and what their own Christian response should be. The continuing dialogue between Pentecostals and popular cultures and religions, and in particular their interaction with the prevailing spirit world that is so evident in many societies worldwide, help clarify the issues involved in formulating an intercultural theology.

Korean Pentecostalism, Shamanism, and Syncretism

Hollenweger was one of the first to see that Pentecostalism was fundamentally altering the character of world Christianity as a whole. His intercultural theology was based on his own experience of Pentecostal churches outside the Western world, at first through his work with the World Pentecostal Fellowship and later with the World Council of Churches. This working experience was also his introduction to the transformation that was happening within world Christianity.

---

[5] Walter J. Hollenweger, *Pentecostalism: Origins and Developments Worldwide* (Peabody, MA: Hendrickson, 1997), 47.

Criticisms of Pentecostal churches have at their basis a belief that these churches do not always represent "true" Christianity because (so the argument goes) pre-Christian beliefs and practices have been absorbed into Christian ones. So, from this perspective, Korean shamanism has been absorbed into Christian practices. However, continuity with pre-Christian ideas does not necessarily mean "syncretism" (in a negative sense) but should rather be seen as an indication of a developing intercultural theology – and, therefore, a positive development. In other words, we should not attempt to dichotomiSe the continuity of the old religion and the discontinuity brought by Christianity – they must be seen as running together in creative tension.

Hollenweger's second major book on Pentecostalism, titled *Pentecostalism: Origins and Developments Worldwide* (1997), updated and developed his earlier ideas with reference to more recent literature. By this time, he had a fully developed theory on the importance of Pentecostalism to intercultural theology. He asked whether the different forms of Pentecostalism worldwide could be regarded as forms of syncretism and answered affirmatively: "So are all forms of Christianity [syncretistic], also and in particular Western Christianity." It is not whether there *is* syncretism but "what *kind* of syncretism" – which leads him to discuss a "theologically responsible syncretism" in assessing Pentecostalism.

Hollenweger was also influenced by other studies at the time. The first critical study of Korean Pentecostalism was conducted by Minjung theologian Kwang-Sun (David) Suh and published by the Christian Academy of Korea in 1981.[6] It focused on the ministry of Yonggi Cho, who was the most prominent Korean Pentecostal leader at the time. Suh and other liberal scholars did not so much accuse Cho of false or "heretical" teaching as to suggest a positive link between Cho's theology and Korean shamanism. In this respect, these scholars might regard Cho as "contextual." Hollenweger took up these ideas. An entire chapter of *Pentecostalism* is titled "Korea: The Oral Shamanistic Culture in Pentecostal Transformation."[7] He acknowledged that the chapter was "heavily based" on the writings of his former Ph.D. student and Korean Presbyterian missionary in Kenya, Boo-woong Yoo.[8] Yoo's doctoral thesis, published in 1988 as *Korean Pentecostalism: Its History and Theology*, is not about Pentecostalism in its present form, but is a reflection on earlier revival movements, the "Korean Pentecost" of 1907 and the mystical "Pentecostal movement" of the 1930s. The only mention of Yoido Full Gospel Church and Yonggi Cho is indirect – in a quotation from Suh.[9] Incredibly, this academic work on "Korean Pentecostalism" only once briefly mentions Yoido Full Gospel Church (hereafter YFGC), the most influential representative of Pentecostalism in Korea. Yoo mainly discusses the relationship between the Korean revival movement in the

---

[6] Reference in Myung Soo Park, "David Yonggi Cho and International Pentecostal Movements," *Journal of Pentecostal Theology* 12:1 (2003), 109.

[7] Hollenweger, *Pentecostalism*, 99–105.

[8] Hollenweger, *Pentecostalism*, 99, n.1.

[9] Boo-Woong Yoo, *Korean Pentecostalism: Its History and Theology* (Frankfurt am Main: Peter Lang, 1988), 206.

Korean Pentecostalism, Shamanism, and Intercultural Theology   269

Presbyterian and Methodist churches and *Minjung* theology. At the end of his work, Yoo refers to the need for "a Pentecostal exploration of Shamanism."[10]

At the same time that Yoo was doing his research in Birmingham, Jae Bum Lee completed a very different Ph.D. study at Fuller Theological Seminary in the USA. The first academic work by a Korean Pentecostal in the English language, Lee's thesis set the pattern for many that followed. He considered the early twentieth-century Korean revival movement as "Pentecostal" and named revival leaders Sun-joo Gil, Ik-doo Kim, and Yong-do Lee as paradigmatic of the Korean Pentecostalism to follow.[11] He drew attention to the fact that Korean revivalism has always been accompanied by what he calls "Pentecostal-type experiences," including Spirit baptism, healing, miracles, and exorcism.[12] This was also a subject close to Younghoon Lee's heart. In 1996, Lee successfully completed his Ph.D. at Temple University in the USA, which gave rise to his book *The Holy Spirit Movement in Korea*, published in 2009. He also traced the beginning of these movements in the early ministries of Gil, Kim, and Lee, but sees these as pre-Pentecostal movements, arguing that Pentecostalism's distinctive is its doctrine of the baptism in the Holy Spirit.[13]

Several Western writers suggest that Korean Pentecostals, in general, and YFGC, in particular, have succeeded because they have combined Christianity with shamanism. Yoo did not do this directly, but his doctoral supervisor, Hollenweger, was probably the first, in his interpretation of Yoo's research. In a footnote, Hollenweger stated that the "famous Korean Pentecostal pastor Paul Yonggi Cho ... could be considered a Pentecostal Shaman par excellence."[14] He suggests that Korean Pentecostalism should be interpreted "with the categories of a Shamanistic culture" rather than from historical and theological categories imposed from outside.[15]

Hollenweger seems to have influenced Harvey Cox, who took up this theme in his *Fire from Heaven*. In a chapter on Korean Pentecostalism (with particular reference to YFGC) entitled "Shamans and Entrepreneurs: Primal Spirituality on the Asian Rim,"[16] he acknowledges the thesis of Yoo in his bibliographical notes at the end.[17] In what is now a well-known passage, Cox says that in his opinion the YFGC "involves a massive importation of shamanistic practice into a Christian ritual."[18] All of this is to support his overarching theory of

---

[10] Yoo, *Korean Pentecostalism*, 223.

[11] Jae Bum Lee, "Pentecostal Type Distinctives and Korean Protestant Church Growth" (Ph.D. thesis, Fuller Theological Seminary, Pasadena, 1986), 180–86.

[12] Jae Bum Lee, "Pentecostal Type Distinctives," 169.

[13] Younghoon Lee, *The Holy Spirit Movement in Korea: Its Historical and Theological Development* (Oxford: Regnum Books, 2009), 71.

[14] Hollenweger, *Pentecostalism*, 100, n 2.

[15] Hollenweger, *Pentecostalism*, 104.

[16] Harvey Cox, *Fire from Heaven: The Rise of Pentecostal Spirituality and the Reshaping of Religion in the Twenty-First Century* (London: Cassell, 1996), 213–41.

[17] Cox, *Fire from Heaven*, 328.

[18] Cox, *Fire from Heaven*, 226.

Pentecostalism as "primal spirituality." Cox assumes that religions succeed when they possess "two capabilities": first, to include and absorb the "old" religions (in this case, shamanism), and second, to prepare people for living in a rapidly changing world. He declares, "Both of these key ingredients are present in Korean pentecostalism."[19] He continues: "One of the key reasons for Korean pentecostalism's extraordinary growth is its unerring ability to absorb huge chunks of indigenous Korean shamanism and demon possession into its worship," of which the YFGC "is an especially vivid case in point."[20]

This idea of a link between Korean Pentecostalism and shamanism has been assumed and perpetuated in Western literature to such an extent that it is now almost taken for granted.[21] Indeed, Korean scholars have debated this issue with Cox himself, and have argued against this simplistic explanation. The so-called "link" with shamanism should be assessed in a quite different way. As Myung Soo Park has pointed out, it is more appropriate to see Pentecostal reactions to shamanism and the teachings of Cho on healing and "threefold blessings" within the context of his contact with international Pentecostalism.[22] In other words, Korean Pentecostalism should be assessed not only from within the internal cultural and religious context of Korea, but also from the external influence of globalisation. Both these elements of continuity and discontinuity with the past are present in Korean Pentecostalism, and they exist in tension with each other.

Most Korean scholars admit that Korean Christianity, like Korean Buddhism, is predated by Korean shamanism, the traditional religion of Korea. Shamanism is the bedrock on which other religions are later built. Younghoon Lee has noted this himself, when he states, "In Korea, shamanism formed the basic background of Korean religions, accepted foreign religions, mixed itself with them, and flourished throughout history. Shamanism is the key element in understanding the religious mentality of the Korean people." This is like what I observed in sub-Saharan Africa, where healers and "witchdoctors" form the basis of a worldview that underlies Christianity. Responses to older religions are based on a particular interpretation of the Bible and are not a simple transfer from one religion to the other.

Hollenweger pointed out that syncretism does not necessarily need to be a negative concept in adapting Christianity to culture.[23] Syncretism is inevitable and unavoidable if Christianity is to be relevant and understandable in its various contexts. Indeed, Western Christianity in all its forms is inherently "syncretistic" in this understanding. Korean Christianity likewise is "syncretistic," not in the negative sense of mixing two religions so that the mixture is unrecognisable as either, but in creative adaptations to traditional religion – in this case, shamanism

---

[19] Cox, *Fire from Heaven*, 219.

[20] Cox, *Fire from Heaven*, 222.

[21] David Martin, *Pentecostalism: The World Their Parish* (Oxford: Blackwell, 2002), 161; Mark R. Mullins, *Christianity Made in Japan: A Study of Indigenous Movements* (Honolulu: University of Hawaii Press, 1998), 175.

[22] Park, "David Yonggi Cho," 110.

[23] Hollenweger, *Pentecostalism*, 132.

Korean Pentecostalism, Shamanism, and Intercultural Theology   271

– so that Christianity becomes understandable and relevant in the Korean context. In other words, the analysis of Korean Pentecostalism should be based on the extent to which it exhibits intercultural theology.

Despite forces of globalisation urging uniformity, Pentecostalism has developed its own characteristics and identities in Korea while establishing transnational connections and international networks. The "local" cannot be separated from the "global," as each has an influence; neither can the "continuous" be separated from the "discontinuous." Culture, including religion, is a dynamic, ever-changing phenomenon. In today's world, there are global forces changing the nature of Pentecostalism in all its variety of different forms. The shapes of what has emerged because of the globalisation process, how these both resemble and differ from the older networks of denominational Pentecostalism, and the extent to which Pentecostalism has permeated and affected the beliefs, values, and practices of other Christians have yet to be analysed fully. Only when these investigations have taken place will we be better able to understand the external forces that forge the religious identities of people and the increasingly important role of Pentecostalism as an expression of intercultural theology.

Recognising Continuity and Discontinuity

Scholarly studies about the expansion of Pentecostalism worldwide have not thoroughly explored a principal reason for its popularity – the extent to which Pentecostalism, through its experience of the Spirit, often unconsciously taps into deep-seated religious and cultural beliefs. Pentecostalism draws from these ancient sources in continuity with them, while simultaneously confronting them in discontinuity, using a biblical rationale for its beliefs and practices. The popularity of Pentecostalism can be more easily understood from this perspective. Pentecostalism makes a radical break with the past, but this does not mean it is either Christianity or the ancient religion. What often appears as continuity, such as the similarities of a Christian healing practitioner with a shaman, is often actually discontinuity because of the interpretation and meaning given to the phenomenon. The reverse is also the case, where practices found throughout global Pentecostalism are invested with new meanings through encounters with a local religious and cultural context. This I have explored thoroughly.[24]

The Holy Spirit occupies an important place in Pentecostalism, both historically with the Holy Spirit movements as outlined by Younghoon Lee, and religiously with its encounter with Korean shamanism. Analyses of Korean Pentecostalism become more meaningful when placed in the context of the shamanistic spirit world that permeates most aspects of South Korean life, even in its highly modern and industrialised society. Pentecostalism and the related Charismatic movement have become two of the most prominent forms of Korean Christianity. Pentecostalism permeates both the historic denominations and independent churches. Worldwide, Pentecostalism has not only contributed to

---

[24] Anderson, *Spirit-Filled World.*

the reshaping of the nature of Christianity but has also left an indelible mark on popular religion and culture. This is no less true of Korea. The power of the Holy Spirit enables Korean Pentecostals to confront all types of evil, including sicknesses and troubles caused by the spirit world surrounding them.

All forms of Christianity are affected by and affect religious beliefs in many fundamental ways. Pentecostalism, both in its similarities and in its differences with local beliefs and rituals has succeeded in remarkable ways to integrate the ancient beliefs throughout the world. The African experiences discussed in my 2018 book have parallels in places wherever a holistic, spiritual universe is central to human experience and beliefs. As anthropologist Adam Ashforth points out, "For most humans … the ultimate source of security is to be found in relations with spiritual powers of various sorts."[25] "Most humans," he continues, live "in a world with a lively appreciation of invisible agencies."[26] The world of evil spirits and demonic forces is believed to be responsible for all kinds of events – including misfortune, illness, poverty, and a host of other social, economic, and political problems bringing spiritual insecurity. These beliefs continue the past beliefs of many generations. In its encounter with this spirit world, Pentecostalism offers radical, discontinuous solutions to all these problems by emphasising the power of the Spirit and the exercise of "spiritual gifts." But in confronting this pervasive spirit world, Pentecostalism also helps to preserve it by recognising its existential reality. Pentecostalism and various forms of Charismatic and Independent Christianity, through their belief in the power of the Holy Spirit, provide a solution to this spiritual conflict and encounter and introduce radical change. It is this confrontation between the old and the new that provides a compelling explanation for the popularity of Pentecostalism outside a Western world that has become rational and secular.

Because Pentecostals believe that they are solidly biblical, most will resist the idea that there are any pre-Christian religious ideas or "syncretism" in their beliefs and practices. This has been repeated time and again by Korean Pentecostal scholars. Pentecostals reject the practices of divination and shamanism while acknowledging the spiritual power behind them that needs to be overcome. Because a spirit-filled world pervades the consciousness of many societies and underlies almost all religious expressions, Pentecostalism acknowledges and addresses needs arising from that spiritual world, often without realising it. It can be considered a culturally and religiously contextual form of Christianity, both interacting with and confronting the spiritual world. Culture and religion are intrinsically linked. Both continuity and discontinuity with the old shamanistic religion are kept in creative tension. Pentecostalism also provides places of spiritual security and personal communities for people unsettled by rapid social and cultural changes.

The Holy Spirit revival movements of the early twentieth century in Korea were filled with spiritual presence. Later, Pentecostalism arrived with enthusiastic promises to meet physical, emotional, and spiritual needs. It offered

---

[25] Adam Ashforth, "AIDS, Religious Enthusiasm and Spiritual Insecurity in Africa," *Global Public Health* 6:2 sup. (2011), S135.

[26] Ashforth, "AIDS, Religious Enthusiasm," S136.

Korean Pentecostalism, Shamanism, and Intercultural Theology   273

solutions to life's problems and ways to survive in a threatening and hostile spirit world, whether or not these solutions were ever realised. Pentecostal preachers proclaimed that the God who saves the "soul" also heals the body and is a "good God" interested in providing answers to human fears and insecurities. They accepted people who feared shamanism and evil spirits as having genuine problems, and they conscientiously tried to find solutions. They proclaimed that the God who forgives sin is also concerned about poverty, sickness, barrenness, oppression by spirits, and liberation from all forms of human affliction and bondage. This all-encompassing message made Pentecostalism attractive to so many.

Pentecostal spirituality has been likened to "primal spirituality" by Harvey Cox, who writes of "the unanticipated reappearance of primal spirituality in our time." He describes this "primal spirituality" as having three dimensions: (1) *primal speech*, found in glossolalia (speaking in tongues), which he describes as "another voice, a language of the heart"; (2) *primal piety*, found in the resurgence of "trance, vision, healing, dreams, dance, and other archetypal religious expressions"; and (3) *primal hope*, which he describes as "pentecostalism's millennial outlook ... that a radical new age is about to dawn."[27] Cox admits that instead of the "death of God" and the decline of religion, something quite different was taking place, a "religious renaissance" throughout the world, touching every sort of religious expression, a period of renewed religious vitality. Cox remarks that "the abstract deity of western theologies and philosophical systems had come to the end of its run."[28] He has rightly described the continuity that exists between Pentecostalism and human religious consciousness. But he runs the risk of advocating an outdated view of religious "primitivism." He also inadvertently has missed the discontinuity that exists simultaneously in the "born-again," radical break with the past that Pentecostalism declares.

Korean Pentecostal spirituality is at an interface between Christianity and the ancient religious world of shamanism, as well as between "historical" and "pentecostal" Christianity. Pentecostal worship often includes a free and spontaneous liturgy that is not hindered by the rigidity that sometimes accompanies older forms of Christian liturgy. This spontaneity also helps remove the sense of foreignness that sometimes accompanies Western forms of Christianity in the Majority World. Pentecostal theologian Amos Yong writes of the importance of a holistic understanding of human religiosity, and that the Pentecostal and Charismatic experience "demands interpretation of the experiential dimension of spirituality over and against an emphasis on textuality in religious life."[29] Pentecostal spirituality reflects the conviction that God is experienced as real through the Spirit, and this is expressed in liturgies that are primarily oral, narrative, and participatory. The Holy Spirit invades all human life.

---

[27] Cox, *Fire from Heaven*, 81–88, 91–92, 96.

[28] Cox, *Fire from Heaven*, xvi, 83, 104.

[29] Amos Yong, *Discerning the Spirit(s): A Pentecostal/Charismatic Contribution to Christian Theology of Religions* (Sheffield: Sheffield Academic Press, 2000), 134, 162, 319.

The popularity of Pentecostalism in Korea can also be attributed to a particularly *contextual* spirituality. Pentecostalism provides for much more than "spiritual" problems alone. Throughout the world, Pentecostalism has been relevant because it has continued some pre-Christian religious expressions and ritual symbols but has transformed them with new meanings. Christianity has been in both a continuous and discontinuous relationship with other, older religions for two millennia. Yong points out that Pentecostals in the Majority World, especially those who are part of Christian minorities, are in constant interaction with other religions. He writes that the experiences of the Holy Spirit common to Pentecostals and Charismatics demonstrate "indubitable similarities across the religious traditions of the world." This opens the way to explore "how the Spirit is present and active in other religious traditions." In their encounter with shamanism, Pentecostals have been challenged and enriched in the content of their proclamation, which without that encounter would have been impoverished and "foreign." Pentecostals offer solutions for life's problems through the indwelling Spirit; they accept them as real problems, conscientiously attempt to provide explanations for them, and expect something to happen to resolve the problems through faith in God.

Until recently, Pentecostals did not talk about their "spirituality," as it was not part of their religious vocabulary. However, "Pentecostal spirituality" has become recognised as a distinctive form of Christian spirituality that can be described through its various activities and rites.[30] But there is no *common* "Pentecostal spirituality," because Pentecostalism throughout the world is extremely diverse. It is more accurate to say that there are different Pentecostal spiritualities with common features, a merging of the "local" with the "global." Even when scholars describe a singular "Pentecostal spirituality" as the experience of God through the Spirit, this transcends cultural boundaries and provides a genuine and flexible encounter with God that is meaningful in its different cultural expressions. Pentecostal spiritualities are centred on the experience of the Spirit that pervades the whole person, makes Jesus Christ more real and relevant to daily life, and inspires testimony, praise, unknown tongues, prophecies, healings, dancing, clapping, joyful singing, and many other expressions that characterise Pentecostalism worldwide. In Korea, these spiritualities are expressed in liturgies that often take on characteristics of Korean culture and are not unaffected by the shamanistic religious tradition that has permeated that culture. The creative tension between the continuity and discontinuity is illustrated in a particular form of Pentecostal spirituality, as in its encounter with Korean shamanism.

Conclusion

Those criticising Korean Pentecostals for their alleged "shamanism" often fail to see that the parallels with ancient religions in these practices are also continuous

---

[30] Daniel E. Albrecht, *Rites in the Spirit: A Ritual Approach to Pentecostal/Charismatic Spirituality* (Sheffield: Sheffield Academic Press, 1999), 9, 14.

Korean Pentecostalism, Shamanism, and Intercultural Theology 275

and compatible with the biblical record. Furthermore, Korean Pentecostals define their practices by reference to the Bible rather than to shamanism, but see their activities as creative adaptations to the local context. It would be more accurate to state that Korean Pentecostalism is in creative tension with shamanism, and is also a reaction to it. Korean Pentecostal scholars could reflect more on the diversity of their cultural and religious past and how this affects their form of Pentecostalism. It is not always helpful to demonise this past, because this will not explain the attraction of Pentecostalism for East Asian peoples deeply influenced by their ancient religions and cultures, even though such a demonisation might help in the religious competition that is a feature of these pluralist societies. But one conclusion that is incontrovertible is that Korean Pentecostals have found both culturally and biblically acceptable alternatives to and adaptations from the practices of shamanism and are seeking to provide answers to the needs inherent in their own context.

I have lived in the Western world for almost three decades and dipped in and out of it for four decades before that. My understanding of religious phenomena outside my context will always be partial. Pentecostal theology in Korea should not reflect a theology born in a totally different context (such as that of the USA), even though cultural radiation from this country has invaded South Korea for over a generation. A theology "made in the USA," whether Pentecostal or otherwise, is a form of cultural and religious colonialism. Korean Pentecostalism now has many gifted scholars who could develop a theology that speaks from a different perspective, reflecting the voice of the poor, a theology of hope for a suffering people, a genuinely contextual theology. The good news of Pentecostalism is that God meets all the needs of believers, including their spiritual salvation, physical healing, and other blessings for material needs, the "three-fold blessing" made popular by Yonggi Cho. South Korea also has experienced the phenomenon of rapid urbanisation, and the Pentecostal churches have provided places of spiritual security and personal communities for people unsettled by rapid social change. As Korean churches become more relevant to their cultural and social context, they become more able to serve the wider society.

Yoido Full Gospel Church and Ecumenism

Cecil M. Robeck Jr.

Requests for Pentecostals to Engage in Ecumenical Dialogue

In 1992, I received an invitation to represent the Pentecostal world in the annual meeting of secretaries of Christian World Communions (CWC), a group of some thirty general secretaries who serve a range of Christian church families. The invitation rightfully belonged to the general secretary of the Pentecostal World Conference (PWC), Rev. Jacob Zopfi (Swiss Pentecostal Mission), though he was not interested in attending any ecumenical meeting. When he ignored this invitation repeatedly, the secretary of the CWCs, Dr. Bert Beach, Seventh Day Adventist, and, the following year, Msgr. John Radano, a representative of the ecumenical office of the Vatican, approached me. Each of them made the case that the secretaries both wanted and needed a Pentecostal voice at the table of its annual meeting. They asked me if I would serve.

After seeking permission from the chairman of the PWC, Rev. Ray Hughes (Church of God, Cleveland, TN), and my general superintendent, G. Raymond Carlson, to accept this invitation, I joined them.[1] This group gathers the general secretaries of global organisations such as the Baptist World Alliance, the Methodist World Council, the Lutheran World Federation (LWF), the World Alliance of Reformed Churches (WARC),[2] Mennonite World Conference, the Pontifical Council for Promoting Christian Unity,[3] and so forth. They meet annually to update each other on their work, to address common issues and concerns at the global level, occasionally with world leaders, and to pray for one another. Among them were two general secretaries who quickly sought me out.

The first request came during the secretaries' meeting in Geneva, Switzerland in 1993, from Dr. Gunnar Stålsett,[4] who asked me if I would be open to the idea of establishing an international dialogue between Pentecostals and the LWF. My

---

[1] I served in that capacity from 1993 through 2022, when I retired, and Rev. David Wells, general superintendent of the Pentecostal Assemblies of Canada and vice-chairman of the Pentecostal World Conference, took my place.

[2] In 2010, the World Alliance of Reformed Churches (WARC) and the Reformed Ecumenical Council (REC) merged to form the World Communion of Reformed Churches (WCRC). That is the current name of the organisation.

[3] In 2022, the Pontifical Council, representing the ecumenical interests of the Vatican, became the Dicastery for Promoting Christian Unity.

[4] Dr. Stålsett was both a politician and a theologian. He served as the head of Norway's Democrat Party, later as the head of the Centrist Party, and as a member of the Norwegian Parliament, representing Oslo. He was a member of the Nobel Peace Prize Committee. From 1998 to 2006, he served as Bishop of Oslo for the Church of Norway.

initial response was to ask him why he thought such a dialogue would be important. He responded immediately.

> The Ethiopian Evangelical Church, Mekane Yesus, is a member of the LWF, yet many Lutherans, especially in Germany, Scandinavia, and the United States do not know how to relate to the Mekane Yesus Church, because it is so different. The Mekane Yesus Church is certainly Lutheran in its core theology, liturgy, and identity, but it is also deeply Pentecostal, welcoming many manifestations of the Holy Spirit, including speaking in tongues, prophecy, healings, falling in the Spirit, and the like. Such manifestations confuse and in some cases scare their European and North American counterparts. You Pentecostals have had long experience with such manifestations, and you could provide both knowledge and wisdom on how we should discern these manifestations in our midst.

I did not hesitate, and told Dr. Stålsett that I would be very pleased to help open such an international dialogue between representative Pentecostals and the LWF. Because of a transition to a new general secretary, Ishmael Noko, and a high priority on completing the "Joint Declaration on the Doctrine of Justification" with the Catholic Church, however, it would be a decade before the official Lutheran–Pentecostal dialogue began.[5] It would finally come under a new general secretary, Rev. Martin Junge.

That same week, Dr. Milan Opočenský, general secretary of the WARC, asked me if I would explore with him the possibility of opening an international dialogue between Pentecostals and representatives from the WARC. The idea of such a discussion with members of the Alliance was also intriguing, especially since Fuller Theological Seminary, where I served as a professor of Church History and Ecumenics, was dominated by a significant number of Reformed faculty members. As a Pentecostal faculty member and associate dean of the School of Theology at the time, I wondered what we Pentecostals might talk about with representatives of the Reformed world. When I asked Dr. Opočenský, "Why do you think we should open such a dialogue?" his immediate response was that we both represent Christian families of churches and that it would be good to get better acquainted with one another.

I have long been convinced that as followers of Jesus, who prayed for unity among his disciples (John 17:21–23), we should build closer relationships with our sisters and brothers across denominational lines. Still, given that, international dialogues are expensive. Because I needed a rationale that I could provide to Dr. Richard Mouw, president of Fuller Theological Seminary, to

---

[5] Because the LWF was busy at the time, the Institute for Ecumenical Research in Strasbourg, France, hosted an unofficial discussion beginning in 2006 through to 2010. The results were published as *Lutherans and Pentecostals Together* (Strasbourg, France: Institute for Ecumenical Research/Pasadena, CA: David du Plessis Center for Christian Spirituality/Zurich, Switzerland: European Pentecostal Charismatic Research Association, 2010). It was subsequently published as "Lutherans–Pentecostals: Lutherans and Pentecostals in Dialogue," in Thomas F. Best, Lorelei F. Fuchs, SA, John Gibaut, Jeffrey Gros, FSC, and Despina Prassas, eds., *Growth in Agreement IV: International Dialogue Texts and Agreed Statements, 2004–2014* (Geneva, Switzerland: World Council of Churches publications, 2017), 2:73–110.

justify my involvement, I told Milan that, while in principle I supported his idea, I needed a better reason. I asked him to identify a problem or a place where there might be conflict between Reformed and Pentecostal churches, where we might make a difference through such a dialogue, and to come back to me when he had one.

A Compelling Request

The following year, 1994, the secretaries of the CWCs held their annual meeting in Istanbul, Turkey. Milan Opočenský and I once again greeted each other warmly. Excitedly, he informed me that he now had a persuasive reason for us to open such an international dialogue. While we spoke of various issues between Pentecostal and Reformed Christians, apartheid in South Africa, and proselytism and prosperity theology in Brazil, he had a more pressing issue in mind. "There is a problem in Korea that needs to be addressed," he began,

> Many Reformed and Presbyterian pastors in Korea are highly critical of Rev. David Yonggi Cho, Pastor of Yoido Full Gospel Church in Seoul. They maintain that some of Pastor Cho's teachings and practices are syncretistic, and from their perspective, not Christian. They accuse Pastor Cho of shamanistic behaviour,[6] and of bringing Confucian practices such as ancestor worship into the church. They reject his "blessing" theology, and view it as a form of prosperity teaching typically embraced by many Neo-Pentecostal and Independent Charismatic churches.[7]

Shamanism has long played an important role within Korean culture. However, many Koreans have been open to the Christian message, especially when the Gospel is preached accompanied by signs and wonders. Both shamanism and Pentecostalism embrace a cosmology that recognises the reality of a spirit world. This worldview is much closer to that found in Scripture than it is to the desacralised, post-Enlightenment, scientific worldview that provides the dominant frame of reference for secular culture today. Jesus and his disciples (Matt 8:16; 10:1; Luke 10:17–20) embraced such a worldview. The Pentecostal message shares this worldview, filled with spirits or demons, that is similar to the shamanist worldview. To be clear, *shamanism* is not a Christian form of spirituality,[8] although some of the experiences and manifestations found among

---

[6] A Shaman is one who, through trance or another altered state of consciousness, claims to have contact with the spirit world. Shamans claim to be able to bring about healing as well as various forms of divination through shamanistic actions.

[7] Daniel J. Adams, "Reflections on an Indigenous Movement: The Yoido Full Gospel Church," *The Japan Christian Quarterly* 57:1 (Winter 1991), 36–45; Mark R. Mullins, "The Empire Strikes Back: Korean Pentecostal Mission to Japan," in Karla Poewe, ed., *Charismatic Christianity as a Global Culture* (Columbia, SC: University of South Carolina Press, 1994), 91–94; Chung Chai-Sik, *Korea: The Encounter between the Gospel and Neo-Confucian Culture* (Gospel and Cultures Pamphlet 16; Geneva, Switzerland: WCC Publications, 1997).

[8] Boo-Woong Yoo, "Pentecostalism in Korea," in Jan A. B. Jongeneel, ed., *Pentecost, Mission, and Ecumenism: Essays on Intercultural Theology: Festschrift in Honour of*

280   *The Holy Spirit, Spirituality and Leadership*

shamans may appear superficially as though they are genuine Charismatic experiences and manifestations given by the Holy Spirit. We can discern the differences by studying Scripture, relying upon the Holy Spirit, and employing the gift of the discerning of spirits (1 Cor 12:10). If Pastor Cho had brought shamanism into Yoido Full Gospel Church, it would be a serious violation of the Gospel. It would need to be condemned.

The second criticism swirling around Pastor Cho's theology was syncretism. *Syncretism* is generally a negative term describing the incorporation of cultural and theological ideas and practices inconsistent with the Gospel, thus changing the nature of its message. The late Professor Walter Hollenweger, a Reformed Church of Switzerland theologian, who had been the pastor of the Swiss Pentecostal Mission in Zürich, Switzerland earlier in his life, but who was always a Pentecostal, posited what he called a "theologically responsible syncretism."[9] I know that many prefer the term *enculturation* when speaking of the interaction between Gospel and culture, but Hollenweger was convinced that even with the change in terminology, for centuries the church had engaged in theologically responsible forms of syncretism, but it had become blind to that reality.

The fact that we have agreed to celebrate the birth of Jesus on 25 December (or with the Orthodox, in early January), for instance, is an example of a theologically responsible syncretism based upon choices early Christian leaders made to celebrate the birth of Jesus around the time of secular winter festivals. By appropriating that date, early Christians *placed* the Gospel message of *the incarnation* of Jesus Christ *at the centre* of their otherwise pagan cultural festivals, and many non-Christians were able to transition easily from their non-Christian past into a Christian future.

Each time we bring the Gospel into a new culture, we must find ways to communicate the message effectively, in order to make it intelligible to that new community and culture. The act intended to make the Gospel intelligible is enculturation. Because various Korean Presbyterian denominations believed that Pastor Cho and Yoido Full Gospel Church were engaged in a theologically *irresponsible* form of syncretism, thereby compromising the Gospel, they distanced themselves from Pastor Cho and Yoido Full Gospel Church, and criticised Cho publicly.[10]

Among the accusations against Pastor Cho regarding syncretism was that he taught ancestor worship. Praying to, appeasing, and worshipping ancestral spirits are common activities within Confucian-dominated Korean culture. What Pastor Cho taught was not the worship or adoration of ancestral spirits, but the veneration of ancestors. There is a significant difference between *adoration* and *veneration*. The third report of the International Roman Catholic–Pentecostal Dialogue made clear that adoration is an act of worship reserved to God alone!

Professor Walter J. Hollenweger (Frankfurt am Main, Germany: Peter Lang, 1992), 172.

[9] Walter J. Hollenweger, *Pentecostalism: Origins and Developments Worldwide* (Peabody, MA: Hendrickson Publishers, 1997), 132–41.

[10] Sheryl Wudunn, "A Surging, Prayerful Force," *New York Times* (25 May 1995), A:3.

Yoido Full Gospel Church and Ecumenism

Veneration involves honouring or paying respect toward someone, in this case, an ancestor.[11] It is fully consistent with the commandment to honour father and mother (Exod 20:12; Deut 5:16), and it is a commandment that, when obeyed, brings the blessing of long life. *It is not* the *worship* of an ancestor.

Pastor Cho believed that he could preach the Gospel within a shamanistic context, moving people from the negative activity of *ancestral worship*, to the positive action of *venerating* or *honouring* their ancestors. His message was fully consistent with the Gospel preached in the power of the Holy Spirit, with Jesus Christ at its centre. Dr. Opočenský and I believed that Pastor Cho's intentions were misunderstood. We hoped that dialogue might help resolve this situation. With this challenge in mind, I quickly agreed to work with him.

The openness of most Korean Christians to deeper experiences of the Holy Spirit begins with their commitment to the Word of God. It is one reason that so many Koreans rise early in the morning for personal prayer, engage in daily prayer services, designate specific places as "Prayer Mountains," spend time praying overnight on Fridays, hold frequent seasonal revivals, and engage in healing ministries. Whether one stands within the Reformed tradition, as may be found within the many Presbyterian denominations in Korea, or one is a member of a Pentecostal congregation, the Word of God and the Holy Spirit always go together.[12]

Establishing the Process

With the encouragement of the WARC Executive Committee, on 8–9 July 1995, Dr. Opočenský and I put together an exploratory meeting at the Assemblies of God College in Mattersey, England. This meeting concluded that there was ample merit to encourage moving ahead with a formal dialogue. Hosted by the Waldensian Church, the first meeting of the dialogue took place in Torre Pellice,

---

[11] "Perspectives on *Koinonia*: The Report from the Third Quinquennium of the Dialogue between the Pontifical Council for Promoting Christian Unity of the Roman Catholic Church and Some Classical Pentecostal Churches and Leaders," 1985–1989, §100. Use of the title "Reverend" in addressing ministers of the Gospel is a form of veneration. The document is available online:
http://www.christianunity.va/content/unitacristiani/en/dialoghi/sezione-occidentale/pentecostali/dialogo/documenti-di-dialogo/testo-in-inglese1.html [Accessed 5 August 2024].

[12] This is affirmed in "Word and Spirit, Church and World: The Final Report of the International Dialogue between Representatives of the World Alliance of Reformed Churches And Some Classical Pentecostal Churches and Leaders 1996–2000," *Pneuma: The Journal of the Society for Pentecostal Studies* 23:1 (Spring 2001), 9–43; *Asian Journal of Pentecostal Studies* 2 (1999), 105–51, and as "Word and Spirit, Church and World: Final Report of the International Pentecostal-Reformed Dialogue," *Reformed World* 50:3 (September 2000), 128–56. This report is also available online at:
http://ecumenism.net/archive/docu/2000_pent_warc_word_spirit_church_world.pdf [Accessed 5 August 2024].

282   *The Holy Spirit, Spirituality and Leadership*

Italy, on 15–21 May 1996, on the topic, "Spirituality and the Challenges of Today." Two months later, the Assemblies of God of Korea joined the National Council of Churches in Korea (NCCK).[13]

Hosted by the Church of God in Christ in Chicago, Illinois, on 11–15 May 1997, the dialogue addressed "The Role and Place of the Holy Spirit in the Church." In Kappel am Albis, Switzerland, on 14–19 May 1998, hosted by the Reformed Church of Switzerland, the dialogue discussed, "The Holy Spirit and Mission in Eschatological Perspective." Because Reformed–Pentecostal relations in Korea continued to be deeply strained, Milan and I decided that it was time for us to meet in Korea. I asked Dr. Wonsuk Ma, a member of the Pentecostal team, to contact Dr. Younghoon Lee, president of the International Theological Institute (ITI) operated by Yoido Full Gospel Church, to see whether Yoido Full Gospel Church would consider hosting the Dialogue.

I had met Younghoon Lee when he was a graduate student at Temple University, where he wrote a fine history of Pentecostalism in Korea.[14] Since I was the co-chair of the Joint Consultative Group, a dialogue between Pentecostals and representatives from member churches of the World Council of Churches (WCC), I had invited him to be one of the Pentecostal participants, and he had readily agreed. After consulting with Pastor Cho, Pastor Cho agreed that the ITI would host the WARC–Pentecostal Dialogue on behalf of Yoido Full Gospel Church, and on 14–20 May 1999, that meeting took place in Seoul.

Because of concerns expressed by many Reformed pastors, the director of the ITI asked us to open up the Dialogue. The steering committee took the unprecedented action of inviting local Pentecostal and Presbyterian leaders and theologians to observe its discussions.[15] The topic in Seoul was "The Holy Spirit, Charisma, and the Kingdom of God." The first five-year round of the Dialogue concluded on 20–24 May 2000, when its participants, hosted by the Presbyterian Church of Brazil, met in São Paulo, Brazil and completed their report.[16]

---

[13] https://n.news.naver.com/mnews/article/001/0004034041?sid=103 [Accessed 5 August 2024].

[14] Younghoon Lee, *The Holy Spirit Movement in Korea: Its Historical and Theological Development* (Oxford: Regnum Books, 2009), is an edited version of the dissertation.

[15] Most international theological dialogues are closed-door events. This allows participants to work undeterred by external forces. Such dialogues are not always popular with all constituencies. Sometimes the fallout from premature news coverage, especially without understanding the theological positions discussed, or the political ramifications of poor reporting, are not understood. In some cases, they have led to disciplinary actions without adequate understanding or evidence. All participants in these dialogues agree that the information in their "Final Report" is fair to critique, but prior to that time, positions expressed should not be treated as though they are final.

[16] "Word and Spirit, Church and World: The Final Report of the International Dialogue between Representatives of the World Alliance of Reformed Churches and Some Classical Pentecostal Churches and Leaders 1996–2000," in *Pneuma: The Journal of the Society for Pentecostal Studies* 23:1 (Spring 2001), 9–43, the *Asian Journal of Pentecostal Studies* 2:1 (January 1999), 105–151, and in the *Reformed World* 50:3

On 12 May 1999, two days before the WARC–Pentecostal Dialogue met in Seoul, Pastor Cho attended the Executive Committee of the World Assemblies of God Fellowship in Honolulu, Hawaii.[17] There he told the committee of the upcoming dialogue and shared his ecumenical aspirations for the Korean Assemblies of God. The leadership of the General Council of the Assemblies of God in the United States did not receive his enthusiasm as good news. They strongly advised Pastor Cho to leave the NCCK, and not to develop any further ecumenical ties.[18] Recognising the historical and cultural differences that distinguish the South Korean context from those found in the North American context, something his North American counterparts failed to see, Pastor Cho stayed the course.

The WARC–Pentecostal Meeting in Seoul

The meeting in Seoul was privileged to have the general secretary, Dr. Milan Opočenský, and his wife, Dr. Jana Opočenská, join with the Reformed team. Their presence signalled the Dialogue's importance to the WARC. Participants experienced a first-hand opportunity to observe members from both the Reformed and Pentecostal communities in Korea. Chaired by the Reverend Abival Pires da Silveira, pastor of Cathedral Evangélica da São Paulo, Brazil, a Presbyterian congregation and myself, discussion focused especially on the gifts or charisms of the Holy Spirit, but various events that took place alongside the Dialogue during that week added a richness to the entire experience.[19]

Members of both teams participated in morning and evening times of common prayer. Most of them attended at least one early morning prayer meeting at Yoido, though a few also visited Yoido's Prayer Mountain, about an hour's drive

---

(September 2000), 128–56. It was published in Jeffrey Gros FSC, Thomas F. Best, and Lorelei F. Fuchs, SA, eds., *Growth in Agreement III: International Dialogue Texts and Agreed Statements, 1998–2005* (Geneva: WCC Publications, and Grand Rapids, MI: William B. Eerdmans Publishing Company, 2007), 477–97, and in Wolfgang Vondey, ed., *Pentecostalism and Christian Unity: Documents and Critical Assessments* (Eugene, OR: Pickwick Publications, 2010), 199–227. It is also available at: http://ecumenism.net/archive/docu/2000_pent_warc_word_spirit_church_world.pdf [Accessed 5 August 2024].

[17] The Assemblies of God World Missions office verified only the date of this meeting and the presence of Pastor David Yonggi Cho.

[18] I received this information from a person on Pastor Cho's staff, who had spoken with Pastor Cho about the meeting.

[19] In 1999, Yohan Hyun presented "The Holy Spirit, Charism and the Kingdom of God from the Reformed Perspective," while Frank D. Macchia addressed "The Struggle for the Spirit in the Church: The Gifts of the Spirit and the Kingdom of God in Pentecostal Perspective." Subsequent to the 1999 meeting in Seoul, these papers were published as Yohan Hyun and Frank Macchia, *Spirit's Gifts – God's Reign* (Theology & Worship Occasional Paper No. 11; Louisville, KY: Presbyterian Church [U.S.A.], Office of Theology and Worship, 1999).

north of the city. Delegates also visited other local congregations, both Pentecostal and Presbyterian. Pastor Cho invited me to preach at Yoido Full Gospel Church on Sunday 16 May 1999. I took as my text Ephesians 4:1–6, in which the Apostle urges the churches in Ephesus to "lead a life worthy of your calling," exercising humility, gentleness, patience, and love, in order to "maintain the unity of the Spirit in the bond of peace."

With the press and television cameras present during some discussions, the steering committee agreed to, and encouraged all participants to accept, interviews when asked. That week, several participants spoke with reporters, allowing them to share their hopes for the Dialogue and to address *some* of the concerns that were present in the Presbyterian and Pentecostal communities in Seoul. Cameras taped interviews, which played in daily Korean television news reports. Newspapers such as the *Kookmin Ilbo* carried stories every day. The decision to open the Dialogue to public scrutiny was risky; however, these concessions allowed the public to see and hear, more or less in real time, how the Dialogue proceeded. They facilitated conversation not only around the immediate dialogue table, but also in Reformed and Pentecostal churches throughout South Korea as their pastors, theologians, and people engaged in extended conversations with one another.

During that week, participants took part in a "Conference on the Holy Spirit." There, a number of Presbyterian pastors, leaders from the NCCK, and a number of Pentecostal pastors heard an address by Dr. Samhwan Kim on "God, the Trinity, and the Holy Spirit Movement in Pentecostalism." I gave the formal response to that address.

On 8–13 November 2002, the Joint Consultative Group met at the Kwang Lim Seminar House, outside of Seoul. I was invited to preach on Christian unity at the Full Gospel Incheon Church, while the other participants attended Yoido Full Gospel Church. The following day the group participated in a theological symposium held at the Tae Jo Dong Full Gospel Church in Seoul, where Dr. Sam-Hwan Kim, director of the ITI, hosted a conference on "Mission in the Age of Globalization." The president of the NCCK as well as three past presidents of two Korean Assemblies of God denominations were present, and the public was invited to observe Pentecostal and ecumenical theologians discuss mission as well as ecumenism. To be clear, while the Korean Assemblies of God did not host an official meeting of the WCC at that time, it did host the dialogue in which representatives from WCC member churches and Pentecostals freely shared their ecumenical experiences and concerns. That week, Rev. Sungkyu Choi was elected president of the NCCK. A month later, on 11 December 2002, Choi, the pastor of Incheon Full Gospel Church in Incheon, Korea, and a disciple of Pastor Cho, was installed in that office.[20]

Over the next several years, the leadership of Yoido Full Gospel Church, including its senior pastor, David Yonggi Cho, and its executive pastor, Dr. Younghoon Lee, continued to develop closer ties between the Korean Assemblies of God, Yoido Full Gospel Church, and the NCCK. Sadly, it was a difficult period, since scandal racked the NCCK during these years, with charges

---

[20] http://www.kyeongin.com/main/view.php?key=249336 [Accessed 5 August 2024].

Yoido Full Gospel Church and Ecumenism   285

of corruption and heresy dividing its ranks. Still, leaders from Yoido Full Gospel Church and from Incheon Full Gospel Church played important roles within the NCCK during this difficult period. Their exposure to the larger ecumenical world also led them to make other inquiries relative to ecumenism. In 2008, Pastor Cho retired, and the Board of Yoido Full Gospel Church chose Dr. Younghoon Lee to succeed Pastor Cho as the senior pastor of the church.

In August 2009, the WCC produced a three-minute and forty-three-second video titled "Welcome to Korea." Through a series of short clips, it reminded viewers of the violence of the Korean War in the 1950s that left the nation deeply divided and the political struggles for democracy in South Korea during the 1970s, and it offered viewers a glimpse of current activities undertaken by the churches of South Korea. The video demonstrated the seriousness with which Korean churches took their role as they invited the WCC to accept Busan, South Korea, as the host city for its tenth Assembly. At minute 2:14 into the video, Pastor David Yonggi Cho appeared, speaking in Korean, with English subtitles, and for the next thirty seconds, he offered the following comment:

> We hope that the 10th Assembly of the World Council of Churches will take place in Korea. The National Council of Churches in Korea and two of its associate organisations, the Assembly of God in Korea and Yoido Full Gospel Church, are fully committed to cooperation for hosting this upcoming event.[21] It's evident that the ecumenical spirit and solidarity will be firmly established by hosting the 10th Assembly of the World Council of Churches.[22]

This video provided a link between the Korean Assemblies of God, the founding pastor of Yoido Full Gospel Church, David Yonggi Cho, and the Central Committee of the WCC. During its deliberations, the Central Committee meeting held in Geneva, Switzerland, voted to accept the invitation to Busan.

By the time this video was shown, Dr. Younghoon Lee had succeeded Cho as senior pastor at Yoido. Dr. Lee had served in multiple positions for the church, including executive pastor, president of its ITI, and president of Bethesda Christian College (now University), a project of Yoido Full Gospel Church in Anaheim, California. He quickly and successfully moved into the significant role for which it seems he had been destined for many years. In 2009, he became the general superintendent of the Korean Assemblies of God. Because of his position within South Korean ecclesial and ecumenical life, Dr. Lee was invited to serve on the Korean Host Committee for the upcoming 10th Assembly of the WCC. The Rev. Dr. Lee, the Rev. Samhwan Kim, founder and pastor of Myung Sung Presbyterian Church, the largest Presbyterian congregation in Korea, and the

---

[21] A more accurate translation of this is: "The Korean Assemblies of God, a member denomination (of the NCCK), and Yoido Full Gospel Church (a congregation of the KAG) are fully committed to cooperation in hosting this upcoming event."

[22] The World Council of Churches supplied this video to Cecil M. Robeck, Jr., who was present when it was shown. The Central Committee of the World Council of Churches subsequently voted to hold the Assembly in Busan, South Korea, on 30 October–8 November 2013. A copy of the video is available at the Assemblies of God's Flower Pentecostal Heritage Center, 1445 Boonville Ave., Springfield, MO. 65802.

Rev. Jong-wha Park served as co-moderators of the Host Committee. The tenth Assembly took place in Busan, South Korea, from 30 October through 8 November 2013.

With the growing interest expressed in a range of WCC Commissions regarding Pentecostalism, it should come as no surprise to find that Pastor Younghoon Lee and Yoido Full Gospel Church would be featured at a plenary worship service on the evening of 4 November 2013. Across the front of the auditorium, a banner proclaimed it as the "2013 WCC 10th Assembly Evening Prayer Meeting" conducted by the "Assemblies of God of Korea." That evening, the hall was packed with several hundred worshippers. Over one hundred Pentecostal pastors from throughout Korea made the trip to participate in the service. A large youthful worship team accompanied Pastor Lee, including musicians and singers. The crowd was filled with expectancy as the choreographed singers led the congregation in a range of contemporary choruses such as "Days of Elijah," "Majesty," "How Great Thou Art," and "Because He Lives," widely known throughout the Christian world. When Pastor Lee came to the pulpit, he preached from a familiar Pentecostal text, Acts 19:1–7.[23] Following his sermon, Pastor Lee led the congregation in praying aloud for several minutes, many in tongues. Two others followed, offering prayers with specific requests. Following the benediction, there was more festive singing and dancing.

Immediately following this service, Younghoon Lee and Yoido Full Gospel Church hosted a dinner in the Grand Ballroom of the Westin Chosun Busan Hotel. About 250 pastors attended in a celebrative atmosphere, while television cameras recorded the event and reporters conducted interviews. Pastor Lee invited me to join him at the head table, where he explained our long personal relationship and told of our shared ecumenical interests.

Shortly after the Busan Assembly, Pastor Lee was also elected president of the NCCK in 2014, where he served three consecutive terms through to 2016. While he was president, some conservative leaders claimed that Yoido Full Gospel Church had joined the WCC, but that was never the case. On 24 July 2015, the church issued a public statement published in the *Kookmin Ilbo* daily newspaper. It decried those who made such claims and asked them to cease from spreading this rumour. The statement went on to distance Yoido from various ideologies found in *some* WCC member churches; notably, religious pluralism, presumably the idea that other religions might be salvific, syncretism, homosexuality, and, with the threats of China and North Korea, politics that leaned towards communism.[24]

While the Korean Assemblies of God still holds membership in the NCCK, in recent years, they have no longer cooperated on either theological dialogue or social projects. Instead, the Assemblies of God has built stronger relationships with another group, the United Christian Churches of Korea (UCCK). The membership of UCCK now has a larger church membership than the NCCK, and

---

[23] A video of the service may be found at
https://www.youtube.com/watch?v=6dYuU7NiDig [Accessed 5 August 2024].

[24] See the *Kookmin-Ilbo Daily*, 24 July 2015. This public statement was published as an advertisement in the newspaper.

it has been able to attract many more conservative churches to cooperate. On 8 December 2022, the UCCK elected Pastor Younghoon Lee to serve as president of the UCCK.[25]

Pastor Lee's ecumenical leadership at Yoido Full Gospel Church demonstrates that ecumenical dialogue can make a difference when Pentecostals are willing to take their rightful seat at the global table of the church. The fact that Yoido Full Gospel Church and its pastors, David Yonggi Cho and Younghoon Lee, were willing to engage in ecumenical dialogue with the WARC led to several important outcomes. It demonstrated that without losing either its identity or its unique Pentecostal witness, the Korean Assemblies of God could become a valued ecumenical partner within the larger Christian community. The success of the Korean Assemblies of God in engaging the larger church world should also be a witness to the World Assemblies of God Fellowship that ecumenical participation does not require compromise of any sort.

Their testimony sends a message that the General Council of the Assemblies of God in the United States or the division of Assemblies of God World Missions should not try to limit the ecumenical decisions of other general councils around the world. Each general council has a unique history, and they have emerged in contexts that differ, sometimes markedly, from those found in the United States. It is not the case that the American experience, in which the 19th-century Social Gospel, the rise of Fundamentalism, the fights between Liberals and Fundamentalists, and even the establishment of the National Association of Evangelicals, should dominate the hopes and dreams of other general councils with their own histories and contexts. All general councils can learn together how best to move forward with respect and without breaking fellowship. The ecumenical choices of Yoido Full Gospel Church and the Korean Assemblies of God have set a precedent that other Pentecostal churches might follow. To what extent Pastor Younghoon Lee may continue to explore other ecumenical options remains to be seen. Still, Yoido Full Gospel Church and the Korean Assemblies of God is a source of hope for the ecumenical future of all Pentecostals.

---

[25] Ruth Wang, "Lee Younghoon, Senior Pastor of YFGC, Elected as President of the Christian Council of Korea," *China Christian Daily* (22 April 2016).
http://chinachristiandaily.com/news/church_ministry/2016–04–22/lee-young-hoon--senior-pastor-of-yfgc--elected-as-president-of-the-christian-council-of-korea-_1072;
https://www.christiantoday.co.kr/news/244219 [Accessed 5 August 2024].

The "Power Paradox" in Spiritual Leadership

Ivan Satyavrata

Introduction

The explosive growth and impact of the Pentecostal movement over the last century has brought attention to the notion of "power" in the life of the church as never before. This is because the "power" motif is a prominent feature of Pentecostal/Charismatic faith and practice. Hymns such as "There is Power in the Blood of the Lamb" and "O Lord Send the Power Just Now" were well-loved favourites of the earlier generation of Pentecostals, replaced in later years by choruses like, "For I'm building a people of power and I'm building a people of praise" and "There is power in the name of Jesus to break every chain," and the list could go on.

Pentecostals are irresistibly drawn to the book of Acts, especially Jesus' promise of the coming of the Holy Spirit in power (Acts 1:8), the spectacular manifestations when the Spirit was poured out on the day of Pentecost (Acts 2:1–4), the accounts of healing, deliverance from demon possession, angelic visitations, and other miraculous interventions in response to prayer. They love to talk about power, are moved by "powerful" preaching, believe that services and prayer meetings must be "powerful" (sometimes measured by the volume of the preacher or pray-er), and get excited at the prospect of "power" encounters.

The explosive growth of the Pentecostal movement and its contribution to the global advance of the Jesus movement is now widely known and chronicled, and the point of its massive impact must hardly be belaboured. But while the phenomenal growth of the Pentecostal movement has done much to revive the church, helped stem the rising tide of liberalism, and restore biblical fidelity in many areas, it has brought with it several aberrations, both by way of doctrinal deviation as well as unhealthy excesses in practice. One of the most widely observed among these is how Pentecostal and Charismatic leaders have gained notoriety for the misuse of power in leadership.

It is neither the author's intent nor essential to this article's aim to cite specific instances of such power abuse. It might suffice to share the summary observation of Pentecostal mission scholar Wonsuk Ma, who writes from his widespread acquaintance with and experience within Pentecostal circles: "Among many positive contributions of the Pentecostal-charismatic movements today, however, bright charismatic 'stars' have fallen on moral grounds … this grave failure is not limited to the 'stars' such as megachurch pastors and televangelists: a lax attitude is also observed among less-than-starry leaders in the Pentecostal-charismatic world."[1]

---

[1] "Tragedy of Spirit-Empowered Heroes: A Close Look at Samson and Saul," in *Spiritus* 2.1–2 (2017), 23–38, accessed 10 July 2023,
https://digitalshowcase.oru.edu/cgi/viewcontent.cgi?article=1009&context=spiritus; for

The mention of "power" generally produces mixed reactions. Some associate power with success and actively pursue it, whether in terms of wealth, position, information, social influence, or spiritual power. Others, however, are cynical about power and view it as self-serving, manipulative, and even inherently corrupt, based on Lord Acton's oft-quoted words: "Power tends to corrupt, and absolute power corrupts absolutely."[2] Power is, however, neutral in and of itself, neither good nor bad. Power is an integral aspect of all types of leadership because it is simply the potential or ability to make things happen, and power is how leaders make things happen. Sometimes, they may mismanage and abuse power, but there's no such thing as leadership without power. Indeed, it is impossible for a leader to accomplish anything if she cannot exercise power. But if properly applied, power can be a positive force for good.

The focus of this article is to explore this built-in tension in the exercise of power by leaders, especially as it applies to Christian leaders who seek to pattern their leadership style after that of Jesus who: "... did not come to be served, but to serve, and to give his life as a ransom for many" (Matt 20:28; Mark 10:45). This tension is perhaps best described in terms of a "power paradox," a term which has come into use both in secular as well as Christian leadership discourse.[3] There is, however, a distinctive connotation to the "power paradox" in leadership when viewed from the perspective of the New Testament. This article suggests that an in-depth grasp of this dimension could correct common misconceptions and perhaps even radically transform how church leaders, in general, and Pentecostal leaders, in particular, view power in leadership. The key guiding question of this inquiry is: how can a biblical understanding of the "power paradox" in leadership help leaders steward responsibly the privilege and burden of power that comes with position, role, charisma, or influence?

An Anatomy of Power

The concept of power is extremely hard to define, as seen from the wide variation in approaches to its definition. Perhaps the most widely known due to its vintage is that of sociologist Max Weber, who defined power as "the probability that one actor within a social relationship will be in a position to carry out his own will despite resistance, regardless of the basis on which this probability rests."[4] French philosopher Michel Foucault sees power as producing reality and a

---

a more strident critique, see Steven Lambert, *Charismatic Captivation: Authoritarian Abuse & Psychological Enslavement In Neo-Pentecostal Churches* (SLM Publications, 2003).

[2] "Letter to Bishop Mandell Creighton, April 5, 1887 Transcript of," published in J. N. Figgis and R. V. Laurence, eds., *Historical Essays and Studies* (London: Macmillan, 1907).

[3] A "paradox" is a concept or reality that combines contradictory features or qualities.

[4] *Economy and Society: An Outline of Interpretive Sociology* (Berkeley: University of California Press, 1978 [1922]), 53.

The "Power Paradox" in Spiritual Leadership   291

ubiquitous means of social control: "Power is everywhere; not because it embraces everything, but because it comes from everywhere."[5]

We have cited Weber and Foucault because of their enormous impact on modern thought. Still, perhaps more germane to our purpose in this article is Jeffrey Pfeffer's definition of power as: "the potential ability to influence behavior, to change the course of events, to overcome resistance, and to get people to do things that they would not otherwise do."[6] John Maxwell sees true leadership power as being exercised through influence: "The true measure of leadership is influence – nothing more, nothing less. If you do not have influence, you will never be able to lead others."[7]

In his study of the power dynamics that regulate the behaviour of religious leaders, Khalid Ehsan differentiates between two distinct but interrelated types of power: *individual charismatic power* – "the capability of an actor to achieve his or her will, even at the expense of others," and *collective structural power* – "a property of the collectivity." He goes on to point out that, while the ongoing tension between these two dimensions of social power is a subject of social science debate, they are not mutually exclusive, and most actions in society are based on a blend of these strategies.

Our focus in this article is on the individual charismatic aspect of power, and a helpful starting point in examining this concept is the widely influential typology of sources of power in leadership developed by social psychologists French and Raven.[8] The six forms of "social power" they identify are summarised below:

1. Coercive power: the use of fear of punishment or threat to force someone to comply against their will, such as loss of employment or reduced wages, excommunication, psychological abuse, and fear of cultic power.
2. Reward power: the use of incentives to induce compliance, such as salaries, bonuses, allocation of resources, access to the leader, public recognition/affirmation for good performance, and expectation of divine blessing/favour.

---

[5] Michel Foucault, *The History of Sexuality*, trans. Robert Hurley (New York: Pantheon Books, 1978), 93; cf. *Discipline and Punish: The Birth of Prison*, trans. Alan Sheridan (New York: Vintage Books, 1979), 194.

[6] *Managing with Power: Politics and Influence in Organizations* (Boston: Harvard Business School Press, 1992), 30.

[7] *The 21 Irrefutable Laws of Leadership* (Nashville: Thomas Nelson, 1998), 11, 20.

[8] Mintzberg calls the French and Raven model "the most widely used categorization of power," and it remains a paradigm that remains largely undisputed in studies of social power: Henry Mintzberg, *Power In and Around Organizations* (Englewood Cliffs, NJ: Prentice-Hall, 1983), 120; cf. Steven R Walikonis, "The Phenomenon of Power in the Church: An Investigation and Analysis of the Relational Dynamics Experienced in the Context of the Assertion of Authority" (D.Min. professional project, Andrews University, 2004), 18.

3. Legitimate power: based on the formal authority derived from a leader's position or role, followers are expected to comply with the leader's will and expectations.
4. Expert power is based on confidence in the leader's specialised knowledge, skills, and abilities.
5. Referent power: based on the personal qualities of a leader that attract their trust, commitment, and respect.
6. Informational power: based on a leader's control over the sources and dissemination of information or powers of persuasion.

Commenting on French and Raven's classification, Ehsan makes the pertinent observation that the controlling factor in all the sources of power is not so much the actual power that leaders possess as the followers' beliefs about them. The leader's power depends to a great extent on the perceptions that followers have of the leader and the relationship between them. But before we go any further, we need to pause and do a "deep dive" into the notion of power itself. For our purpose, it is essential that we delineate an explicitly Christian understanding of power.

In his in-depth treatment of the power motif, Andy Crouch sees power as "a fundamental feature of life" and makes a compelling case for us to view power as a *gift*, rooted in creation and intimately tied to the role human beings play as image bearers.[9] Flawed though it is as a result of the Fall, this gift of power can be redeemed and restored to serve our Creator's original intent as an empowering and flourishing instrument in our world. Human beings are thus "agents of creativity in a universe designed to create more and more power ... image bearers [who] do not exist for their own flourishing alone, but to bring the whole creation to its fulfilment."[10]

Crouch's conception of power is not, however, naively optimistic. He concedes the common perception of power as dangerous, even acknowledging that the whole history of power can sometimes be seen as "one long story of perversion and betrayal."[11] However, he effectively counters the Nietzschean cynical claim that power is simply an instrument of manipulation in the universal and perpetual struggle for dominance between human beings. For him, the deepest truth about the world is that "Love transfigures power. Absolute love transfigures absolute power ... The power to love, and in loving, to create together, is the true power that hums at the heart of the world."[12]

It is difficult to capture Crouch's thought without using his own vividly descriptive prose, but although his argument is not explicitly framed along the lines of a biblical exposition, his description is deeply rooted in and infused with biblical content. We will explore another source of biblical corroboration for this notion of power subsequently, but at this stage in applying this understanding to *individual charismatic* leadership, we view it through this essentially positive

---

[9] *Playing God: Redeeming the Gift of Power* (Downers Grove, IL: IVP, 2013), 12.

[10] Crouch, *Playing God*, 34–35.

[11] Crouch, *Playing God*, 37.

[12] Crouch, *Playing God*, 45, 52.

lens. Power is a gift bestowed by God on human beings, his image bearers, for the purpose of flourishing – an instrument for creating, empowering, adding value and meaning to all of life.[13]

By this definition every human being has access to some measure of power at some level, within the family, place of occupation, or within society. Leaders, however, are privileged with more power than the average person – legitimate, expert or referent power – or by virtue of wealth, caste, or social status which enables them to exert reward/coercive power. The greater "burden" of power leaders carry thus places on them greater responsibility for proper stewardship of their power.

The Misuse and Abuse of Power

The common cynicism regarding power and leadership is well-founded. Power in the wrong hands can be extremely dangerous and its dark side is highlighted in a famous quote sometimes ascribed to Abraham Lincoln: "Nearly all men can stand adversity, but if you want to test a man's character, give him power."[14] The misuse or abuse of power occurs when power is applied inappropriately by corrupt means or for unethical purposes. The misuse and abuse of power by those in some form of leadership is sadly common; we live with it every day and are either the victims or perpetrators.

A leader's over-estimation of his own value, along with the misconception that he is the rightful owner of power, is what usually leads to the abuse of power. All leaders, at any level, are susceptible to various forms of power abuse, from enjoyment of unfair benefits of the privileges that come with power to coercive force, sexual harassment, psychological manipulation, and even violence. University of California psychologist Dacher Keltner cites studies that show that those possessing the power of wealth, education, or corporate position are more likely to engage in unethical behaviour, such as taking bribes or cheating on taxes, and self-serving behaviour that increases their personal compensation at the expense of company profit and reputation.[15]

Charismatic leaders tend to be more susceptible to power abuse due to their extraordinary appeal. Followers are drawn to the leader's personal qualities and swayed by their exceptional abilities, achievements, giftings, teaching, or powers of persuasion. They are consequently able to inspire followers to make unusual sacrifices and to persevere in the face of great hardship or opposition.

---

[13] "Remove power and you cut off life, the possibility of creating something new and better in this life and recalcitrant world … Power is for flourishing – teeming, fruitful, multiplying abundance." Crouch, *Playing God*, 25, 35.

[14] More likely the words of the nineteenth-century American politician Robert G. Ingersoll, *Reuters Fact Check*, accessed 20 July 2023, https://www.reuters.com/article/factcheck-abrahamlincoln-power-idUSL1N2PA1V7.

[15] Dacher Keltner, "Don't Let Power Corrupt You," *Harvard Business Review* 94 (October 2016), accessed 10 July 2023, https://hbr.org/2016/10/dont-let-power-corrupt-you.

Charismatic leaders raise people's aspirations for a better future but are just as likely to be tyrannical as they are heroic.

Power is seductive. As leaders get bigger titles, offices, and financial and other benefits, it's easy for egos to become inflated and for hubris to set in. They have a strong need to be in control of people, to win every argument, and have the last word in every situation. Before long they become overly preoccupied with the privileges that come with the power of leadership, and protecting that power soon becomes an obsession. They become jealous and insecure when others get recognition for their success or achievements. This is when they begin to surround themselves with sycophants who keep stroking their egos and who in turn receive special treatment as reward for their "loyalty." But this is a shallow loyalty, a form of manipulation in the "power games" that people play to ensure their survival, greater privilege, or promotion.[16]

Ideally, every pastor, priest, elder, deacon, teacher, or any other person in a position of influence in the church should exercise power in ways consistent with the teachings of Jesus. The painful reality, as any honest churchman would admit, is that the abuse of power regrettably can be observed within the church as well. We all have witnessed, to some extent, the inappropriate use of power in church leaders, perhaps even on occasion within ourselves.

Certain abuses in Christian leadership are unique to spiritual leadership. These have sometimes been characterised as "spiritual" abuses in which a person in need of help, support, or spiritual empowerment is mistreated with the opposite effect of weakening, undermining, or decreasing her spiritual empowerment. In his analysis of power abuse in the local church, Beasley-Murray observes: "It is about relating in ways which in some way diminishes the other, rendering them to some degree impotent and powerless. It is about manipulation and control."[17]

Abuses within the church and Christian organisations take various forms, many of which overlap with those which occur in the secular world and include: authoritarianism, intimidation and mistreatment of subordinates, use of power for personal benefit, self-preservation, various forms of misconduct and corrupted character traits inconsistent with Christian principles. While some forms of power misuse such as financial misappropriation or sexual abuse may be easily identified, the substitution of one's opinion with God's will is an abuse that is difficult to detect. The misuse of "God's will," placing submission to pastors or church leaders on the same level as submission to God or implying the

---

[16] Bill Treasurer, "When Leadership Turns Dangerous," *Forbes* (12 December 2018), accessed 12 July 2023,
https://www.forbes.com/sites/forbescoachescouncil/2018/12/12/when-leadership-turns-dangerous/?sh=67209aaa55f3.

[17] Paul Beasley-Murray, *Power for God's Sake: Power and Abuse in the Local Church* (Carlisle, PA: Paternoster, 1998), 8.

use of God's authority to manipulate an individual, is a common instrument of such "cultic" power abuse by religious leaders.[18]

"Treasure in Jars of Clay": The Leadership "Power Paradox"

In his influential study, *The Power Paradox: How We Gain and Lose Influence*,[19] Dacher Keltner applies the term "power paradox" to capture his radical reframing of the power construct. Keltner is convinced that the common premise that power is essentially corrupt is based on a misunderstanding of the true nature of power. Based on twenty years of research on how power is shaped, he sees it as a positive and socially constructive force, the ability to do good for others, expressed in daily life.

According to Keltner, people usually gain power through traits and actions such as empathy, collaboration, fairness, selflessness, and sharing, that advance the interests and add value to the lives of others. However, when they start to feel powerful or enjoy a position of privilege, those qualities begin to fade. They begin displaying socially harmful behaviours and by losing sight of the very behaviours that helped them to gain power in the first place, allowing corruption and power abuse into their lives. This eventually results in them losing power at work, in family life, or among friends. Keltner terms this phenomenon, "the power paradox." Keltner's book thus deals with how we can obtain and maintain power, avoid its abuse, and learn how to deal with the power paradox.

In *The Leadership Paradox: Becoming Great Through Service*, George Flattery's excellent exposition of the "servant-leadership" theme, based on Matthew 20:20–28, he uses the term "paradox" (more frequently in its adjectival form, "paradoxical") to indicate how the route to leadership begins with servanthood: "Paradoxically, the one who wants to be great must be the servant of all and the one who wants to be first must be the slave. By implication, the paradox of leadership is that leaders become great through service."[20]

I would like to suggest that the application of "paradox" to the biblical ideal of leadership goes deeper to the notion of power at the heart of leadership. This is most clearly expressed in one of the Apostle Paul's "hardship catalogues"[21] found in 2 Corinthians 4:7–12:

---

[18] Zorislav Plantak, "Ethical Analysis Of Abuses Of Power In Christian Leadership – A Case Study Of 'Kingly Power' in The Seventh-day Adventist Church" (Dissertations, Andrews University, 2017), 11–15.

[19] Penguin Books, 2017.

[20] Springfield, MO: Network211, 2016, vii.

[21] In Hellenistic philosophical literature, a hardship catalogue emphasises how the sage was self-sufficient in spite of the outside afflictions that he or she had to endure, while Paul stresses his dependency on God and his conformity to the image of Christ; some scholars see Paul as making use of this genre in this context in several places in his Corinthian correspondence, where he lists the hardships he underwent in the service of the Gospel. John T. Fitzgerald, *Cracks in an Earthen Vessel: An Examination of*

But we have this treasure in jars of clay to show that this all-surpassing power is from God and not from us. We are hard pressed on every side, but not crushed; perplexed, but not in despair; persecuted, but not abandoned; struck down, but not destroyed. We always carry around in our body the death of Jesus, so that the life of Jesus may also be revealed in our body. For we who are alive are always being given over to death for Jesus' sake, so that his life may also be revealed in our mortal body. So then, death is at work in us, but life is at work in you (2 Cor 4:7–12).

In his commentary on this passage, Murray Harris observes: "No person was more aware of the paradoxical nature of Christianity than Paul. And perhaps none of his epistles contains more paradoxes than 2 Corinthians."[22] Paul's description here may appropriately be regarded as paradigmatic, reflective of a feature that is consistent with a pattern that runs all through the New Testament: the power paradox in leadership. Fee observes that while this passage is commonly seen as an account of Paul's suffering and hardship for the sake of the Gospel, this must be understood rather as illustrating his experience of "empowering in the midst of weakness."[23] In contrast to his detractors who base their self-commendations on the pride of their "powerful" visions, revelations, and accomplishments, Paul rests his claim to apostleship on "God's power" working through his weakness. Fee thus asserts that "Weakness/hardship and Spirit-empowering go together in Paul's thinking."[24]

The first paradox, "treasure in jars of clay," is foundational to the others that follow: the relative ordinariness of the receptacle is contrasted with the inestimable value of what it carries within, to emphasise that the "all-surpassing power" is only and all God's. The four vivid antitheses that follow illustrate both the weakness of Paul and God's preserving power: "hard pressed ... but not crushed; perplexed, but not in despair; persecuted, but not abandoned; struck down, but not destroyed" (2 Cor 4:8–9). The next two verses highlight the inherent paradox in how both the death and resurrection-life of Jesus were simultaneously evident in Paul's experience (4:10–11). But then in the following verse Paul makes the climactic assertion which takes us to the heart of the meaning of the "power paradox" in Christian leadership: "So then, death is at work in us, but life is at work in you" (4:12). This is where any notion of Christian leadership finds both its starting point and ultimate destination – *the cross!*

Paul summarises this truth more succinctly in the account of his struggle with his "thorn in the flesh" in which Christ's answer to Paul's pleas for deliverance was simply: "My grace is sufficient for you, for my power is made perfect in weakness" (2 Cor 12:9). Paul's response then expresses his own realisation of

---

Catalogues of Hardships in the Corinthian Correspondence, SBL Dissertation Series 99 (Atlanta: Scholars Press, 1988).

[22] Frank E. Gaebelein, ed., *The Expositor's Bible Commentary*, vol. 10 (Grand Rapids, MI: Zondervan, 1976), 342.

[23] Gordon Fee, *God's Empowering Presence: The Holy Spirit in the Letters of Paul* (Peabody, MA: Hendrickson, 1994), 333.

[24] Fee, *God's Empowering Presence*, 333.

The *"Power Paradox" in Spiritual Leadership*   297

this "power paradox": "That is why, for Christ's sake, I delight in weaknesses, in insults, in hardships, in persecutions, in difficulties. For when I am weak, then I am strong" (2 Cor 12:10). What does this "power-in-weakness" notion mean for our approach to leadership power in the church? In concluding his discussion on 2 Cor 4:7–12, Fee observes:

> What is striking in all this is the inclusion of the powerful working of the Holy Spirit in the midst of a list that fully affirms weakness ... the Spirit in Paul leads not to triumphalism, but to triumph in Christ ... even in the midst of those things that others reject or avoid as signs of weakness and powerlessness. For Paul the power lies ... not in deliverance from hardships, but in the powerful working of the Spirit that enables and empowers him for ministry even in the midst of such adversity.[25]

Sadly, most contemporary models of church leadership seem to have failed to grasp this "paradox" at the heart of the New Testament notion of power in leadership. Instead, the power of the Holy Spirit and the delegated authority which church leaders exercise over the flock is often confused with the hubris that accompanies a leader's increase in power due to a rise in position, growth of the church, or exceptional spiritual giftedness. A notable case in point which has been carefully analysed is the Seventh Day Adventists' "kingly power" controversy.[26]

Pentecostals and Charismatics, however, are especially susceptible to this danger, as evangelists, prophets, and pastors whom God uses in healing, exorcism, prophecy, and other supernatural gifts tend to develop an aura around them as people in turn place them on a pedestal. They eventually acquire demi-god or guru-like status and a heady cocktail of giftedness, success, growing access to wealth, and social recognition makes them intoxicated with power. The resultant sense of infallibility, invincibility, and lack of accountability is a slippery slide on which many leaders go down into power abuse and spiritual shipwreck.

But there is a liberating burst of freedom that comes from embracing the "power paradox" – the joyful discovery that the true secret of any great leader's power is that when you feel the weakest, that's when you really are the strongest ... for his strength is made perfect in your weakness! That is the ultimate bedrock of the "power paradox" in leadership – a reminder that the power we possess as leaders is really "treasure in jars of clay ... this all-surpassing power is from God and not from us" (2 Cor 4:7).

Where the "Power Paradox" Meets "Basin and Towel" Leadership

We must now return to the guiding question of this inquiry: how can a biblical understanding of the "power paradox" in leadership help leaders steward responsibly the privilege and burden of power that comes with position, role, charisma, or influence? As we have seen, a leader's power lies in her ability to

---

[25] Fee, *God's Empowering Presence*, 335.

[26] Plantak, *Ethical Analysis*, 30–33.

influence the actions and opinions of people – to get people to follow! Leadership is power, and power is what leaders use to fulfil their responsibilities towards people and organisations. Powerful leaders get followers to vote them into power, empty their bank accounts for a cause, become volunteer slaves, even lay down their lives for them. Tragically, sometimes church leaders want to look like leaders in the world, like corporate CEOs, powerful politicians, or a special class with "guru-like" status. Sometimes people follow us, of course, but for the same reasons that they follow politicians, corporate heads, and gurus: because they see us wielding power – the power of money, position, or spiritual magic.

In contrast, let us see what Jesus' power consciousness led him to do: "Jesus knew that the Father had put all things under his power, and that he had come from God and was returning to God; so he got up from the meal, took off his outer clothing, and wrapped a towel around his waist" (John 13:3–4). Jesus' act of foot-washing occurs as a prelude to what is commonly referred to as Jesus' Farewell Discourses (John 13–16), representing Jesus' parting words to his disciples before he begins his journey to the cross. This was not just a symbolic gesture of humility; this was the means he chose to use to engrave the heart of his message on the hearts and minds of his disciples, a vivid and powerful lesson for every leader in any sphere of life. Three key features of Jesus' power consciousness in this passage take us to the heart of Jesus' ideal of leadership, which leaders who want to follow Jesus' servant-leadership model should seek to emulate.

Self-Awareness

"Jesus knew that the Father had put all things under his power, and that he had come from God and was returning to God" (John 13:3). Jesus knew who he was, where he had come from, why he was here, and where he was going. Sadly, most leaders have never seriously faced the question: *who am I?* It is not about what title, degrees, position I hold; not what family, club, or social group I belong to; not how much wealth or property I own, or what car I drive. It is not even about how many people follow me on Facebook, Twitter (now X), or Instagram. My true identity as a Christ-follower can and must be defined by one thing alone: *who I am in God's eyes when everything else is stripped away from me?*

Every individual's true value is rooted in the fact he/she is the crown of creation, made in the image of God. The cross further deepens my sense of worth and identity when I realise that God values me enough to die for me, that my adoption into God's family has been paid for with the precious blood of Christ, that I am now a child of God and my Father is the Ruler of the universe. Furthermore, he has endowed me with his blessed Holy Spirit, bestowed me with gifts, and has a plan and purpose for my life. Beyond all that, he loves me as I am, accepts me as his child just as I am, and has bound me to himself in an unconditional, indissoluble, eternal covenant relationship. A critical safety net to self-awareness is the discipline of genuine accountability, grounded in the biblical principle of mutual submission (Eph 5:21). Leaders who lack adequate self-awareness, as well as meaningful accountability, set themselves up for inevitable failure regardless of how successful they appear to be from the outside.

Security

Lack of self-awareness leads to one of the worst diseases from which any leader can suffer: *insecurity*. There are a wide range of symptoms to this disease, such as when you see people around you as a threat if they happen to be good or even better than you at something, when you cannot bear even the slightest criticism, when you find it hard to celebrate another person's success while you struggle to make it. Jesus' supreme act of servanthood flowed out of his strength and security grounded in his *identity* as God's Son sent on a *mission*, for which "the Father had put all things under his power"; he had come to this world with a clear *purpose*, and his *destiny* was sure, "he had come from God and was returning to God" (John 13:3).

Your security is based not on your wealth, education, title, or position, but on your essential identity as a child of God. A secure leader has nothing to prove because his identity and purpose are centred on God. A secure leader is big enough to acknowledge his weaknesses, smart enough to correct them, and strong enough to embrace them. At the end of the day, he feels no pressure to impress or please anyone but God. That makes her free to love and serve people and focus on fulfilling God's purpose for her life.

Selflessness

Jesus' self-awareness and security in God freed him to pick up the towel and basin and perform the most menial of slave duties. Most New Testament scholars view Jesus' act in John 13 as pointing towards his cleansing sacrifice on the cross, capturing the very heart of his message and ministry, which is all about *selfless, loving service*. The foundational event of our faith rehearsed in the great Christological hymn in Philippians reminds us that the incarnation was the supreme self-giving act (Phil 2:3, 5–8). That is why Jesus issues this stern warning to his disciples: "You know that the rulers of the Gentiles lord it over them, and their high officials exercise authority over them. Not so with you. Instead, whoever wants to become great among you must be your servant" (Matt 20:25–26).

Self-preservation – the need to take care of myself, my well-being, and my interests – is the greatest hindrance to effective leadership. Jesus' act of foot-washing pointed forward to the cross, by which Jesus invites his followers to set aside the instinct for self-preservation just as he did and to lay our lives down for one another. By his death on the cross, Jesus showed us what true love is: pouring out your life in sincere, costly service to the other (1 John 3:16).

How should leaders use their power over people responsibly? A self-aware, secure, and selfless person will be an effective leader because he/she will have the right disposition towards the power that every leader wields in some measure. The absolute standard here is Jesus. Jesus was driven by his pure and deep love for his followers in his exercise of power over people (John 13:1). Jesus' love for people did not allow him to force or manipulate them into doing what he wanted them to do. Leaders who follow Jesus are "basin and towel" leaders who reflect the central truth of the Gospel, *the cross*. The real power of every leader who follows Jesus is the power of *the cross*, one person giving his life to another.

Conclusion

Being in a position of power gives a church leader a tremendous opportunity to make a difference in the lives of others. How do you want to use your power as a leader? You can use it to exploit people, lord it over them, get them to serve you, to further your own interests, and to promote yourself; or, you can use it to serve and empower others, to see others grow, to invest in and build others, and seek to better their lives. Is the world becoming a better place because of your power? Are you using your power to fight injustice, serve the poor, spread the good news, and dispense goodness in an evil world?

The Lord of the universe holds every person accountable for how we use whatever power we may wield over others at any level of influence in the family, government, church, or corporate world. God gives leaders the power to enable us to build the lives of others, empower the powerless, draw people closer to God's Kingdom, and create a better future for them. But the truly great leaders – leaders who lead well, finish well, and leave a lasting legacy in the service of Christ's Kingdom – are those who know that their power resides in jars of clay, those who see their power as ultimately belonging to and coming from God.

An Emmaus Walk with Ancient Mothers and Fathers: From the Sawdust Trail to the Ecumenical Patriarchate

Harold D. Hunter

Introduction

This study highlights four primary areas of interest in Eastern Orthodoxy: the 2016 Holy and Great Council, primacy, ecumenism, including dialogue with other religions, and care for God's creation. These topics properly align with the address by Ecumenical Patriarch Bartholomew I on the day of his enthronement, which focused on theology and liturgy, Orthodox unity and cooperation, ecumenism, interfaith dialogue, and protection of the environment. Patriarch Bartholomew is counted as the 269th successor to Saint Andrew and has served one of the longest tenures of any ecumenical patriarch.

Among the questions that need attention is that of Christian unity. Although Pentecostals are not in a position to lecture anyone on this issue, what can be said of the Orthodox? The crisis surrounding the autocephalous Orthodox Church of Ukraine is a case in point that exploded when Russia invaded Ukraine in 2022 with the support of the Moscow Patriarchate. The distance between the Ecumenical Patriarch and Moscow Patriarch Kirill on this unprovoked invasion can be measured in light years.

It has often been said that outsiders do not know how to determine a Pentecostal position on given issues. This is understandable if one counts 600–700 million made of groups more diverse than what is often labelled Protestant. However, it must be said that it is terribly unclear to Pentecostals about who speaks for the Orthodox. While the Ecumenical Patriarchate has a place of honour as first among equals, the reality is quite different, as seen in the 2016 "Holy and Great Council" in Crete.

If one were to judge by stereotypes based on headlines and select photos, there is little common ground between Eastern Orthodox and Classical Pentecostals. However, growing academic and ecumenical literature from both traditions suggests this image must change. Essential parts of the Ecumenical Patriarch's mission captured in his enthronement address are treated in a published book review of his biography by John Chryssavgis.[1] For example, Pentecostals can resonate with Chryssavgis's description of the Ecumenical Patriarch's take on ecumenism this way:

---

[1] Harold D. Hunter, "John Chryssavgis, Bartholomew: Apostle and Visionary" *Pneuma Review* (January 2016) at http://pneumareview.com/journey-with-the-orthodox-biography-of-ecumenical-patriarch-bartholomew-reviewed-by-harold-d-hunter [Accessed 5 May 2024].

... he shuts the door to any caricature of Christian unity as sweepingly blending all Christian teachings into one or as superficially rendering everyone uniform. Dialogue and reconciliation do not imply parity among denominations or unity as confessional adjustment. Nor again do they entail acquiescence to doctrinal relativism or resignation to denominational minimalism.[2]

This study will provide some context to the informal talks between the Ecumenical Patriarchate and Classical Pentecostals that ran from 2010 through 2012. The first meeting was hosted by the Ecumenical Patriarchate at the Phanar in Constantinople. Co-chairs for the first round were the late Metropolitan Professor Gennadios of Sassima and Harold D. Hunter. The reimagined talks resumed in 2017, just prior to the annual American Academy of Religion (AAR)/Society for Biblical Literature (SBL) conference hosted by the Holy Cross Orthodox School of Theology. Co-chairs of those talks were Brandon Gallaher and Harold D. Hunter.

My early days as a Pentecostal evangelist in the late 1960s were mostly in modest Western-style church buildings. However, my father's ministry included multiweek-long revivals where some locations used a tent that had sawdust. Illustrative of the surprises is the story of my preaching ministry, which started as a Pentecostal evangelist in an exclusive-body ecclesiology Pentecostal church. The Ecumenical Patriarch made it possible for me to go to Mount Athos, perhaps the only or at least the first Pentecostal to visit this sacred space, where I stayed in more than one monastery. The extraordinary guide was Professor Petros Vasillious. I celebrated Pascha more than once with the Ecumenical Patriarch at St. George, witnessed the "Service of the Holy Light," better known as the "Miracle of the Holy Fire," at the Church of the Holy Sepulchre in Jerusalem after meeting with Patriarch Theophilus. I also twice celebrated Christmas with Patriarch Krill at the magnificent Cathedral of Christ the Saviour Cathedral in Moscow.

"The Spirit Blows Where It Will" (John 3:8): A Historical Overview

In response to the remarkable presence of Pentecostals at the 2022 General Assembly of the World Council of Churches (WCC), I opened a blog for its website by saying:

As a Pentecostal, I have "dreamed dreams" and had visions aplenty, but often it has been the WCC that brought those dreams and visions to life. Karlsruhe '22 fulfills a vision that I took with me to Geneva in 1989 in a meeting with then-general secretary Emilio Castro. During that visit, I called on the WCC to bring together 120 Pentecostal scholars from around the world to the WCC 7th Assembly, known as Canberra '91. Before the WCC 11th Assembly in Karlsruhe, Germany had come to an end, it was obvious that the Pentecostal presence this time was elevated in more than one way.[3]

---

[2] John Chryssavgis, *Bartholomew: Apostle and Visionary* (Nashville: Thomas Nelson, 2016), 74.

[3] Harold D. Hunter, "Pentecostals at the WCC 11th Assembly in Karlsruhe, Germany 2022," https://www.oikoumene.org/blog/pentecostals-at-the-wcc-11th-assembly-in-

An Emmaus Walk with Ancient Mothers and Fathers

Monsignor Peter Hocken and I put together a Theology Track at "Brighton '91" that featured Professor Jürgen Moltmann. The primary conference sponsor was the International Charismatic Consultation on World Evangelization (ICCOWE), led at that time by Anglican Michael Harper, who would later become an Orthodox priest. Presenters were Roman Catholic, Orthodox, Protestant, and Pentecostal. This invitation-only event was the first global conference for Pentecostal scholars. Money was raised to strike a balance between the Global North and the Global South with not only presenters but those in attendance. Simultaneous translation was provided in four languages.

The book *All Together in One Place*, reprinted in 2019 with a new foreword, explains why no invitation was extended to anti-apartheid Pentecostal pastor Frank Chikane, who went on to become a top leader with Apostolic Faith Mission (South Africa) International and the WCC. Also noted is why no one from Palestine was invited as a speaker. From Brighton '91 onward, with three Orthodox presenters, I have never put together a conference without Orthodox participation, the last being Oxford 2012, which featured the late Metropolitan Professor Kallistos Ware.[4]

There were subsequent conferences of a similar nature sponsored by ICCOWE/International Charismatic Consultation (ICC) in Prague and Malta that included the Metropolitan Kallistos Ware and Metropolitan Hilarion Alfeyev.[5] Relations between Pentecostals and the Orthodox moved forward positively through mutual involvement in the WCC and various national councils of churches. The WCC began consultations with Pentecostals in 1996, which brought Orthodox and Pentecostals to the same table. These consultations evolved into the WCC–Pentecostal Joint Consultative Group. There has also been cross-fertilisation at WCC's General Assemblies, Central Committee meetings, WCC Faith and Order, the National Council of Churches of Christ USA's Faith & Order, Edinburgh 2010 Centennial, and the WCC Conference on World Mission and Evangelism held 8–13 March 2018 in Arusha, Tanzania.

---

karlsruhe-germany-2022 [Accessed 5 May 2024]. When the WCC did not authorise a special Pentecostal event with Canberra '91, I moved the first global conference for Pentecostals and friends to what has been known simply as Brighton '91. An account of my call to ministry that involved an indigenous woman is found in Harold D. Hunter, "Pentecostal Ecumenical Pioneers: Select Case Studies in Leadership," in Elorm Donkor and Clifton Clarke, eds., *African Pentecostal Missions Maturing: Essays in Honor of Apostle Opoku Onyinah* (Eugene, OR: Wipf & Stock, 2018), 102–20. That study starts with the prophecy over David DuPlessis.

[4] Harold D. Hunter, "Foreword" to the 2018 reprint edition of Peter Hocken and Harold D. Hunter, eds., *All Together in One Place* (Eugene, OR: Wipf & Stock, 2019), 1–9. Papers from Oxford 2012 were published in Neil Ormerod and Harold D. Hunter, eds., *The Many Faces of Global Pentecostalism* (Cleveland, TN: CPT, 2013).

[5] Harold D. Hunter and Cecil M. Robeck, eds., *The Suffering Body: Pentecostal Perspectives on Violence Around the World* (Milton Keynes, UK: Paternoster, 2006), 228.

In recent years, there has been positive movement in the Christian Churches Together in the USA, the Christian Churches Together in England, and the Global Christian Forum. In January 2009, a conference on Receptive Ecumenism in Durham (UK) featured Metropolitan Kallistos Ware and Veli-Matti Kärkkäinen as keynote speakers. It was here that I was able to resume conversations with Metropolitan Kallistos Ware about relations between the Orthodox and Pentecostals.

In June 2009, I was granted a private audience with Ecumenical Patriarch Bartholomew. One immediate result was the launching of informal talks between the Ecumenical Patriarchate and Pentecostals for the next three years. The co-chairs for these talks mentioned in the biography of the Ecumenical Patriarch were the late Metropolitan Gennadios of Sassima and me.[6] I wrote the following in an initial letter to the Ecumenical Patriarch proposing the talks:

> I am emboldened in this quest by reading in your book *Encountering the Mystery* that Ecumenical Patriarch Jeremiah II broke new ground in the 16th century "Augsburg–Constantinople" encounter. Paraskevè Tibbs projects that perhaps Melanchthon himself recast the Augsburg Confession in Greek for the benefit of this significant exchange.[7]

Any observer of mainstream media can observe how the West is quick to point to the exploits of Pope Francis while paying less attention to the Ecumenical Patriarch, even when the two were involved in joint ventures like the 2016 refugee outreach in Lesbos. This media inequality, however, has never drawn criticism from Constantinople nor support from the Vatican. This was on display again during the June 2018 WCC celebration of their 70th anniversary with the stark contrast between media attention for Pope Francis versus the Ecumenical Patriarch.

In 2014, International Pentecostal Holiness Presiding Bishop A. D. Beacham, Jr., went to the Phanar to celebrate Pascha at the Patriarchal Church of St. George. Despite many long services during Holy Week, with some that lasted past midnight, Ecumenical Patriarch Bartholomew welcomed Bishop and Mrs. Beacham into his office. One of the most memorable moments was the Ecumenical Patriarch telling Bishop Beacham that sitting on the patriarchal throne – which has suffered greatly since the collapse of the Byzantine Empire – has taught him the true meaning of patience. As Archdeacon John Chryssavgis points out, Ecumenical Patriarch Bartholomew has an icon of Saint Hypomone ("patience") in his office. Those who saw the Ecumenical Patriarch interview by Bob Simon on CBS "60 Minutes" (2009) will remember that the Ecumenical Patriarch said he felt he had been "crucified" by the social-political reality

---

[6] Chryssavgis, *Bartholomew*, 76.

[7] Harold D. Hunter letter, 21 June 2009, to the Ecumenical Patriarch. Eve Tibbs, "Patriarch Jeremias II, the Tübingen Lutherans, and the Greek Version of the Augsburg Confession: A Sixteenth Century Encounter," unpublished paper (9 March 2000) for Dr. Nathan P. Feldmeth, Fuller Theological Seminary, CH-502 Medieval–Reformation History, 11–15.

An Emmaus Walk with Ancient Mothers and Fathers 305

inherent with life at the Ecumenical Patriarchate at the Orthodox "Jerusalem," namely Constantinople (Istanbul).

The initial direct talks between Pentecostals and the Ecumenical Patriarchate that ran from 2010 to 2012 were approved by the Holy Synod and processed through their ecumenical committee at Constantinople that was led by Metropolitan Anthanasios of Chalcedon. In due course, a letter of confirmation was received from the Ecumenical Patriarch that brought a Pentecostal team to Istanbul on 3–7 October 2010. In the 2010 meeting, participants were welcomed by the Ecumenical Patriarch. Metropolitan Professor Anthanassios of the Senior See of Chalcedon served as president of the Orthodox team, with Harold D. Hunter as president of the Pentecostal team. The discussions focused on identifying for the Orthodox who their Pentecostal partners might be and who they represent, the appropriate methodology to be used, and the next steps. Recommendations from the Orthodox participants were taken to the Holy Synod and approved. The second round convened 28–29 October 2011 in Heraklion, Crete. Our gracious host was the late Archbishop Irenaios.

The third in a series of conversations between the Ecumenical Patriarchate and Pentecostals convened 27–28 October 2012. The European Pentecostal Seminary, a Pentecostal institution in Knebis, Germany, near Stuttgart in the Black Forrest, hosted the event. Metropolitan Professor Gennadios and Harold D. Hunter served as co-chairs of the two teams. Pentecostal team members were Simon Chan (Singapore), Daniela Augustine (Bulgaria), Dale Coulter (USA), and Olga Zaprometova (Russia). Members of the Orthodox team were Georges Tsetsis (Switzerland) and Konstantinos S. Kenanidis (Crete). Georges Lemopoulos (Switzerland) sent his apologies. A wide range of topics were discussed, including matters such as that of Pentecostal churches joining the WCC, which surfaced during the 2012 WCC Central Committee meeting in Crete. Simon Chan, professor of Theology at Trinity Theological College in Singapore, presented a paper for the Pentecostal team entitled "The Nature of the Church: The Holy Spirit and Spiritual Life," which was subsequently published in the January 2013 issue of the *Cyberjournal for Pentecostal-Charismatic Research.* Chan's excellent paper brought high praise from all the participants, which resulted in rich discussions. The Orthodox team did not present a formal paper.

It was mutually agreed at Knebis that the conversations would not convene in 2013. This reflected external events involving both groups, such as the WCC General Assembly in Busan and the Pentecostal World Conference in Kuala Lumpur. When it came time to work toward resuming the conversations in 2014, the Ecumenical Patriarchate decided to suspend conversations with Pentecostals. Conversations between the Ecumenical Patriarchate and Baptists and Methodists were likewise suspended.

It seemed a sincere hope of all concerned that a way forward could be found to keep alive conversations between the Ecumenical Patriarchate and Pentecostals. Informal efforts continued, and these matters were addressed by personal contacts during the WCC General Assembly that met from 30 October to 8 November 2013 in Busan, South Korea. During a 2019 conversation with Metropolitan Gennadios in Istanbul, he proposed a new start of the original talks to be considered by the Ecumenical Patriarch. Gennadios's notion of resuming the 2010–2012 unofficial talks with the Ecumenical Patriarchate was separate from all other engagements. I had been scheduled to meet with Ecumenical Patriarch Bartholomew at the Phanar, but events with Pope Francis in Rome delayed his return to Istanbul. Unfortunately, these were also days of ill health for Gennadios, which resulted in his death on 1 June 2022. Yet even in the shadow of his imminent demise, he arranged for me to have a private audience with the Ecumenical Patriarch at the Phanar in April 2022.

The reimagined Eastern Orthodox–Classical Pentecostal talks resumed in 2017 just prior to the annual AAR/SBL conference hosted by the Holy Cross Orthodox School of Theology. Co-chairs of those talks were Brandon Gallaher and Harold D. Hunter. Although none of those presentations were published, the group cast a vision for what was to follow. Holy Cross was an excellent host, extending every courtesy to us.

The second meeting of the Orthodox–Pentecostal Academic Dialogue was held on 16 November 2018 at the Iliff School of Theology, Denver, Colorado, in conjunction with the 2018 Annual Meeting of AAR/SBL. As host for this round, Pentecostals were gifted a beautiful room for our meeting at Iliff School of Theology by Dean Boyung Lee.

The steering committee for the second meeting consisted of Brandon Gallaher, Harold D. Hunter, Paul Ladouceur, and Daniela C. Augustine. The subject for discussion at the second meeting on 16 November 2018 was "Spiritual Experience." The meeting heard and discussed two papers: "The Experience of God as Light in the Orthodox Tradition," prepared by Paul Ladouceur; and "Pentecostalism and Experience: History, Theology, and Practice," prepared by Lisa P. Stephenson.

The papers and the discussion suggested several promising avenues of convergence in the understanding of experience in the two Christian traditions, avenues which could be further explored in future meetings. Rico Monge and Veli-Matti Kärkkäinen led the prayer and Bible reflection services, which concluded the meeting. The papers were published in the *Journal of Pentecostal Theology* 28:2 (Fall 2019), after editor Lee Roy Martin was approached about such a possibility. I wrote the following to the Ecumenical Patriarch, which was acknowledged by return mail:

> … [we] published in the September 2019 edition of the *Journal for Pentecostal Theology*. The lead articles are from the 2018 edition of the Orthodox–Pentecostal Academic Dialogue. There is a preface published with the articles that grounds these talks in the earlier informal conversations with the Ecumenical Patriarchate. Those talks were co-chaired by Metropolitan Gennadios and me.

The third round of the Orthodox–Pentecostal Academic Dialogue convened on 22 November 2019 at the University of San Diego, California, in conjunction with the 2019 annual meeting of AAR/SBL. The subject for discussion was "Mediation in the Christian Life." The Pentecostal paper by Chris Green and the Orthodox paper by Philip LeMasters were both published in the *Journal of Pentecostal Theology* 30:1 (May 2021). The University of San Diego gifted ideal space for the day-long meeting.

There are unique aspects of the Eastern Orthodox–Classical Pentecostal talks compared to Pentecostal dialogues with the Vatican, World Communion of Reformed Churches (WCRC), and Lutheran World Federation (LWF). The Pentecostal World Fellowship (PWF) had originally officially endorsed only the informal talks between the Eastern Orthodox Ecumenical Patriarchate in Constantinople and the Pentecostal team that I led. Due to my personal contacts, the ongoing talks (2017–2019) initially kept the PWF connection while benefiting from the blessings of the Ecumenical Patriarch. Those connections came to an end in 2020. Each member of the Pentecostal team in the 2010–2012 talks had a letter of endorsement from the highest authority in their community, including Russia, Bulgaria, Finland, Singapore, and the USA. The Pentecostal team had elections for moderator and the steering committee that decided on venue and presenters while the team decided on new or replacement members of their team.

Authoritative Voices

Pentecostals have a global vision when projecting their mission as being present in all UN-recognised countries of the world. I was raised in a small Pentecostal church with a global vision on display at the annual international conference. Part of what propelled them to go to remote corners of the world was the belief that they were the One, Holy, Catholic, and Apostolic Church. It was projected that millions of Christians would one day be united with the "One Fold" (i.e., that specific Pentecostal church), before the return of Christ.

In the prestigious International Orthodox Theological Association (IOTA) conference in Iasi, Romania, in January 2019, up to forty countries were present, yet this illustrates that the Orthodox do not have a global "outreach" vision. There was almost no one from Africa, none from Latin America, and almost none from Asia. The Oriental Orthodox representation would have helped with at least Africa. IOTA followed with a second "Mega Conference" in Volos, Greece. The January 2023 conference was the largest gathering of scholars of Orthodox Christianity in more than one hundred years, with more than four hundred attendees from forty-five countries.

I witnessed a miniature example of related issues during one of my 2011 visits to Oxford, where I spent time with Metropolitan Professor Kallistos Ware. I went to the church he started near Oxford University, and there was a note on the door that essentially announced that those who were loyal to the Moscow Patriarchate rather than the Ecumenical Patriarchate would be meeting elsewhere. Even this small intimate building could not keep everyone together.

Archdeacon Chryssavgis, among others leading Eastern Orthodox voices, has referred to the Holy and Great Council that met in Crete as a historic Pan-Orthodox Council unlike anything seen by the Orthodox for at least one century, if not an entire millennium. However, Oriental Orthodox were not part of this General Council. It should be noted that the WCC reserves the term "inter-Orthodox" when referring to all twenty-first-century Orthodox churches.

During multiple visits to Russia and Belarus initiated in 2011, one hears the constant refrain that the Moscow Patriarchate is the Third Rome and that it should become the seat for the Ecumenical Patriarchate, thus replacing Constantinople. In 2018, the chasm between Constantinople and Moscow drew international attention. The Ecumenical Patriarchate granted autocephaly status to the church of Ukraine. The result was that Moscow had broken communion with the Ecumenical Patriarchate. At the start, very few Eastern Orthodox Patriarchates have loudly taken a position on this sharp divide. However, the leading role of Patriarch Kirill supporting Putin's murderous invasion of Ukraine has left little middle ground.

The Eastern Orthodox churches in play do not reach Western media, in part due to location and language. However, public discussions about the Moscow Patriarchate involving the WCC were anything but tame. This includes the 2022 WCC Central Committee meetings and then the 31 August–8 September 2022 WCC General Assembly in Karlsruhe. Prior to arriving at Karlsruhe, there was a vocal movement to remove the Russian Orthodox Church as a member of the WCC. One group of Orthodox scholars created, signed, and promoted their version of the Barmen Declaration, known as "A Declaration of the 'Russian World' (RUSSKII MIR) Teaching." It was broadcast through social media and published on 13 March 2022 by the Orthodox Christian Studies Center at Fordham University, which showed that the events of 24 February 2022 had exploded a bomb.[8]

The biography of the Ecumenical Patriarch by Chryssavgis highlights strains among the fourteen autocephalous churches, in particular, the ongoing tension between Constantinople and Moscow. The book notes that the Ecumenical Patriarch alone can declare a church autocephalous. Thus, the 1960 granting of autocephaly to the Orthodox Church of America by the Patriarch of Moscow is deemed uncanonical. At the same time, the four dissenting autocephalous churches that stayed away from Crete 2016 (The Holy and Great Council), give fodder to those outsiders who view Eastern Orthodox churches as simply a federation of churches. It would seem there is no unanimity among the Eastern Orthodox on the notion that "first among equals" has real consequences even when qualified as neither commanding nor compelling. Chryssavgis himself warns about autocephaly of ethnophyletism. One advantage for the Ecumenical Patriarchate is that it lacks the kind of nationalistic political pressure of many other Orthodox Patriarchates.[9]

In a 2016 interview in Boston, Chryssavgis expertly pointed out that, while no tradition, regardless of its ecclesiology, is spared inward tensions, the Orthodox model that allows open conflict of the kind associated with the "Third Rome" (Moscow) over against perceived encroachments like the "Ravenna Document" – which has been marginalised of late – is obviously not hidden from public view. Chryssavgis goes so far as to say that this is the way the conciliar

---

[8] The article remains online and available to sign, as I did early on, at https://publicorthodoxy.org/2022/03/13/a-declaration-on-the-russian-world-russkii-mir-teaching/ On 6 February 2023, this same website published "Why Have You Forgotten the Truth of God?" by Sergei Chapnin, addressed to Orthodox hierarchs.

[9] Chryssavgis, *Bartholomew*, 151–57.

model looks, and it should be appreciated even by those who confer primacy on the Bishop of Rome or any other hierarch. Chryssavgis stands fast by the notion that the history of the church is never without synods and primates, a point that has been challenged by Pentecostal theologians such as me.[10] Although the failures of Pentecostals are widely known, particularly in an age ruled by social media, the issues raised here deserve continued thoughtful consideration.

Care for God's Creation

Pentecostals, who constantly measure themselves against magisterial Protestants, need to look closely at the record of the Green Patriarch. He has made creation care a hallmark of his tenure as the Ecumenical Patriarch. Chryssavgis is more than justified to devote an entire chapter to this critical theological issue.

Mainstream media coined and then conferred the title "Green Patriarch" in recognition of the Ecumenical Patriarch's unique contribution. This unpretentious yet telling title was recognised in the White House in 1997 by Al Gore, vice president of the United States. True to this landmark distinction, in 1997, the Ecumenical Patriarch would equate abuse of God's creation as sin. This public stand was rightly lauded by environmental activists from around the world.[11]

The July 2006 "blessing of the waters" on the Amazon River attracted international media attention. The Ecumenical Patriarch was welcomed as "the Patriarch of the Amazon." He responded by enlarging on the significance of the baptism of Christ in the Jordan River: "In our encounter with the indigenous peoples of this region, we witnessed and felt their profound sense of the sacredness of creation and of the bonds that exist between all living things and people. Thanks to them, we understand more deeply that, as creatures of God, we are all in the same boat: *estamos no mesmo barco!*"[12]

It should be emphasised that the Ecumenical Patriarch sought to bring accountability for God's creation first to the Orthodox. In 1992, soon after his election as Ecumenical Patriarch, he brought together an unprecedented Synaxis of Primates at the Phanar. All the assembled prelates endorsed 1 September as a day of "Pan-Orthodox prayer for God's creation." The Ecumenical Patriarch put it this way when clarifying the Scripture phrase "stewards of creation": "… we are called to offer creation back to God as priests, just as the priest in the Eucharist offers the bread and wine to God, who in turn transforms them into his body and blood for the life of the whole world. So, rather than speaking of becoming 'stewards of creation,' it may be more helpful to speak of becoming

---

[10] Harold D. Hunter interview with John Chryssavgis, meeting at Boston, MA, on 19 December 2016.

[11] Chryssavgis, *Bartholomew*, 173–76.

[12] Chryssavgis, *Bartholomew*, 194.

'priests of creation' in accordance with our donation and vocation to be part of the 'royal priesthood.'"[13]

In many early ecumenical events involving Pentecostals, there were those who would wish to reduce Pentecostals to their distinctives and think there is nothing else to say about the living communities. At the start of my ecumenical journey in the late 1970s and 1980s, I focused on Pentecostal distinctives, but it was ongoing ecumenical encounters that moved me to research other aspects of global Pentecostalism for professional papers and publications outside the Global North. While teaching at the Pentecostal Theological Seminary, Cleveland, Tennessee in the 1980s, I lectured on ecotheology. Creation Care was highlighted at Brighton '91, and I lectured about climate justice at Pentecostal schools in various parts of Latin America, Asia, and Europe starting in the early 1990s.

I expanded this call with a workshop at the October 2022 Pentecostal World Conference hosted by Yoido Full Gospel Church and at Brunnen at the September 2022 WCC General Assembly in Germany. There once was hope to make inroads into the WCC Commission on Climate Justice and Sustainable Development that the 15–18 June 2022 Central Committee put on the agenda for the 2022 WCC General Assembly. I was present as a delegated observer when this commission was approved in Karlsruhe during the WCC's eleventh General Assembly.

With the approval of the PWF Executive Committee and advisory board that met during the 2022 Pentecostal World Conference in Seoul, I now chair the PWF's Creation Care Task Force. This working group of ten persons from around the world openly seeks to engage the United Nations Environment Programme (UNEP) and the ecumenical annual festival running from September 1 – October 4 known as the "Season of Creation", in addition to Pentecostal dialogue partners like the Vatican, the Ecumenical Patriarchate, the WCRC, and the LWF. While the World Evangelical Alliance, along with most Christian global communions, are accredited with the UN, this is not the case with the PWF. Since the PWF is not accredited with the UN like our ecumenical partners, no one representing the PWF could gain access to privileged areas during COP28, the 2023 United Nations Climate Change Conference.[14]

The series of Zoom sessions in 2021, titled "Faith and Science: Toward COP26," organised by the Vatican, the Italian Embassy to the Holy See, and the British Embassy to the Holy See became a most fascinating encounter on the ecological training ground. A select group of perhaps fifty global faith leaders from all religions, along with eminent scientists, met each month by Zoom with

---

[13] Chryssavgis, *Bartholomew*, 203–4.

[14] The lack of UN accreditation is also problematic for the PWF World Mission Commission Network of Relief and Development Partners. See Mikael Jägerskog, "Pentecostal World Fellowship (PWF)/Pentecostal Relief and Development Partners (PRDP) advocacy update, December 2023," email sent 7 December 2023. I serve on the advisory committee for the "Season of Creation" project at https://seasonofcreation.org/about/ accessed on 5 August 2024.

translation of various languages. David Wells and I represented the PWF. This series culminated in a 4 October 2021 meeting at the Vatican with Pope Francis. The Holy Father delivered our "Joint Appeal" to His Eminence Alok Sharma, president of COP26, the United Nations Climate Change Conference held in Glasgow, Scotland, on 1–12 November 2021. The gathering attracted many of the world's top political leaders from over one hundred countries that participated.[15]

The disproportionate impact of climate change on the poor and marginalised is emphasised in *Laudato Si* and echoed in a wide range of actions taken by the Green Patriarch, Ecumenical Patriarch Bartholomew. During the 2020 organisational phase, a "COP26 Faith Event: Final Non-Paper"[16] was circulated to those invited to the select group. The thesis stood tall on the following assertion that would be the cornerstone to the "Joint Appeal" to all faith traditions and governments to protect the poor and marginalised:

> The global temperature has already increased by one degree Celsius above the twentieth century average. With present National Determined Contributions (NDCs), the temperature will rise by 3 degrees, which will be catastrophic for the entire planet – humans, animals, and plants – especially the marginalised and poorest communities. COP26 aims to galvanise action to limit the rise to well below 2 degrees Celsius, and preferably 1.5 degrees Celsius.

During the 2021 Zoom sessions of faith leaders organised by the Vatican working toward COP26, scientists focused on the food humans eat, the clothes humans wear, biodiversity, transportation, carbon neutral, divesting from fossil fuels, and moving toward investment in green energy. Oxford University economist Kate Raworth gave a ground-breaking presentation on an economy of life emphasising thriving over growing, which was warmly received by the faith leaders who were willing to challenge the axioms of capitalism.[17] Professor Riccardo Valentini's explosive presentation shocked some when he said that there are almost as many people in the world who die of obesity (29 million) as

---

[15] William "Billy" M. Wilson is chair of the Pentecostal World Fellowship and president of Oral Roberts University in Tulsa, OK. ORU has a school of Global Environmental Sustainability. The ORU academic journal for religion, *Spiritus,* has published articles on Creation Care and ORU Professor of Religion Jeffrey Lamp has published more than most while assisting ORU students in such publications including *Spiritus*. One such example is Kathry Moder, Megan Munhofen, Cade Rich, Nathan Von Atzigen, Jeffrey S. Lamp, "Creation Care as Caring for Human Beings," *Spiritus* 5:1 (2020), 137–50. This article adopts a pro-life narrative to chase Oklahoma politicians involved in determining the amount of mercury that is legally allowed.

[16] "COP26 Faith Event – Final Non-Paper" circulated 2020 by the Vatican's Secretaries of Relations with States, the Italian Embassy to the Holy See and the British Embassy to the Holy See.

[17] Here are links to data related to Raworth's paper:
https://www.ted.com/talks/kate_raworth_a_healthy_economy_should_be_designed_to_t hrive_not_grow?language=en and https://time.com/5930093/amsterdam-doughnut-economics/ [Accessed 5 May 2024].

malnutrition (36 million) each year. He also mentioned that many modern city dwellers have little understanding of where food comes from. Considering the ecological impact of meat, Valentini argued that we need to get our food from trees and change our diet.

The First World Assemblies of God Prayer Rally held in 1994 in Seoul witnessed the importance of prayer for God's creation. Within two years, Dr. David Yonggi Cho, with the influence of Professor Jürgen Moltmann on what was known as the world's largest church, established a ministry team at Yoido Full Gospel to address environmental concerns. When enumerating six priorities of ministry at the 1999 Full Gospel Inchon church, Dr. Song Kyu Choi listed creation as number five.

The first academic article by a PWF-type Pentecostal was published in South Korea as "Pentecostal Healing for God's Sick Creation?"[18] On 21 May 1991, Dr. Younghoon Lee provided information about Yoido Full Gospel Church. Pastor

---

[18] By Harold D. Hunter in *The Spirit and the Church* 2:2 (November 2000), 145–67. My paper read at the 1998 Pentecostal World Conference in Korea was the basis of my article that was published in Korea. The useful study by Jonathan W. Rice, "Ecology and the Future of Pentecostalism: Problems, Possibilities, and Proposals" in *Pentecostal Mission and Global Christianity* (2005), edited by Wonsuk Ma, Veli-Matti Kärkkäinen, and Asamoah Gyadu, unfortunately gets the chronology wrong by pointing first to Amos Yong in 2005 and never mentions my article. It did not help subsequent contributions that the journal that published my article was in Korea and stopped publication after a few years when the sponsoring Foursquare seminary closed unexpectedly. Anyway, Rice starts with Amos Yong, *The Spirit Poured Out on All Flesh: Pentecostalism and the Possibility of a Global Theology* (Grand Rapids, MI: Baker Academic, 2005), 300. Then he goes on to Wonsuk Ma, "The Spirit of God in Creation: Lessons for Christian Mission," *Transformation* 24/3 & 4 (July & Oct 2007), 227. Next up is Steven M. Studebaker, "The Spirit in Creation: A Unified Theology of Grace and Creation Care," *Zygon: Journal of Religion and Science* 43:4 (December 2008), 943–60. And so on. However, the correct sequence had already been published by A. J. Swoboda's early work, as he confirmed when I first met him at SPS. Compare these surveys to Anita Davis, "Pentecostal Approaches to Ecotheology: Reviewing the Literature." Swoboda labels my work exploratory, but I remain convinced that healing is a motif that resonates with our community. I also took note that the language was used with the unique group of global faith leaders of all religions organised in 2021 by the Vatican depicted in this article. Prior to my *The Spirit and the Church* article, *Pneuma* published Jean-Jacques Suurmond, "Christ King: A Charismatic Appeal for an Ecological Lifestyle," *Pneuma: Journal for the Society for Pentecostal Studies* 10:1 (1998), 26–35. Suurmond told me he does not identify as a Pentecostal. Also note ecology sections in Harold D. Hunter, "Musings on Confessing the One Faith," *Pneuma: The Journal of the Society for Pentecostal Studies* 14:2 (Fall 1992), 207, and Harold D. Hunter, "The Reemergence of Spirit Christology," *EPTA Bulletin* 10:1 (1992), 54.

An Emmaus Walk with Ancient Mothers and Fathers　　　　313

Choi highlighted this concern in an address to the WARC–Pentecostal Dialogue that met on 14–20 May 1999 in Seoul, Korea.

According to University of South Africa professor M. L. Daneel's presentation at the Theological Stream of Brighton '91, in the discussion of water baptism, one group of African Initiated Church candidates in Zimbabwe confess not only personal sins, but things like "I chopped down thirty trees, but did not plant any," and "I ruined the topsoil." Then there is the Lord's Supper. A monstrous fire is built, and thousands go running around this huge fire, yelling out their sins. Along with familiar confessions to adultery, jealousy, and stealing are wailings over ecological wizardry. Before taking the elements of communion, they must pass through a series of symbolic gates of heaven. Each gate has prophets who discern hidden sins not confessed when running around the bonfire. Those hidden sins include ecological sins![19]

Final Reflection

No table is more ecumenical than where faith leaders of all religions gather to heal the sick planet. These final reflections show that I have been working to be consistent with a statement I wrote thirty years ago at the invitation of Professor Jürgen Moltmann, which was slightly revised in 2010:

> Profoundly relevant for an answer to this question is the theological diversity contained in the canonical record. Ernst Käsemann brought to the 1963 Montreal conference on Faith and Order his publicized view that the New Testament canon does not dismiss but in fact contains "the basis for the multiplicity of the confessions." Coping with the additional realities of diverse cultural and social contexts also strengthen[s] the argument of Jürgen Moltmann that the church should not be seeking "uniformity but should be working through the ecumenical movement to expand its range of unlikeness." Contact alone is not compromise. As has been said by the Waldensians in Italy, no one church has all the marks of the church, and the more we fellowship with other churches, the more we represent the body of Christ rather than compromise the unity of that body.[20]

---

[19] M. L. Daneel, "African Independent Church Pneumatology and the Salvation of all Creation," in *All Together in One Place*, 98–128.

[20] Harold D. Hunter, "Global Pentecostalism and Ecumenism: Two Movements of the Holy Spirit?" in Wolfgang Vondey, ed. *Pentecostalism and Christian Unity: Ecumenical Documents and Critical Assessment* (Eugene, OR: Pickwick Publications, 2010), 20–33. The original article is Harold D. Hunter, "We Are the Church: New Congregationalism," in Jürgen Moltmann and Karl-Josef Kuschel, eds., *Concilium: Revista Internazionale di Teologia* 3 (1996), 17–21. This volume was devoted to the topic "Pentecostal Movements as an Ecumenical Challenge."